Lord Seaforth

Lord Seaforth

Highland Landowner, Caribbean Governor

Finlay McKichan

EDINBURGH
University Press

For Joan

Edinburgh University Press is one of the leading university presses in the UK. We publish academic books and journals in our selected subject areas across the humanities and social sciences, combining cutting-edge scholarship with high editorial and production values to produce academic works of lasting importance. For more information visit our website: edinburghuniversitypress.com

© Finlay McKichan, 2018

Edinburgh University Press Ltd
The Tun – Holyrood Road
12 (2f) Jackson's Entry
Edinburgh EH8 8PJ

Typeset in 11/13 Sabon by
Servis Filmsetting Ltd, Stockport, Cheshire,
and printed and bound in Great Britain

A CIP record for this book is available from the British Library

ISBN 978 1 4744 3847 6 (hardback)
ISBN 978 1 4744 3848 3 (paperback)
ISBN 978 1 4744 3849 0 (webready PDF)
ISBN 978 1 4744 3850 6 (epub)

The right of Finlay McKichan to be identified as author of this work has been asserted in accordance with the Copyright, Designs and Patents Act 1988 and the Copyright and Related Rights Regulations 2003 (SI No. 2498).

Contents

Figures and Tables

Tables

Acknowledgements

The author of a work of this sort owes debts of gratitude to many people, and it is a pleasure to acknowledge them. My principal academic acknowledgement is to Dr Annie Tindley, who heroically read each chapter in draft and gave invariably constructive comment. Her encouragement and practical help played a large part in the completion of the project. My thanks for reading drafts are due also to Dr John MacAskill and Dr Douglas Lockhart for the sections on kelp and planned villages respectively. I am indebted to Castle Fraser, and especially to Jean Jolly, for giving me pointers to and extracts from the Fraser papers in Aberdeen University Special Collections and transcripts held at the castle. I also wish to thank Dr Aonghas MacCoinnich for his advice on the origins of the Mackenzie kindred and for drawing to my attention Seaforth papers in the Mitchell Library and Dr Iain Davidson for his advice on Seaforth's hearing and speech loss. I am grateful to the anonymous readers of the proposal for this volume, whose suggestions have made it a better book than it would otherwise have been.

I have greatly appreciated the encouragement and advice of Professor Eric Richards, and it has been a privilege to have the support of the doyen of Highland Clearance studies. I am also grateful for the encouragement of Professor John Mackenzie, my friend and classmate in the Glasgow University Honours History class of 1964. Dr Bill Inglis has given me regular encouragement, especially valued at times when it was most needed. I have had helpful advice also from Dr Tony Cooke. My sincere thanks are due also to the editors of my journal articles, Professor Ewen Cameron, Dr Catriona Macdonald and

Professor Marjory Harper and the anonymous readers of these articles for collectively teaching me the techniques of modern academic publishing. I would like to thank Anita Joseph for the great care and skill with which she has acted as copy-editor.

The most pleasurable aspect of a historian's craft is working in archives. I am especially grateful to the staff of the National Records of Scotland in Edinburgh (where I must be one of the longer-serving customers) and of The National Archives at Kew. However, I have also had invariably courteous assistance in the National Library of Scotland, the British Library, Aberdeen University Special Collections, the Mitchell Library, the Royal Society Library, the Barbados Department of Archives and the Barbados National Library.

My formal acknowledgements for the reproduction of illustrations are given in the figure captions. However, I would like to especially thank for their generous permissions the Hon. Rory Guinness, Mr Andrew Matheson, Brahan, and the National Trust for Scotland.

May I acknowledge the great contribution made to this project by my wife, Joan. Her encouragement and good nature have made it possible. It has been a pleasure to be accompanied by her on research trips to Barbados and (many times) to London. Joan has also made an important practical contribution by using her drawing-office training in making the maps and her teacher's training to check my spelling and syntax by reading everything in draft.

Preface

Francis Humberston Mackenzie (1754–1815, from 1798 Lord Seaforth) inherited the Seaforth estate, comprising the island of Lewis and lands in mainland Ross-shire, in 1783. What might be expected of a Highland landowner, subsequently a peer, of his time? He came to his estates at a time when many Highland proprietors were increasing their incomes by letting to commercial sheep farmers and moving the inhabitants to the coast or off the estate. Despite being profoundly deaf, he served as MP for the county of Ross from 1784 to 1790 and from 1794 to 1796. MPs could, if they supported ministers faithfully, win re-election by securing government and military posts for voters (or for relatives or friends of voters). From 1793 to 1815 Britain was almost continuously at war with revolutionary and Napoleonic France. Landed proprietors, especially Highland ones, could make money by raising regiments. Seaforth was governor of Barbados from 1801 until 1806, only a year before the abolition of the British slave trade. Enslaved labourers on the island were unsettled by the hope that emancipation might follow or even accompany this. However, plantation slavery was still making good profits for planters, who expected that the island would be governed in their interests. Seaforth tried to solve serious financial problems by setting up cotton plantations in the frontier territory of Berbice, Guyana, in which it was alleged that conditions for enslaved labourers were especially hard.

Perhaps surprisingly, Seaforth regarded himself, and was seen by others, as a humanitarian. It will be argued in this book that in many respects (although not all) his policies and behaviour ran contrary to what would be expected of a man of his background and position. He was far from being a stereotypical Highland proprietor, intent on maximising his income at any cost to his people, or a stereotypical Caribbean governor, allowing the sugar planters to determine policy. He also aspired to be an untypical and caring plantation owner. He was unique in his time in filling a colonial governorship while suffering from his disability. This book is based on the belief that case studies of this type lead to a more nuanced view of topics such as Highland land management and the Clearances, Scottish electoral politics, participants in plantation slavery and colonial governance than has often been given by historians. It aspires to cast fresh light on these. It is not the sort of biography which gives a chronological coverage of the subject's life. It places Seaforth in the context of the dramatic changes of his time nationally and internationally and the extensive historiography these have encouraged. The Conclusions sections provide links between the themes and give pointers to other chapters in which the overarching issues are addressed. It should be noted that 200 years ago British people commonly described other racial groups in terms which are now regarded as inappropriate or even offensive. Such terms are used here only in direct quotations from persons featured in the book.

1 Early Days

A short distance from the entry to the National Gallery of Scotland is one of its largest pictures, twelve by seventeen feet. It attracts attention by its size and by the dramatic scene it depicts. Hunting dogs have brought a magnificent stag to bay. A richly dressed man is underneath the stag and holding out his arm to protect himself. This is Alexander III, King of Scots, who reigned from 1249 to 1286. Horsemen are making frantic efforts to save him, but cannot get close enough. The hints of tartan on their clothing and the mountains in the background suggest that this is taking place in the Highlands. The drama is enhanced by lowering clouds. The foreground is dominated by a well built and muscular figure. He is holding the stag's antlers with one hand and with the other is about to plunge a spear into it and thus, we are led to believe, save the king. This is Colin Fitzgerald, according to legend the founder of the Mackenzie kindred. For this service he is said to have received from Alexander the lands of Kintail, which was certainly the country from which the Mackenzies sprang. The picture was commissioned in 1784 by Francis Humberston Mackenzie, who had succeeded one year earlier to the Mackenzie chief-ship and a large estate in Ross-shire. He is the subject of this book, and it was characteristic of him that the painting was intended to make a big impression without concern for cost. It was displayed in the Royal Academy exhibition in London and was said to have been admired by King George III. It was the work of the king's official history painter Benjamin West and the fee was 800 guineas, almost as much as West's annual fee from the king. Equally characteristically, there is evidence that

Figure 1.1 *Alexander III of Scotland Rescued from the Fury of a Stag, by the Intrepidity of Colin Fitzgerald (The Death of the Stag)*, 1786, by Benjamin West. (Courtesy National Galleries of Scotland, NG2448. Purchased with the aid of the National Heritage Memorial Fund, the Art Fund (William Lang Bequest), Ross and Cromarty District Council and Dennis F. Ward 1987.)

Seaforth may never have paid for it. Although intended to hang in Brahan Castle, the family seat in Ross-shire, after the exhibition the painting returned to West's studio and remained there throughout Seaforth's life.[1]

Is there any evidence that the scene in the picture ever occurred or that the Mackenzies were in possession of Kintail in the late thirteenth century? How had they emerged as major landowners in Ross-shire and what were the estates to which Francis Humberston Mackenzie succeeded? Alexander Mackenzie of Kintail is the first chief (c.1430–c.1475) who can be credibly identified, in a note of a charter of 1463–4, some two centuries after Alexander III's encounter with his alleged saviour Colin Fitzgerald. The story about Colin Fitzgerald first appears in a series of manuscript genealogies and histories of the Mackenzies written in the mid seventeenth century and intended (inter alia) to claim a long-standing loyalty of the family to the Crown.[2] One of the purposes of the picture was to emphasise loyalty to the Hanoverian kings of a family which had fought for the Jacobite 'James VIII' as recently as 1719.

By the end of the sixteenth century the Mackenzies had acquired the lands of Lochbroom in Wester Ross and Brahan (in Strathconon) and other lands in Easter Ross, including Chanonry (Fortrose). By the early seventeenth century their Kintail heartland had expanded to include Lochalsh and in 1610 their growing power and influence with the Crown was recognised by the creation of Kenneth Mackenzie as Lord Mackenzie of Kintail.[3] Aonghas MacCoinnich has argued that the Mackenzies, like the Campbells, took full advantage of James VI's strategy of expropriation of troublesome clans under cover of the need to 'civilise' them.[4] Kenneth was granted the island of Lewis by royal charter in 1610, invaded the island and after the death of the last Macleod chief in 1613 had complete control. Colin Mackenzie became an earl in 1623, took his title from Loch Seaforth in Lewis, but built his seat at Brahan near Dingwall.[5] This was the period at which the Mackenzie lands were at their greatest extent. Lands were lost due to the civil wars of the next century and especially participation in the Jacobite risings.

In 1689 Kenneth, fourth earl of Seaforth, fought for James VII against King William III in the Irish campaign which confirmed James's loss of the throne. In 1714 William and his consort Mary were followed on the throne of what was, after 1707, the United Kingdom by George I, the first king of the Hanoverian dynasty. Earl Kenneth's first son William, the fifth earl, fought for 'James VIII' against George I in the 1715 rising, lost many of his clansmen at the battle of Sheriffmuir and was declared by act of attainder to be a traitor and thus in law forfeited his estates. His final attempt in the 1719 rising to restore his king and his legal right to his own lands ended in defeat at the battle of Glenshiel on Seaforth territory. In 1741, the year after Earl William's death, the Seaforth lands were bought back from the state for his son, Kenneth Lord Fortrose, for £25,109. This marked the formal acceptance by the Seaforth family of the Hanoverian dynasty in the person of George II, and Kenneth (whatever his private loyalties) was prudent enough to keep well clear of the 1745 Jacobite rising.[6] The repurchase also created a debt which, as will be shown in Chapters Two and Four, was a continuing and indeed growing financial burden on the estate.

The Seaforth family illustrated a sequence followed by other Highland chiefly dynasties involved in the Jacobite risings – forfeiture of titles and lands, followed by, after a considerable interval, acceptance of the Hanoverian monarchy, and restoration, at considerable cost, to its favour and to their ancestral estates. Another local example was the Mackenzies of Cromarty, who had estates scattered across Ross-shire at Coigach on the west coast, Strathpeffer and, in the east of the county, Tarbat. They had fought for the Stuarts in 1689, but the real disaster for them was the third earl of Cromarty's somewhat half-hearted participation in the 1745 rising (he did not fight at Culloden). The earl narrowly escaped with his life, but he was reduced to abject poverty by the annexation of his estates to the Crown. It is clear that participation in the risings was followed by financial disaster for Jacobite landowning families. Both the Seaforth and Cromarty estates emerged indebted from forfeiture, and neither of the restored proprietors did much to refill the estate coffers. Cromarty spent heavily renovating Tarbat House and incurred heavy obligations to the family of his wife, whom he married three years before his death but who outlived him by fifty-six years.[7] His near contemporary, Kenneth Earl of Seaforth, as will be shown, devoted much of his time to a cultured and sometimes scandalous life abroad and died in 1781 leaving debts of almost £71,000.

Francis Humberston Mackenzie's father, William Mackenzie, was the son of the third earl's fourth son. As such he had no reason to suppose that he would succeed to the Seaforth estates or dignities, and had to make his own way in the world. One effective way of doing this was to marry Mary, the daughter and heir of Matthew Humberston, proprietor of the Humberston estate in Lincolnshire. There were four children of this marriage, of whom Francis (born 1754) was the second son.[8] Mary was a formidable lady, who will play a significant part in this story. She was outspoken in her letters to Francis even when he had become the chief of the clan Mackenzie and proprietor of the Seaforth estate. She outlived two of her children and died in 1813, only two years before Francis. The cost of maintaining her in some style in London for all these years was an unanticipated financial burden on the estate, and the late payment of her annuity was regularly a matter of contention.[9] In 1792 she turned down Francis' suggestion that she relocate to Brahan, where her upkeep would have been much cheaper. She believed the idea of living there permanently to be unthinkable and argued that the cost of travelling there and back would outweigh any saving.[10]

Francis' father William did not share his wife's longevity and died in 1770. However, he did have some positive characteristics which Francis was to inherit. He had, according to his tombstone, 'a passion for military glory'. In 1738 he joined a Scottish Jacobite company in the Russian service[11], in which he held a colonel's commission. In 1745 he became a major in the Earl of Louden's Highland Regiment of Foot (the 54th), showing a willingness to bear arms for the Hanoverian kings considerably earlier than the main line of the Seaforth family. He served in the British army on the continent.[12] He was an example of the increasing tendency of the sons of Highland gentry to serve in the British army as a route to social respectability and a gentlemanly lifestyle.[13] After the War of the Austrian Succession ended in 1748 he was put on half pay and in 1750 or 1751 he went to Bombay to take up a command in the army of the East India Company. Ill health obliged him to retire early and he then displayed a pleasure in reading which was to be shared by Francis.[14]

Relatively little is known about Francis Humberston Mackenzie's early life. He was the second son of a gentry family and there would not have been the same need to create and preserve records as when he later became a clan chief, proprietor of a great Highland estate, peer of the realm and colonial governor. The Lincolnshire Archives contains no substantial Humberston estate or family archive. On the other hand, he was the descendant of a Scottish earl and it is known that as a young boy he was a page of honour to George III, presumably shortly after his accession in 1760. The king remembered this association with kindness in 1793 and it is likely that Francis' enthusiastic loyalty to him stemmed from his recollection of this time.[15] His memories of early childhood would be especially rosy as, at about the age of twelve, occurred a disaster from which he suffered severely. He caught scarlet fever and as a result lost his hearing completely and for life.[16] This is not unknown as a side effect, but more unusually he also developed a speech defect which lasted for many years. It is possible that this was a psychosomatic reaction to sudden deafness. Those who have become deaf face greater communication and psychological issues than those born deaf because they remain 'culturally hearing'.[17] As a boy of intelligence and imagination, who could understand the implications and foresee the consequences, this would be a particularly serious blow.

A remarkable story, and it may be no more than this, was told by the husband of Seaforth's great-granddaughter about his deafness.[18] The story is that, while he was in a dormitory of schoolboys suffering from scarlet fever, he had a dream. In the dream a hideous old woman went round the boys. She drove a wooden peg into the heads of some boys, and these subsequently died. Others she touched, and these recovered, but with a disability. When she came to Seaforth she felt his ears, and during the illness he became profoundly deaf. We will never know whether he had such a dream, but it is possible that the story was passed down from him. According to this account, he could never in later years forget the terror of the moment when the old woman approached him. This does sound like a story told by him. If so, it was not his only attempt to build a narrative round his deafness. In this case, its purpose could be to show that he was privileged to survive and that this must have been for a reason, to achieve great things. And indeed he was to become a member of parliament and governor of Barbados. This is the sort of rationalisation that a man of great energy might make to explain the apparent disaster of his deafness.

Francis' preferred methods of communicating were reported by John Knox, who visited him at Seaforth Lodge in Lewis in

1786: 'The usual way of conversing with him is by writing or by the fingers at which his family and intimate acquaintances are very expert, and he is equally quick in anticipating their meaning'.[19] His skills in signing were either learned from or developed by Thomas Braidwood, then the most noted British teacher of a wealthy deaf clientele and a pioneer in this area. After his death Braidwood's family, who named Seaforth as one of his pupils, claimed that Braidwood's methods made deaf people 'capable of bearing a general competition with the rest of mankind'.[20] In some respects Seaforth was certainly able to do this. Sometimes in society he had the benefit of conversing with people used to signing. For example, in 1795 he visited Arniston, home of the Dundases and one of the leading political salons in Scotland. He reported that 'Mrs Dundas talked on her fingers', and he met two or three others there who could do this. He seems to have been less at ease with those with whom he was unfamiliar or whose tact and courtesy could not be relied on. A few days before the visit to Arniston, finding beds at military posts on his journey south from Brahan, he was pleased that the commander gave orders that there should be 'no teasing [me] to join the mess (which he saw I did not like)'. He was on occasion very frank to his wife about his sense of impairment. In London, he went to the theatre to see Mrs Siddons perform and confessed, 'I seldom felt my own distress so keenly – I was so affected by her acting that I quite longed to hear.'[21] He remained profoundly deaf, and as late as 1794 it was possible for a London newspaper to comment that he 'has been deaf and dumb from birth'.[22] However, in 1790 a newspaper reported an apparently articulate speech by him at the Ross-shire election.[23] According to a 1799 report, he addressed 'a few appropriate words' at the presentation of colours to the 2nd North British Militia.[24] In both of these cases his words could have been carefully rehearsed. Nevertheless, it seems clear that in later years his power of speech improved and then, if not before, he was able to hold his own in society. One of his obituaries referred to 'his delightful talents for society . . . and his faculty of diffusing grace and lustre over every topic, whether of instruction or amusement'.[25]

How unusual was it for a man with Seaforth's disabilities to be prominent in public life? No other governor has been identified who was profoundly deaf through most of his life and only one politician. He was Lord Archibald Hamilton (1770–1827), brother of the tenth duke of Hamilton and MP for Lanarkshire from 1802 until his death.[26]He argued for political reform and was almost always opposed to the government. He even refused office when his Whig friends were in office in 1806–7. Accordingly, he never had the executive responsibilities which Seaforth carried as a regimental commander, lord lieutenant and colonial governor. Seaforth appears to have been unique in his time in occupying a prominent position in politics and government while suffering from his disabilities.

The only contemporary reference which suggests that Francis Humberston Mackenzie attended one of the great English public schools comes from a letter he wrote to Lord Hobart in 1801 in which he addressed him as 'my old schoolfellow'.[27] Hobart entered Westminster School in 1770 at the age of ten, at which time Francis would have been sixteen. There is no reference to Francis in a published Westminster School register, which, it would be fair to assume, is reasonably complete.[28] There is some evidence to suggest that he might have been a pupil at Harrow School. His lifelong friend, Charles F. Greville (1749–1809), second son of the first earl of Warwick and Brooke, was a pupil at Harrow in 1764 when he was fifteen and Francis was ten. Although the published registers do not show Francis as a pupil at Harrow, the lists prior to 1770 are fragmentary. It may also be significant that he sent his own two sons William and Francis to Harrow.[29]

Is it possible to surmise what may have been the pattern of his education? It was not unknown at that period for boys of elite families to be tutored at home. This was the experience of Alexander Mackenzie Fraser, from 1785 Seaforth's brother-in-law and, like Greville, a very close friend.[30] Public schools of the time were rough places. They had the reputation of being 'communities of undisciplined young barbarians, precocious in the knowledge and practice of ill living'.[31] If a boy was thought to have a delicate physique he might well be tutored at home. An example of a boy who was withdrawn from school was Robert Stewart, the future Lord Castlereagh, who as foreign secretary played a large part in rearranging the states of Europe at the Congress of Vienna after Napoleon's fall in 1815. Between the ages of eight and ten he attended Armagh Grammar School, but subsequently was tutored privately at his family's Irish seat, Mount Stewart.[32] With his deafness and speech defect Francis would be an obvious candidate for home tutoring. It may be

Figure 1.2 The young Francis Mackenzie, later Lord Seaforth, pastel by Mrs Hoare. (Reproduced by generous permission of the Hon. Rory Guinness.)

that he did attend Harrow, but not for long. At best, school lists were compiled annually. A boy who did not attend for a full year might well be unrecorded. Seaforth's disability would make it difficult to survive in such an environment for long. It is possible that he caught scarlet fever at Harrow and then went home. What can be made of Seaforth's claim to have been at Westminster School with Hobart? By 1770 he was sixteen and it is possible that an attempt was made to prepare him for the wider world by sending him there. It is true that he does not appear in the Westminster lists. Here also he may have missed the list by not being in attendance for a full year, either because he could not cope or because money was short after his father died on 12 March 1770.

In a biographical document which Seaforth seems to have written, or at least added to personally, there is a reference to his service in the Royal Navy as a young man. This states that he was a midshipman 'and served for many years in the Medway sixty four gun ship bearing Admiral Mann's flag under Captain W. Affleck . . . and afterwards several other ships between the years 1774 and 1781'.[33] His naval service appears to have begun in 1774 at the age of twenty. This was very late to become a midshipman, fourteen usually being the latest age, and this would undoubtedly be due to his disability. At this time the appointment of midshipmen was in the hands of individual captains and it has been suggested that the 1770s were a period when gentry and aristocratic backgrounds played a particularly important part. Presumably the Humberstons had connections with a captain, probably Captain Affleck of the *Medway*, who was willing to overlook Francis' age and disability.[34] It was far from unique to remain a midshipman at twenty-seven due to such misfortunes (for an aspiring naval officer) as a prolonged peace or a lack of influential sponsors.[35] It may seem surprising that a man who was profoundly deaf and had a speech defect was able to respond to and issue orders in the hectic environment of a large sailing ship at sea and in action. Understandably, he appears never to have passed the lieutenant's exam, which was the formal gateway to an officer's career and which would certainly have required the use of senses which he had lost.[36] There are other references to his sea-going days and much evidence that he was familiar with navigation and other maritime matters. In 1795 he referred in a letter to his wife to 'Admiral Morgan, your cousin and my old shipmate'.[37] A more questionable reference comes from John Knox, who in 1786 visited him on behalf of the British Fisheries Society in his summer quarters on the island of Lewis. He made a boat trip with him and described him as an experienced seaman who 'when very young served in the Royal Navy'. He stated that his loss of hearing had been caused by the noise of cannon in a naval engagement with the French.[38] It can only be assumed that Seaforth made this claim (possibly after a good dinner) to mask his embarrassment, but there is no other evidence to support it. What does exist is a great deal of evidence of Seaforth's expertise in ship-handling and navigation. For example, on a voyage home from Barbados in late 1803 and early 1804 he kept a diary in the form of a letter to his wife. He regularly recorded weather states, with the effects of these, and longitude and latitude readings. He doubted the competence of the master and crew and, as the ship approached the entrance to the English Channel, complained they were not taking or recording proper bearings. 'The wind is directly in our teeth and blows a gale. If it continues we shall tomorrow be worse off than we were this day week'.[39] That the master took the ship within a mile of the Scilly Island rocks would seem to confirm that Seaforth really did have the greater command of navigation.

Is it possible to know how much Francis as a midshipman would be in action, a time when his disability would be a real handicap? Newspapers of the period report on the activities of HMS *Medway*.[40] In May 1774 Admiral Mann was shortly to hoist his flag aboard her at Spithead, after which she would be bound for the Mediterranean to be stationed there for three years. Francis almost certainly sailed with her and served during her deployment as flagship of the Royal Navy's Mediterranean squadron, which concluded at Spithead in March 1778. From the outbreak of the American War of Independence in 1775 one of the principal duties of the squadron was to intercept American privateers active in the Mediterranean and also American merchant vessels carrying sugar, other foodstuffs and tobacco cargoes to Mediterranean ports and sometimes war stores on the return voyage. The squadron called at ports such as Gibraltar, Malaga, Genoa, Leghorn (Livorno) Naples and Port Mahon (Minorca), the principal British naval base in the western Mediterranean. The *Medway* made regular visits to Mahon to replenish her stores.[41] Visits to Mahon were sufficiently frequent for Mackenzie to become a member of the Masonic lodge there. Shortly before the squadron returned home in 1777, it issued a certificate to 'our trusty and well beloved brother Francis Mackenzie Esq ... a regular, registered Master Mason belonging to our lodge [who] always behaved himself as became the character of a worthy mason and brother'.[42] He had clearly begun his lifelong membership of the freemasons and was in good standing with them. This certificate also confirms that he was with the Mediterranean squadron at that time.

Admiral Mann claimed great success in taking prizes but, according to one of the papers, not as many as could have been captured by a larger squadron (he had only three ships, the *Medway* and two frigates). Shortly after, it was reported that the squadron was to be reinforced with three men of war. Towards the end of the tour of duty the *Morning Chronicle* commented that Mann 'has paid great attention to his duty and behaved in a manner also on shore that reflects great honour on the Navy of England'.[43] This suggests that operations were conducted on land and at sea. While there are also references to capturing pirate galleys from Algiers and a report in January 1777 of an action with three Spanish men of war in the Straits of Gibraltar, it seems clear most of the hostilities were with American ships. There appears to have been plenty of action for Mann's squadron, but mostly for frigates. Life on a ship of the line was regarded, except in a major fleet action, as less exciting and less dangerous.[44] Although in his subsequent career Francis displayed no lack of physical courage, it may be that he was placed on a ship of the line because in action his disability would be a handicap and danger to himself and to his shipmates.

Is it possible to see the influence of Seaforth's naval years in later life? He had a very hierarchical view of society and a belief that orders should be obeyed (both orders given to him and by him). It is likely that this was at least reinforced by service in the Royal Navy. He may also have learned from Admiral Mann a concern for the welfare of those for whom he was responsible. In the early autumn of 1777 Mann wrote to the naval officer at Mahon that 'His Majesty's squadron under my command is much distressed from want of beds, hammocks and slops' and asked that all those in the store should be sent to Gibraltar. Slops were seamen's robust working clothes. He asked that 'shoes and such slops as may be useful in the approaching winter' should be sent.[45] Seaforth had a strongly mercantilist view of trade and mercantile activity and with that a belief that British shipping should be supported and rivals discouraged. This was becoming unfashionable even when he was young, and it may have been developed by a naval service which seems mainly to have involved policing merchant ships. In particular, there is a clear link to a marked prejudice against Americans which he demonstrated in later years. In 1808 he wrote that the 'Yankees are really between ignorance and vanity something worse than half mad'.[46] This attitude had considerable political significance when he was governor of Barbados (1801–6) and tried to limit access by American ships and cargoes. It seems highly likely that his dislike of Americans was derived from the long periods at sea in the Mediterranean in the 1770s chasing American ships and often being outwitted by them.

Are there other pointers in Seaforth's early life which explain aspects of his later career? He developed a great pride in the heritage of the clan Mackenzie, probably through his father, who lived until Seaforth's seventeenth year. Perhaps because both were far removed from the Highlands geographically, and from the main line of the Mackenzie chiefs, Seaforth grew up with what was becoming an old-fashioned view of the nature of a clan and the powers of its chief. It will be shown in Chapter Two that this affected in important ways his attitude to the clan lands and to the tenants who lived on them. He also inherited from his father an ambition for military renown which was likely to be sadly compromised by his disability. This topic will be introduced in Chapter Six. Experts explain that those who (like Seaforth) become profoundly deaf find it harder to adjust than those who are born deaf. Illustrations have been given to show that the adult Seaforth felt his disability deeply. It may be that this caused, or at least exacerbated, a tendency to impatience and high-handedness which he sometimes demonstrated. It will be argued that it also led to a strong ambition to excel. This could be a positive pressure in encouraging him to use his considerable abilities to the full. His policies in Barbados were nothing if not ambitious, as will be shown in Chapters Seven and Nine. On the other hand, it was a damaging force in leading him (as shown in Chapter Four) to adopt a lifestyle which he could not afford and a level of expenditure which greatly increased his debts.

Notes

1. Clifford, T., M. Gallagher and H. Smailes, *Benjamin West and the Death of the Stag* (Edinburgh, 2009), pp. 5, 11–15, 17–19.
2. MacCoinnich, A.,'"Kingis rabellis" to Cuidich' n' Righ; the emergence of Clan Choinnich, *c*.1475–1508' in S. Boardman and A. Ross (eds), *The Exercise of Power in Medieval Scotland, 1200–1500* (Dublin, 2003), pp. 176–8, 182.

3. Munro, J., 'The Mackenzies' in R. D. Oram and G. P. Stell (eds), *Lordship and Architecture in Medieval and Renaissance Scotland* (Edinburgh, 2005), pp. 276–8, 281–2.
4. MacCoinnich, A., *Plantation and Civility in the North Atlantic World :The Case of the Northern Hebrides, 1570–1639* (Leiden, 2015), p. 189.
5. MacCoinnich, A., 'Siol Torcail and their Lordship in the Sixteenth Century' (Lewis: Islands Book Trust, 2007), pp. 10–11, 13–17.
6. Mackenzie, A., *History of the Mackenzies* (Inverness, 1894 edn), pp. 281–3, 291–8, 324, 326.
7. Richards, E. and M. Clough, *Cromartie: Highland Life 1650–1914* (Aberdeen, 1989), pp. 51–2, 55–60, 62–3, 67–8, 96, 99, 102–4.
8. Mackenzie, *History of the Mackenzies*, p. 331.
9. For example, Edinburgh, National Records of Scotland (NRS), GD46/15/1/11, Mrs Mary H. Mackenzie to F. H. Mackenzie, 19 December 1793.
10. NRS, GD46/17/4/289–90, Mrs Mary H. Mackenzie to F. H. Mackenzie, 19 January 1792.
11. Macinnes, A., 'Jacobites and Empire: Highland Connections, 1707–1753', paper at ESHSS Conference 'The Scottish Highlands: an Historical Reassessment?', September 2012.
12. NRS, GD46/17/2, 'Statement of lineage of Mackenzie, Earl [sic] of Seaforth', n.d., but apparently about 1807.
13. Nenadic, S., *Lairds and Luxury: the Highland Gentry in Eighteenth-Century Scotland* (Edinburgh, 2007), pp. 14, 98–9.
14. NRS, GD46/14/11/46, MS genealogies and biographical notes of the Mackenzies of Seaforth, etc., n.d., but post 1815 and pre 1840s.
15. NRS, GD46/6/25/7, A. Brodie to F. H. Mackenzie, 15 February 1793.
16. Chichester, H. M., 'Mackenzie, Francis Humberston, Baron Seaforth and Mackenzie of Kintail (1754–1815)', rev. J. Spain, *Oxford Dictionary of National Biography (ODNB)*, Oxford, 2004, online edition, <www.oxforddnb.com>, article no. 14126, accessed 29 September 2004.
17. Graham, B. and M. M. Sharp-Pucci, 'The special challenge of late-deafened adults: another deaf way' in C. J. Erting, R. C. Johnson, D. L. Smith and B. D. Snider (eds), *The Deaf Way: Proceedings from the International Conference on Deaf Culture* (Washington DC, 1994), pp. 505–6. The author is indebted to Dr Iain Davidson for this reference and for suggestions on the causes and consequences of Seaforth's disability.
18. Macrae, N., *Highland Second-Sight* (Dingwall, 1909), pp. 167–9.

19. Knox, J., *A Tour through the Highlands of Scotland and the Hebride Isles in 1786* (Edinburgh, 1787, reprint 1975), p. 185.
20. Hutchison, I., *A History of Disability in Nineteenth-Century Scotland* (Lewiston, NY, 2007), pp. 179–80; NRS, GD46/17/37/642–4, 'The case of the Family and Descendants of Mr Thomas Braidwood', London, 1811.
21. Edinburgh, National Library of Scotland (NLS), MS 6396, fos 21, 24, 30, F. H. Mackenzie to Mrs Mary Mackenzie, 10 and 13 October, 14 November 1795.
22. *Oracle and Public Advertiser,* British Library Burney Collection of 17th and 18th Century Newspapers online (BCN), 5 March 1794, accessed 9 December 2010.
23. *Gazetteer and New Daily Advertiser,* 28 July 1790 (BCN), accessed 8 December 2010.
24. *Star,* 24 December 1799, *Morning Herald,* 25 December 1799 (BCN); accessed 6 December 2010.
25. Barron, J., *The Northern Highlands in the Nineteenth Century: Newspaper Index and Annals,* (Inverness, 1903), vol. 1, pp. i, 80, 82.
26. Barker, G. F. R., 'Hamilton, Lord Archibald (1770–1827)', rev. H. C. G. Matthew, *ODNB,* online edition, <www.oxforddnb.com>, article no. 12051, accessed 21 June 2011.
27. London, The National Archives (TNA), CO28/67, fo. 168, Lord Seaforth to Lord Hobart, 29 December 1801.
28. Thorne, R., 'Robert Hobart 4th Earl of Buckinghamshire (1760–1816)', *ODNB,* online edition, <www.oxforddnb.com>, article no.13396, accessed 31 March 2008; Barker, G. F. R. and A. H. Stenning (eds), *The Westminster School Register from 1764 to 1883* (London, 1892), pp. v, 114.
29. Gun, W. T. J., (ed.), *The Harrow School Register, 1571–1800* (London, 1934), pp. xiii, 12; Welsh, R. C., (ed.), *The Harrow School Register 1801–1883* (London, 1894), p. 22.
30. Massie, A. W., 'Alexander Mackenzie Fraser (1758–1809)', *ODNB,* online edition, <www.oxforddnb.com>, article no. 10103, accessed 15 July 2009.
31. Adamson, J. W., *English Education 1789–1902* (Cambridge, 1930), pp. 54–7.
32. Bew, J., *Castlereagh Enlightenment, War and Tyranny* (London, 2011), pp. 15–16.
33. NRS, GD46/17/2, 'Statement of lineage of Mackenzie, Earl [sic] of Seaforth'.
34. Cavell, S. A., *Midshipmen and Quarterdeck boys in the British Navy, 1771–1831* (Woodbridge, 2012), p. 210.
35. Rodger, N. A. M., *The Command of the Ocean: A Naval History of Britain 1649–1815* (London, 2005 edn), pp. 381–2.

36. Pappalardo, B., *Royal Navy Lieutenants' passing certificates, 1691–1902* (Kew, 2001).
37. NLS, MS 6396, fo. 27, F. H. Mackenzie to Mrs Mary Mackenzie, 30 October 1795.
38. Knox, *A Tour through the Highlands of Scotland*, p. 185.
39. NLS, MS 6396, fos 39–41, Lord Seaforth to Lady Seaforth, 19 January 1804.
40. *London Chronicle*, 31 May 1774, 9 November 1775, 21 January 1777, 4 and 9 September 1777; *General Evening Post*, 2 March 1776, 15 June 1776, 5 October 1776; *St James Chronicle*, 9 December 1775, 22 June 1776, 22 October 1776, 22 November 1777; *Morning Chronicle*, 5 February 1777; *Daily Advertiser*, 4 and 29 November 1777; *Say's Weekly Journal*, 14 February 1778; *Public Advertiser*, 13 August 1777, 24 March 1778 (BCN, all accessed 15–16 November 2010).
41. TNA, ADM106/1225, fos 434 and 437, M. Warren, HM Naval Officer at Port Mahon, to Principal Officers and Commissioners of HM Navy, Navy Office, London, 23 September and 31 October 1774.
42. NRS, GD46/17/5, Certificate and recommendation by Lodge No. 1 of Minorca, 22 April 1777.
43. *Morning Chronicle*, 30 September 1777 (BCN), accessed 16 November 2010.
44. Cavell, *Midshipmen and Quarterdeck Boys*, p. 16.
45. TNA, ADM106/1240, fo. 134, R. Mann, Vice Admiral of the White, to Mr Warren, HM Naval Officer, Port Mahon, 19 September 1777; Rodger, *Command of the Ocean*, pp. 190–1.
46. NRS, GD46/17/28/57, Lord Seaforth to Inglis, Ellis and Co., 7 November 1808.

2 Land Management and Clanship in the 1780s and 1790s

Inheriting a Highland estate

The son of the Kenneth Mackenzie who, as has been seen in Chapter One, remained loyal to the government during the 1745 rising, was created earl of Seaforth in the peerage of Ireland in 1771. He spent much of his time abroad living the expensive life of what has been described as 'a cultured expatriate'.[1] A small picture in the Scottish National Portrait Gallery shows him presiding over a musical party in his villa in Naples in 1771. The performers are believed to be the composer Mozart (then aged fifteen) and his father.[2] In 1777 he escaped his debts by crossing the English Channel to France, accompanied by his mistress Harriet Powell. He subsequently married Harriet, a marriage which was without issue.[3] Harriet died in December 1779 and Kenneth wrote that 'I shall endeavour to bear with resignation the fate that Heaven has allotted to me'.[4] In 1780 he decided to sell the Seaforth estate to Thomas Frederick Humberston as a solution to his financial problems and probably also because of his lack of a male heir. Frederick was Francis' elder brother.[5] The Ross-shire estate still comprised a handsome part of the Seaforth patrimony – Lewis, Kintail (with Glenshiel), Lochalsh and a number of smaller properties in Easter Ross around Brahan and Fortrose.[6]

It was the intention to partially finance the Ross-shire purchase by selling Humberston's Lincolnshire estate, which might be expected to raise about half the cost.[7]

It was not until January 1781 in London that Frederick was able to meet Earl Kenneth, who had been with his regiment in

Guernsey, to finalise the deal. Frederick was in a hurry as he knew that he and his regiment were about to sail for India. He reported to George Gillanders, the estate factor, 'I have now taken the weight of his debts and of possession of the Estate upon myself.' Lord Seaforth had 'done everything required of him in a most pleasant manner'.[8] Well he might. The arrangement was that Frederick borrowed back the purchase price of £100,000 from the earl at 5 per cent. This effectively meant that he paid Earl Kenneth (and after Kenneth's death in 1781, his heir, Lady Caroline Mackenzie) annual interest of £5,000.[9] Frederick regretted that 'I could otherwise wish much to have been precisely informed of the net income of the estate'.[10] When Gillanders, whom he reappointed factor, subsequently produced this, the free rental after payment of ministers' stipends, etc. was £4,085.[11] The income of the Ross-shire estate was, therefore, less than the interest payment to Earl Kenneth. This disastrous decision, exacerbated by the failure to sell the Humberston estate until 1788, created a burden which was to have a serious effect on the estate's finances well into the next century.

When Earl Kenneth died Frederick inherited the chiefship, but not the earldom, which could only descend through the direct male line. Frederick was now in India, serving as lieutenant colonel commandant of the 100th Regiment of Foot. In April 1783 the ship on which he was travelling was attacked by a Maharatta fleet. A desperate resistance was maintained for four hours against overwhelming odds before the ship was captured. He was shot through the body with a four-pound canonball and died of his wounds.[12] When, months later, news of this reached Britain, Francis knew that he had succeeded to the chiefship of the Mackenzies and to the ownership of the Seaforth lands in Ross-shire. He was part of recognisable trends in coming to his estates because of the failure of the main line to reproduce and in the fusing of Celtic and English elites in marriage.[13] Another example was William Johnston (1729–1805), of a Border gentry family, who married an English heiress, Frances Pulteney and was made rich by this alliance.[14] As Francis' lands were heavily indebted he had a challenging inheritance. And there was for him another bitter legacy. The family regarded Frederick's death as heroic and his service in India as highly honourable. He described how in his command in Calicut he 'drove the Enemy out of the country, defeated them in three actions, in one of which I killed Hyder's brother in law . . . and by this means got possession of a large and fertile tract of territory'.[15] The consequence for Francis (hereafter referred to as Seaforth) was that he developed a strong ambition to emulate the command skills and courage under fire of his brother and, prior to that, of his father Major Mackenzie. But who would entrust troops in action to a man who was profoundly deaf?

Attitudes to clanship and 'improvement' – people or sheep?

Traditionally, under the concept of *duthchas* (trusteeship over the lands occupied by the clan), the chief's role was to provide protection to the members of the clan. Allan Macinnes has shown that this was already breaking down in the seventeenth century. Chiefs became involved in commercial enterprises, often initially through the droving trade. They socialised with other members of the Scottish landed elite and were increasingly absent from the clan lands. They accumulated debts, partly as a result of the seventeenth-century civil wars, and had to service them. These trends accelerated in the eighteenth century and, Macinnes argues, in the aftermath of the 'Forty-Five the clan elite throughout Scottish Gaeldom abandoned the traditional idea of trusteeship'.[16] The traditional Highland economy came under strong pressure from that of the rapidly industrialising United Kingdom to increase production of wool, beef and kelp, a pressure exacerbated from 1793 by the effects of the wars with revolutionary and Napoleonic France. Macinnes's view is that in the late eighteenth century chiefs subordinated, if not threw over, their personal obligations as protectors of their clansmen. Competitive bidding on the expiry of leases was seen as leading to rent rises, the growth of single-tenant farms (often sheep farms tenanted by outsiders), the virtual elimination of the traditional multiple-tenant communal township and the creation of crofting townships. The period has been called 'The First Phase of Clearance'.[17] This view has been supported by many historians.[18] James Hunter argues that 'by the eighteenth century's end any lingering traces of a patriarchal outlook had been strictly subordinated to the pursuit of profit'.[19] Peter Womack states that Highland chieftains 'learned to think of themselves as individual proprietors rather than as trustees of a collective inheritance'.[20] An example of such a proprietor was Duncan Macdonald of Glengarry, who from 1782 introduced large-scale sheep farms to Glengarry and subsequently to Knoydart, evicting his small tenants, many of whom emigrated to Canada.[21]

The judgement of modern historiography is that Glengarry's view predominated among late-eighteenth-century Highland chiefs.[22] However, Seaforth was different. One of his landowning neighbours in Ross-shire complained of his 'foolish ideas of chieftaincy, long since abandoned by men of sense'.[23] It was perhaps because he was born and brought up in England and had an old-fashioned view of chiefship that he adopted the role of *caber feidh* or hereditary chief of the clan Mackenzie with great seriousness. His Highlandism translated into a significant (even if not consistent) measure of practical concern for his clansmen. His attitudes and actions had much more in common with that high priest of Highlandism, David Stewart of Garth, who criticised 'the system of overlooking the original occupiers and of giving every support to strangers'.[24] Like Seaforth, he had traditional views of his duties to his tenants, was unable to repay inherited debts and sought financial salvation in a West Indian governorship.[25] In 1804 Seaforth wrote to the home secretary that on estates where large-scale sheep farming had not been introduced 'the proprietors are often under the necessity of sacrificing their own interest to provide for this population'.[26] This was a fair description of his own record, although it will be seen that he was often given contrary advice and was sometimes tempted to bring in sheep farmers. Seaforth was not alone among Highland proprietors in 'sacrificing their own interest'. For example, successive dukes of Hamilton in this period, refused to bring in Lowland sheep farmers to displace local residents on the Isle of Arran. They were, however, wealthier than Seaforth.[27] The earls of Breadalbane were criticised by one of their advisers for feeling 'indifferent to what was passing around them' and for 'not wishing to increase their revenues by dispossessing the families who resided upon their property' due to 'a mistaken feeling of compassion to the small farmers'.[28] The fourth duke of Gordon was opposed to large-scale sheep farming throughout the late eighteenth century. As David Taylor has explained, he hoped to raise regiments and 'decided that his future ... lay more in the patriotic rearing of men than sheep'.[29] Other proprietors reluctant to introduce sheep (including Seaforth) may also have been influenced by the potential of their estates for military recruitment.

Seaforth's policy towards his small tenants should be placed in the context of the especially rapid population growth which was taking place in the north-west Highlands. It has been calculated that the Highlands and Hebrides had the highest rate of population increase in Scotland in the 1790s at 15.5 per thousand of population, the next highest being the western Lowlands at 13 per thousand.[30] The population of the whole of Ross and Cromarty rose by 17 per cent between Alexander Webster's enumeration in 1755 and the figures given in the 1790s by parish ministers in the Old Statistical Account. This average conceals substantial variations, as shown in Table 2.1. In the Easter Ross parish of Urray (which contained Brahan Castle) there was a decline of around 24 per cent due, according to the minister to 'the annual emigration to the South Country in harvest' and army enlistment.[31] In almost all the Wester Ross parishes containing Seaforth lands and also in Lewis there was a substantial increase, in most cases between 20 and 45 per cent. Two may have suffered from miscalculation. The minister of Lochalsh was himself puzzled that, despite a considerable emigration in 1770 and large military recruitment, the increase

Table 2.1 Population of selected Ross-shire parishes, 1755 and 1790s.

Parish	1755	1790s	% change (+ or −)
Easter Ross			
Urray	2456	1860	−24.26
Wester Ross			
Glenshiel	509	721	+41.65
Kintail	698	840	+20.34
Lochalsh	613	1334	+117.61
Lewis			
Barvas	1995	2006	+0.55
Lochs	1267	1768	+39.54
Stornoway	1812	2639	+45.64
Uig	1312	1898	+44.66

Sources: J. G. Kyd, *Scottish Population Statistics including Webster's Analysis of Population 1755* (Edinburgh, 1952), pp.61–2; *Statistical Account of Scotland*, vols VI, VII, XI, XIX (1793–7), <http://stat-acc-scot.edina.ac.uk/link/1791–99/ Ross>, accessed 19 April 2017.

for his parish seemed so high.[32] The apparent failure of the population of Barvas to increase is out of line with the other Lewis parishes, in all of which the increase was around 40 per cent. This was higher than on the island of Skye, whose population grew over the same period by approximately 27 per cent according to a recent estimate. This may be because emigration from Skye was estimated in the 1790s to have been 2,400.[33] As will be shown, emigration from Lewis then was probably not much more than 800. These figures for Wester Ross and Lewis represent very significant growth, especially considering that in 1783 there was a calamitous harvest failure caused by an ash cloud following the Laki volcanic eruption in Iceland.[34] The reasons for population growth are complex. A significant factor was the increasing use from the 1780s of inoculation against smallpox, a disease which had killed children in particularly large numbers. Another was the cultivation of the potato which, according to Thomas Pennant, who toured the Highlands in the early 1770s, was widespread (but not universal) in Ross-shire by then, allowing denser settlement.[35]

Despite the population pressures Seaforth resisted expulsive clearance and was slow to introduce large-scale sheep farming. Some time prior to 1786 he refused offers of double rent from south-country sheep farmers for lands in Kintail and replied to George Jeffrey, the factor who had received the offer, that 'he neither would let his lands for sheep pasture, nor turn out his people, upon any consideration, or for any rent that could be offered'.[36] In 1787 there was a general sett (or re-letting) of the estate. A London newspaper, reporting this sett, commented that 'a spirit of philanthropy directed his management, founded on the situation of his country and the disposition and circumstances of the people'. On this occasion sheep farmers offered triple rent for Kintail lands, which was again refused. The report argued that, had the offer been accepted, 'the people must have emigrated in a body to the wilds of America', that Seaforth had accepted a very moderate increase of rent 'and permitted every man to possess the land his ancestors had lived on for generations'.[37] Reflecting on this later he commented that he had acted against advice because 'I was so anxious to keep together the people I looked on as heritably attached to my family'.[38]

The rent rises in Lewis do not appear to have been as moderate as this report suggested. They ranged from 24 per cent in Ness

Figure 2.1 Map of the Isle of Lewis, showing parishes and selected farms and townships, c.1800 (© Joan C. McKichan)

and Stornoway to 34 per cent in Uig and 36 per cent in Lochs and Carloway.[39] What could be regarded as philanthropic is that the number of tenancies in Lewis remained roughly the same through the 1780s. In 1789 the number of tenants in Uig was twenty-six (one less than in 1783), in Barvas twelve (the same) and in Lochs twenty-two (three more than in 1783). A detailed examination of about half the tenancies in Uig in 1783 and 1787 indicates a high degree of continuity in the names of both the farms and the tenants in both larger and smaller tenancies. The exceptions are two joint farms, in which the name of the lead tenant had changed.[40] It was, therefore, not unfair for the 1787 newspaper report to claim that, after the sett of that year, each man possessed the same land as before. But this was at a substantially higher rent.

On many Highland and Hebridean estates in the first half of the eighteenth century large parcels of land were let to tacksmen on favourable terms, many on very long leases and some even over several generations. These were the men who in the past had acted as the officers of the clan regiment and were often related, even if remotely, to the chief. In return for military service these tacks had often been under-rented. However, tacksmen were reputed to exact high rents from their sub-tenants and so to cream off much of the profit of the estate.

The general view has been that, as proprietors became more commercially minded in the later eighteenth century, they had a strong incentive to remove these tacksmen or radically review their leases.[41] As James Hunter puts it, 'most tacksmen were unwilling or unable to make the necessary adjustment ... Tacksmen's tenancies were therefore ended and the lands offered to the highest bidder'.[42] Recent work on the lands in Badenoch owned by the duke of Gordon has revealed a set of entrepreneurial tacksmen who struggled very hard to keep up with the commercial economy as cattle graziers and agricultural improvers. The estate relied on them for their commercial enthusiasm and reserves of capital and as middle managers well into the nineteenth century.[43] On the Seaforth estate also, in the late eighteenth century, there were larger tenants holding their tacks for long periods, some of whom were actively involved in commercial activities and could be described as middle managers.

Table 2.2 shows that there were seventeen Lewis tacksman families who held tenancies throughout the period 1755 to 1791. Two of the highest-rented in 1755 were Gress and Back (John McIver, £40) and Kneep and Berve (Duncan and William McLennan, £31). The farm of Linshader was held by Donald McAuley in 1755 (£11) and by George McAuley

Table 2.2 Families holding tenancies on Lewis in 1755 and 1791

Parish/District	Tenant/s 1755	Possession 1755	Rent 1755 (£ s d)	Tenant/s 1791	Possession 1791	Rent 1791
Uig	Donald McAulay	Linishader	11.3.4	George McAulay	Linishader & Callernish	84.0.0
Do.	John Nicolson & brother	Cairnish etc.	16.11.2	John Nicolson	Cairnish etc.	26.5.0
Do.	Duncan & William McLennan	Kneep & Berve	31.13.4	Duncan & Donald McLennan	Berve & Kneep	67.0.0
Do.	Donald McAulay	Brenish etc.	26.5.9	Don. McAulay & Widow McAulay	Brenish	36.7.0
Do.	Aulay McAulay	Breasklet	11.2.3	William McAulay	Breasklet	27.3.0
Do.	Donald & John McLeod	Pabay	13.7.9	Donald McLeod	Pabay	26.0.0
Stornoway	Roderick McIver	Two Tolstays	22.4.5	John McIver Jun. & Widow	South & North Tolstay	45.3.0
Do.	John McIver	Gress & Back	40.0.9	Evander McIver	Gress & Back	94.10.0
Do.	William McIver	Upper Coll	10.11.1	William McIver	Upper Coll	29.0.0
Do.	Alexr Morrison	Shader etc.	12.17.9	John Morrison	Shader & Sheshader	30.0.0
Lochs	Mr Colin McKenzie (Rev.)	Keose & Valtos	31.15.7	Alexr & Roderick Mackenzie	Valtos & Buinish	28.19.0

(*Continued*)

Table 2.2 (Continued)

Parish/District	Tenant/s 1755	Possession 1755	Rent 1755 (£ s d)	Tenant/s 1791	Possession 1791	Rent 1791
Do.	Donald McKenzie	Leurbost	11.8.3	Allan & John Mackenzie	Rainish & Leurbost	74.0.0
Barvas	John Ross	Mid Borve	6.17.0	Donald Ross & Widow	Mid Borve & Begargary	28.10.0
Ness	Donald Morrison	North Dell	14.10.0	Allan Morrison	North Dell	35.0.0
Do.	Donald Morrison	Cross	9.17.6	Angus & Allan Morrison	Cross	22.1.0
Do.	William Murray relict	Rona & Swanibost	21.3.4	Rory & John Murray	Swanibost	39.15.0
Do.	Kenneth Morrison	Lionel	10.13.4	Alex. Morrison	Lionel	28.0.0

Source: National Records of Scotland, GD427/4/2, GD427/16/5.

for at least twenty-five years (1766–91). George was able to add Callernish by 1776 and was very active in the management of Seaforth's kelp business. The enlarged holding was rented at £84 in 1791, representing 10.8 per cent of Uig's rental. Also in Uig, the parish with the best kelp shores, the Nicolson family were tacksmen throughout the years 1755–91. John Nicolson held Edrechile from, at the latest, 1776, followed by Kenneth from, at the latest, 1783.[44] Kenneth was appointed kelp overseer for Barvas and Stornoway parishes in 1795, and was described as the only man capable of so acting 'both for firmness and his knowledge of shipping the kelp'.[45] These were classic examples of the new-style tacksmen who Andrew Mackillop has described as 'elite tenantry as developers of capital reserves and as the region's primary entrepreneurial class'.[46] A tacksman on Seaforth's Wester Ross estates who was able to adjust to new times and also become a middle manager was Archibald Macrae of Ardintoul in Lochalsh. The Macraes had long been allies of the Seaforth chiefs in Wester Ross. Archibald not only retained his tack into the early nineteenth century, but was also factor for Seaforth and then, on the sale of Lochalsh in 1801, to the new proprietor Hugh Innes.[47]

As tacksmen, George Gillanders and his son Alexander were special cases. They held land in several Lewis parishes. In Lochs alone they held three tenancies in 1783 totalling £77, which represented 20 per cent of the rental of the parish, and they seem to have under-rented their own tenancies. For example, the rent of Gravir and St Colums (Lochs), held by George Gillanders, increased only fractionally between 1776 (£22 6s 8d) and 1791 (£23 10s 8d). By contrast, the overall rental for Lochs increased by 36 per cent in 1787. George and Alexander Gillanders also held substantial tacks in Stornoway parish – by 1791 Aignish, Arnish, Gameray, Melbost and Upper Bybell – with combined rental £165 or 32 per cent of the parish rental.[48] They owed their power and wide acres to their factorial role. The position of tacksmen on Lewis to some extent paralleled that on Tiree. In 1768–9 half the island was held by twelve larger farmers, usually on a nineteen-year tack, and thus described as 'tacksmen'. Eric Cregeen described these as 'a powerful and privileged class of upper tenants'.[49]

A feature of the Gillanders' factorship in the 1770s which Seaforth was determined to avoid was emigration. There had been an emigration from Lochalsh to North America in 1770, described as 'considerable',[50] and one from Lewis in 1773, when between 700 and 800 people had sailed from Stornoway for North America. The newspaper report of this event stated that the emigrants 'complained much of the oppression they laboured under which, they say, obliged them to leave their native country'.[51] This is clearly a reference to the regime of George Gillanders. George became factor of Lewis in 1761 and from 1765 had responsibility also for the mainland estates. His son Alexander was factor of Lewis from 1775. Earl Kenneth, who was rarely in Ross-shire, appears to have had complete confidence in George Gillanders. When a new sub-factor was to be appointed, he told him, 'I shall approve of your choice on this occasion as I entirely trust to you.'[52] When Frederick Mackenzie Humberston acquired the estate in 1781 he associated Alexander with George in the factorial commission and assured George, 'I have every confidence both in your ability and integrity.'[53] However, the father and son continued to attract criticism. In 1788 Charles Greville, one of Seaforth's greatest friends, recommended that he make Seaforth Lodge in Lewis his principal residence. He argued this would be 'a benefit to the improvement of the Island tenfold of that it would be if the same amount was employed through the agency of factors' and that this 'would make persons inclined from oppression to emigrate select the Lewis as an asylum'.[54]

In 1792, an informed observer of the efforts by Mrs Mackenzie to set up spinning schools (which will be discussed later in this chapter) insisted that fair prices must be set in contrast to 'exploitation by the superior or the superior's man of business in selling to and buying from the inhabitants'.[55] Why was Seaforth, who aspired to be a supportive proprietor, slow to tackle the behaviour of the Gillanders' management? He could not be accused of ignoring Lewis. In the 1780s he spent most summers at Seaforth Lodge. As will be shown in Chapter Three, he put a considerable effort into the scheme to establish a fishing village at Loch Roag. He devoted a large amount of time in 1787 to a general sett. While he had in mind the bigger picture of how Lewis might be developed, he seems not to have addressed the day-to-day behaviour of his agents. He did not suffer from lack of energy or of good intentions, but at this time his focus was on his political, family and social life, much of which was conducted in London. It was not until the death of Alexander in 1794 and his father's retiral in 1796 that the factorial regime of the Gillanders dynasty in Lewis came to an end. As Eric Richards has pointed out, it was not unusual for Highland factors to become figures of hatred among the people of their estates.[56]

Before Frederick sailed for India in 1781, an Act of Parliament was secured to permit the entail on the Humberston estates in Lincolnshire to be broken so that they could be sold to pay off part of the purchase price of the Seaforth estates in Scotland.[57] Therefore, when Francis succeeded in 1783 there was a mechanism in place to restore the estate's finances. His advisers pressed, 'it will be necessary for Mr Mackenzie . . . to determine a sale of some of the estates.'[58] However, land sales did not take place until the late 1780s and the debt burden increased. This was one factor, together with his extravagance and inherited debts, in bringing about in 1788 the first of many financial crises, which will be discussed in Chapter Four. In the event only the Lincolnshire estate was sold (in late 1788).[59] A year later the East India Company paid almost £23,000 to settle at last the balance of his brother's Indian estate.[60] These two events averted the immediate crisis, but were insufficient to give sound foundations for the future. In May 1788 Charles Greville advised that Kintail and Lochalsh should be sold to provide funds to invest in the potentially profitable island of Lewis. However, Francis' pride in his heritage made him unwilling to sell the lands from which the Seaforth Mackenzies had sprung. 'As common business', he explained, 'I would sell these estates, but as the head of a Family and of a Clan I would not.'[61] Thus, family pride prevented him in the 1780s from establishing large-scale sheep farms or selling Lochalsh and Kintail. Seaforth did accept one economy recommended by Greville.[62] He left Parliament in 1790 and made his main residence Seaforth Lodge in Lewis.[63]

Multiple pressures in the 1790s

Seaforth sought advice, not only from his estate factors, who tended to recommend sheep farming, but also from authorities who did not. Notably, in 1790 he received a long letter of advice from George Dempster of Dunnichen, the agriculturalist,

economic commentator and politician. Seaforth and he were in
touch as fellow directors of the British Fisheries Society and (in
the late 1780s) as fellow Whig MPs.[64] He had high hopes for
Lewis now that Seaforth had made it his principal residence. He
wrote, 'I envy you and your lady as primitive king and queen,
legislators and benefactors of your people, who will thrive
under your genial influence.' He encouraged road-building by
promising that he would visit Lewis 'when you can whirl me
with safety in your phaeton from Stornoway to Loch Roag'. He
hoped that in Lewis settlements would soon be seen where hitherto cattle had their summer pastures, and that limestone would
be found to provide fertiliser for the new fields. However, he
also knew of the reputation of the Lewis factors and encouraged
the settlement of attornies, 'whom the poor resort to in cases of
oppression'.[65]

Dempster also shared Seaforth's ambition to discourage
Highland emigration to North America. He criticised John,
nineteenth Macdonald of Clanranald, for the treatment which
had recently caused the people of the island of Eigg to emigrate.
He was alleged to have spent more time in Geneva than in
Scotland,[66] and after his death in 1797 his debts were estimated
at £57,605.[67] Another Hebridean proprietor from whose estate
there was emigration at this period was Roderick Macneil of
Barra, fortieth chief (1755–1822, and thus an almost exact contemporary of Seaforth). He created larger farms and moved the
old tenants to smaller and poorer holdings. A total of around
300 people are reckoned to have emigrated from Barra to Prince
Edward Island in 1790 and 1792.[68] Dempster was clear that,
in contrast, Seaforth shared his own horror of emigration. It is
noteworthy that this was before the outbreak of war with revolutionary France in 1793 made it potentially very profitable to
retain population to recruit soldiers and process kelp. Seaforth
was given credit for this by sympathetic observers. In 1791 one
of these commented:

> He has in his retirement from political life been incessantly employ-
> ing himself in improving the island of Lewis ... the improvements
> he has made in two years excite astonishment ... He deserves also
> to be mentioned in this band of patriots who ... do not consider
> their extensive possessions are given them solely for their own
> benefit, and who disdain to increase their revenues by banishing the
> people'.[69]

A similar comment on Seaforth was made almost ten years later. A correspondent, who recommended in 1800 that inland Lewis should be let entirely to sheep farmers, admitted that 'the proprietor may not be disposed to break the strong ties of affection which unite ten thousand people to the place of their nativity'.[70]

No evidence has been found of major emigrations from the Seaforth estates in the 1780s or 1790s. The first emigration in Seaforth's time seems to have been the departure of two ships from Lewis to America in late 1802, when he was in Barbados and after the Peace of Amiens removed temporarily the need for military and naval recruits. This was happening throughout the Highlands. The correspondent who reported this to him in Barbados added 'the setts of Lords Breadalbane and Macdonald lately made and those about to be so by Duke Gordon, Lochiel, Macintosh etc. will occasion great displacement of people and consequent emigration, which is a mania'.[71] This confirms a suggestion by James Hunter that the Peace of Amiens in 1802/3 renewed emigration from the Highlands, which had been curtailed since the outbreak of the French War in 1793.[72] In 1804 Seaforth opposed (successfully) a proposal to pay the passage of families of recruits to the Royal Canadian regiment on the grounds that it would encourage 'endless future emigration' and the creation of more sheep farms. Another concern, he admitted, was that more conventional recruitment would suffer.[73]

It is evident that in the 1790s Seaforth was increasingly torn between commercial considerations and concern for his small tenants. He provided a report, probably in early 1794, for incorporation into Sir John Sinclair's General View of the Agriculture of the Northern Counties and Islands of Scotland (1795). By this time his view was that 'a conjunct farm is a cantonment of wretches who quarrel together' and that 'lasting improvements in agriculture can only be expected from men of much larger funds than can possibly be attracted to a small highland farm'. On the other hand he believed that 'to dismiss all supernumeraries is a harsh remedy – the more humane one is to suffer the inconvenience patiently and wait for an opportunity of disposing comfortably of those who must go'.[74]

Seaforth liked to appear an authority on agriculture, and two of his proposers for election to the Royal Society in 1794 were leading improvers, Arthur Young and Sir John Sinclair.[75] By 1799 he was one of five vice presidents of the Highland Society of Scotland, which met in Edinburgh.[76] This was formed in 1784 on similar lines to the Highland Society of London (1778). Both had an elite memberships dedicated to 'Highlandism'. It has been suggested that this was an attempt to establish 'Scoto-Britishness' as a distinctive Scottish identity within the British state and was expressed through the promotion of Highland culture and the Highland economy.[77] The Edinburgh Society had a greater reputation for making practical suggestions for agricultural improvement. A few years earlier George Dempster had complained to him, probably mainly about the London Society, that 'they encourage the bagpipe to drown out the noises and groans of the people'.[78] However, Seaforth's status as a vice president of the Highland Society was downgraded in 1800 to one of ten extraordinary directors on the grounds that he was only occasionally in Edinburgh to attend meetings.[79]

In the early 1790s Seaforth was forced by financial problems to consider at least the possibility of clearance. He was not unaware of the rent increases which could be achieved by introducing sheep. His interest in sheep was illustrated in 1795 when he became an 'extraordinary director' of the Society for the Improvement of British Wool, chaired by Sir John Sinclair.[80] At several times the introduction of sheep farms was suggested by his advisers. A sale in Lewis was contemplated in 1793–4 and a draft advertisement suggested that the parishes of Uig and Lochs would be particularly suitable for conversion into sheep walks.[81] In the event, successful recruitment for the 78th Regiment appeared to ease the immediate pressure and no sale took place.[82] Not only was the regiment expected to be profitable, but it also gave a positive incentive to retain population. As George Gillanders put it, 'now is the time that men is preferable to gold'.[83] At the 1793 Glenshiel sett, Seaforth's factor Peter Fairbairn led him to expect that

> Matters can be so brought about as to introduce sheep farming, secure a handsome augmentation, and continue your tenants ... some of the Glenshiel people begin cordially to relish sheep farming and hope they will all come into it with little difficulty.[84]

In fact this optimism was misplaced. Small tenants lacked the capital, expertise and marketing facilities required for sheep farming,[85] and Seaforth was unwilling as yet to evict in order to introduce sheep. He later alleged that at the 1793 sett the

Glenshiel tenants had banded together so as not to compete against one another for the new leases.[86] This was written many years later (1811) after many disappointments. What he may have forgotten in 1811, but was probably influenced by in 1793 and 1794, was the ability of small tenants to provide sons for his regiment, the 78th. In Lochalsh in 1794, rent rises were modified in return for a high level of recruitment and Andrew Mackillop has suggested that a direct undertaking was obtained that land could be retained by those supplying recruits.[87] There is evidence elsewhere in the Highlands of small tenants becoming more assertive and willing to bargain in the 1790s. David Taylor has shown how in Badenoch they took advantage of high cattle prices to haggle with drovers and the demand for recruits to bargain over bounties and land in return for enlistment.[88]

One of the features of Highland estates in the First Phase of Clearance was the increasing frequency of competitive bidding for leases and elimination of multiple-tenant communal townships in order to create large single-tenant farms and crofting townships.[89] Rent rises, and thus presumably a process of competitive bidding, had been taking place on the Seaforth estate since the middle of the eighteenth century. This is shown by Table 2.3.

As might be expected, the largest increases coincide with periods of rising prices for cattle. That, in the 1760s, reflects the expansion of the Highland cattle trade in the more settled political conditions in the Highlands from the 1750s and also the epidemic of cattle plague in England between 1745 and 1757.[90] Conversely, the 1770s was a decade in which there

Table 2.3 Total rental of Lewis parishes, 1755–1803

Year	Rental (to nearest £)	Incremental % increase	Cumulative % increase
1755	1536	—	—
1766	2145	39.64	39.64
1776	2296	7.03	49.47
1787	2884	25.60	87.76
1799	4436	53.81	188.80
1803	5476	23.44	256.51

Source: National Records of Scotland, GD427/4/2 (1755), GD427/5/5 (1766), GD427/11/7 (1776), GD427/15 (1787), GD46/20/4/1/4 (1799), GD46/20/4/1/16 (1803).

were six years of poor cattle prices, and thus limited opportunity for rent increases. Although climatic conditions were poor in the early 1780s, there was a sustained run of favourable cattle markets in the second half of the decade, reflected in a rent rise in 1787 which was substantial but not as high as the 1760s.[91] The most substantial increase of all, in the 1790s, was a consequence of the great increase in livestock prices created by the French Revolutionary War. The rental of Lochalsh rose from £582 in 1780 to £1,299 in 1800, an increase of 123 per cent. Colin Mackenzie, Seaforth's second cousin and Edinburgh law agent, when in 1797 he was trying to sell Lochalsh, wrote of 'the great rise since 1780 proving how certainly progressive the Rent of a Highland property is'.[92] The rental of Lewis rose from £2,212 in 1783, when Seaforth inherited, to £4,472 in 1801, an increase of 102.16 per cent.[93] It seems that these rent increases were at the lower end of the spectrum. The rental of the Cromarty estate rose over a similar period (1780–1806, and before it had extensive sheep farms) from £1,250 to £4,500 or 260 per cent.[94] A still more striking comparison is with the 740 per cent increase achieved by sheep farming on parts of Glengarry between the 1770s and 1802.[95] Over a similar period (1776–1802), the Lewis rent increase was 95.42 per cent.[96] Seaforth would not have accepted the view of modern historians such as Charles Dodgshon that the interests of landowners and their lesser tenants were now irreconcilable.[97]

Similarly, the number of tenancies remained roughly the same – for example, in 1789 the number of tenants in Uig was 26 (27 in 1783), in Barvas 12 (the same in 1783) and in Lochs 22 (19 in 1783).[98] This does not suggest the widespread creation either of larger farms or of small ones on the coast for kelping tenants. However, rentals can mask the actual tenurial structure and a single tenant might have several communal townships on his tack.[99] To complicate matters further, it has been shown that in Lewis in the second half of the eighteenth century there was a continual process of shifting settlement. Some townships survived, but others disappeared and new ones were established.[100] It is likely that this reflected changes in pasture quality and the needs of kelp processing.

In 1792 Seaforth's wife Mary proposed (undoubtedly with his approval) setting up spinning schools on Lewis,[101] although the main demand was for linen thread to be woven and finished in the distant Lowlands.[102] In his submission to the Board of

Agriculture in 1794 Seaforth argued that, if population was to be preserved in the Highlands, manufactures must be introduced. However, he also mentioned the problems arising from distance from markets and bad roads.[103] Mary's plans involved trespassing on the authority and interests of the Gillanders family. An informed observer (an official from the Society for the Propagation of Christian Knowledge) commended her 'laudable intentions for the introduction of knowledge and industry into the hitherto neglected island', but criticised former manipulation of prices by the factors.[104] By February 1794 Alexander Gillanders, any overt obstruction by him having dissolved, reported that the spinning schools in Stornoway and Bernera were particularly successful.[105] In 1799 and 1800 the estate was paying spinning mistresses at Uig, Carloway, Shawbost and Borve.[106] James Headrick, the agricultural commentator from whom Seaforth commissioned a report on Lewis in 1800, thought that their introduction of spinning had done much good in giving employment to the women.[107] Lady Seaforth was determined that the scheme should be continued after she moved to Barbados in 1801. Colin Mackenzie reported that the issue of monopoly had again arisen (on this occasion due to the activities of the Stornoway merchant P. Downie), and a new agent was to be appointed. His duty was 'to see people have fair play . . . and encourage the competition which must be for the benefit of your poor islanders'.[108] However, the linen spinners of Lewis were always at a competitive disadvantage. Linen weaving was carried out in the Lowlands, and rural spinners in Angus, Perthshire, Dunbartonshire, Argyllshire and even Easter Ross had lower transport costs and thus a clear advantage over those in Lewis.[109]

Seaforth's record in capital investment was patchy. He extended his holdings in Easter Ross around Brahan, an area which was believed to be more capable of improvement than the west-coast lands. Ussie, to the north of Brahan, was purchased as early as 1784 and Moy, to the west, in 1794.[110] In 1795 extensive new farm buildings were being planned for Balnain and Dunglast near Brahan. These had the prospect of attracting higher rents, but the same could not be said for the building programme of churches and schools in Lewis. Fairbairn argued in 1795 that this should be completed before any new projects of the sort were contemplated.[111] A better investment might have been in roads. In 1787, when the directors of the

British Fisheries Society visited Lewis, they discovered that there were 'yet no roads made in the country'.[112] Around 1809 Lewis was still described as being entirely destitute of roads, with the exception of a road from Stornoway to Barvas, begun in 1793 'and not yet nearly finished'.[113] However, it was not easy to attract skilled contractors to a remote island at a reasonable price. One contractor, H. Sinclair, and his assistant McPherson had been employed on the Barvas road in 1796 at £100 per mile. When the estate attempted to complete the road in 1798, they offered to contract for twice the previous rate. Sinclair was working on Highland roads and McPherson threatened to go off to the Crinan Canal.[114] Some deal must have been made with Sinclair because he was paid £261 in 1798 and £450 in 1799 for road-making in Lewis.[115] Seaforth was persisting with the Barvas road, but was apparently unwilling or unable to invest enough to complete it.

There is evidence that Seaforth was among the proprietors who were slow to eliminate multiple-tenant townships, which survived in significant numbers after 1800. In Ussie, which had been purchased to be more productive than the heavily peopled west-coast lands, an expert survey in 1802 criticised the large number of small tenants.[116] In 1807 the Croe lands in Kintail were referred to as 'chiefly intermixed and occupied by small tenants'.[117] James Headrick's report on Lewis in 1800 made clear that, among the small tenants, multiple tenancy was still the norm, and he was horrified by the extent of it. He wrote that 'I have often seen what is called runrig . . . where different people cultivated ridges which were intermixed. But I never saw sixteen or eighteen cultivators concerned in the culture of the same ridge'. He recommended the division of runrig farms into crofts 'by which each man might work for himself, and not be confused and jumbled among his neighbours' and that many small farmers would be better employed as fishermen or day labourers and could be given about four acres to keep a cow and grow potatoes.[118] However, a recent study of land use in Lewis suggests that the replacement of communal holdings by crofts did not occur generally until the 1820s and indeed in the Park area of south-east Lewis not until around 1850.[119]

One aspect of Headrick's advice was adopted. He wrote that 'the greatest part of the parishes of Lochs and Uig are best adapted for sheep'. In 1802, when Seaforth was in Barbados, six farms in the parish of Lochs were amalgamated in the Valamos sheep farm, the only one established on the estate in Seaforth's time. The rental increased from £145 to £317, or 140 per cent, compared to the 47 per cent increase which had been achieved the previous year in a more limited reorganisation in a sett of Glenshiel (which will be discussed in Chapter Four).[120] This illustrates the financial rewards which could have been open to Seaforth if he had fully taken aboard Headrick's proposals and, like so many other Highland proprietors, established more than one large-scale sheep farm and hastened to abolish joint farms.

Lord Macdonald's lands on Skye and North Uist offer an interesting parallel to Lewis. They had been surveyed and valued by J. Blackadder in 1799. He, like Headrick, recommended the abolition of runrig and of joint farms. Larger farms, initially one or two of them for sheep, were to be tenanted by farmers from outside the Highlands. The displaced families would be settled on crofts by the seashore (in North Uist for kelpers). It was expected that the rental of the Skye estate would increase from £5,500 to £9,690 or 76 per cent. In 1801, 267 of his Skye tenants were given notice to quit. The consequence was widespread opposition reflected in petitions and preparations by many, especially in the parishes of Sleat and Strath, to emigrate to America. Macdonald was horrified at the potential loss of his kelping labour force and postponed the planned completion of the scheme until a year later (Whitsun 1804). By this time the passing of the Passenger Vessels Act of 1803, under pressure from Highland proprietors, made it much more expensive to emigrate.[121] However, Macdonald seems, like Seaforth, to have had contradictory policies. In 1803 he instructed his factors 'to place in each farm as many tenants as can be properly accommodated in it ... without regard to the additional increase of rent ... his object being to give situations to as many families of the actual natives and inhabitants of Skye as can be supported in comfort'.[122] When Blackadder returned in 1811 to survey Lord Macdonald's estate he indicated that most townships were still in runrig.[123]

Conclusions

How can we assess Seaforth's management of his Ross-shire estates in the period from 1783, when he inherited them, until his departure for Barbados in February 1801 and on what criteria can a judgement be made? It would be fair to judge first how far he kept to his own principles. He had a conservative world view which was reflected in a lack of enthusiasm for the free play of market forces. Thus his views were less those of Adam Smith and more akin to Adam Ferguson. He shared Ferguson's disapproval of the individual who 'considers his community only so far as it can be rendered subservient to his personal advancement and profit'.[124] Historians of this period have generally argued, as James Hunter has, that 'most Highland landlords had no interest in their estates or tenantries other than as sources of ready cash'.[125] However, Seaforth did have a paternalistic concern for those for whom he felt responsible. He believed himself to be a humanitarian and was so regarded by others. Possibly his disability gave him empathy for others who suffered under disadvantages. More specifically, he had a firm belief in the value of clanship, no longer shared by the majority of his contemporary Highland proprietors, and a strong wish to protect the clan lands he had inherited and the interests of his clansmen and tenants, including small tenants. At one level he may be thought to have adhered to these principles well. He refused graziers' offers for Glenshiel in 1784 and 1787 and until 1802 (despite repeated recommendations from his advisers and limited attempts to introduce sheep farming) no large-scale sheep farm was established on his estates. He was, contrary to expert advice, slow to eliminate multiple-tenant townships in favour of large single-tenant farms. He discouraged emigration, despite substantial natural increase in population. Despite frequent advice to the contrary, the only part of his Ross-shire estate which he sold before 1801 was a small amount of land around Fortrose and Rosemarkie in Easter Ross in 1798,[126] although, as will be shown in Chapter Four, he was trying to dispose of Lochalsh from the late 1790s and ultimately did so in 1801.

However, he was not an unqualified admirer and supporter of his clansmen and small tenants. He did not take decisive action to deal with the grievances in Lewis in the 1780s against the Gillanders factors. Nor did he remain long an enthusiast of multiple-tenant townships, as shown by his report to Sir John Sinclair, probably written in early 1794. It was later in that year that the Glenshiel tenants, he subsequently claimed, had banded together not to compete for leases. He wrote that, after his protection of them in the 1780s, this was 'hurtful to his happiness and feelings'.[127] His attitudes and policies increasingly became commercial. This was unavoidable in view of his large inherited debts and his extravagant lifestyle, which will be considered in Chapter Four. Rents rose substantially across the estate, the consequence of a degree of competitive bidding. To some extent these reflected the higher prices his tenants received for cattle and other produce, but they were much lower than those achieved by proprietors who let their glens to commercial sheep breeders.

Seaforth's principles were almost certainly unrealisable in the economic and demographic circumstances of the Highlands in the late eighteenth century and with his levels of debt and expenditure. As Sir John Sinclair put it in 1795 he, and some others, were Highland proprietors who 'may be desirous of having the full value of their property, but cannot think of parting with their people'.[128] The result was that customary and commercial pressures pulled him in different directions, which led to contradictions and ambiguities in his policies.[129] It can be argued that, until he sailed for Barbados in February 1801, he managed to keep the show on the road by retaining the bulk of the estate, avoiding large-scale clearance and also achieving the extravagant lifestyle and social position he aspired to. However, this was a high-wire balancing act, which resulted in great stress for him and his advisers. Chapter Four will analyse how lifestyle and estate management policies led to financial crises and pressure for land sales. Whether the balancing act was to be of long-term benefit to him, his family or his clansmen was an open question at the turn of the nineteenth century. This will be answered in Chapters Eleven and Twelve, when his estate management policies after his return from Barbados are considered. However, a nuanced study of the first two decades of his estate management reveals a man very different from the stereotype figures of a Highland proprietor and clan chief of the period. Two of his attempts to develop the economy of Lewis, fishing and kelp gathering, are of such a significant nature that they will be addressed separately in Chapter Three.

Notes

1. Mackenzie, A., *History of the Mackenzies* (Inverness, 1894 edn), pp. 328–9, 334.
2. Clifford, T., M. Gallagher and H. Smailes, *Benjamin West and the Death of the Stag* (Edinburgh, 2009), p. 14.

3. Carter, H. B., *Sir Joseph Banks, 1743–1820* (London, 1988), pp. 152–3.
4. Edinburgh, National Records of Scotland (NRS), GD427/305/2 and /5, Kenneth Earl of Seaforth to G. Gillanders, 24 December 1779, 1 February 1780.
5. Mackenzie, *History of the Mackenzies*, pp. 330–1.
6. NRS, Register of Sasines Ross-shire Abridgements, no. 126, 17 November 1785.
7. NRS, GD46/17/2, Minute of sale between Earl of Seaforth and T. F. Mackenzie Humberston, 1780.
8. NRS, GD427/306/5, Col. T. F. M. Humberston to G. Gillanders, 18 January 1781.
9. NRS, Register of Sasines Ross-shire Abridgements, nos 2 and 3, 9 February 1781; no. 72, 12 October 1782.
10. NRS, GD427/306/5, Col. T. F. M. Humberston to G. Gillanders, 18 January 1781.
11. NRS, GD427/306/7, 'Gross rent of the Seaforth estate', n.d., but clearly 1781.
12. Mackenzie, *History of the Mackenzies*, pp. 333–4.
13. Colley, L., *Britons: Forging the Nation 1707–1837* (London, 1994 edn), pp. 156–7, 159.
14. Rothschild, E., *The Inner Life of Empires* (Princeton, 2011), pp. 19–20, 29, 64.
15. Castle Fraser, Mackenzie Fraser Papers (C. F. Papers), Lt Col. T. F. M. Humberston to 'B', 20 January 1783.
16. Macinnes, A. I., *Clanship, Commerce and the House of Stuart, 1603–1788* (East Linton, 1996), pp. 2–3, 172, 210, 233.
17. Macinnes, A. I., 'Scottish Gaeldom: The First Phase of Clearance', in T. M. Devine and R. Mitchison (eds), *People and Society in Scotland, Volume 1, 1760–1830* (Edinburgh, 1988), pp. 71–2, 74.
18. Dodgshon, R. A., *From Chiefs to Landlords: Social and Economic Change in the Western Highlands and Islands, c.1493–1820* (Edinburgh, 1998), pp. 107–8; Devine, T. M., *Clanship to Crofters' War: The Social Transformation of the Scottish Highlands* (Manchester, 1994), pp. 43–4; Devine, T. M., *The Scottish Nation 1700–2000* (London, 1999), p. 173.
19. Hunter, J., *The Making of the Crofting Community* (Edinburgh, 1976), p. 13.
20. Womack, P., *Improvement and Romance – Constructing the Myth of the Highlands* (Basingstoke, 1989), p. 115.
21. McLean, M., *The People of Glengarry: Highlanders in Transition, 1745–1820* (Montreal, 1991), pp. 68–9, 74–5.
22. For the spread of large-scale sheep farming in the Highlands in the late eighteenth century see Richards, E., *A History of*

the Highland Clearance: Agrarian Transformation and the Evictions, 1746–1886 (London, 1982), pp. 183–92.

23. Sir A. Mackenzie of Coull in 1791, quoted in Thorne, R. G., *The House of Commons 1790–1820* (London, 1986), vol. 2, p. 573.

24. Stewart, D., *Sketches of the Character, Manners and Present State of the Highlanders of Scotland* (Edinburgh, 1822), vol. 1, p. 168.

25. Robertson, J. I., *The First Highlander: Major-General David Stewart of Garth CB* (East Linton, 1998), pp. 87–8, 95–6, 102–6, 123, 170.

26. NRS, GD46/17/10, Lord Seaforth to C. Yorke, 23 April 1804.

27. Little, J. I., 'Agricultural Improvement and Highland Clearance: The Isle of Arran 1766–1829', *Scottish Economic and Social History*, vol. 19, 1999, pp. 137, 145.

28. Dodgshon, *From Chiefs to Landlords*, p. 242.

29. Taylor, D., *The Wild Black Region: Badenoch 1750–1800* (Edinburgh, 2016), p. 166.

30. Flinn, M. (ed.), *Scottish Population History from the 17th Century to the 1930s* (Cambridge, 1977), p. 270, table 4.4.5.

31. *Statistical Account of Scotland (OSA)*, vol. VII (1793), p. 253, <http://stat-acc-scot.edina.ac.uk/link/1791-99/Ross>, accessed 19 April 2017.

32. *OSA*, vol. XI (1794), p. 425.

33. Miller, E., 'A community approaching crisis: Skye in the eighteenth century' in C. Dyer et al. (eds), *New Directions in Local History since Hoskins* (Hatfield, 2011), pp. 132–3.

34. Tindley, A. and H. Haynes, 'The River Helmsdale and Strath Ullie, *c*.1780–*c*.1850: a historical perspective of societal and environmental influences on land management', *Scottish Geographical Journal*, vol. 130, 1, 2014, p. 42.

35. Richards, E. and M. Clough, *Cromartie: Highland Life 1650–1914* (Aberdeen, 1989), pp. 113, 120.

36. Knox, J., *A Tour Through the Highlands and the Hebride Isles in 1786* (Edinburgh, 1787, reprint 1975), p. 125; Rev. J. Macrae, *OSA*, vol. VII, p. 128.

37. *Morning Chronicle*, 3 August 1787, British Library Burney Collection of 17th and 18th Century Newspapers online (BCN), accessed 7 December 2010.

38. NRS, GD46/17/36, Lord Seaforth to C. Mackenzie, 1 July 1811.

39. NRS, GD427/15, Rental of Lewis Crop 1787.

40. NRS, GD427/14/8, Rental of Lewis Crop 1783; GD427/15, Rental of Lewis Crop 1787; GD427/16/2, Rental of Lewis Crop 1789.

41. Dodgshon, *From Chiefs to Landlords*, pp. 237–8; Macinnes, *Clanship, Commerce and the House of Stuart*, pp. 145–6.

42. Hunter, *Making of Crofting Community*, p. 13.
43. Taylor, *The Wild Black Region*, pp. 176, 208, 223–4, 252–4.
44. NRS, GD427/4/2, 'Lewis Rental as presently payed by tacksmen and tenants', 1755; /5/5, Lewis Rental 1766; /11/7, Rental of Lewis Crop 1776; /16/5, Rental of Lewis 1791.
45. NRS, GD46/17/13, P. Fairbairn to F. H. Mackenzie, 20 April 1795.
46. Mackillop, A., *'More Fruitful than the Soil': Army, Empire and the Scottish Highlands, 1715–1815* (East Linton, 2000), p. 154.
47. NRS, GD427/212/12, A. Macrae to G. Gillanders, 22 October 1792; *Aberdeen Journal*, 9 September 1801, 19th Century British Library Newspapers online (19BLN), accessed 3 February 2011.
48. NRS, GD427/11/7, Rental of Lewis Crop 1776; /14/8, Rental of Lewis Crop 1783; /16/5, Rental of Lewis 1791.
49. Cregeen, E. R., A. Tindley (ed.), 'The Creation of the Crofting Townships in Tiree', *Journal of Scottish Historical Studies*, vol. 35, 2, 2015, pp. 165–9.
50. Downie, Rev. A., *OSA*, vol. 11, p. 425.
51. *London Evening Post*, 17 July 1773 (BCN), accessed 27 March 2013.
52. NRS, GD427/305/5, Earl of Seaforth to G. Gillanders, 1 February 1780.
53. NRS, GD427/306/3, /5, T. F. M. Humberston to G. Gillanders, 26 November 1780, 18 January 1781.
54. NRS, GD46/17/4/164, 'Charles Greville's idea of my affairs given at the meeting of my brother's executors. May 1788'.
55. NRS, GD427/226/21, J. Kerr to P. Downie, 22 March 1792.
56. Richards, E., *The Highland Estate Factor in the Age of the Clearances* (Isle of Lewis, 2016), pp. 9–12.
57. NRS, GD46/1/8/6–7, Will of T. F. M. Humberston (recorded Bombay, 30 June 1783).
58. NRS, GD46/17/4/58–60, 'Memo concerning the affairs of the late Col. Mackenzie of Seaforth, 1783'.
59. NRS, GD46/17/4/216, V. Gibbs to F. H. Mackenzie, January 1789 and /219, F. H. Mackenzie to W. Dixon, 17 February 1789.
60. NRS, GD46/17/4/253, D. Scott, India House to F. H. Mackenzie, 22 December 1789.
61. NRS, GD46/17/4/165, 'Charles Greville's idea of my affairs, given at the meeting of my brother's executors, May 1788'.
62. Ibid.
63. Chichester, H. M., 'Mackenzie, Francis Humberston, Baron Seaforth and Mackenzie of Kintail (1754–1815)', rev. J. Spain, *Oxford Dictionary of National Biography (ODNB)*, Oxford, 2004, online edition, <www.oxforddnb.com>, article no. 14126, accessed 29 September 2004.

64. Lang, A. M., 'Dempster, George, of Dunnichen (1732–1818)', *ODNB*, online edition, <www.oxforddnb.com>, article no. 7472, accessed 10 July 2015.
65. NRS, GD46/17/4/303, G. Dempster to F. H. Mackenzie, 13 January 1790.
66. Dressler, C., *Eigg: The Story of an Island* (Edinburgh, 1998), p. 57.
67. NRS, GD201/1/365/1, 'State and view of Clanranald's Affairs as at 1st January 1797'.
68. Branigan, K., *The Last of the Clan* (Stroud, 2010), pp. 25–28.
69. P. Frazer to Capt. J. W. Payne, 11 September 1791, in A. Aspinall (ed.), *Correspondence of George, Prince of Wales*, vol. 2 (London, 1965), p. 194.
70. Dodgshon, *From Chiefs to Landlords*, p. 242.
71. NRS, GD46/17/23/140, J. E. Fraser of Reelig to Lord Seaforth, January 1803.
72. Hunter, *Making of Crofting Community*, p. 23.
73. NRS, GD46/17/10, Lord Seaforth to C. Yorke, 23 April 1804.
74. Glasgow, Mitchell Library, Mackenzie Miscellanea (ref. 591706, –711, –837), 'Humble hints for Doctor Walker's use so far as relates to Ross-shire', n.d.
75. London, Royal Society Library, EC/1794/05, election certificate of Francis Humberstone Mackenzie, 26 June 1794.
76. *Whitehall Evening Post*, 17 January 1799 (BCN), accessed 6 December 2010.
77. McCullough, K. L., 'For the Good and Glory of the Whole': The Highland Society of London and the Formation of Scoto-British Identity' in J. A. Campbell, E. Ewan and H. Parker, *The Shaping of Scottish Identities: Family, Nation and the Worlds Beyond* (Guelph, ON, 2011), pp. 199–204.
78. NRS, GD46/17/4/309, G. Dempster to F. H. Mackenzie, 13 January 1790.
79. *Caledonian Mercury*, 18 January 1800 (19BLN), accessed 3 February 2011.
80. *Oracle and Public Advertiser*, 19 February 1795 (BCN), accessed 9 December 2010.
81. NRS, GD46/17/80/59–61 'To be sold by private bargain – the Parishes of Uig, Barvas and Lochs', n.d.
82. NRS, GD46/17/3, P. Fairbairn to F. H. Mackenzie, 20 February 1794.
83. NRS, GD46/17/3, G. Gillanders to F. H. Mackenzie, 8 February 1794.
84. NRS, GD46/17/3, P. Fairbairn to Seaforth, 23 October 1793.
85. Gray, M., *The Highland Economy 1750–1850* (Edinburgh, 1957), pp. 90–1.

86. NRS, GD46/17/36, Lord Seaforth to C. Mackenzie, 1 July 1811.
87. NRS, GD46/17/11, Advertisement for sale of Lochalsh 1798, C. Mackenzie to J. Gibson, 17 December 1798; Mackillop, 'More Fruitful than the Soil?', pp. 160–1.
88. Taylor, The Wild Black Region, pp. 182–3, 246.
89. Macinnes, 'Scottish Gaeldom: The First Phase of Clearance', pp. 71, 83, 86.
90. Hamilton, H., Economic History of Scotland in the Eighteenth Century (Oxford, 1963), p. 91.
91. Taylor, The Wild Black Region, pp. 182–3.
92. NRS, GD46/17/18, C. Mackenzie to Lord Seaforth, 14 September 1797; GD46/20/4/1/13, State of Rental, etc., Crop 1800.
93. NRS, GD427/14/8, Rental of Lewis Crop 1783; GD46/20/4/1/7, Rental of Lewis Crop 1801.
94. Richards and Clough, Cromartie, pp. 131–2, 144.
95. McLean, People of Glengarry, pp. 74–5.
96. NRS, GD427/11/7, Rental of Lewis 1776; GD46/20/4/1/9, Rental of Lewis 1802.
97. Dodgshon, From Chiefs to Landlords, p. 243.
98. NRS, GD427/14/8, Rental of Lewis Crop 1783; GD46/20/4/1/16, Rental of Lewis Crop 1803.
99. Richards and Clough, Cromartie: Highland Life, p. 131.
100. Campbell, S. D., 'Post-medieval settlement in the Isle of Lewis: a study in adaptability or change?', Proceedings of Society of Antiquaries of Scotland, vol. 139, 2009, pp. 320–7.
101. NRS, GD427/226/21, J. Kerr to P. Downie, 22 March 1792.
102. Gray, Highland Economy, p. 139.
103. Mitchell Library, Mackenzie Miscellanea, 'Humble hints for Doctor Walker's use'.
104. NRS, GD427/226/21, J. Kerr to P. Downie, 22 March 1792.
105. NRS, GD46/17/15, A. Gillanders to Mrs Mary Mackenzie, 25 February 1794.
106. NRS, GD46/1/562/2, Charge and Discharge Lewis crop 1799; GD46/1/326, State of Rents, Public Burdens, etc. of Island of Lewis, crop and year 1800.
107. Headrick, J., Report on the Island of Lewis (Edinburgh, 1800), p. 27.
108. NRS, GD46/17/20, C. Mackenzie to Lord Seaforth, 10 January 1801.
109. Gray, Highland Economy, pp. 138–9.
110. NRS, GD46/17/3, P. Fairbairn to F. H. Mackenzie, 30 March 1794; GD46/17/14, G. Gillanders to Lord Seaforth, 4 November 1800.
111. NRS, GD46/17/15, P. Fairbairn to F. H. Mackenzie, 1 December 1795.

112. NRS, GD9/1/109, Journal of British Fisheries Society Directors Tour, 1787.
113. GD46/17/80/45–58, Detailed specification for intended road Stornoway–Kenhulairick Bay, with economic case for new roads Lewis, n.d.
114. NRS, GD46/17/18, P. Fairbairn to Lord Seaforth, 7 March 1798.
115. NRS, GD46/1/562/1–2, Charge and discharge Lewis crops 1798, 1799.
116. NRS, GD46/20/4/1/15, 'Contents and Estimate of lands of Ussie, made out 1802 by George Brown'.
117. NRS, GD46/17/31, W. Mackenzie to Lord Seaforth, 20 March 1807.
118. Headrick, *Report on the Island of Lewis*, pp. 20–2, 28.
119. Randall, J., *The Historic Shielings of Pairc* (Laxay, Isle of Lewis, 2017), pp. 8, 24, 32–3.
120. NRS, GD46/20/4/1/16, Rental of Lewis 1803; GD46/17/19, C. Mackenzie to Lord Seaforth, April 1801.
121. Hunter, *Making of Crofting Community*, pp. 19–21.
122. Richards, *Agrarian Transformation and the Evictions*, pp. 145–6.
123. Dodgshon, *From Chiefs to Landlords*, p. 190.
124. Herman, A., *The Scottish Enlightenment: The Scots' Invention of the Modern World* (2006 edn, London), pp. 206–7, 211–12.
125. Hunter, *Making of Crofting Community*, p. 33.
126. NRS, GD46/17/11, C. Mackenzie to Lord Seaforth, 6 June 1798.
127. NRS, GD46/17/36, Lord Seaforth to C. Mackenzie, 1 July 1811.
128. Sinclair, Sir J., *General View of the Agriculture of the Northern Counties and Islands of Scotland* (Edinburgh, 1795), pp. 111–12.
129. On this see F. McKichan, 'Lord Seaforth and Highland Estate Management in the First Phase of Clearance (1783–1815)', *The Scottish Historical Review*, vol. 86, 1, no. 221, April 2007, pp. 64–8.

3   Riches from the Sea?

As has been seen in Chapter Two, Seaforth became more ambivalent about his small tenants. Nevertheless, unlike most Highland proprietors, he continued to be loath to break up multi-tenant townships and to introduce large-scale sheep farms. He was, however, well aware that he needed to increase his income. His brother-in-law the London lawyer Vicary Gibbs believed that he depended too much on untested new projects rather than savings. He advised him, 'Don't lay plans only for improving your income and diminishing your expenses, but while you are attending to the former project, do something in execution of the latter, which is much the most material'.[1] He was certainly happier planning a project than economising. He and his advisers were agreed that economic development and income growth were more likely to be achieved on Lewis than on the Wester Ross lands. In 1788 his close friend and confidential adviser Charles Greville actually recommended selling Lochalsh and Kintail to provide capital to improve Lewis.[2] When he became proprietor the best prospect for the development of Lewis seemed to him to be fishing.

The Lewis fishing industry

In 1786 Seaforth subscribed for ten £50 shares in the 'British Society for Extending the Fisheries and Improving Sea Coasts of the Kingdom' (the British Fisheries Society). This was newly established as a joint-stock company to develop fisheries in the north-west Highlands.[3] Only the duke of Argyll and his sons subscribed more. The duke became governor and Seaforth a director. The origins of the Society are to be found in a report in 1785 by Dr James Anderson to the Lords of the Treasury[4] and the work of John Knox, who became a roving investigator for the Society. In the aftermath of the loss of the American colonies, they were determined to strengthen the 'metropolitan' empire of the British islands, especially by developing the economy of its more remote regions. The encouragement of fishing in the north-west Highlands and islands would create a nursery for seamen (especially for the Royal Navy), make the Highlands prosperous and civilised and thus reduce the incentive to emigrate, consolidate the Union and discourage tendencies to political separation (like the Jacobite movement). To achieve this, the fiscal–military state of the UK would have to spend on grants and bounties in addition to war and debt payments. However, this should not only be a state enterprise. The fiscal backing of the state should be combined with investment by landowners in fishing villages, in which poor Highlanders would be resettled. This was put in place by two statutes of 1786, which provided for a new type of bounty and for the establishment of the Society.[5]

Since 1750 'tonnage bounties' had been paid after each fishing voyage to vessels over a certain size. The purpose had been to encourage busses on the model of the Dutch vessels which had for long operated around the northern coasts of Scotland. Busses were decked sea-going boats designed to both catch and cure mainly herring. However it was alleged, notably by Adam Smith, that their owners were often aiming to catch the bounty rather than fish and that frequently, and illegally, they got most of their loads from small local boats fishing inshore. It was now argued that bounties should be paid also to the open inshore boats. 'Barrel bounties' were accordingly introduced (initially at a rate of one shilling per barrel) for any fisherman or curer.[6]

Seaforth was quick to develop further the last earl's efforts to make Stornoway an important base for the buss fishery. In 1785 he announced that, to encourage the fishing trade, he would feu ground on liberal terms for houses for 'skilful and industrious persons who may be inclined to settle there'.[7] He drew up a street plan for stone houses and, further from the centre, for 'neat and uniform' houses with garden ground for 'fishermen and mechanics', and planned the rebuilding of the church and the erection of a townhouse.[8] When the directors of

Figure 3.1 *A View of Stornoway*, 1798, by James Barret, showing herring busses inside the harbour and in the bay. (Courtesy National Galleries of Scotland, PG3291.)

the British Fisheries Society visited Stornoway in July 1787 they were delighted by what they saw. In a journal kept by Lachlan Mactavish for the duke of Argyll, he wrote with enthusiasm of the slated houses built for the buss owners and merchants, the substantial output of dried fish, the busy harbour and the energetic preparation for the new fishing season. Stornoway made them 'entertain more sanguine hopes of the designs of the Society than they had hitherto done'.[9] Seaforth continued to promote the buss trade. For example, in 1789 he encouraged the Stornoway merchants to use a superior quality of salt for curing by subsidising the initial consignment.[10] In 1796 Stornoway's 'principal inhabitants' owned about thirty decked vessels of between twenty and eighty tons, 'employed in the summer in the herring bounty-fishing and at other times in the coasting trade'.[11]

The Stornoway trade was one in which the capital was raised and the profits went to men of means who owned busses. The British Fisheries Society's aim was to provide a market for the owners of small open boats, often crewed by a group of joint tenants and launched from the beach of a coastal township. Hitherto these had sometimes been owned by tacksmen, who might claim a big portion of the catch. Alternatively, it might be owned jointly by three or four joint tenants, but would only fish close to that particular township.[12] Seaforth was keen to provide better options for these fishermen. There seemed to be a real opportunity on the west side of Lewis, where it was reported in 1785 that 'vast quantities of herrings are set into Loch Rogue, but there are no fishing vessels on the coast'.[13] At the Lewis sett of 1787 he was reported to have the aim of freeing 'the fishermen ... from the yoke of the richer farmers, and he has accordingly given only temporary leases for three years, that he may have time fully to digest his plan in their favour, and be ready to take advantage of any public encouragement'.[14] His plan was to establish a fishing village at Loch Roag, and the 'public encouragement' he looked for was that it should be one of the villages to be established by the British Fisheries Society.[15] The directors of the Society believed that small boats could operate in sea lochs, catch more cheaply and bring fish ashore to be cured. For this purpose fishing stations would be required to store salt and barrels, provide a labour force for gutting and curing and hopefully guarantee the quality of the product.[16]

Seaforth failed to interest the directors of the Society in a village at Loch Roag when they visited Lewis in 1787. However, he did not give up. Later in 1787 he tried to establish the viability of the Lewis boat fishery by chartering a yawl. Seven seamen were paid wages in cash and oatmeal for a period of up to eleven weeks, part of which was spent on the Lochs coast (on the east side of the island) and part in Loch Roag.[17] The following year he formally offered the Society a site on the banks of Loch Roag or Loch Carloway 'as the Directors and their surveyor may judge most adapted to furnish a station for a village', promising to build a road from the east side of the island. The directors thanked him for his liberality, but advised that they were unable to take immediate advantage of it and would send a surveyor. By this time the Society had committed to fishing stations at Ullapool, Tobermory, Loch Bay (Skye) and Canna. Robert Fraser was sent to Loch Roag in August 1788 and reported that, although it offered an excellent harbour, the soil was very shallow and poor.[18] The directors believed that a successful fishing village would need to have good agricultural land nearby. To make a living settlers would require to grow crops as well as be involved in the fishing.[19] Seaforth's case may also have been damaged by his political opposition to William Pitt's government, which will be analysed in Chapter Five. However, he was still not discouraged in his ambition to make Loch Roag into a fishing centre. In his letter of advice on Lewis, written in 1790, George Dempster of Dunnichen encouraged the Loch Roag project (despite being a director of the British Fisheries Society) as a means of discouraging emigration.[20] The following year a sympathetic observer claimed that 'the hopes of the people [of Lewis] for his continued attention have entirely prevented the spirit of emigration from extending its self to that island'.[21] When in 1793 consideration was briefly given to selling part of Lewis, the draft advertisement claimed that 'the benefits which may be derived from the celebrated herring fishing in Loch Roag are so obvious that it is needless to do more than mention them'.[22]

Later in 1793, the Loch Roag project reappeared in a different form. Seaforth entered a partnership with Bailie Alexander MacIver of Stornoway. The aim of the Loch Roag Fishing Establishment was to develop fishing from open boats, but not to establish a village. Accounts have survived for the season 1794–5. The investment in barrels, salt and storehouses was £160 3s 6d each and the profit for each that season (after payment of freight costs and salt duty) £43 9s 5d. Fish were sold at Liverpool, Dublin and Belfast. However, sales receipts of cod and ling were about £240 and, disappointingly, of herring less than £70.[23] The movements of herring were always unpredictable and the export trade in cured herring at this period (for example, for consumption by slaves in the Caribbean) was centered on the Clyde and would have incurred high transport costs from Lewis.[24]

Should the Loch Roag Establishment have been more successful? In December 1795 Peter Fairbairn, in an unusually critical letter to his master, implied that Seaforth had not made his promised investment. He forecast serious consequences if 'we fail in appearing with the necessary supply of money'.[25] Seaforth may have been right to be cautious. The yields of the Lewis herring fishing were clearly declining in the late 1790s,[26] a trend from which the Stornoway busses also suffered.[27] In early 1796 a good fishing was despaired of for the season and the poor tenants were not benefitting as had been hoped. On the contrary, they had lost by spending to prepare for a fishing which did not materialise and, worse, by the loss of a Barvas boat and its crew of six in November 1795 in tragic circumstances. It overturned as the wives and families watched it attempt to leave the Barvas shore to join the herring fishing in Loch Roag. Four of the dead were brothers and the other two father and son.[28] Although the ling fishery was good in that year, an inventory for a public roup in July 1797 of the barrels and salt in the storehouses at Duhob and Valtos suggests that Seaforth was pulling out of the joint venture.[29] Maciver continued the Loch Roag curing business for a while, but by 1800 it had ended.[30] Seaforth was aware that kelp prices were beginning to rise rapidly and, in contrast to fishing, offered a high income from Lewis without major investment.[31] Another problem may have been that there was no sheltered water off the west coast of Lewis and it was thus less suitable for open boats. A similar issue was faced by the fifth duke of Argyll in trying for twenty years after 1773 to set up a fishing village at Scarinish on the island of Tiree. Good catches were being found on the Tiree banks by decked boats from elsewhere, but the Tiree men could not afford to buy such vessels.[32]

What does a study of the Lewis fishing suggest about Seaforth's skill in devising and implementing economic development schemes? The greatest success was in the Stornoway buss fishery, which had been set under way by previous proprietors. As with subsequent and much more expensive schemes, Seaforth demonstrated initially an exaggerated and almost naive optimism. Chapter Eight includes an analysis of a similar approach to the very damaging purchase of plantations in Berbice (Guyana) in 1801. John Knox describes him mounting personal fishing expeditions near Stornoway to demonstrate potential catches.[33] His plans for a west-coast small-boat fishery did not take into account the need for fishing villagers to have some agricultural land. The herring fishery, on which the plans were primarily based, was highly unpredictable. Weather conditions off the west coast of Lewis were often unfavourable. Like the linen industry which (as has been shown in Chapter Two) his wife attempted to encourage with spinning schools, the principal markets were distant and expensive to access from Lewis. It may be that in this era of enthusiastic aristocratic improvers, not only Seaforth, but also his advisers exaggerated the economic potential of Lewis. As has been seen, Dempster, a very noted improver, encouraged the Loch Roag project.[34] What may be argued on Seaforth's behalf is that he appears to have withdrawn finance earmarked for Loch Roag in 1795 when he began to understand the much greater potential of kelp for income creation.

A financial lifeline from the shores – the kelp industry

The Seaforth family's advisers, notably the Gillanders dynasty of factors, were clear that Lewis was the part of the estate with potential for economic development. Although Earl Kenneth spent much time away from the United Kingdom, he had, prior to selling the estates in 1780, inaugurated two industries on Lewis which appeared to have clear prospects. These were fishing and kelp. As early as 1767 Alexander Gillanders was supplying oatmeal to small tenants on Lewis to manufacture kelp.[35]

If fishing was given less priority by Francis Humberston Mackenzie in the late 1790s it was because kelp now seemed the best way to win extra revenue and to create employment. Kelping involved the laborious gathering and burning of seaweed to produce an alkaline extract used in the manufacture of soap and glass. It developed in the west Highlands from the mid eighteenth century, especially in the Long Island, first on North Uist and Berneray and subsequently in Lewis, and to a lesser extent on the mainland. From the 1770s domestic production of kelp was protected from foreign competition by duties on imported barilla, which came mainly from Spain and Tenerife, which had twice the alkali content of kelp and was of more uniform quality. Kelp became the principal source of alkali, especially for the Liverpool soap boilers. What has been described as a 'patriotic partnership' between government and proprietors developed from about 1775 to 1815. By this kelp production was protected by duties in return for the proprietors supporting the fiscal–military state by retaining sufficient population to provide large numbers of recruits to the army and navy.[36] Kelp gathering was apparently an ideal industry for an indebted west Highland coastal estate with a large number of underemployed tenants and sub-tenants. It required virtually no capital investment. Labour requirements were mostly between June and August, that is, before harvest. The seaweed was cut in damp conditions and ropes attached for it to be hauled ashore by hand or by ponies. It was then laid out to dry. When dry it was burned on the shore in rough kilns made from stones. It had to be stirred continuously, day and night, until it melted. The cooled and hardened product was reckoned to have about one twentieth of the weight of the original seaweed. The work was not only arduous and unpleasant, with many hours spent in evil-smelling smoke which irritated the eyes, it also required skill to ensure that the product did not include stone and sand which would reduce its value. Chartered small ships visited the individual kelping locations to load the extract.[37]

When the Humberston Mackenzies got control of the Seaforth estate (1781) the anticipated annual kelp output of Lewis was 112 tons.[38] This was a relatively small output compared to further south on the Long Island. Lord Macdonald's North Uist estate produced 400 tons in 1770 and by 1790 the remarkable figure of 1,200 tons.[39] The Lewis output edged upwards in the 1780s and in 1789, 197 tons were loaded. The main centre of production was Loch Roag (123 tons) on the west coast, with 46 tons from Loch Erisort and 27 tons from Loch Seaforth on the east coast.[40] Precise figures are available for Mull kelp until 1797. The price was about £3 to £4 per ton until it rose to £7 in 1777 during the American War of Independence, dropped slightly to a plateau of about £5 in the 1780s, then rose to £6 6s in 1795 after the outbreak of the French Revolutionary War and to £8 8s in 1797.[41] The trend in Lewis was similar, as shown in Table 3.1. Net receipts (after deduction of manufacturing costs, mainly wages) rose rapidly in 1795 to £1,589 and in 1798 to £2,453. The year 1798 was the best one yet, with a profit of £8.45 per ton on 290 tons.[42] Although a magnificent return on a limited investment, this was significantly less than from the Clanranald estate, comprising Arisaig and Moidart, the Small Isles, South Uist and Benbecula. There, 620 tons of kelp were produced in 1797, giving a profit of £4,600.[43]

The downside of relying on kelp revenue was its unpredictable swings.[44] The price varied depending on production levels and on market sentiment, in particular the prospects of peace

Table 3.1 Gross and net receipts of Lewis kelp, 1794–9

Year	Gross receipts (to nearest £)	Net receipts (to nearest £)
1794	1481	1105
1795	2253	1589
1796	1755	1400
1797	1929	1667
1798	2978	2453
1799	2062	1767

Source: National Records of Scotland, GD46/13/126, State of Lewis kelp, 1794–9.

(which would make it easier to import soda) or war. Seaforth took an increasing personal interest in what became a major source of income. In 1795 Peter Fairbairn urged him to make a speedy deal for the sale of that season's Lewis kelp 'as the offers are good and should there be a peace, or near prospect of it, they may fall'.[45] In 1796 his advice was 'as a continuance of the War is now confirmed . . . you need not hurry an agreement with any of the offerers for they will most probably still advance their offers'.[46] This was sound policy. An initial offer of £7 10s per ton was ultimately topped by one of £9 9s.[47] Net receipts in Lewis dropped in 1799 to £1,767, but by 1809 had reached the remarkable level of £5,572, with an increased output (486 tons) at a higher average price (£11.87 per ton).[48] As Dodgshon puts it, in this period 'few Hebridean summers would have seen wholly clear skies, as the smoke from kelp burning billowed out along the coast'.[49]

Many criticisms have been made of the way proprietors managed the kelp business to maximise their own profits, allegedly adversely affecting the kelpers in different ways. These will be addressed in turn in relation to the Seaforth estate, focussing mainly on Lewis, the centre of its kelp trade. It has been argued that the landlords built local monopolies, which channelled most of the income to their own pockets. It is certainly true that they controlled the sale of kelp from their estates. Often they paid agents a commission on the final selling price to charter ships and pay insurance to transport the kelp and sell it in the main commercial centres, such as Liverpool, London, Hull or Leith.[50] The practice of the Seaforth estate was to sell the kelp to the agent, the price received by the estate being that payable on delivery to the agent's ships on the coast. For example, the £5 10s per ton received for Lewis kelp in 1789 was the sum contracted for by the agent, Angus Campbell of Ensay. An advantage of this arrangement for a cash-strapped proprietor like Seaforth was that the agent would often make a cash payment on account at the time of signing the contract – £500 by Campbell in 1789. It also made sense for the estate's ownership of the kelp to end on loading. The navigation of small sailing vessels round the shores of the Hebrides and Highlands was a dangerous business and in 1789 one of Campbell's ships was lost on the Caithness coast.[51]

It cannot be denied that proprietors controlled the kelp trade to maximise their own profits and that kelpers did not receive their share of rising prices. Indeed wages were relatively static. In 1794 the cost of production (mainly wages) of Lewis kelp was £1.44 per ton when the net receipts (profit) were £4.25 per ton. In 1799 the cost of production was only slightly higher at £1.81 when net receipts had almost doubled to £8.45 per ton.[52] This confirms Hunter's claim that across the kelping areas wages were little affected by rising prices.[53] In Lewis part of the wage was paid in oatmeal, the quantity varying according to the difficulty of the shore. In 1800, for example, 6.5 stones of oatmeal were paid per ton of kelp at Loch Roag, 6.5 or 8 stones in Lochs depending on the location and 9 stones at Valamos.[54] Peter Fairbairn criticised the practice of giving kelpers oatmeal on credit. As he put it, 'some under pretence of becoming manufacturers would get into your debt by taking up meal' and then not delivering the corresponding amount of kelp.[55] Throughout the kelping areas, in the settlement at the end of the season, the kelper's rent might be set against their earnings, often substantially reducing the cash payment.[56] While kelpers may not have benefitted from rising prices, the trade did insulate them, at least to some extent, from harvest failure and famine. There is evidence that in the famine years of 1782–5 kelp income enabled lairds to import grain for their tenants. Furthermore, the cash element of the kelper's income, even if small, might make it possible to buy hitherto unattainable luxuries such as tea.[57]

It has been argued that initially proprietors tended to let kelp manufacture to large tenants on whose tacks the shores were situated, but later created small coastal plots to let directly to the kelpers in order to be able to oblige small tenants to engage in kelping.[58] For example, in 1800 the fifth duke of Argyll let two coastal farms in Tiree to sixteen small tenants as their kelp income would enable them to pay more in rent than the previous gentleman farmer. By 1806 most of the coast of that island was held by small tenants and the proportion of land held by tacksmen had dropped from three-quarters to around one half.[59] The Seaforth estate certainly worked initially through tacksmen, using them in part as managers. For example, George Macaulay, regarded as the local expert on kelp manufacture, reported, 'I am vext the remainder of . . . Seaforth's kelp did not answer as well as it ought, but I'll make the rascals make up the remainder this season.'[60] Reference has been made in Chapter Two to the long-standing tacks of the Macaulays and the Nicholsons in Uig, the main centre of the kelp trade. Representatives of these families continued to play a major part in the Lewis kelp trade as tacksmen and as Seaforth's kelp overseers. The evidence does not suggest that small coastal tenancies on Lewis were being created in this period by the estate as a matter of policy. The number of tenancies increased in Lochs only from nineteen in 1783 (the year Seaforth inherited) to twenty-six in 1802 and in Uig from twenty-seven in 1783 to thirty-four in 1803. The Lewis rental for 1803 (the only one after 1791 which names tenancies) shows in Lochs just three 'farms' rented at less than £15 out of twenty-two and in Uig eight of thirty-five. This does not suggest there was a large number of small tenancies.[61] Admittedly, this evidence must be qualified by two considerations. The rental does not make clear whether these were single-tenant farms or multiple-tenant townships nor whether there were sub-tenancies on what the rental shows as a single-tenant farm.

Inaclete on the outskirts of Stornoway was one place where the Seaforth estate may have envisaged the creation of kelping tenancies. In 1795 a new village was being started there, with lots being allocated to tenants moving from Goathill. Fairbairn reported in April 1795 that he had let forty-nine lots and hoped soon to have another fifty available.[62] As their plots were small, the villagers would need a variety of sources of income, and it may be that one of them was intended to be manufacturing kelp during the brief summer season. However, by 1819 their main occupations were as seamen and fishermen.[63] An allegation linked to the creation of small kelping tenancies across the Hebrides is that kelping tenants were rack-rented (rents being raised to a level unrelated to the land's intrinsic agricultural value). This charge has been made specifically against Macdonald of Clanranald, proprietor of South Uist and Benbecula.[64] On the Seaforth estate there is no doubt that rents were increasing, but the shortage of detailed Lewis rentals makes judgements difficult. Between 1791 and 1803 the percentage increase in the total rent of the two principal kelping parishes (Uig, 71 per cent; Lochs, 76 per cent) was higher than in the other three rural districts (Carloway, 63 per cent; Barvas, 61 per cent; Ness, 67 per cent).[65] However, the differences are not so great as to prove that in this period rack-renting in the kelping districts of Lewis was widespread or extensive.

It is certainly true that by the mid 1790s the estate, in an attempt to maximise the profits offered by the French

Revolutionary War, was attempting to direct the labour of the small tenants on Lewis. It was not finding this easy. A vivid account is given in a long letter from Peter Fairbairn to Seaforth in April 1795. Except at Loch Roag, he 'found the manufacturing for the ensuing season ... rather critical'. In previous years the Lochs kelp had been manufactured by Uig men, but they were increasingly unwilling to cross the island to do so. In 1794 they had refused 'until absolutely beat and forced by Mr Gillanders', who happened to be touring the district to recruit for the second battalion of Seaforth's regiment. This year the Lochs people would have to be made to manufacture themselves 'what is adjacent to their respective farms, which they can easily do without detriment to their fishing, having but small proportions [of kelp shore] to each family'. Fairbairn envisaged that the aversion to kelping he had encountered at Lochs would be repeated at Barvas, which was 'in a sort of infant state, from the ignorance and backwardness of the people'. It would be very difficult to break them in 'as they detest the business beyond measure, but their antipathy must either be surmounted or you cannot make kelp in that parish to any advantage'. Stornoway was in a similar position and he had engaged to supervise these two districts Kenneth Nicolson (a member of the Uig tacksman family), 'the only man capable of acting as overseer ... both for firmness and his knowledge of shipping the kelp'.[66] By 1800 kelping had become sufficiently important for supervision of the kelpers of Lewis to become closer and more systemised. Manufacturing was done by the tenants of the farms adjacent to the shores 'as they may be arranged by the overseer'. The estate's official in each district of Lewis, the ground officer, acted as kelp overseer. He gave instructions on the work to be done, checked quality and authorised payment.[67]

It has also been alleged that proprietors took over the kelp industry by establishing legal rights to the seaweed and thus took control of all its productive and marketing sequences.[68] The crux of this is the claim that proprietors won unchallenged control of the foreshore. Recent research suggests that this position was not established generally until after the peak years of the kelp industry.[69] In the case of the Seaforth estate, it has been claimed that a standard regulation that tenants should not cut any sea-ware fit for making kelp (meaning that the estate monopolised its use) was already underway in 1766.[70] It is true that in 1793 Seaforth ordered the enforcement of his instructions that tenants should not encroach on the seashore reserved for his kelp.[71] However, this did not mean that he had a monopoly of the shore. In 1794 the estate stated that 'the tacks contain no clause respecting the sea-ware, further than that the lands are let as formerly possessed' and the most essential of these privileges was taking sea-ware for manure. Each year the boundaries were lined out between the tenants' sea-ware and what could be used for kelp burning.[72] The island of Mull has been claimed to be an unusual example of small tenants enjoying free rights of using the weed on their land.[73] However, it would appear that on Lewis in the 1790s they had the right to use half the weed. It seems to have been about fifteen years later that Seaforth's agents attempted to tie small tenants down to regulations which would give the estate complete control by trying to prevent kelp being used for any purpose other than manufacture.[74]

The need to maintain a kelping workforce was an important reason why proprietors in the north-west Highlands and Islands, including Seaforth, opposed emigration at this period. As has been seen in Chapter Two, this led to the Passenger Vessels Act 1803 which, under the guise of improving medical and dietary provision, made a passage more expensive and thus more difficult to access.[75] Seaforth was in Barbados when this Act was passed, but he enthusiastically supported it. In 1804 he lamented 'that restless wish for change and that spirit of discontent' which caused emigration.[76] The suggestion that he actually encouraged the growth of the population of Lewis is more difficult to prove.[77] Further south on the Long Island, landlords undoubtedly crowded their lands to provide a sufficient labour force to expand production and to ensure that the rent could only be paid by working kelp. Population increase between 1755 and 1811 has been calculated as 118 per cent in South Uist, 102 per cent in North Uist, but a more modest 58 per cent in Lewis.[78] In Lewis, the parishes of Uig and Lochs, being the main centres of kelping, would be the most likely to be affected by any policy of deliberate population increase. The population of Uig increased from 1,898 in 1792 to 2,086 in 1801 (10.7 per cent) and of Lochs from 1,768 to 1,875 (an almost identical 10.6 per cent).[79] These are substantial increases over a period of only nine years, and it may be that, because of the needs of kelping and army recruitment, Seaforth felt that he had no need to discourage the trend. His successor, James Stewart-Mackenzie, admitted in 1822 that the high wartime price of kelp had encouraged proprietors to keep kelp workers on their estates.[80]

The Lochalsh and Kintail kelp contracts were of the type where an annual rent of the shores was agreed. For season 1795 this yielded £307.[81] This modest figure confirms the view that on the mainland the burning kilns were more scattered and their output less significant in the local economy.[82] In December 1795 a Mr Maclean offered £150 per annum for nine years, starting season 1796, with a break for each party every three years. This was less than had been received in 1795 (£340 from Anderson). Fairbairn advised Seaforth to accept immediately, which he did, as 'good prices will not stand long, very probably'.[83] The attraction was presumably the long-term contract while wartime conditions still applied. Lack of skilled labour was a problem at Lochalsh. Maclean withdrew at the first option, after the 1798 season. For 1799 the only bidder, John Elder from Skye, would offer the same rent (£150) for only one year, or £120 annually for three years. He put this down to 'the extreme difficulty of getting manufacturers in the present times, the country being drained of them by the war, etc.'[84] Lochalsh had been particularly forthcoming in supplying recruits for the two battalions of Seaforth's regiment (the 78th Foot) in 1793 and 1794. By 1801, with prices dropping, the sale of the Kintail crop was not even attempted.[85]

Conclusions

Seaforth's record in economic development was distinctly patchy. His encouragement of the Stornoway buss fishery was successful, but of limited benefit to his revenues and achieved a strictly local increase in employment. Small-boat fishing and linen spinning in Lewis created limited employment and were, with the benefit of hindsight, probably not good prospects for growth at that time. Seaforth's greatest commercial success was the expansion of the Lewis kelp industry in the 1790s, and by the turn of the century this trade was by no means yet at its peak. Kelp revenue played an important part in his financial survival For example, in 1799 the rental of Lewis was a little over £4,000, Lewis kelp income £1,767 and debt interest £5,680, leaving the rental of Lochalsh and Kintail (£3,021) to meet all expenses and annuities.[86] For this reason, it is probably the activity in which he showed least concern for the welfare of his small tenants. They were obliged to participate in a trade they heartily disliked, and he, like other kelp proprietors, creamed off for himself the vast bulk of the revenues. On the other hand, historians have suggested a standardised and oppressive form of kelp management which is not fully reflected on the Seaforth estate. In this period there is no evidence from Uig and Lochs, the principal kelping parishes, of rent levels very much higher than in other Lewis parishes (rack-renting). Nor is there evidence of the large-scale creation of small direct tenancies on the coast as a means of ensuring a sufficient kelp labour force. In Chapter Two it was argued that, in giving access to land, Seaforth was considerably more benevolent to small tenants than the generality of Highland proprietors. Even in kelp sales, in which he was at his most entrepreneurial, the suggestion in this chapter is that he treated them less oppressively than other accounts claim was the norm. The consequences for his finances of the rise and fall of kelp prices will be considered in Chapters Four and Eleven.

It is clear that in this period Seaforth followed advice to concentrate development schemes on Lewis, which was seen as being the part of the estate with the greatest economic potential, and that the economy of Wester Ross was relatively neglected. In 1788 his friend and adviser Charles Greville recommended that he sell Lochalsh and Kintail in order to have enough capital to improve Lewis and held out an attractive prospect of what could be achieved there by 'a man of sense and spirit', mainly through the fisheries.[87] Probably it was not only sentiment which led him to retain the Wester Ross properties in the 1780s and 1790s (as referred to in Chapter Two). They enabled him to create votes and were fertile recruiting grounds for his regiment, issues which will be addressed in Chapters Five and Six. However, they do appear to have been deprived of significant capital investment until fishing villages were begun at Dornie and Bundalloch in Kintail. This was in part a reaction to clearance carried out by the new owner after the sale of Lochalsh and adjoining parts of Kintail in 1801.[88] How Seaforth broke his embargo on Wester Ross sales will be discussed in Chapters Four and Eleven.

Notes

1. Edinburgh, National Records of Scotland (NRS), GD46/17/4/264–5, V. Gibbs to F. H. Mackenzie, 21 April 1787.
2. NRS, GD46/17/4/165, 'Charles Greville's idea of my affairs . . . May 1788'.
3. *General Evening Post*, 13 June 1786, British Library Burney Collection of 17th and 18th Century Newspapers online (BCN), accessed 7 December 2010.
4. Anderson, J., *An Account of the Present State of the Hebrides and Western Coasts of Scotland* (Edinburgh, 1785).
5. Gambles, A., 'Free Trade and State Formation: The Political Economy of Fisheries Policy in Britain and the United Kingdom, circa 1750–1850', *Journal of British Studies*, vol. 39, 3, 2000, pp. 293–300, 302–3.
6. Forte, A. and J. R. Coull, 'Fishing and Legislation' in J. R. Coull, A. Fenton and K. Veitch (eds), *Scottish Life and Society: A Compendium of Scottish Ethnology*, vol. 4 (Edinburgh, 2008), pp. 175–6.
7. *Morning Herald* and *Daily Advertiser*, 7 April 1785 (BCN), accessed 7 December 2010.
8. Knox, J., *A Tour through the Highlands of Scotland and the Hebride Isles in 1786* (Edinburgh, 1787, reprint 1975), pp. 182–3.
9. NRS, GD9/1/108–9, 'Journal of the proceedings of the Directors of the British Society since their departure from Aros in Mull 1 July' (Journal Directors BFS Tour, 1787).
10. NRS, GD427/138/2, F. H. Mackenzie to A. Gillanders, Stornoway, 7 April 1789.
11. Mackenzie, Rev. C., *Statistical Account of Scotland* (*OSA*), vol. XIX (Edinburgh, 1797), pp. 242, 256, <http://sta-acc-scot.edina.ac.uk/link/1791–99/Ross>, accessed 19 April 2017.
12. Coull, J. R., 'Fishery Development in Scotland in the Eighteenth Century', *Scottish Economic and Social History*, vol. 21, 2001, pp. 13–14; Gray, M., *The Fishing Industries of Scotland, 1790–1914* (Aberdeen, 1978), p. 104.
13. *London Chronicle*, 6–8 January 1785 (BCN), accessed 27 March 2013.
14. *Morning Chronicle*, 3 August 1787 (BCN), accessed 7 December 2010.
15. NRS, GD9/1/96–112, Journal Directors BFS Tour, 1787.
16. Coull, 'Fishery Development in Scotland', pp. 3, 9–11, 14; Dunlop, J., *The British Fisheries Society, 1786–1893* (Edinburgh, 1978), pp. 22–3.

17. NRS, GD46/13/145/2, 4 January 1788, 'Accounts paid Seaforth's fishers and crew to Loch Roag, anno 1787'.

18. Dunlop, *British Fisheries Society*, pp. 92–3.

19. NRS, GD9/1/109–110, Journal Directors BFS Tour, 1787; Gray, *Fishing Industries of Scotland*, p. 103.

20. NRS, GD46/17/4/306–9, G. Dempster to F. H. Mackenzie, 13 January 1790.

21. P. Frazer, Ullapool, to Capt. J. W. Payne, 11 September 1791 in A. Aspinall (ed.), *Correspondence of George, Prince of Wales, 1770–1812*, vol. 2 (London, 1964), pp. 194–5.

22. NRS, GD46/17/80/59–60, 'To be sold by private bargain the parishes of Uig, Barvas and Lochs in the island of Lewis', n.d.

23. NRS, GD46/17/11, Accounts of Loch Roag fishing establishment, 1794–5; Dunlop, *British Fisheries Society*, pp. 95–6.

24. Gray, M., *The Highland Economy 1750–1850* (Edinburgh, 1957), pp. 110–11.

25. NRS, GD46/17/15, P. Fairbairn to F. H. Mackenzie, 1 December 1795.

26. NRS, GD46/17/15, P. Fairbairn to F. H. Mackenzie, 3 December 1795, 12 and 31 January 1796; GD46/17/13/131, P. Fairbairn to F. H. Mackenzie, 27 December 1796; Dunlop, *British Fisheries Society*, p. 96.

27. Rev. C. Mackenzie, OSA, vol. XIX, p. 242.

28. NRS, GD46/17/15, P. Fairbairn to F. H. Mackenzie, 13 December 1795; GD46/17/13, 21 January 1796.

29. NRS, GD46/17/11, P. Fairbairn to F. H. Mackenzie, 18 July 1797; GD46/1/561/1, 'Inventory of casks and salt lying in the store houses at Loch Rogue to be sold by public roup at Stornoway Court House, 26 July 1797'.

30. NRS, GD46/20/4/1/4, State of Rents Lewis, 1800; GD46/1/326, State of Rents, Public Burdens, etc., Lewis, 1800.

31. NRS, GD46/17/15, P. Fairbairn to F. H. Mackenzie, 2 May 1795 and 24 April 1796.

32. Cregeen, E. R., A. Tindley (ed.), 'The Creation of the Crofting Townships in Tiree'. *Journal of Scottish Historical Studies (JSHS)*, vol. 35, 2, 2015, pp. 173–4.

33. Knox, *Tour through the Highlands*, pp. 195–6.

34. NRS, GD46/17/4/306, G. Dempster to F. H. Mackenzie, 13 January 1790.

35. NRS, GD427/136/1, G. Macaulay, Loch Rogue, to A. Gillanders, Stornoway, 12 June 1767.

36. Thomson, W. P. L. and J. R. Coull, 'Kelp' in J. R. Coull, A. Fenton and K. Veitch (eds), *Scottish Life and Society: A Compendium of Scottish Ethnology*, vol. 4 (Edinburgh, 2008), pp. 151–2, 158.

MacAskill, J., 'The Highland Kelp Proprietors and their Struggle over the Salt and Barilla Duties, 1817–1831', *JSHS*, vol. 26, 2006, pp. 60–1, 64.

37. Gray, *Highland Economy*, pp. 124–9.
38. NRS, GD427/136/22, G. Macaulay to A. Gillanders, 23 April 1781.
39. Gray, *Highland Economy*, p. 126.
40. NRS, GD427/138/4, A. Campbell, Ensay to F. H. Mackenzie, 28 March 1789; /9, A. Gillanders to A. Campbell, 22 October 1798.
41. Cregeen, E. R. (ed.), *Argyll Estate Instructions: Mull, Morvern and Tire 1771–1805* (Edinburgh, 1964), p. 188.
42. NRS, GD46/13/126, State of Lewis kelp from 1794 to 1799.
43. NRS, GD201/1/365/2, 'State of Clanranald's Affairs Jan. 1798'.
44. Mackillop, A., '*More Fruitful than the Soil': Army, Empire and the Scottish Highlands, 1715–1815* (East Linton, 2000), pp. 134–5.
45. NRS, GD46/17/15, P. Fairbairn to F. H. Mackenzie, 2 May 1795.
46. NRS, GD46/17/15, P. Fairbairn to F. H. Mackenzie, 24 April 1786.
47. NRS, GD46/17/15, P. Fairbairn to F. H. Mackenzie, 1 May 1796; C. Mackenzie to F. H. Mackenzie, 12 June 1796.
48. NRS, GD46/13/127, Account of sale of Lewis kelp 1809.
49. Dodgshon, R. A., *No Stone Unturned: A History of Farming, Landscape and Environment in the Scottish Highlands and Islands* (Edinburgh, 2015), p. 303.
50. Gray, *Highland Economy*, pp. 128–9.
51. NRS, GD427/138/3, A. Campbell to A. Gillanders, 11 May 1789; /4, A. Campbell to F. H. Mackenzie, 28 March 1789.
52. NRS, GD46/13/126, State of Lewis kelp from 1794 to 1799.
53. Hunter, J., *The Making of the Crofting Community* (Edinburgh, 1976), pp. 17–18.
54. NRS, GD46/1/326, State of Rents, Public Burdens, etc. of Island of Lewis crop and year 1800.
55. NRS, GD46/17/3, P. Fairbairn to F. H. Mackenzie, 1 March 1794.
56. Hunter, *Making of Crofting Community*, p. 18.
57. Thomson and Coull, 'Kelp', p. 160.
58. Gray, *Highland Economy*, pp. 130–1; Thomson and Coull, 'Kelp', p. 153; Hunter, *Making of Crofting Community*, p. 16.
59. Cregeen, 'Creation of the Crofting Townships in Tiree', p. 180.
60. NRS, GD427/136/24, G. Macaulay, Loch Rogue to A, Gillanders, 10 May 1782.
61. NRS, GD42714/8, Rental of Lewis Crop 1783; GD46/20/4/1/16, Rental of Lewis Crop 1803.
62. NRS, GD46/17/15, P. Fairbairn to F. H. Mackenzie, 6 April 1795.
63. NRS, GD46/17/45, 'Note of Lewis rentals, 1819'.
64. Hunter, *Making of Crofting Community*, p. 18; Gray, M., 'The Kelp Industry in the Highlands and Islands', *Economic History Review*, New Series, vol. 4, 2, 1951, p. 204.

65. NRS, GD427/16/5, Rental of Lewis Crop 1791; GD46/20/4/1/16, Rental of Lewis Crop 1803.
66. NRS, GD46/17/13, P. Fairbairn to F. H. Mackenzie, 20 April 1795.
67. NRS, GD46/20/4/1/14, Lewis, State of Rents 1800.
68. Hunter, *Making of Crofting Community*, p. 16.
69. MacAskill, J., '"The most arbitrary, scandalous act of tyranny": The Crown, private proprietors and the ownership of the Scottish foreshore in the nineteenth century', *The Scottish Historical Review*, vol. 85, 2, 2006, p. 279.
70. Gray, *Highland Economy*, pp. 131–2 and 'The Kelp Industry', p. 200; Dodgshon, R. A., *From Chiefs to Landlords: Social and Economic Change in the Western Highlands and Islands, c.1493–1820* (Edinburgh, 1998), p. 240.
71. NRS, GD46/17/3, A. Gillanders to F. H. Mackenzie, 18 April 1793.
72. NRS, GD46/17/2, 'Printed case 1794 re Lewis kelp'.
73. Gray, 'The Kelp Industry', p. 200.
74. NRS, GD46/17/80/211–2, n.d., but from position in volume apparently *c.*1810.
75. Macinnes, A. I., 'Scottish Gaeldom: The First Phase of Clearance' in T. M. Devine and R. Mitchison (eds), *People and Society in Scotland, Volume 1, 1760–1830* (Edinburgh, 1988), p. 86.
76. NRS, GD46/17/10, Lord Seaforth to Charles Yorke, 23 April 1804.
77. Macdonald, D., *Lewis: A History of the Island* (Edinburgh, 1978), p. 88.
78. Gray, 'The Kelp Industry', pp. 204–5.
79. 1792, *OSA*, vol. XIX, p. 276 (Lochs), p. 283 (Uig); 1801: Macdonald, *Lewis*, p. 50.
80. MacAskill, 'The Highland Kelp Proprietors', p. 64.
81. NRS, GD46/17/15, P. Fairbairn to F. H. Mackenzie, 26 November 1795.
82. Gray, *Highland Economy*, p. 127.
83. NRS, GD46/17/15, P. Fairbairn to F. H. Mackenzie, 3 December 1795; GD46/17/11, Advertisement for the sale of Lochalsh, 1798.
84. NRS, GD46/17/18, P. Fairbairn to F. H. Mackenzie, 27 December 1798.
85. NRS, GD46/17/19/356, C. Mackenzie to Lord Seaforth, 20 October 1801.
86. NRS, GD46/20/4, Rental of Lewis, Lochalsh and Kintail 1799; GD46/17/11, State of Lord Seaforth's debts 1799–1800.
87. NRS, GD46/17/4/163–5, 'Charles Grenville's idea of my affairs . . . May 1788'.
88. NRS, GD46/17/20/204–5, C. Mackenzie to Lord Seaforth, 24 November 1801.

4 Lifestyle, Debts and First Land Sales

Lifestyle

In Chapters Two and Three it has been shown that Seaforth's land-management policies and concept of his role as clan chief caused him to accept a lower level of income (with the exception of kelp revenue) than many of his fellow Highland proprietors. The rational consequence of this would have been a more modest lifestyle. However, his lifestyle was far from modest. In this chapter the nature of and motivations for his lifestyle will be analysed and also the consequences of successive debt crises for his estate in the period to his departure for Barbados in 1801.

It was suggested in Chapter One that Seaforth's deafness caused him greater psychological problems than a person born deaf because he was 'culturally hearing'. The theory was also advanced that his survival from the scarlet fever which caused his deafness gave him the impression that he had been thus privileged in order to achieve great things. That he was a man of considerable ability was demonstrated by his scientific achievements, and this was an activity on which he spent large sums of money, especially in the 1780s. In 1794 he was elected a fellow of the Royal Society, the citation referring to him as 'a gentleman well versed in various branches of Natural knowledge'.[1] Election depended on the approval of Sir Joseph Banks, virtual director of the Royal Botanic Garden at Kew and president of the Royal Society.[2] Banks believed in the role of amateur scientists from elite society, like himself, whose aim was to harness science for the benefit of their own estates and the economy at large. Seaforth met, not only his social, but also his scientific criteria. Like Banks he was interested in the natural sciences, especially botany, and also zoology and geology, which lent themselves more to the collection of objects and scientific data than to the abstract theorising of the mathematical sciences.[3] He was an avid collector of botanical, zoological and geological specimens, and supplied mineral samples to their mutual friend Charles Greville, who himself had a very fine collection of minerals. Seaforth also shared Banks's enthusiasm for voyages of scientific exploration. Banks had made his name by participation in Captain Cook's Pacific Ocean voyage of 1768–71.[4] They corresponded about Seaforth's proposed two-season scientific tour of the Western Isles, the Faroes and Iceland. In addition to the expense of his sloop, *Mary*, he employed two scientific assistants, one of whom was nominated by Banks.[5] Seaforth was proud of the results and had sought the botanical specimens which were of primary interest to Banks.[6] The proposed visit to the Faroes and Iceland did not happen, almost certainly because the next season, 1788, coincided with Seaforth's first major financial crisis. It is likely that a particular attraction of scientific work for him was that, for much of it, and especially for the background reading, his deafness was not an issue. He built up a considerable library of scientific books at Brahan Castle and, when in 1801 their sale was being considered to raise cash, he made clear how much they meant to him. He explained to Greville, 'I cannot converse like other people and these were my friends . . . I have now lost in a moment what I have been twenty years collecting and their loss has taken from me all relish for a pursuit which filled up many weary moments of a miserable life.'[7] Friends came to the rescue to save him from this.[8]

Even more important to Seaforth than his scientific interests was his family life. Although most of the surviving letters are from him to his wife, it is clear that there was a warm and continuing affection between them. He married in 1782 Mary Proby, cousin of the earl of Carysfort.[9] Mrs Mackenzie (from 1798, Lady Seaforth and known in the family as Mira) spent substantial amounts of time in the Highlands at Brahan and on Lewis at Seaforth Lodge. When he was away on parliamentary, military and estate business Seaforth wrote to her frequently. He usually addressed her as 'Dear Life'. In 1791 he wrote from Edinburgh, 'I must scribble a little to you from time to time as it is now my greatest pleasure to chat with you and think of you and our Dear little ones.'[10] When in 1793 it was confirmed that Seaforth would not have to go overseas with his regiment, Mira's sister, Cathleen Proby, wrote to him expressing relief that Mira would not be deprived of 'her greatest comfort and delight, viz. your society'.[11] They were compatible in many ways. They shared the same aspirations for their estates and their inhabitants. As has been shown in Chapter Two, Mira was active in encouraging linen manufacture in Lewis. An unhelpful shared interest was the couple's enjoyment in spending money which they did not have. In 1790 Seaforth's sister, who lived in London, complained she was being plagued by a tradesman for payment of £200–£300 of goods ordered by Mira six or seven years previously.[12] Seaforth clearly had a warm personal relationship also with his children and took a keen interest in their progress. In letters to Mira he often referred to them as their 'litter' – for example in 1791 when telling her he was bringing presents for them to Seaforth Lodge.[13] Contrary to suggestions that aristocratic fathers were uninterested in female children[14], he wrote in 1793 to Mira, 'tell little Mary [now aged almost 10] her letter was the prettiest she could write and if she hereafter shows as much desire to act like a good girl as she expresses wishes to act like a big lad she will make me completely happy.'[15] The quality of Seaforth's family life was commented on even by those who were not friends or allies. In the hotly contested Ross-shire election of 1809, an elector advising that he would not be voting for Seaforth's candidate, nevertheless referred to the 'reciprocity of affection and duty and fine domestic happiness' of the Seaforth family.[16]

It may seem surprising that a man who was so concerned for his wife and children as Seaforth lived so consistently beyond his means that long-held landholdings were sold off, thus accelerating a process by which the estate was gradually lost in the nineteenth century.[17] He was far from unique among Highland proprietors in extravagantly financing his social aspirations and accumulating debt despite benefitting from rises in commodity prices.[18] They could not escape the social pressures of British landed society, which judged status by the level of expenditure on housing, dress and entertaining.[19] It will be argued that in Seaforth's case there was a particular pressure – that an able and energetic man felt a strong need to excel to compensate for his profound deafness and speech problems. Seaforth lived in

London, the centre of elite social life, for at least half the year while MP for Ross-shire from 1784 to 1790 and from 1794 to 1796. He lived in fashionable districts in the West End – for example in the 1780s and 1790s around Berkeley Square and Grosvenor Square.[20] He sought thereby, not only prestige, but also political influence. Houses of this sort permitted the scale of entertaining which helped to secure these ambitions.[21] Status was also sought by his commission to Benjamin West for the painting (referred to in Chapter One) showing the legendary Colin Fitzgerald saving King Alexander III from a stag, which was shown at the Royal Academy exhibition in 1786. It was intended to demonstrate the alleged ancient origins of the clan Mackenzie, their supposed loyalty to the Crown and to establish Seaforth as a patron of the arts.[22]

Seaforth's ambition was to restore the peerage which had died with Earl Kenneth in 1781.[23] In 1788, his mother wrote 'when you see Lord Selkirk talk to him about claiming the Title'. This letter appears to refer also to the gambling habits of his London circle.[24] That he in his young days was one of the group around George, Prince of Wales, was confirmed by his daughter Caroline in 1812. She complained that 'his oldest most intimate friend should not be invited' to one of the many parties held by George, now Prince Regent, at Carlton House.[25] Alexander Mackenzie's *History of the Mackenzies* (first published in 1879) suggested that 'the recreation of the Court was play . . . he [Seaforth] heedlessly ventured and lost'.[26] Two pieces of contemporary evidence tend to confirm his gambling losses. A statement in his own hand shows his personal debts to have increased from £4,000 in December 1786 to £10,000 a year later.[27] The letter from his mother in July 1788, when he was at Brahan, advised him not to hurry back to London, 'and, as to your friends (or rather your Enemys) who crowd so unseasonably on you, turn them all out'.[28] This seems likely to refer to gambling companions. It appears that Seaforth's urge to excel in London brought him into what has been called 'a boozy and masculine sociability . . . in a culture of debt common among the landed classes'.[29]

In order to economise Seaforth moved his main residence to the island of Lewis when he left Parliament in 1790. Life at Seaforth Lodge was not exactly frugal. John Knox, who visited in 1786, described how the Seaforth family lived in what he describes as 'more than Asiatic luxury in the simple produce of his forest, his heaths and his shores – beef, mutton, veal, lamb, pork, venison, hare and every sort of fowl. Fish were caught daily for him and thrown in a heap near the kitchen'.[30] Mrs Mackenzie made some attempt to save in 1790. One male and three female servants and a boy were to be employed.[31] This was certainly modest compared to the eight male (five of them outdoor) and nine female servants employed at Brahan in 1785–6.[32] However, Mira's list of their duties suggests that the economy consisted mainly in each servant covering more than at Brahan. Seaforth Lodge was fitted out in some style and at some expense. In 1793 Seaforth was worried that, as a result of the pillage which might be done by a French privateer in the area, 'I shall suffer most for my furniture and plate, books, etc. to the amount of some thousands value'.[33] He believed that he and his family deserved a certain standard of life irrespective of their financial circumstances. However, this was not just a demonstration of extravagance. Status was at risk if visitors were not met by certain standards of sociability and taste and a certain level of consumption. For example James Boswell, a real weather vane of metropolitan taste, and Dr Samuel Johnson visited Sir Alexander Macdonald, a Highland chief of similar rank to Seaforth, at Armadale in 1773. Boswell remarked that although Macdonald was English-educated and had an English wife, the house and its hospitality were no better than a tenant could have given and he was 'quite hurt with the meanness and unsuitable appearance of everything'.[34] Even if visitors were few on Lewis, such a reaction would be very damaging to the Seaforth family's social status, especially as they hoped to elevate it to the peerage.

In the 1790s Seaforth's social aspirations to shine among the Highland (and indeed Scottish) landed elite expanded further, and the attempts to economise did not last long. As will be explained in Chapter Five, he now settled his differences with the political manager of Scotland, Henry Dundas (and thus with the prime minister, William Pitt) and, as a consequence, was commissioned in 1793 and 1794 to raise two battalions of foot soldiers. This brought him to the centre of the Scottish political and military establishment and made the long-held ambition of restoring the peerage a realistic prospect. The rapprochement with Dundas and Pitt resulted in Seaforth returning, now in their interest, as the MP for Ross-shire between 1794 and 1796.[35] This required him to live for part of the year in London and to spend accordingly. He bought a new London house in Hereford Street, near Grosvenor Square, making Colin Mackenzie 'truly anxious to relieve [him] from possible embarrassment about the £2,000 you want for your house'. The most likely lender had declined because 'if he is to reside in London it will not strengthen his security'.[36] Metropolitan living was not a recipe for economy.

The mid 1790s also saw increasingly expensive participation by Francis and Mira in elite social life in the Highlands. He played a prominent part as a steward in the Northern Meeting, the highlight of the proprietors' social calendar, held over a week of expensive celebrations in Inverness every September. In 1795 the Mackenzies evidently put on a good show as 'to Mrs Mackenzie of Seaforth and a very respectable party of ladies and gentlemen from Ross-shire the meeting was much indebted'.[37] This sort of sociability was inevitably expensive, but it is clear that friends regarded Seaforth and Mira as being particularly extravagant. In 1795 they were invited to visit the Halls of Dunglass, near Dumbarton. Sir James Hall was, like Seaforth, an amateur scientist.[38] In extending the invitation, Lady Hall wrote that she was aware 'you have servants and postillions and waiting maids and trunks and band boxes and portmanteaus and imperials, etc., etc.'.[39]

Seaforth was determined to play the role of chief, which was seen to have been neglected by Earl Kenneth through spending much of his time abroad.[40] Brahan must now become the political, military and social centre of the county. In Easter Ross, the houses of Cromarty, Invergordon, Tulloch, Foulis and Novar all became elegant mansions during the thirty years after the 1745 rising.[41] Brahan must not be eclipsed. Seaforth's marriage into an English aristocratic family must have increased pressure to update and extend his Highland seat. He accordingly renovated and added to Brahan Castle to reflect design trends in England and Scotland and filled it with fine furniture, carpets, porcelain and paintings.[42] A similar process can be seen in Ireland, where aspiring landowners whose estates were remote from the metropole were emulating English models of gracious country living. The high point in big house construction in Ireland was from the early eighteenth to the mid nineteenth centuries with, as in the Highlands of Scotland, a particular boom in the late eighteenth century as rent levels rose. Some houses were built from scratch and in other cases,

as with Seaforth and more commonly in the Highlands, existing houses were renovated and extended. Sometimes as part of
this process, as at Brahan, the gardens of big houses were also
remodelled along the most fashionable lines.[43] The promise in
1796 of a peerage[44] made it seem necessary to prepare seriously
for more stylish living and hospitality. A substantial extension to Brahan, known during design and construction as 'the
Kitchen Wing', was being planned from late 1795. This wing
also included, on the third floor, a nursery and children's bed-
rooms. Mrs Mackenzie insisted that the headroom on this floor
be increased from eight-and-a-half feet to ten feet.[45] Seaforth
was offered two plans of the east front and chose the more
expensive – with turrets in the middle.[46] Ironically, in the same
month Colin Mackenzie was struggling to renegotiate his debts.
He wrote, 'I cannot dissemble or conceal the extreme difficulty of procuring money' and warned that the creditors might
force land sales at disadvantageous prices.[47] This is further evidence of Seaforth's determination to secure the style of living
to which he believed his family was entitled regardless of his
financial position.

A fine building required fine contents. Among the many
pieces ordered were, in 1796 from the London sculptor John
Bacon, a chimney piece with carved figures, pilasters for the
library and a monument to his brother Frederick.[48] Substantial
expenditure on the garden was not only to impress visitors,
but also to satisfy Seaforth's great enthusiasm for gardening,
derived from his botanical studies. He was a follower of the
'expressive' style led by Capability Brown, in which the viewer
reacted personally to a supposedly natural, but in reality highly
planned, landscape.[49] The grounds and garden appear to have
been under continuous development in the 1790s.[50] In 1795
a temple was being built and reference was made to 'the new
garden'.[51] In 1796 a ha-ha was built.[52] In 1798 the new shrub-
bery was being planned. In 1799 an external consultant, John
Johnstone, was brought to Brahan to advise on another new
garden. He recommended that the lawn should come right up
to the house and approved the position of new shrubberies.[53]
The cost of draining, earth-moving, fences and gravel walks was
estimated at £916.[54]

In 1799 Colin Mackenzie criticised the size of the Brahan
staff and argued that, if Seaforth gave up his 'permanent and
expensive establishment', there it would still be possible for

he and his wife to pay occasional visits.[55] How far was this concern justified? In 1797–8 eight male servants were declared at Brahan for tax purposes – a butler, two footmen, a coachman, a postilion, a groom, a gardener and a gamekeeper. This was not as many as Sir Hector Munro of Novar, near Alness, who had nine male servants, the largest establishment in Ross-shire.[56] Seaforth undoubtedly envied Novar's wealth acquired by questionable means while soldiering in India, and regarded him as an arriviste on the make. Although Novar came from a minor Ross-shire gentry family, his father had been a merchant. Now, as returning Indian nabobs tended to do, he was trying to establish himself among the elite of Ross-shire society.[57] Seaforth and he had also been political opponents since 1784. Novar was one of the first proprietors in Ross-shire to let his lands to sheep farmers and was at the centre of the sheep riots in 1792.[58] There were thus numerous reasons for Seaforth to disapprove of him.

Despite Seaforth's increasing financial problems and Novar's much deeper pocket, Seaforth was trying to keep up with him in his establishment at Brahan. The total of male servants in 1797–8 had been maintained at the same level as 1785–6 (eight), and the number of footmen had increased from one to two.[59] Tax rates were higher for male servants on the grounds that they represented conspicuous consumption. A similar story of county rivalries can be seen in the Carriage Tax Returns. By 1797–8 there were a number of Ross-shire notables, for example Seaforth's political rival Sir Charles Ross of Balnagown, who had one carriage, a four-wheeler. Only two had two carriages – Seaforth and Novar, further evidence that theirs was the leading social rivalry. Novar may have had more male servants, but Seaforth won the carriage stakes. Both of Seaforth's carriages had four wheels, but only one of Novar's (the other presumably being some sort of gig).[60]

Seaforth's determination to take a leading role in the society and politics of Ross-shire was resented by others. One was an elderly soldier, Major General Sir Alexander Mackenzie of Coull, whose family had purchased Strathconon from Earl Kenneth about 1770. In 1792 he wrote to a neighbouring proprietor with many indirect (and a few direct) criticisms of Seaforth. He objected to those who 'consider the fortune of a friend as a bank they have a right to draw on' (an obvious reference to Seaforth's extravagance and borrowings). After a meeting of the county freeholders at Tain in 1792, he commented that 'the Pride of Seaforth never shone so bright, certainly never so absurdly.'[61] Ambition and energy over-rode rational restraints in spending.

Debts and financial pressures

Seaforth's financial problems caused by inherited debt, land-management policies and high levels of expenditure, culminated in 1788 in what was to be the first of many crises. The urgency of the situation had been clear to Seaforth's brother-in-law and London lawyer Vicary Gibbs for fully a year. He wrote to him in April 1787:

> I do not like to enter upon the state of your affairs with you because our opinion of them differs very widely . . . The same course pursued for a definite portion of time, and that not a very long one, will lead you to the end. This is not my language, but that of all who know anything of you here [London] . . . They will not say this to you lest it should offend you, but they all say it . . . consider the family you have and are likely to have . . . for God's sake stop your hand before it is too late.[62]

This seems to indicate an unwillingness to face up to financial realities, in particular to make economies and an impatience when anyone ventured to point out these realities. It seems likely that Gibbs's highly critical tone was a response especially to Seaforth's gambling.

Seaforth did get as far as to write in his own hand three possible methods of dealing with his debts, which included potential sales of all properties except Lewis and Brahan. In a 'Memorandum of my Affairs and intended arrangements', written by him in December 1787, he calculated that the total debt was now £147,911. Of this £98,400 was on the Scottish estate (that is, only slightly reduced from the purchase price of £100,000). The Lincolnshire estate was mortgaged for £12,000. Payments still due by him for his late brother's legacies amounted to £10,300. Two major loans from private individuals totalled £7,211. The capital required to support his mother's annuity of £500 per annum was estimated at £10,000. Seaforth's personal debts were also calculated at the suspiciously round figure of £10,000. Current expenditure included, not only the family's living expenses, but also building works at Brahan, gambling losses and the cost of maintaining the sloop *Mary* at Stornoway.[63]

Seaforth's calculations do not reflect the complexity, nor probably the extent, of his borrowing. The statement made at the beginning of 1787 is described by himself as 'rude sketch not accurate'. In particular, with the exception of the £5,000 interest due annually to Lady Caroline on the purchase price of the Ross-shire estate, it does not give a clear indication of the cost of servicing debt. If 3 per cent interest is conservatively estimated on the remaining £48,000 of debt, the annual payment on that would be £1,440. The total annual interest due would therefore be about £6,440. Table 4.1 shows what Seaforth described as 'the present free rental' of the Ross-shire estate. It includes the unpredictable kelp income and makes no allowance for arrears. Even so the total, £5,995, was barely sufficient to meet interest charges.[64] The income of the English estates was about £1,600, far short of what was needed to pay his living costs and other expenses (not specified in his calculations). How, therefore, were interest payments met? The answer was by further borrowing. Seaforth's calculation in December 1787 includes in the debts 'Col. Mackenzie's advance for interest £5,211'. His brother-in-law appears, therefore, to have made a loan to meet the greater part of that year's interest payments.

By May 1788, Gibbs was finding greater difficulty than usual in negotiating Seaforth's bills to extend his credit.[65] It was in the same month that his close friend and adviser Charles Greville

Table 4.1 'Free rental' of Ross-shire estates (in £ sterling) as calculated by Seaforth, early 1787

Lewis	2525
Kintail	1400
Kildun, Ussie, Dingwall, etc.	500
Mains of Brahan	300
Fortrose	110
Value of Lewis kelp	1000
Value of Kintail kelp	110
Feu duties	50
Total	5995

Source: National Records of Scotland, GD46/17/4/78.

recommended the sale of Lochalsh and Kintail, which, as has been seen, he was unwilling for sentimental reasons to do.[66] He now accepted that the Lincolnshire estate, Humberston, should be sold. However, there followed an unseemly and protracted wrangle with his mother and her legal representatives. Mrs Mackenzie Senior's annuity of £500 was secured on the Humberston revenues. Seaforth had for some time been proposing to transfer this burden to the dubious security of the Ross-shire rents.[67] Her legal advice, understandably, was that the encumbrances of the Scottish estate made this imprudent.[68] Seaforth's relations with his mother were at times less than cordial. Some of the tension was over payment of her annuity, which was a significant drain on the estate. In 1792 she wrote to him that 'I hope you will immediately order it to be paid as there will be very disagreeable consequences ... if you do not'.[69] The implied threat of legal action can have done little to improve their relationship.

In early October 1788, Mrs Mackenzie Senior threatened to leave the country on a visit to France. Gibbs was terrified that she would go before agreement had been reached and wrote to Seaforth, 'this is of such importance to you ... it would be worth your while to go to London on purpose. At all events keep your temper with her.' She finally agreed at the end of October and Humberston, with the adjoining estate of Somerby, was sold by the end of 1788 for £49,000.[70] Despite Charles Greville's recommendation to sell them, the Wester Ross properties and Fortrose were retained at this time. The arrival in December 1789 of the balance of his brother Thomas Frederick's Indian estate (£23,000) enabled Seaforth to maintain this stance.[71] Seaforth therefore benefitted from the great ingress of capital from India in the eighteenth century charted by George McGilvary. This was made possible by the employment of family members in one of the countries which provided the best opportunity for the speedy acquisition of riches.[72] Unlike many other proprietors, the funds were used by Seaforth primarily to support debt rather than to invest in income generating improvements.

One of Greville's recommendations which he did adopt was to retire from Parliament at the next general election (1790) and take up what was expected to be a more economical way of life at Seaforth Lodge. As has been seen, the need to maintain certain standards of taste and consumption meant that the Seaforth family's mode of living there was only relatively economical. In any case, it remained the family's full-time residence for less than three years. The outbreak of war with revolutionary France in 1793 brought Seaforth back to the mainland to raise a line regiment, and to return to Parliament and to London society between 1794 and 1796.[73] As has been shown above, the promise of a peerage created a perceived need for even more stylish living and the expensive extension to Brahan Castle was begun in 1796. Was there reason to suppose that there were increasing income streams to justify such expenditure?

It is telling that the estate papers do not include regular statements of income and expenditure on a consistent basis nor a clear and comprehensive list of debts. The income from Lewis kelp gave the greatest grounds for optimism. The gross receipts increased from about £1,080 in 1789[74] to £2,253 in 1795 (the year in which planning of the kitchen wing began) and were to grow further to £2,978 in 1798.[75] The gross land rental of Lewis rose significantly from £2,212 in 1783[76] to £2,925 in 1791.[77] However, over these signs of income growth hovered the spectre of debt interest payments. Colin Mackenzie from time to time warned Seaforth that the estate income was insufficient to do much more than service the debt. For example, in 1800 he advised that £5,293 had been paid in debt interest in the previous year and that the free rental for the current year was estimated at only a slightly higher sum than that (£6,666).[78] In addition to debt interest, there were regular demands for repayment, which often could be met only by taking out new loans, usually at increased interest rates. David Taylor has questioned Professor Devine's claim that Highland landowners of this period were subject to irresistible social and thus financial pressures. He argues that, in the case of the fourth duke and duchess of Gordon, they were repeatedly warned by their estate officials of the likely consequences of their extravagance, but were conscious and willing agents of continuing and indeed increasing expenditure. The duchess is reckoned, between 1791 and 1809, mainly on her role as a leading political hostess in London, to have spent £112,000 or 20 per cent of the estate expenditure.[79] Because of his inherited debts Seaforth could not have contemplated spending on this level, but he does seem to have shared the Gordons' wilful refusal to match expenditure to income.

Days of reckoning – the first great land sale

From the mid 1790s Seaforth's advisers were again urging him to make land sales to ease his debt problems. The improvident purchase of the Hereford Street house in 1795 was in many ways a catalyst. Colin Mackenzie wrote that 'it must indeed be a very embarrassing and disagreeable thing if the money is not raised'. A sudden demand by his creditors might be fatal.[80] After months of struggling Colin managed to borrow the purchase price of £2,000 (£1,000 from his own father, the Edinburgh lawyer Alexander Mackenzie).[81] To add to the crisis, Exchequer officials threatened legal action over non-payment of Lewis feu duty due to the Crown,[82] the accumulated arrears of which amounted by 1796 to between £4,000 and £5,000 (at least half the annual revenue of the estate).[83] Colin had to explain that, in the third year of war, Seaforth's loans were much harder to renegotiate. High interest was available with complete safety in government bonds, which made it less attractive to lend to a heavily indebted Highland landowner. He recommended land sales because of 'the trouble and distress which a load of debt exposes you to in times when money is much in demand' and dreaded 'Mr Pitt's further loans, which . . . give so great a temptation to your creditors to call for their money'.[84]

Such a call occurred in the autumn of 1796. Embarrassingly, Seaforth was sued by a junior officer in his own regiment, Lieutenant William Gray Polson, for repayment of a loan of £3,000 made in 1794 and secured, as most of his borrowing was, on the entire Ross-shire estate. Interest had only been paid up to October 1795. Repayment was now being sought from the estate lands by legal process.[85] The problem, as usual, landed in the lap of Colin Mackenzie. He wrote, 'Polson's debt gives me great uneasiness . . . I must not hide that all my exertion may prove fruitless.'[86] In addition to the Hereford Street purchase, this was the year when the new wing at Brahan was being built. In early November 1796 a loan of £1,500 was secured from the Inverness banker Shaw[87] and at least a temporary accommodation seems to have been made with Polson's representatives.

In early November 1795 Colin Mackenzie, in an attempt to talk up Seaforth's credit worthiness, argued that the annual rental of the estate was 'not less than £8,000' and that in addition £2,500 could be expected from kelp.[88] However, only two weeks later his father wrote to Seaforth that an expected £3,000 remittance from the estate would be only £2,000, 'which with the balance of the kelp money will not make up the interest due to Lady Caroline and the creditors on the estate'.[89] The short-term solution to this emergency was to borrow from family members, some of them close family. Nine days later, Colin reported that 'sums I have received are £1,000 from Kenneth Mackenzie at Millbank my uncle [which] will accordingly bear interest to him, and £1,000 from my uncle the colonel [Alexander Mackenzie, Seaforth's brother-in-law, who had lent also in the 1787–8 crisis] and your sister's money'.[90] Constant effort was required to raise loans, many from members of the extended family and other Mackenzie proprietors in Ross-shire, the traditional sources of lending for Highland chiefs.[91] The Register of Sasines shows such lenders being given security on the Seaforth estate – for example, in 1796 Alexander Mackenzie, for £1,000, the uncle of Sir Kenneth Mackenzie of Gairloch and Thomas Mackenzie of Ord, both also for £1,000.[92] By 1800 Seaforth was even driven to borrow £1,000 from his father-in-law, Dean Proby.[93] In 1801 the largest debt due by him in Scotland was £3,400 borrowed in 1796 from the heirs of his former Lewis factor Alexander Gillanders.[94]

If the long-term solution, frequently advised, was to sell land, which might Seaforth be persuaded to part with? In 1795 Colin suggested 'a sale of the parish of Lochalsh alone, which is a fine estate, quite separate and distinct from Kintail and possessing neither the advantage of high and incalculable improvability as Lewis nor the attraction like Kintail of being the most ancient grant to your ancestors'.[95] In other words, Lewis was too potentially profitable to sell. Kintail, he assumed, was off limits for sentimental reasons. Lochalsh he thought should sell for £40,000. However, there were difficulties. Seaforth was now lobbying hard for the peerage which would establish the social pre-eminence of his house in Ross-shire. A complicated deal was in the making, which included an assurance to Dundas of the full weight of Seaforth's political support. Votes in county elections depended on freehold of land and Seaforth had been active in creating fictitious freeholds on the basis of his wide acres. Selling land meant losing votes and the prospect of this might sink the peerage deal. As Colin put it, when trying to renegotiate loans in the spring of 1796, 'I wish to God your great object were attained so that you might with propriety make a sale . . . I can perfectly feel . . . your anxiety on the pleasing object in view, which a sale of . . . any considerable part of your estate might injure', but pointed out that the attacks of creditors might be even more damaging.[96] The peerage negotiations being now at a critical stage, he advised Seaforth three weeks later that a sale 'might be laid hold of by Administration as pretence for breach of their engagement'.[97] However, after a further week the deal was done and the newspapers reported that Seaforth would be one of a new creation of peers.[98] An advertisement for the sale of Lochalsh was subsequently published.[99] This was not a novel or unique dilemma. In the 1760s and 1770s the Grant of Grant family delayed land sales needed to reduce their debts in order to protect their political influence in Inverness-shire and Moray.[100]

Surprisingly, in view of Seaforth's previous views, the sale was offered, not only of Lochalsh, but also of Kintail. Even more surprisingly, it suggested that 'Glenshiel . . . would form the most desirable sheep walk in Scotland and of course would afford a very considerable increase of rent'.[101] How can this be squared with his long-held wishes to protect his tenants and preserve his ancestral lands? The explanation may have been sheer financial desperation. Word came in November that the government would give no relief in the long-running case on the Lewis feu duties. As the prime minister put it, Seaforth was 'already in line for a favour of the highest consequence'.[102] On top of all this, there was a serious concern that a major creditor Mrs Scott would attempt to arrest the estate rents.[103] There were to be other occasions, notably his purchase of a slave plantation in 1801, when imminent financial disaster led him to take decisions apparently at variance with his humanitarian approach.

There was no sale, for which there are a number of possible reasons. The lands had been used as security for so many debts that purchasers might be concerned whether what they were buying was uncontested ownership.[104] Peter Fairbairn, the estate factor, saw 'no prospect of a sale unless there should be a peace very soon'.[105] A potential purchaser had withdrawn because of the failure of preliminary peace negotiations and consequent depression of stock prices, his money being tied up in stocks which could not be sold without loss.[106] Colin Mackenzie had to respond to a complaint on behalf of another interested party that Lochalsh was 'at present low rented'. He explained that 'in making the last sett his Lordship was obliged to submit to some loss in consideration of the alacrity with which his people had enlisted in his regiment newly raised'.[107] It appears that in the 1794 sett Seaforth had given leases to Lochalsh tenants in return for supplying recruits for the second battalion of the 78th Regiment.[108] In the autumn of 1799 a friend of George Gillanders was in the offing as a possible purchaser. Colin was concerned that he might be frightened off by an unwillingness by Seaforth to bargain over the asking price of £40,000.[109] It may be that Seaforth, having been brought to advertise the properties, was still loath to conclude a sale. But the pressure from Colin was relentless, and even Lewis was not out of the frame. About a month before Seaforth set sail for Barbados, Colin thought there was a prospect of selling the island to Lord Armadale for £105,000.[110]

The reason for Colin's determination was that the financial situation was worsening, notwithstanding the highest-yet profit from Lewis kelp of £2,453 in 1798.[111] He was worried by the unpredictability of some of the interested parties, notably Lady Caroline Mackenzie. She was seen by Colin (and also Seaforth) as eccentric and dangerous because she was willing to take legal measures and was an enthusiast of French republicanism. Colin commented that 'there must be something fascinating in Republicanism since her Ladyship appears to have imbibed it even amidst the horror of Revolution ... but I dread her proceeding more than any of the rocks your estate has hitherto weathered' and warned that she could arrest the rents.[112] Seaforth was certainly not indifferent to his financial problems. In April 1799 Colin wrote to him, 'I am sorry to know that it [his pecuniary situation] is such ... as sometimes to excite in your mind the most poignant uneasiness.' What could be done? For all his 'uneasiness' radical retrenchment was not seen as an option. Colin assured him in the same letter that 'I am not going to propose any rigid schemes of economy such as your rank and situation might render difficult'.[113]An insight into how Seaforth was in the habit of maintaining his 'rank and station' is given by a letter from a London coach manufacturer. He claimed to have been supplying coaches to him for thirty years 'in the best manner', but was disappointed by the lack of orders in 1800. He tried to tempt him by offering a coach in stock with bear skin seat covering and harness with silver coronets. Seaforth's own crest could be reproduced.[114]

Colin Mackenzie believed it was absolutely crucial that Lochalsh be sold. If it raised £40,000, that would reduce the capital debt from £107,600 to £67,600. If, in addition, about £4,500, the gross rent of Lewis, was put each year into a sinking fund, the remaining debt could be dissolved in thirty years. Colin was uncharacteristically lyrical about the prospect thus offered. 'That sacrifice made [Lochalsh] ... all the rest of your noble possessions may be preserved, may be rendered free from encumbrance, perhaps while you yourself may have the joy to witness it ... certainly at the date when your son will have only reached mature years'. In case this was too distant a prospect, he added that the immediate benefit of a sinking fund would be to restore his credit and reduce 'clamourous and importunate demands'.[115] Emergency measures had to be taken regularly to raise cash. In 1798 the lands around Fortrose were hurriedly sold to a Ross-shire neighbour, Mackenzie of Flourburn (the first sale by Seaforth of part of his Highland estate). The £3,000 raised was earmarked to pay off one debtor, but much larger sums than this were needed.[116] Another emergency measure was an auction held in August 1799 by Christie's of the contents of Seaforth's London house at Hereford Street, Grosvener Square. The advertisement gives an indication of his taste for fine wines:

SALE BY AUCTION by Mr Christie on the premises August 14 and the following day – all the neat household furniture and variety of other effects; also a capital assortment of choice wines, consisting of remarkably high flavoured claret, hock, vin de grave, East India Madeira, excellent sherry, capital old port, the whole of the first quality.[117]

In October 1799, Colin asked for a meeting with Seaforth at which

We could ... examine and discriminate the various branches of expenditure and point out those in which there appeared excess, not with the fear of vain regrets for what is past, but of establishing useful practical rules for the future, but if we are not at the same time enabled ... to commence the delightful work of dissolving the debts themselves, if instead of this we are goaded by the clamour of so importunate a creditor as Lady C, it is obvious that we shall have done little toward your present ease or the benefit of your family.[118]

Seaforth was not a natural or willing economiser and the sinking fund never got off the ground. In January 1800, with Lochalsh still unsold, Colin wrote of 'the great uneasiness I feel at the pressure which seems to weigh on you at the moment'.[119] The demands for 1800 were estimated to be £6,665, which did not exceed 'the utmost expectations' from the rents of Lewis, Kintail, Lochalsh and Brahan.[120] Increasingly Seaforth's mind moved to other methods of restoring his finances, namely securing a remunerative Caribbean governorship and making money by owning a Caribbean plantation. Colin hoped that 'the consequence will be your return in few years enabled to pay off all your debts and preserve your noble estate in your family'.[121]

There were doubts in at least one of Seaforth's circle as to whether it was right to sell the Wester Ross lands. George Gillanders, the long-serving factor, was now retired and no longer felt obliged to give the soundest financial advice. He may also have thought that the large loan of £3,400 which his family had made to Seaforth, still outstanding, entitled him to express an opinion.[122] He wrote that he never wished Lochalsh or Kintail to go out of the family 'having been the family's property for centuries ... they are the flower of Highlanders, and what our ancestors would have purchased with blood and treasure'. This was a very direct appeal to sentiment and tradition.[123] However, no such doubts crossed the mind of Colin Mackenzie, the man in the front line of shoring up the chief's finances. About six weeks before the new governor set sail for Barbados, Colin wrote, 'I wish to God a sale could be effected in one or other of these quarters ... [Lochalsh, Kintail or Ussie] for without it I see nothing to be looked for but difficulty and vexation.'[124]

In the event, Lochalsh was sold to Hugh Innes for £38,000. Seaforth made the terms of sale on 10 February, a few days before he left London for his transatlantic voyage.[125] However, Innes was to pay for Lochalsh in instalments, with the first of £17,000 being paid within four months and the next not until January 1802.[126] This was insufficient to solve the immediate issue, which was a short-term but serious cash-flow problem. When he left Britain Seaforth faced demands which were between £8,000 and £9,000 greater than the likely incomings, and Lady Caroline was one of the creditors.[127] Colin commented later on 'the poignant feelings to which your situation gave rise at the time of your sailing'.[128] Seaforth was aware before he left that further lands needed to be sold. In April three Kintail farms adjoining Lochalsh were purchased by Innes for £7,200. Colin admitted to his fellow trustee Vicary Gibbs that he might have got a higher price, but the advantage over the Lochalsh sale was expected to be that the money would be paid very soon. As he put it 'prompt payment is requisite to save Lord Seaforth's credit . . . it relieves pretty much the violent pressures under which we laboured'.[129] In the event, £3,000 was paid at Whit 1801 as arranged, but the balance due in August was still outstanding in mid October.[130] These sales in Wester Ross were made on a strictly commercial basis under extreme financial pressure and, as has been shown in Chapter Three, were followed by clearances by the new owner, Hugh Innes. Colin's conscience (and presumably Seaforth's) was eased by trying to make to make room for as many as possible of those cleared in the fishing villages then being lotted at Dornie and Bundalloch on remaining Seaforth land in Kintail.[131]

Seaforth's confusions and contradictions when under pressure were well illustrated by a sett which took place in Kintail in the early spring of 1801 (after his departure for Barbados, but clearly in accordance with his orders). His advisers expected that a similarly commercial approach would be taken as in the sale of Lochalsh. In July 1800, Peter Fairbairn recommended that nine months' notice should be given to Glenshiel tenants to remove at Whit 1801 and thereby 'to require them to give in proposals which, should they come short of expectation, would give good reasons to hold the country out to strangers'.[132] By strangers he clearly meant sheep farmers, as he had recommended in 1794. The advertisement for the 1801 sett was consequently an invitation to sheep farmers. It suggested that Glenshiel was 'perfectly well known to many sheep farmers as being uncommonly well adapted for a sheep walk'.[133] However, as the date of the sett and of Seaforth's departure approached fast, Colin Mackenzie still wanted to have a clear steer on the matter. He wrote that it was 'a subject on which I have not yet got any orders, but which required immediate steps'. The tenants must have been aware of what was in the wind and a letter indicating their unwillingness to move was received from the Kintail tacksman, Archibald Macrae. Colin had little sympathy with this and made clear to Seaforth the instructions he was seeking. He wrote that:

> It is a distressing thing to find the people bent on staying to their ruin. I ... wish that the people could in considerable numbers be prevailed on to become villagers. Many of them might I think be taken care of by the sheep farmers and placed on small improvable spots suggested by Headrick [the agricultural commentator]. They might be taken bound to enclose these crofts to pay their rent in turnips, potatoes and hay to the sheep farmers.[134]

What Colin was proposing for Glenshiel was a classic clearance to bring in sheep farmers. However, he gave Seaforth one escape route, a previous land sale. Seaforth took this route. Although no reply from him has been found, it is clear that, as he sailed from Portsmouth on 13 February[135], he had left orders that Glenshiel should not be cleared now that Lochalsh had just been sold.

What happened in Glenshiel at Whit 1801 was that the new leases required sheep farming, but were given to the most promising of the original farmers as multiple tenants, which limited the rental increase considerably. Colin reported to Seaforth that the initial intention was to obtain exactly double rent. This was based on the recommendation of the famous sheep farmer Thomas Gillespie of Glenquoich in Glengarry[136] that five of the seven existing farms should be rearranged into three and let to single tenants. In the event it was decided to divide the glen into six farms 'as a greater number of farms enables us to accommodate more people ... To have let each farm to a single tenant would have left twenty-one unprovided for, and besides our knowledge of your wish to dispossess none if a reasonable attention to your interests would permit it'. The new farms were given to between two and four tenants and the rental increase was said to be £490 (an increase of 47 per cent or less than half of what had been envisaged). Even so, there were some casualties. Twelve tenants, 'those that seemed in point of substance unfit for following the sheep system', were concentrated on Morvich. This was a clearance, but a relatively limited one. It was still hoped that sheep farming could be introduced. The tenants, except on Morvich, were bound by the new leases to 'proceed to stock with sheep and uphold the stock in the manner practised on duly regulated sheep farms'.[137] However, it considerably frustrated the estate managers, who had been pressing for almost a decade for a more radical reorganisation of Glenshiel, and on this occasion were supported by expert advice. It is clear that Seaforth had only considered this under severe financial pressure, and when this was eased he pulled back. In his report on the sett Colin stated that 'we found ourselves tied up by an express promise given at the former sett to give the tenants of these farms a preference to strangers, reserving only a right to new model the farms'.[138] There is a suggestion that at the 1794 sett he had given some sort of undertaking to the Glenshiel tenants in return for recruits.[139]

Conclusions

From a strictly commercial point of view, part of the gains of selling Lochalsh in 1801 were promptly squandered on the Glenshiel sett, which reflected Seaforth's determination not to evict the existing tenants in favour of a Lowland sheep farmer. There is no doubt that external pressures pushed Seaforth in opposite directions, and he was never to resolve the dilemma between them. Commercial pressures pointed to evictions and/ or land sales which, if pursued consistently, would have been likely to make him a much richer man and to finance the style of living to which he aspired for himself and his family. In Chapter Two it was argued that he largely resisted such pressures in the 1780s and 1790s (except in relation to kelp production) because of his traditional view of clanship. On the other hand, political pressures gave influence and honours, and with them the social esteem which he craved, to a 'man rich' proprietor who retained his lands and his people and used them to recruit for the army, as will be shown in Chapter Six. The constant and worsening financial problems analysed in this chapter illustrate well the perils which faced Highland proprietors whose social and political aspirations exceeded their income. On the other hand, there was a danger of elite families being shamed socially by living modestly. Seaforth believed that such a fate must be avoided at all costs if the family was to be restored to its rightful place in Ross-shire and nationally.

How unusual was Seaforth among Highland proprietors of the time in suffering financial problems caused by extravagance

and accordingly being forced into land sales? Maclean of
Drimnin's relatively small estate was sold in 1798 because
of his extravagance.[140] A closer parallel is presented by the
estate of Macdonald of Clanranald, comprising Arisaig and
Moidart, the Small Isles, South Uist and Benbecula. Ronald
George Macdonald shouldered a substantial debt, £56,263,
when he inherited the estates as a minor in 1797.[141] The estate
was forced into trust in 1811.[142] The consequence, as in the
case of the Seaforth estate, was land sales – first the islands of
Muck and Shona in 1812 and ultimately most of South Uist
in 1838–9.[143] Clanranald and Seaforth would appear to have
been guilty of similar extravagance. Of Clanranald's 1812 debt,
£2,606 was outstanding on a house at Arisaig designed by the
Edinburgh architect James Gillespie Graham.[144] Clanranald is
claimed to have dissipated his kelp revenue at the gaming tables
of Brighton while in the circle of the Prince of Wales.[145] In
both cases their sales were insufficient to avert further crises
before long. Unusually, Macleod of Dunvegan's sale of Glenelg
in 1810 cleared his father's debts and by 1820 his estate was
unencumbered, but was in serious debt again by the 1840s.[146]
Another major island proprietor, Lord Macdonald, benefitted
from kelp receipts from North Uist of £14,000 in 1812 and
when the *New Statistical Account* was compiled in the late
1830s virtually all of the estate there and in Skye was still in
his hands.[147] In parting with Lochalsh in 1801 Seaforth was,
therefore, a decade before the other early sales of this period
by major west Highland landowners (Macleod in 1810 and
Clanranald in 1812).

Most sales made by Highland landed families in the first half
of the nineteenth century took place later, especially from the
late 1820s after kelping became unprofitable.[148] The sixth duke
of Argyll is reckoned to have reduced the substantial fortune of
his family by £2 million by his conspicuous consumption and
Morvern had to be sold in 1819.[149] Barra was sold by McNeill
in 1837.[150] Alastair Ranaldson Macdonell, fifteenth chief of
Glengarry, was known for his extravagant display, although it
was not until 1840, twelve years after his death, that substantial sales of Glengarry lands were made.[151] That Seaforth was
obliged to sell land earlier than other chiefs suggests that there
were particular elements in his financial problems. One was
an especially large inherited debt (at £100,000 almost twice
that of Clanranald). However, the fundamental problem was

his unusual degree of extravagance, which not only prevented him reducing the debt, but actually increased it, the capital debt being calculated at £107,600 in 1799. This is explained by his psychological need, created by his deafness, to be seen to excel. The political activities which seemed to him to justify a high level of expenditure will be discussed in Chapter Five. Whether his recruiting activities for the army on balance helped his finances is a central issue of Chapter Six. His attempt to escape from his financial problems by acquiring land in Berbice, Guiana, to establish cotton plantations will be examined in Chapter Eight. The continued financial pressures which led to further land sales in Wester Ross will be considered in Chapters Eleven and Twelve.

Notes

1. London, Royal Society Library, EC/1794/05, election certificate of Francis Humberstone Mackenzie, 26 June 1794.
2. Gascoigne, J., 'Banks, Sir Joseph, baronet (1743–1820)', *Oxford Dictionary of National Biography (ODNB)*, online edition, <www.oxforddnb.com>, article no. 1300, accessed 30 April 2009; Carter, H. B., *Sir Joseph Banks, 1743–1820* (London, 1988), pp. 149, 154.
3. Withers, C. W., *Placing the Enlightenment: Thinking Geographically about the Age of Reason* (Chicago, 2008), pp. 57–8.
4. Gascoigne, J., *Joseph Banks and the English Enlightenment* (Cambridge, 1994), pp. 70, 110–12, 258.
5. London, British Library (BL), Add. MS 33978, fos 107–8, 127, 118, F. H. Mackenzie to Sir J. Banks, 1 March, 31 May and 5 May 1787.
6. Glasgow, Mitchell Library, bound volume 'Mackenzie Miscellanea', refs 591706, –711, –837.
7. BL, Add. MS 42071, fo. 288, Lord Seaforth to C. F. Greville, 21 March 1801.
8. NRS, GD46/17/19/39, B. Proby to C. Mackenzie, 10 April 1801.
9. Chichester, H. M., 'Mackenzie, Francis Humberston', *ODNB*, online edition, <www.oxforddnb.com>, article no. 14126, accessed 29 September 2004; Mackenzie, A., *History of the Mackenzies* (Inverness, 1894 edn), p. 337.
10. Edinburgh, National Library of Scotland (NLS), MS 6396, fo. 9, F. H. Mackenzie to Mrs Mary Mackenzie, 19 May 1791.
11. NRS, GD46/15/1–2, Cathleen Proby to F. H. Mackenzie, 5 April 1793.

12. NRS, GD46/17/4/282, F. Gibbs to F. H. Mackenzie, 14 December 1790.
13. NLS, MS 6396, fos 9–10, F. H. Mackenzie to Mrs Mackenzie, 19 May 1791.
14. Tague, I. H., 'Aristocratic women and ideas of family in the early eighteenth century' in H. Berry and E. A. Foyster, (eds), *The Family in Early Modern England* (Cambridge, 2007), p. 195.
15. NLS, MS 6396, fo. 13, F. H. Mackenzie to Mrs Mary Mackenzie, 24 February 1793.
16. NRS, GD46/17/35/159, J. Anderson to Lord Seaforth, 8 October 1809.
17. McKichan, F., 'Lord Seaforth and Highland Estate Management in the First Phase of Clearance (1783–1815)', *The Scottish Historical Review (SHR)*, vol. 86, 1, 2007, pp. 61–3, 66–7.
18. Hunter, J., *The Making of the Crofting Community* (Edinburgh, 1976), p. 7; E. Richards, *The Highland Clearances: People, Landlords and Rural Turmoil* (Edinburgh, 2000), p. 75; Nenadic, S., *Lairds and Luxury: The Highland Gentry in Eighteenth-Century Scotland* (Edinburgh, 2007), p. 206.
19. Devine, T. M., *Clearance and Improvement: Land, Power and People in Scotland, 1700–1900* (Edinburgh, 2006), pp. 194–6.
20. NRS, GD46/17/4/61, W. Dixon to F. H. Mackenzie, Mount Street, Berkeley Square, 31 January 1784; *True Briton*, 7 August 1799, British Library Burney Collection of 17th and 18th Century Newspapers online (BCN), accessed 6 December 2010, sale of wine and furniture at Lord Seaforth's house, 17 Hereford Street, Grosvenor Square.
21. Nenadic, S. (ed.), *Scots in London in the Eighteenth Century* (Lewisburg, 2010), pp. 14, 31.
22. Clifford, T., M. Gallagher and H. Smailes, *Benjamin West and the Death of the Stag* (Edinburgh, 2009), pp. 5, 11–15, 17–19.
23. Chichester, 'Mackenzie, Francis Humberston', *ODNB*, online edition, article no. 14126, accessed 29 September 2004.
24. NRS, GD46/17/4/161, Mrs Mary H. Mackenzie to F. H. Mackenzie, 22 July 1788.
25. NRS, GD46/17/29, Caroline Mackenzie to Lady Hood, n.d., but from context June 1812.
26. Mackenzie, *History of the Mackenzies*, p. 343.
27. NRS, GD46/17/4/74–6, 'State of my Affairs, Nov. 1786', /258, 'Sketch Seaforth's Affairs, Dec. 1787'.
28. NRS, GD46/17/4/161, Mrs Mary H. Mackenzie to F. H. Mackenzie, 22 July 1788.
29. Rendall, J., 'The Reputation of William Cullen (1710–1790): Family, Politics and the Biography of an 'Ornate Physician', *SHR*, vol. 93, 2, 2014, p. 276.

30. Knox, J., *A Tour through the Highlands of Scotland and the Hebride Isles in 1786* (Edinburgh, 1787, reprint 1975), pp. 184–9, 194–6.
31. NRS, GD427/212/18, Mrs Mary Mackenzie to George Gillanders, n.d., but from context clearly around 1790.
32. NRS, E326/5/5/166, Male Servants Tax, E326/6/2/109, Female Servants Tax, Ross and Cromarty, 1785–6.
33. NRS, RH2/4/71/300, Home Office: Correspondence, Letters and Papers, Scotland, F. H. Mackenzie to Lord A. Gordon, 30 June 1793.
34. Nenadic, *Lairds and Luxury*, pp. 178–9.
35. Thorne, R. G., *The House of Commons 1790–1820* (London, 1986), vol. 2, pp. ii, 572.
36. NRS, GD46/17/15, C. Mackenzie to F. H. Mackenzie, 5 June 1795.
37. *Oracle and Public Advertiser*, 10 November 1795 (BCN), accessed 9 December 2010.
38. Brown, I. G., 'James Hall's Paris Day', *Scottish Archives*, vol. 17, 2011, p. 13.
39. NRS, GD46/17/4/462–3, Lady H. Hall to F. H. Mackenzie, 18 April 1795.
40. Mackenzie, *History of the Mackenzies*, pp. 328–9, 334.
41. Mowat, I. R., *Easter Ross 1750–1850: the Double Frontier* (Edinburgh, 1981), p. 90.
42. Colley, L., *Britons: Forging the Nation 1707–1837* (London, 1994 edn), p. 159.
43. Dooley, T. E. M., *The Decline of the Big House in Ireland: A Study of Irish Landed Families* (Dublin, 2001), pp. 28–9, 271; Nenadic, *Lairds and Luxury*, pp. 160–1.
44. NRS, GD46/14/2/2, H. Dundas to F. H. Mackenzie, 23 April 1796.
45. NRS, GD46/17/15, P. Fairbairn to F. H. Mackenzie, 13 December 1795.
46. NRS, GD46/17/15, P. Fairbairn to F. H. Mackenzie, 26 April and 26 May 1796.
47. NRS, GD46/17/15, C. Mackenzie to F. H. Mackenzie, 4 April 1796.
48. NRS, GD46/17/4 /334–5, 338–9, J. Bacon to F. H. Mackenzie, 27 May 1796 and n.d.
49. Hunt, J. D., *Gardens and the Picturesque: Studies in the History of Landscape Architecture* (Cambridge, Mass., 1992), pp. 75–6.
50. McKichan, F., 'Lord Seaforth (1754–1815): The Lifestyle of a Highland Proprietor and Clan Chief', *Northern Scotland*, New Series, vol. 5, 2014, p. 60.
51. NRS, GD46/17/13/108, P. Fairbairn to F. H. Mackenzie, 6 August 1795; /111, 'State of Gardener's Account, 30 May–15

August 1795'; /114, P. Fairbairn to F. H. Mackenzie, 22 October 1795.

52. NRS, GD46/17/15, P. Fairbairn to F. H. Mackenzie, 26 May 1796.

53. NRS, GD46/1/347, J. Johnstone, 'Observations on the state of the grounds round Brahan Castle and hints for further improvement', 12 October 1799.

54. NRS, GD46/1/347, 'Estimate of ground work of the new garden at Castle Brahan', December 1799.

55. NRS, GD46/17/14, C. Mackenzie to Lord Seaforth, 7 November 1799.

56. NRS, E326/5/27/131, Male Servant Tax Rolls, Ross and Cromarty, 1797–8.

57. Mackillop, A., 'The Highlands and the Returning Nabob: Sir Hector Munro of Novar, 1760–1807', in Harper, M. (ed.), *Emigrant Homecomings: The Return Movement of Migrants 1600–2000* (Manchester, 2005), pp. 238–41, 245–7, 251–3.

58. Richards, E., *A History of the Highland Clearances: Agrarian Transformation and the Evictions, 1746–1886* (London, 1982), pp. 255–6.

59. NRS, E326/5/5/165, Male Servant Tax Rolls, Ross and Cromarty, 1785–6.

60. NRS, E326/8/19/135, Ross-shire Carriage Tax Rolls, 1797–8.

61. BL, Add. MS 39195, fos 39–41, Sir A. Mackenzie of Coull to J. R. Mackenzie of Suddie, 12 December 1792.

62. NRS, GD46/17/4/264–5, V. Gibbs to F. H. Mackenzie, 21 April 1787.

63. NRS, GD46/17/4/78–81, 'Memorandum of my Affairs and intended arrangements, Decr. 1787'; /258, 'Sketch Seaforth's Affairs, Dec. 1797'.

64. NRS, GD46/17/4/ 77–8, 'My Affairs beginning of 1787, rude sketch not accurate'.

65. NRS, GD46/17/4/168, V. Gibbs to F. H. Mackenzie, 19 May 1788.

66. NRS, GD46/17/4/164–5, 'Greville's idea of my affairs, May 1788'.

67. NRS, GD46/17/4/133, 'Case for consideration of Mr Scott, 7 June 1787'.

68. NRS, GD46/17/2, Opinion of J. Scott, 7 June 1787.

69. NRS, GD46/17/4/288, Mrs Mary H. Mackenzie to F. H. Mackenzie, 19 January 1792.

70. NRS, GD46/17/4, V. Gibbs to F. H. Mackenzie; /181, October 1788; /183, 10 October 1788; /189, 28 October 1788; /216, January 1789; GD46/17/4/219, F. H .Mackenzie to W. Dixon, 19 February 1789.

71. NRS, GD46/17/4/253, D. Scott, India House to F. H. Mackenzie, 22 December 1789.

72. McGilvary, G. K., *East India Patronage and the British State: The Scottish Elite and Politics in the Eighteenth Century* (London, 2008), pp. 187, 190, 206–7.

73. Chichester, 'Mackenzie, Francis Humberston', *ODNB*, article no. 14126, accessed 29 September 2004.

74. NRS, GD427/138/9, A. Gillanders to A. Campbell, 22 October 1789.

75. NRS, GD46/13/126, State of Lewis kelp from 1794 to 1799.

76. NRS, GD427/14/8, Rental of Lewis 1783.

77. NRS, GD427/16/5, Rental of Lewis, crop 1791.

78. NRS, GD46/17/11, C. Mackenzie to Lord Seaforth, 13 November 1800.

79. Taylor, D., *The Wild Black Region: Badenoch 1750–1800* (Edinburgh, 2016), pp. 186–7, 249–50.

80. NRS, GD46/17/15, C. Mackenzie to F. H. Mackenzie, 15 and 19 May 1795.

81. NRS, GD46/17/15, C. Mackenzie to F. H. Mackenzie, 7 November 1795.

82. NRS, GD46/17/15, A. Mackenzie, Edinburgh, to F. H. Mackenzie, 10 June 1795.

83. NRS, GD46/17/2, A. Brodie to F. H. Mackenzie, November 1796.

84. NRS, GD46/17/15, C. Mackenzie to F. H. Mackenzie, 27 October 1795.

85. NRS, GD46/1/15, Copy of Adjudication 20 September 1796 at instance of Lieut. W. G. Polson, his commissioners and factor, against F. H. Mackenzie of Seaforth.

86. NRS, GD46/17/15, C. Mackenzie to F. H. Mackenzie, 17 September 1796.

87. NRS, GD46/17/15, P. Fairbairn to F. H. Mackenzie, 1 November 1796, G. Gillanders to F. H. Mackenzie, 8 November 1796.

88. NRS, GD46/17/15, C. Mackenzie, Memo, Edinburgh, 4 November 1795.

89. NRS, GD46/17/15, A. Mackenzie, Edinburgh to F. H. Mackenzie, 20 November 1795.

90. NRS, GD46/17/15, C. Mackenzie to F. H. Mackenzie, 29 November 1795.

91. Devine, *Clearance and Improvement*, p. 200; Mackillop, A., *'More Fruitful than the Soil': Army, Empire and the Scottish Highlands, 1715–1815* (East Linton, 2000), pp. 135–6.

92. NRS, Register of Sasines Ross-shire Abridgements, no. 473, 26 January 1796; nos 488 and 489, 28 June 1796.

93. NRS, GD46/17/19/222, Receipt Seaforth's Commissioners to Dean of Lichfield, 15 June 1801.
94. NRS, GD46/17/15, G. Gillanders, Highfield to F. H. Mackenzie, 22 May 1796; GD46/17/19/364, 'State of Lord Seaforth's affairs made up to 15 October 1801'.
95. NRS, GD46/17/15, C. Mackenzie to F. H. Mackenzie, 15 October 1795.
96. NRS, GD46/17/15, C. Mackenzie to F. H. Mackenzie, 4 April 1796.
97. NRS, GD46/17/15, C. Mackenzie to F. H. Mackenzie, 26 April 1796.
98. *Lloyd's Evening Post*, 4 May 1796 (BCN), accessed 9 December 2010.
99. NRS, GD46/17/15, C. Mackenzie to F. H. Mackenzie, 10 October 1796.
100. Mackillop, A., 'The Political Culture of the Scottish Highlands from Culloden to Waterloo', *The Historical Journal*, vol. 46, 3, 2003, p. 518.
101. *Morning Chronicle*, 26 November 1796 (BCN), accessed 9 December 2010.
102. NRS, GD46/17/2, A. Brodie to F. H. Mackenzie, November 1796.
103. NRS, GD46/17/15, C. Mackenzie to F. H. Mackenzie, 15 December 1796.
104. NRS, GD46/17/15, C. Mackenzie to F. H. Mackenzie, 7 and 29 December 1796
105. NRS, GD46/17/11, P. Fairbairn to F. H. Mackenzie, 18 July 1797.
106. NRS, GD46/17/11, C. Mackenzie to Bain, Esq., Dorset, 15 December 1798.
107. NRS, GD46/17/11, C. Mackenzie to J. Gibson W.S., 17 December 1798.
108. Mackillop, *'More Fruitful than the Soil'*, pp. 160–1.
109. NRS, GD46/17/14, C. Mackenzie to Lord Seaforth, 28 October 1799.
110. NRS, GD46/17/14, C. Mackenzie to Lord Seaforth, 29 December 1800.
111. NRS, GD46/13/126, State of Lewis kelp from 1794 to 1799.
112. NRS, GD46/17/18, C. Mackenzie to Lord Seaforth, 4 December 1798.
113. NRS, GD46/17/14, C. Mackenzie to Lord Seaforth, 24 April 1799.
114. NRS GD46/17/11, Mr Forster to Lord Seaforth, 15 January 1800.

115. NRS, GD46/17/14, C. Mackenzie to Lord Seaforth, 24 April 1799.
116. NRS, GD46/17/11, C. Mackenzie to R. Mackenzie, 1 May 1798; C. Mackenzie to Lord Seaforth, 22 May 1798; petition by D. Hossack and J. Holm, tenants in Rosemarkie, to Lord Seaforth, 5 June 1798.
117. *True Briton*, 7 August 1799 (BCN), accessed 6 December 2010.
118. NRS, GD46/17/14, C. Mackenzie to Lord Seaforth, 28 October 1799.
119. NRS, GD46/17/14, C. Mackenzie to Lord Seaforth, 9 January 1800.
120. NRS, GD46/17/11, C. Mackenzie to Lord Seaforth, 13 January 1800.
121. NRS, GD46/17/14, C. Mackenzie to Lord Seaforth, 21 June 1800.
122. NRS, GD46/17/19/364, 'State of Lord Seaforth's affairs made up to 15 Oct. 1801'.
123. NRS, GD46/17/14, G. Gillanders to Lord Seaforth, 1 January 1799.
124. NRS, GD46/17/14, C. Mackenzie to Lord Seaforth, 26 December 1800.
125. NRS, GD46/17/19/111, C. Mackenzie to V. Gibbs, 21 April 1801.
126. NRS, GD46/17/19/363, 'State of Lord Seaforth's affairs made up to 15 Oct. 1801'. Innes took sasine on 19 February 1802 (NRS, Register of Sasines, Ross-shire Abridgements).
127. NRS, GD46/17/19/107–8, C. Mackenzie, report to V. Gibbs, 21 April 1801.
128. NRS, GD46/17/20, C. Mackenzie to Lord Seaforth, 11 June 1801.
129. NRS, GD46/17/19/95, /108–13, C. Mackenzie to V. Gibbs, 21 April 1801; Register of Sasines, Ross-shire Abridgements, 1 February 1802. The Kintail farms were Fadoch, Killelan and Corriedoine.
130. NRS, GD46/17/19/363, 'State of Lord Seaforth's affairs made up to 15 Oct. 1801'.
131. NRS, GD46/17/20/204–5, C. Mackenzie to Lord Seaforth, 24 November 1801.
132. NRS, GD46/17/11, P. Fairbairn to Lord Seaforth, 9 July 1800.
133. *Caledonian Mercury*, 8 December 1800, 19th Century British Library Newspapers online, accessed 3 February 2011.
134. NRS, GD46/17/20, C. Mackenzie to Lord Seaforth, 10 January 1801.
135. NRS, GD46/17/16, List of dates of journey to Barbados, 1801 (in Seaforth's hand).
136. Richards, *Agrarian Transformation and the Evictions*, pp. 198, 209.

137. NRS, GD46/17/19/230, 'Abstract of Glensheal leases granted April 1801'.
138. NRS, GD46/17/19/77–9, 82–4, C. Mackenzie to Lord Seaforth, April 1801.
139. Mackillop, *'More Fruitful than the Soil'*, p. 161.
140. Devine, *Clearance and Improvement*, p. 195.
141. NRS, GD201/1/365/1, State and view of Clanranald's affairs, 1 January 1797.
142. NRS, GD201/1/365/9, State and view of the affairs of R. G. Macdonald Esq. of Clanranald, 8 June 1812.
143. Devine, *Clearance and Improvement*, pp. 193, 211, 213–15.
144. NRS, GD201/1/365/8, List of debts due by Clanranald, 8 June 1812; Miers, M., *The Western Seaboard: An Illustrated Architectural Guide* (Edinburgh, 2008), p. 129.
145. Dressler, C., *Eigg: The Story of an Island* (Edinburgh, 1998), pp. 64, 67.
146. Devine, *Clearance and Improvement*, pp. 194, 197.
147. *New Statistical Account of Scotland*, vol. XIV, 169, 176 (North Uist); 224 (Portree); 265 (Kilmuir); 289 (Snizort); 318 (Sleat); 364–5 (Strath), <http://stat-acc-scot.edina.ac.uk/link/1834-45/Inverness>, accessed 30 October 2011.
148. Devine, *Clearance and Improvement*, pp. 193–7.
149. Ibid., p. 188, 195.
150. Ibid., p. 216.
151. Richards, *Agrarian Transformation and the Evictions*, pp. 216, 449–50.

5   Local and National Politician, 1783–1800

Winning the votes

In 1782 a group of fourteen mostly minor landowners from Ross and Cromarty complained that 'the abuse through creation of nominal and fictitious qualifications has of recent years grown to such an enormous height as actually to deprive the real proprietors of land of their constitutional rights'. The electors were supposed to be landowners in the county. However, they alleged that, of the eighty-three electors in Ross-shire, forty-two had no property in the county and voted on fictitious qualifications. They demanded that such electors be struck off.[1] What was the basis of their complaint? The Scottish parliamentary franchise gave votes in county seats to freeholders (owners) of land valued at £400 Scots or 40 shillings of 'old extent'. In Scottish legal theory, land was held from a 'superior', thus 'superiority' was the technical term for ownership of land. A large landowner, like Seaforth, had more than enough land to qualify for a vote and he could give or sell superiorities worth £400 Scots to relations or friends. No land changed hands, and the superiorities were therefore described as fictitious. The holder of such a superiority simply had a legal document which enabled him to vote, and he would be expected to cast his vote for the candidate supported by the real owner of the land. This practice had become increasingly common in the third quarter of the eighteenth century.[2]

Kenneth Earl of Seaforth spent much of his time abroad and thus lost much of his influence in Ross-shire politics. It was noted in 1772 that 'he has not Ross-shire at command from his neglect of his clan'.[3] When the Humberstons acquired the Seaforth estate they were determined to rectify this situation and restore the Seaforth political influence.[4] After inheriting the estate in 1783 Francis Humberston Mackenzie was MP for Ross-shire between 1784 and 1790, and 1794 and 1796. Creating fictitious votes had to be supported by legal documentation to survive the rigorous examination they would get from opponents at the annual head court, which admitted electors to the roll. This could only be drawn up by specialist lawyers whose services were not cheap.[5] For example, the duke of Gordon spent £1,600 in 1790 alone in the creation of fictitious votes in the north-east of Scotland.[6] Why did landowners like Seaforth go to this sort of expense? Andrew Mackillop has shown that in the later eighteenth century many Highland proprietors spent more than they could afford to control the election of MPs and secure political influence. They aimed to secure state patronage for themselves and their clients. Successive major wars and the growth of what has been called the 'fiscal–military state' greatly increased the number of posts for army and navy officers and also for excise officers, which were filled by political patronage. By voting for their patron's candidate, impoverished Highland landowners could secure a livelihood for their relatives and dependants.[7] The Scottish MPs of the eighteenth century have been described as going south 'above all for the sake of the spoils they could bring home'.[8] However, it has also been argued that 'alongside the evident hunger for office and official favour amongst the Scottish political classes there existed a clear sense of a Scottish "national interest"'.[9] For example, although the establishment of the British Fisheries Society in 1786 was designed to strengthen the Union after the loss of the American colonies and Seaforth hoped it would benefit him by setting up a fishing station on Lewis, the Society and its bounties to fishermen were of general benefit to the Highlands.[10]

Entering politics

As a delayed consequence of the loss of the American colonies, George III was reluctantly obliged in February 1783 to allow his bête noire Charles James Fox and the Whigs into government. However, in the following December he dismissed this government on the grounds that Fox's East India bill would have given ministers control of Indian appointments, would reduce the power of the Crown, and was thus unconstitutional. The young William Pitt became prime minister. The king's manoeuvre was also constitutionally dubious, so on both sides there were issues of great principle as well as personal rivalry and antipathy. In March 1784 Pitt sought a parliamentary majority in a general election.[11]

These rivalries were reflected at local level in Ross-shire. As has been seen in Chapter Four, Seaforth was one of the social circle around the Prince of Wales of which Fox was a leader. His admiration for Fox was such that he once reported to his wife, 'I have bought a charming picture of a fox and I look at it almost with adoration.'[12] His opponent in the Ross-shire constituency in 1784 was a judge, John Mackenzie Lord Macleod, MP since 1780, cousin and political supporter of Henry Dundas.[13] Dundas, the right-hand man of Pitt in the Commons, was one of the leading supporters of the king in using his prerogative to keep Fox out of office. He was also in the process of building up his political control of Scotland, which involved trying to wrest political control from the Whig aristocrats, like Seaforth, whose wide acres enabled them to create large numbers of fictitious votes.[14]

On the eve of the Ross-shire poll, George Mackenzie, Lord Macleod's brother, wrote to Sir Roderick Mackenzie of Scatwell, 'Your voice is earnestly called for, it may and probably will fix whether the real or fictitious voters are to carry the County of Ross.' He appended a list of the 'real' voters which showed the sides equal on eleven votes each.[15] Seaforth was reported to have won 'comfortably', which must mean that his fictitious votes carried the poll. William Adam, the Scottish political agent for the Whigs, claimed that Seaforth had 'by far the most considerable estate and interest' in Ross-shire, but Lord Ankerville would probably oppose him in another election 'from an aversion to his great interest founded on liferent votes'.[16] By 1788 Seaforth was reckoned to have twenty-four Ross-shire votes under his direct control.[17] When in 1790 he stood down from the House of Commons to economise, he set out to secure his replacement by Adam.[18] Although he made extensive use of fictitious votes, he still needed the votes of independent freeholders. During the 1790 election he wrote to his young daughter Mary in London:

Your poor papa is just now tired to death, he is canvassing for
the election and never stays two days in a place, but hurries back-
wards and forwards, and then is often obliged to do all over again.
Sometimes it rains and blows and is so cold as he rides, then he
writes [canvassing letters], oh! He does write.[19]

This laborious canvassing paid off and Adam was elected unopposed.[20] Adam described Seaforth as 'the object of such general
admiration and respect, not by his own family only, but by
all names and descriptions of gentlemen'.[21] This view was not
shared by all the gentry of Ross-shire. One complained that in
this election 'a chieftain willed it and Mr Adam was elected to
please him'. He added that 'the pride of Seaforth never shone so
bright, certainly never so absurdly'.[22]

A deaf MP

To Francis Humberston Mackenzie, as an able and energetic
young estate owner who was determined to restore the ancient
prestige and influence of his family, the political route offered
great attractions. But could a man who was profoundly deaf
act as an MP? John Robinson, an electoral expert and adviser
of Pitt, had believed that 'as the chief of the Mackenzies ...
is deaf and dumb, it is unlikely he will think of coming into
Parliament'.[23] This greatly underestimated the man, who was
to serve a total of eight years in Parliament and over five as
governor of Barbados at a critical time. Although his speech
improved somewhat he remained profoundly deaf throughout
his life. It must have required enormous courage to enter and
survive in the intensely speech-dominated world of politics.

How effectively was Seaforth able to operate as a politician?
Understandably he does not appear to have taken an active
part in parliamentary debates. However, his speaking voice
seems to have improved. A speech by him in the 1790 Ross-
shire election was described as 'elegant and concise' in a report
which described an articulate and far from concise address.[24]
This could have been carefully rehearsed. By the mid 1790s,
he was able to conduct interviews regularly and successfully.
In July 1795, after lobbying for the promotion of his brother-
in-law Alexander Mackenzie, he wrote to Henry Dundas that,
had he known that he was at home at Wimbledon, he would

have 'taken a ride to communicate my wish ... in person'. He did have an interview on the matter with the Duke of York, the commander-in-chief.[25] Later in 1795, Sandy (now Colonel) asked him to come to London to oppose a plan to merge the two battalions of his regiment, arguing, 'I know your presence will do more to bring the matter to a happy conclusion in one day than all you can say on paper for twelve months.' Sandy did not treat Seaforth to insincere flattery, begging also that 'if you write to any of the official people on the subject it may be with temperance'.[26] Seaforth's temper was not always under control, but it seems that by the mid 1790s he was able to make his views known effectively in a face-to-face situation. He had by now become a regular operator in the world of back-stairs influence. His balance of political skills and handicaps was reflected also in his governorship of Barbados, as will be shown in Chapters Seven, Nine and Ten.

An enemy of government

It has been suggested that a factor which motivated Scottish MPs was that they could not afford the luxury of opposition and also win acceptance as social equals by the English elite.[27] Seaforth wished to have both the spoils and the social acceptance, but paradoxically did not at first seek to attract the official favour which would win these rewards. This is another way, in addition to his land-management policies (discussed in Chapter Two) and his response to the needs of enslaved and free people of colour in Barbados (the subject of Chapter Nine) in which he differed from stereotyped views of men in his position. His outspoken mother wrote to him in 1792, 'I think you had better wheel about to the right, you might be a gainer then by your Politicks, hitherto you have been a loser.'[28] Seaforth had been elected to Parliament in 1784 as an opponent of Henry Dundas and, therefore, of William Pitt. There was an element in his character which led him at times to put principle, as he saw it, before his pragmatic interests. He also wished to stand by his friends. Throughout that Parliament (to 1790) he appears to have remained a faithful member of the Whig opposition and, especially, an admirer of Charles James Fox. Two issues illustrate this.

Pitt believed that the fundamental cause of Irish discontent was poverty, and in 1785 framed ten propositions substantially reducing duties on manufactures and produce exchanged between Great Britain and Ireland. Opposition quickly developed among British commercial and manufacturing interests fearful of Irish competition. Fox proposed and carried amendments which introduced a wide range of exceptions, which it was impossible to get through the Irish parliament. In consequence the scheme had to be abandoned.[29] Seaforth voted with Fox and thus helped to destroy the Irish scheme.[30] What were his motives? As he shared Pitt's ambition to hold together what remained of the British empire, his vote might be seen as unprincipled loyalty to Fox. However, as has been shown in Chapter Two, he was not an enthusiast of the new doctrines of free trade being propounded by Adam Smith. He did not believe (as Pitt did) that both Britain and Ireland would benefit from free trade. In this case, therefore, he had a genuine dislike of the government's proposals in addition to a desire to support his political mentor Fox.

In late October 1788, King George III was afflicted by what his doctor described as 'an agitation of spirits nearly bordering on delirium'. If the king was incapacitated for long the Prince of Wales was expected to become regent. It was highly likely that he would dismiss Pitt and install in government his political allies, the Portland Whigs. Fox suggested that the prince would be entitled to assume the regency without the approval of Parliament. This was quite contrary to the Whigs' devotion to parliamentary sovereignty as established by the Glorious Revolution of 1688.[31] Speaking in the Commons with 'eloquence scarcely ever paralleled', he argued that the Prince of Wales had 'unquestionable pretensions' to a sole and unlimited regency.[32] Pitt procrastinated on the issue, successfully moving in December that the Lords and Commons should determine the appointment of a regent and his powers. In the nick of time for Pitt, the king miraculously recovered.[33] Seaforth, despite the dubious tactics which had been used by Fox, followed him into the lobby.[34] Clearly Seaforth's support in the regency crisis for Fox and the prince was not the way to secure Crown patronage, now firmly in the hands of Pitt, and in Scotland of Dundas.

Lack of patronage is likely to have been one reason for Seaforth's failure in burgh elections in the 1780s. Burgh MPs were elected by town councils through commissioners. By 1786 Seaforth had established a strong influence in the burgh of Dingwall, four miles from Brahan.[35] He financed burgh projects.

For example, he contributed £100 in 1788 towards the cost of a new water supply for Dingwall.[36] Dingwall was one of the burghs in which it has been said 'the parliamentary franchise was an important source of revenue as well as of largesse for the leading councillors'.[37] In other words, votes were won by payments to individual town councillors. Evidence of this is that Sir George Mackenzie of Coull, who would have liked to become an MP, was not prepared to attempt the Northern Burghs because 'my small fortune will not admit of interference with them'.[38] It was less easy for one man to control the election of a burgh than a county MP as the burghs were arranged into groups or districts[39], in this case Tain, Dingwall, Dornoch, Wick and Kirkwall. This was particularly challenging as the district was heavily influenced by the Sutherland family and Sir John Sinclair. As allies of Dundas they secured the election in 1786 and again in 1790 of Charles Lockhart Ross of Balnagown, a grand-nephew of Dundas. He was to become a long-standing political rival of Seaforth.[40] In the 1786 burgh elections Seaforth also suffered from inexperience. He announced his support for Balnagown's opponent too late, with the result that an excessive amount of time was devoted to influencing the Dingwall councillors and Tain, which was vital, was lost.[41]

The French Revolution and Seaforth's reconciliation with government

Seaforth's political stance changed dramatically in early 1793, and by the time the French Republic declared war on Britain in February of that year he was a supporter of Henry Dundas and of Pitt's government. It has been argued that in politics he was a man of principle, so what were the factors which brought about this dramatic volte-face? Events in France were the principal cause. In April and May 1791 there was a series of increasingly emotional confrontations in the House of Commons between Burke and Fox, the two most eloquent Whig leaders, respectively opposing and supporting French developments.[42] At this time Seaforth still supported Fox and thus his approval of the French Revolution.[43] During 1792 events both at home and in France increased the concerns of those (like Seaforth) who had a fundamental interest in the existing property and social system.

On 2 June, the king's birthday, an Edinburgh mob attacked Dundas's house in George Square and burned him in effigy.[44] Seven weeks later a Society of the Friends of the People was set up in Edinburgh to campaign for democratic reform on the model of earlier societies in England.[45]

The abolition of the French monarchy and declaration of a republic was followed by the massacre of aristocrats in September 1792 and French promises to export their revolution. Understandable concerns were now raised among landowners in Britain for their property and personal safety. In December, with Louis XVI now on trial for his life, the more conservative Whigs around the duke of Portland refused to back Fox in opposing defensive measures taken by the government. The Whig party was clearly falling apart. In the Whig Club, Fox provocatively toasted 'equal liberty to all mankind'.[46] Seaforth's conservative world view and interests as a major landed proprietor made it natural that he should resent and fear what the French Revolution had turned into. As he put it, writing to Adam, 'I can bear these French dogs hardly better than Burke; dancing I might agree to learn from them, but damn their politics.'[47] He was torn between his politics and friends of many years on the one hand and his view of society and concern for the safety of his estates and his family on the other. In December a convention of radical societies was held in Edinburgh and listened to fiery rhetoric from a young advocate, Thomas Muir.[48] During the autumn and early winter of 1792, trees of liberty, the French symbol of *liberté, égalité, fraternité*, were set up in many towns and villages throughout Scotland. Government was informed that when the news reached Perth of the French capturing Brussels, 'the lower classes of people talk of nothing but Liberty and Equality – No Dundas . . . No King.'[49]

There followed a negotiation between Seaforth and Dundas, an intermediary in which was Alexander Brodie, MP for Elgin Burghs. He was a long-standing friend of Seaforth and fellow horticulturalist, but also a supporter of Dundas and Pitt. A letter, written by Brodie from London on the last day of 1792, was a lightly bated hook. It advised Seaforth that war was now inevitable and that many of his friends were supporting the precautions being taken by Pitt. A Scottish militia was being contemplated, together with lords lieutenant in Scottish counties (a title to which Seaforth might reasonably aspire).[50] At some point Brodie delivered to Dundas a message from Seaforth, possibly after the execution of Louis XVI on 21 January, indicating his willingness to support the government in the national emergency. The response, on 30 January, was a more precise offer. When a Scottish militia was ultimately established Dundas intended to offer Seaforth the lord lieutenancy of Ross-shire 'as the person he conceived best entitled to that dignity'. Fencible regiments (for home defence) were to be raised and 'Mr Dundas asked me if I thought you would be disposed to raise a regiment of that description'. The dukes of Gordon and Buccleuch and the countess of Sutherland were to raise similar regiments.[51] This was calculated to appeal to Seaforth's military ambitions and vanity (as he was still a commoner). The government funds to raise and maintain the regiment made it potentially profitable. At a Ross-shire county meeting at Tain, Seaforth spoke in favour of resolutions supporting the government in the national emergency. A week later (during which news reached London that the French Convention had declared war on Britain and Holland) Brodie sent him a message from Dundas:

> Mr Dundas is pleased at present with your approbation of the measures of Government. It is because he considers you respectable – not because he adds ... more votes to his list of supporters in parliament – nor has his conduct at this time proceeded from any expectation of any such acquisition.[52]

As a leading Scottish Whig, Seaforth was quite a catch, but to reel him in it was necessary to let him think (even if he did not quite believe) that the national emergency was the sole motivation. This was backed up by an even better military offer, to raise what would be the first regiment of the line of the war, that is, one on the permanent establishment and available for overseas service. It would be more prestigious and potentially more profitable than a regiment of fencibles.[53] Seaforth was now being initiated into Dundas's Scottish circle. Brodie wrote that he 'is now much gratified in having your approbation as a public man'. He had mentioned Seaforth to King George. The king, who must have previously regarded him as one of his most intransigent Scottish opponents, had recalled with kindness that Seaforth had as a young boy been a page to him.[54]

Later in 1793 William Adam, who remained a friend of Fox and a Whig, alleged that some of his former allies were using the war with France 'as a golden bridge to pass to places, pensions, contracts, honours and titles, without the loss of character which ought to attend such conduct'.[55] Did Seaforth abandon long-standing allies and principles in order to secure ministerial favour and the rewards that it brought? It is fair to say he supported the Whig party until it was clearly disintegrating. He did not cement his alliance with Dundas until the French Republic declared war on Great Britain, threatening to export revolution. He saw it as patriotic to support the common effort when the nation was under threat. As he put it to Portland, 'it is really needful to be on the watch against the insidious plans of our enemies, both foreign and domestic, and it is entirely on that ground that I now support ministry.'[56] On the other hand, it was not until July 1794 that most of the moderate Whigs followed their leader Portland into the government camp.[57]

Dundas believed that in this emergency the 'fiscal–military state' needed the unity of its principal stakeholders. Some, like Seaforth, the inheritors of wide acres and a long military tradition, could become successful regimental recruiters, as will be shown in Chapter Six. Dundas also relied on the great landowners to contribute to the maintenance of order at home through the system of lords lieutenant, introduced in Scotland in 1794. The campaign in the Low Countries was not going well.[58] An all-British convention of the Society of the Friends of the People met in Edinburgh at the end of 1793, was broken up and its organisers transported. Although it has been doubted if there were in Scotland many active supporters of the French revolutionaries,[59] what Dundas wanted from the new lords lieutenant was intelligence of seditious activities. Their role was 'the preservation of internal tranquillity against any who, either in conjunction with Foreign Enemies or actuated by their own evil disposition, might be inclined to disturb it'.[60] Their appointment has also been seen as establishing clearer leadership in Scottish local government, with a reporting line directly to the home secretary.[61] These posts were given to the most elevated of Scotland's landed elite, and that Seaforth was given the position for Ross-shire was a recognition of his political and social leadership of the county.[62] Another benefit was that his patronage in the county was increased by his authority to create deputy lieutenants.

Return to the Commons

In 1794 Seaforth replaced William Adam in the Ross-shire seat in what was for each of them a painful and embarrassing process. He considered it his patriotic duty after the outbreak of war with France to ensure that the Ross-shire MP should be a supporter of that war. A year earlier he had written to Adam that 'for the present I have promised my support to ministry and I am determined to give it fully, fairly and faithfully'.[63] If so, inability to hear debates does not excuse his failure to vote once in the major Commons divisions between 1794 and 1796.[64] He had ulterior motives for wanting to return to Parliament. He was increasingly in favour with Dundas (and therefore Pitt) and had recently been presented to the king at a royal levee.[65] He had three major issues to negotiate with government. How far did membership of the Commons enable him to convert favour into political clout?

Firstly, he was facing demands from the Exchequer for substantial arrears (dating back to Earl Kenneth's time) on feu duties due to the Crown from Lewis. In 1794 the Exchequer revived the suit to meet the needs of wartime finance.[66] Seaforth, only three months back in Parliament, sought Dundas's aid. The reply was a characteristically tactful exercise in prevarication, written in his own hand. He would take the earliest opportunity of laying the matter before the prime minister, but 'we are at present so occupied with the business of the greatest moment that I shall not be able as yet to talk with Mr Pitt on the subject'.[67] In June 1794 the French armies were advancing into the Low Countries and threatening Holland, believed to be critical to Britain's defence. Pitt was using this threat to persuade the Portland Whigs to join the government.[68] In the autumn of 1796 Seaforth made another approach to Dundas, this time through Brodie. Dundas gave the impression that he had done his best 'but Mr Pitt found [the arrears], upon enquiry, to amount to 4 or 5 thousands and did not think himself at liberty at this period to recommend the grant of so large a sum'.[69] This indicates that Seaforth's transfer of loyalty to Dundas and Pitt did not give him unlimited influence. It appears that he was strung along on the Lewis feu duties until the June 1796 general election was safely over. He was also unsuccessful in 1795 in his attempt to prevent the merger of the two battalions of the 78th Regiment, which he had only recently raised. As will be shown in Chapter Six, the Duke of York as commander-in-chief was reducing the number of recently created Scottish and Irish battalions, including clan regiments raised by private military patronage. Nevertheless, Seaforth was able to secure an interview with the duke[70] and was at least able to prevent complete disbandment, a fate which overtook some of the recently created regiments.[71]

Seaforth had already received signals that his influence was likely to be effective in what to him was by far the most important issue. Pitt said that he could not excuse the feu-duty demand, 'particularly to a person on whom it was intended to confer another favour of the highest consequence'.[72] This favour was the peerage which he had long coveted to give him increased status in elite society and clear superiority in Ross-shire. In early 1796 Dundas saw the forthcoming election as an opportunity to complete his control of the Scottish parliamentary seats. One piece in his jigsaw was to put Sir Charles Lockhart Ross, his grand-nephew, into Seaforth's Ross-shire seat.[73] A deal was in the making for Seaforth to receive a peerage in return. However, the process was not speedy, and any delay put Seaforth under serious financial pressure. Creditors were more than usually pressing and Colin Mackenzie was pushing hard for land sales. He wrote to Seaforth, 'I wish to God your great object were attained so as you might with propriety make a sale.'[74] The sale of land would involve the loss of votes in Ross-shire. What Seaforth had to offer Dundas was, not only his acquiescence in the election of Lockhart Ross, but also the votes at his command. It was a race against time to get the election past and the peerage decided before financial disaster occurred. Colin feared that 'sale of part might be laid hold of by Administration as pretence for breach of their engagement'.[75] The deal was finalised in London in April 1796. Dundas wrote remarkably frankly that he would support Seaforth's elevation, 'attended with expressions of attachment on yours, and a declaration of a determination to render your local influence everywhere conversant to my wishes'.[76] In other words, the grant would be in return for his electoral support in Ross-shire and the Northern Burghs.

Since becoming an ally of Pitt and Dundas, Seaforth's influence in the Northern Burghs had greatly increased. This transfer of loyalty gave him access to Crown patronage and made possible an electoral pact by which Seaforth and the Sutherland family would nominate a candidate for the Northern Burghs at alternate elections.[77] It has been argued recently that burghs in this period were not necessarily in the pocket of local landowners, although that scholar concedes that small market towns in rural areas resisted landed influence less readily.[78] Dingwall was dominated by the Seaforth family, but not under its absolute sway.[79] For example, in 1796 George Gillanders (his old chief factor) asked him to support Donald Cameron to become clerk to the justices of the peace. Cameron was 'really attached to your interest in the Council . . . and needs assistance, for ought I learn here are underhand dealings among them'.[80] He was 'now at my lug expecting your immediate attention to him'.[81] Local jobs thus had to be found for councillors or their relatives.

Even the promise of both the Northern Burghs and the Ross-shire seat did not secure immediate ennoblement for Seaforth. The king was unhappy about making too many peerages, and Seaforth was told he might have to wait three years.[82] However, the deal was honoured.[83] Seaforth was on the spot to ensure that his influence was effective in the 1796 general election. Gillanders hoped to see him, 'but not to interfere with your present political hurry'.[84] Colin Mackenzie had a slight concern that 'the candidate will be unpopular in the West', but trusted that 'since Sir C has your patronage his election will be unanimous'.[85] The bulk of Seaforth's lands, and therefore of his 'unmanufactured' votes, were in the west, whereas Lockhart Ross was an Easter Ross proprietor. Colin need not have worried. Sir Hector Mackenzie of Flowerdale (a west-coast proprietor) promised that 'with regard to Sir Charles Ross I will do as you wish'.[86] Charles Mackenzie of Kilcoy wrote, 'I candidly and freely at once promise my vote to Sir Chas as you wish it . . . though not intimately acquainted with him.'[87] Kilcoy is in south-east Ross-shire, and his ready adherence illustrates that in 1796 a coalition was created of the Mackenzie lairds of Wester and Easter Ross. One reason was that both the patron and the candidate were firmly in Dundas's camp, and could expect to share in the distribution of patronage to which he had access in the British service and the East India Company. Another reason was certainly Seaforth's superiority in fictitious votes. Lockhart Ross was elected unopposed. Seaforth's contribution to winning the Northern Burghs for Dundas's candidate was equally easily accomplished. The town council of Dingwall actually made him its delegate at the election.[88] Dornoch was controlled by his ally the countess of Sutherland, and Tain by Lockhart Ross. Three of the five burgh votes were thus secure for William Dundas, and again there was no contest.[89]

Out of Parliament, but not out of influence

Dundas supporters won forty-three of the forty-five Scottish seats in 1796, which has been seen as the climax of his Scottish political career.[90] His debt to Seaforth was repaid sooner than promised. His peerage was announced in the *London Gazette* in October 1797. In February 1798 he was created a British peer as 'Lord Seaforth, Baron Mackenzie of Kintail in the County of Ross' by kissing the king's hand, and the following month took his seat in the House of Lords.[91] Colin Mackenzie's father Alexander described the peerage as 'a just acknowledgement of your personal merit and spirited support for the constitution of our country'.[92] This may read today as an ironic commentary on the deal. However, in addition to delivering votes to Dundas, Seaforth had also transferred his support to the government at the point in 1793 when the state and entire social system appeared to be threatened by revolutionary France. And he had subsequently recruited two line battalions for the French War, as will be shown in Chapter Six. He defended his position frankly to a would-be candidate by writing, 'I am to be made a British peer and I need not say I feel myself bound by every tie of common gratitude to do my utmost to support the interest and wishes of Mr Dundas.' He then claimed somewhat disingenuously that Dundas had imposed no condition.[93]

Seaforth's mother's characteristically caustic comment on the peerage was that 'a title in the family ... may be bought too dear and this is only tinsel in comparison with your interest in the county'.[94] However, events showed that Seaforth's dominance of Ross-shire politics did not depend on him remaining a member of the House of Commons. William Dundas was successfully re-elected for the Northern Burghs in December 1797, MPs appointed to office being obliged to seek re-election.[95] He wrote to Seaforth in a letter (which he asked him to burn) that '. . . Though I have not had Dingwall's answer . . . you will fair make me perfectly secure there'.[96] The sale of Lochalsh in 1801 reduced Seaforth's stock of fictitious votes. Nevertheless, in the 1802 general election, held when he was in Barbados, his influence was still strong. Sir Charles Lockhart Ross was re-elected for the county and Lady Sutherland's candidate for the Northern Burghs (as had been arranged in their agreement). In each case they were unopposed.[97]

Seaforth's influence at Westminster also survived when he was no longer an MP. In the spring of 1799, with Lochalsh still unsold, his creditors were becoming ever more pressing. Colin Mackenzie wrote, 'I need say nothing of the distress consequent on your lordship's present situation in regard to pecuniary matters . . . as sometimes to excite in your mind the most poignant uneasiness.'[98] He began to think of a colonial governorship as a means of restoring his finances and to lobby in Whitehall. He wrote to Mira from London in June, '<u>I shall succeed</u>, but office people are so dreadfully slow I dread to think of time.'[99] However, he had important contacts in London. Not only was Henry Dundas still keen to retain his goodwill. The secretary of state for the Home Department, whose brief included the colonies and colonial appointments[100], was the duke of Portland, Seaforth's party leader in the 1780s and early 1790s. In addition, his long-standing friend Charles Greville was willing to act as a go-between with the powerful men who would make the appointment. He had been active in politics and an MP in the 1770s and 1780s and thus understood the system and knew its leading figures.[101] Seaforth was hoping for the highly remunerative governorship of Jamaica. In May 1800 Colin Mackenzie wrote, 'I truly rejoice at the prospect of so flattering and lucrative appointment as you mention,'[102] and in June, 'I trust the consequence will be your return in a few years enabled to pay off all your debts and preserve your noble estate in your family.'[103] But the question was which appointment was open to him. A meeting between Seaforth and Portland had resulted in a misunderstanding about what was on offer. Portland now asked Greville to tell Seaforth that 'the government of Barbados, which is . . . the second best thing in my gift . . . was the government which I had in contemplation for him'.[104] Seaforth accepted Barbados and took the oaths as governor and captain general at a council at St James's Palace on 20 November.[105] His political influence and contacts, therefore, were insufficient to secure his preferred governorship of Jamaica but, four years after leaving the Commons, were able to win for him the second prize of Barbados. It has been suggested that in the posts Henry Dundas secured for Scots he 'was able to pick and choose, not solely ensuring rewards to political clients and associates, but also to some extent on the basis of talent, ability and experience'.[106] It may be that Seaforth was appointed partly on the grounds of his intelligence and energy. As will be shown in Chapters Seven, Nine and Ten he was to have an impact on Barbadian political life which was far beyond what the planters who dominated the island expected of a governor, especially one who was profoundly deaf.

Conclusions

Andrew Mackillop's contention that politics continued to be a dominant issue in the Highlands after the battle of Culloden is confirmed by this case study of Seaforth's political activities in the 1780s and 1790s.[107] The conventional explanation for his efforts to control elections has been that patrons like him wished to access the gravy train that government could offer, opportunities which grew in this period as the 'fiscal–military state' expanded.[108] This patronage was, of course, sought by Seaforth and provided him (at least from 1793) with the means of dominating the landed society of Ross-shire in a way to which he believed his family's heritage entitled him. However, he does not entirely fit the stereotype outlined above. Until 1793 he opposed the government at least in part on grounds of principle and in so doing damaged his political and material interests. This denied or at least strictly limited his access at that stage to Crown patronage, as his clear-sighted and caustic mother pointed out to him in 1792.[109] There is a parallel between this and his reluctance to evict his small tenants, which (as explained in Chapter Two) would have greatly increased his income. Recent researchers have countered the argument that the motivation for promoting publicly funded projects was the private benefit of the applicants by pointing out that these projects were also in the wider national interest (local, Scottish and British).[110] As has been shown in Chapter Three, Seaforth's directorship of the British Fisheries Society did not bring what he requested for his own estate – a fishing village at Loch Roag. This may have been in part a consequence of his then opposition to government. If so, he was pursuing contradictory aims, and not for the last time. His contrasting treatment of Lochalsh and Glenshiel in 1801, analysed in Chapter Four, is another example of such a contradiction in his policies as he faced competing pressures.

Seaforth's switch to support Dundas and Pitt in 1793 certainly gave him access to the gravy train, which was mainly but not invariably to his advantage. It is true that he immediately received the potentially profitable offer of a commission to raise a regiment of the line and a second battalion the following year. As will be argued in Chapter Six, it is doubtful if this turned out to be of financial benefit. He was not able to protect both battalions of the 78th from the Duke of York's cull of privately raised regiments in 1795, but their merger ensured that the regiment survived. He was strung along by the government on the long-running issue of the Lewis feu duties until his support had been delivered in the 1786 general election. Thereafter, however, he was able to play the system successfully to win two great prizes – in 1797 the long-sought peerage and in 1800 the governorship of Barbados (accepted by him less enthusiastically, but regarded as essential to his financial survival). As will be shown in Chapters Seven and Nine he greatly regretted that he was unable to dispense as governor of Barbados the sort of patronage which he had benefitted from in Britain. There is evidence that at home he was regarded as a skilled political operator. In 1805, when he was in Barbados, a bill was being promoted to finance the building of bridges over the Ross-shire rivers Conon and Orrin. Sir George Mackenzie of Coull commented that 'we have missed Seaforth terribly in this business'.[111]

There is a good case for arguing that his transfer of support to Dundas and Pitt in 1793 was on grounds of public policy, namely that the outbreak of war with revolutionary France made it necessary. While this might be seen as protecting his private and class interest, for him this was very much a matter of fundamental principle. Pitt's success in protecting the established order in Britain attracted in Seaforth a loyalty as firm as he had previously given to Fox. When Pitt and Dundas resigned in February 1801 over the king's refusal to accept Catholic emancipation,[112] he wrote to Dundas, 'the same motives that made me quit a former opposition to join your and Mr Pitt's standard will make me ambitious of being numbered among your friends whether you are in or out of place.'[113] How far this was honoured when he returned from Barbados will be seen in Chapter Eleven.

Notes

1. Edinburgh, National Records of Scotland (NRS), GD427/183, Minutes of Freeholders, etc. of Ross and Cromarty, 6 November 1782.
2. Fry, M., *The Dundas Despotism* (Edinburgh, 1992, 2004 edn), pp. 46–7, 61, 84.
3. Mackillop, A., 'The Political Culture of the Scottish Highlands from Culloden to Waterloo', *The Historical Journal*, vol. 46, 3, 2003, p. 527.
4. NRS, GD427/306/3, T. F. M. Humberston to G. Gillanders, 26 November 1780.
5. Mutch, A., 'A Contested Eighteenth-Century Election: Banffshire, 1795', *Northern Scotland*, New Series, vol. 2, 2011, pp. 28–9.
6. Taylor, D., *The Wild Black Region: Badenoch 1750–1800* (Edinburgh, 2016), p. 185.
7. Mackillop, 'Political Culture of the Scottish Highlands', pp. 511, 514–6, 521–3.
8. Fry, *The Dundas Despotism*, p. 55.
9. Harris, B., 'The Scots in the Westminster parliament and the British state in the eighteenth century' in J. Hoppit (ed.), *Parliaments, Nations and Identities in Britain and Ireland, 1660–1850* (Manchester, 2003), pp. 126–7.
10. Gambles, A., 'Free Trade and State Formation: The Political Economy of Fisheries Policy in Britain and the United Kingdom, circa 1750–1850', *Journal of British Studies*, vol. 39, 3, 2000, pp. 293–7, 302, 304.
11. Namier, Sir L. and J. Brooke, *The House of Commons 1754–1790* (London, 1964), vol. 1, pp. 87–9.
12. Edinburgh, National Library of Scotland (NLS), MS 6396, fo. 10, F. H. Mackenzie to Mrs Mary Mackenzie of Seaforth, 19 May 1791.
13. Namier and Brooke, *House of Commons 1754–1790*, vol. 1, p. 494.
14. Fry, *The Dundas Despotism*, pp. 61, 84, 95.
15. London, British Library (BL), Add. MS 39191, fos 97–9, G. Mackenzie to Sir R. Mackenzie, 21 April 1784.
16. Namier and Brooke, *House of Commons 1754–1790*, vol. 1, p. 495.
17. Thorne, R. G., *The House of Commons 1790–1820* (London, 1986), vol. 2, p. 572.
18. Wilkinson, D., 'Adam, William (1751–1839)', *Oxford Dictionary of National Biography* (ODNB), Oxford, 2004,

online edition, <www.oxforddnb.com>, article no. 108, accessed 28 February 2012.

19. NRS, GD46/17/9/1, F. H. Mackenzie to Mary F. E. Mackenzie, 14 November 1790.

20. *Gazetteer and New Daily Advertiser*, 28 July 1790, British Library Burney Collection of 17th and 18th Century Newspapers online (BCN), accessed 7 December 2010.

21. Thorne, *The House of Commons 1790–1820*, vol. 4, p. 494.

22. BL, Add. MS 39195, fos 41–2, Sir A. Mackenzie of Coull to J. R. Mackenzie of Suddie, 12 December 1792.

23. Namier and Brooke, *House of Commons 1754–1790*, vol. 3, p. 86.

24. *Gazetteer and New Daily Advertiser*, 28 July 1790 (BCN), accessed 7 December 2010.

25. NRS, GD51/6/210, F. H. Mackenzie to H. Dundas, 22 July 1795.

26. NRS, GD51/1/658/2, A. Mackenzie to F. H. Mackenzie, 27 September 1795.

27. Murdoch, A., *'The People Above': Politics and Administration in Mid-Eighteenth-Century Scotland* (Edinburgh, 1980), p. 124.

28. NRS, GD46/17/4/289, Mrs Mary H. Mackenzie to F. H. Mackenzie, 19 January 1792.

29. Hague, W., *William Pitt the Younger* (London, 2004), pp. 185–9, 195–6.

30. Namier and Brooke, *House of Commons 1754–1790*, vol. 3, p. 86; Ginter, D. E. (ed.), *Voting Records of the House of Commons, 1761–1820* (London, 1995), vol. 5, p. 288.

31. Hague, *William Pitt the Younger*, pp. 252, 256, 258–61, 264–6.

32. *Caledonian Mercury*, 20 December 1788 (NLS microfilm Mf. N.776).

33. Namier and Brooke, *House of Commons 1754–90*, vol. 3, p. 86.

34. Ginter, *Commons Voting Records*, vol. 5, pp. 305, 307.

35. Thorne, *The House of Commons 1790–1820*, vol. 2, p. 572.

36. Macrae, N., *The Romance of a Royal Burgh: Dingwall's Story of a Thousand Years* (1923, reprint Wakefield: EP Publishing, 1974), p. 237, Dingwall Town Council Minutes, 30 June 1788.

37. Ferguson, W., 'Dingwall Burgh Politics and the Parliamentary Franchise in the Eighteenth Century', *The Scottish Historical Review (SHR)*, vol. 38, 1959, pp. 106–7.

38. Castle Fraser, Mackenzie Fraser Papers (C. F. Papers), G. Mackenzie to Maj. Gen. A. Mackenzie, 24 February 1804.

39. Fry, *The Dundas Despotism*, pp. 77–8.

40. Namier and Brooke, *House of Commons, 1754–1790*, vol. 1, pp. 511–2.

41. NRS, GD46/17/4/357, D. Ross to F. H. Mackenzie, 27 June 1786.

42. Hague, *William Pitt the Younger*, pp. 288–9.
43. NLS, MS 6396, fo. 8, F. H. Mackenzie to Mrs Mary Mackenzie, 16 May 1791.
44. Logue, K. J., *Popular Disturbances in Scotland, 1780–1815* (Edinburgh, 1979), pp. 144–7.
45. Fry, *The Dundas Despotism*, pp. 167–8.
46. Hague, *William Pitt the Younger*, pp. 314–24.
47. Thorne, *The House of Commons 1790–1820*, vol. 4, p. 495.
48. Fry, *The Dundas Despotism*, p. 169.
49. Logue, *Popular Disturbances*, pp. 148–9.
50. NRS, GD46/6/25/1, A. Brodie to F. H. Mackenzie, 31 December 1792.
51. NRS, GD46/6/25/2, A. Brodie to F. H. Mackenzie, 30 January 1793.
52. NRS, GD46/6/25/5, A. Brodie to F. H. Mackenzie, 11 February 1793.
53. NRS, GD46/6/25/6, A. Brodie to A. Mackenzie of Balmudithy, 15 February 1793.
54. NRS, GD46/6/25/7, A. Brodie to F. H. Mackenzie, 15 February 1793.
55. Wilkinson, 'Adam, William', *ODNB,* online edition, article no. 108, accessed 28 February 2012.
56. Thorne, *The House of Commons 1790–1820*, vol. 4, p. 495.
57. Fry, *The Dundas Despotism*, pp. 186–7.
58. Hague, *William Pitt the Younger*, pp. 365–6.
59. Fry, *The Dundas Despotism*, pp. 171–2.
60. Quoted Logue, *Popular Disturbances*, p. 77. See also Harris, B., *The Scottish People and the French Revolution* (London, 2008), p. 124.
61. Wold, A. L., *Scotland and the French Revolutionary War, 1792–1802* (Edinburgh, 2015), pp. 20–1.
62. Thorne, *The House of Commons 1790–1820*, vol. 4, p. 494.
63. Thorne, *The House of Commons 1790–1820*, vol. 2, p. 573; vol. 4, p. 495; Wilkinson, 'Adam, William', *ODNB*, online edition, article no. 108, accessed 28 February 2012.
64. Ginter, *Commons Voting Records*, vol. 5, pp. 353–95.
65. *Lloyd's Evening Post*, 3 January 1794 (BCN), accessed 9 December 2010.
66. NRS, GD51/9/60/2, Petition of F. H. Mackenzie to Lords of Treasury, 29 September 1794.
67. NRS, GD46/17/2, H. Dundas to F. H. Mackenzie, 18 June 1794.
68. Hague, *William Pitt the Younger*, pp. 355–9.
69. NRS, GD46/17/2, A. Brodie to F. H. Mackenzie, 6 October 1796 and November 1796.
70. NRS, GD51/6/210, F. H. Mackenzie to H. Dundas, 22 July 1795.

71. Cookson, J. E., *The British Armed Nation, 1793–1815* (Oxford, 1997), pp. 147–8.
72. NRS, GD46/17/2, A. Brodie to F. H. Mackenzie, November 1796.
73. Fry, *The Dundas Despotism*, pp. 194, 201–2.
74. NRS, GD46/17/15, C. Mackenzie to F. H. Mackenzie, 4 April 1796.
75. NRS, GD46/17/15, C. Mackenzie to F. H. Mackenzie, 24 April 1796.
76. NRS, GD46/14/2/2, H. Dundas to F. H. Mackenzie, 23 April 1796.
77. Thorne, *The House of Commons 1790–1820*, vol. 2, p. 620.
78. Harris, B., 'Landowners and Urban Society in Eighteenth-Century Scotland', *SHR*, vol. 92, 2, 2013, pp. 234, 250.
79. Ferguson, 'Dingwall Burgh Politics', pp. 100, 106.
80. NRS, GD46/17/15, G. Gillanders to F. H. Mackenzie, 22 May and 10 September 1796.
81. NRS, GD46/17/15, G. Gillanders to F. H. Mackenzie, 23 September 1796.
82. NRS, GD46/14/2/2, H. Dundas to F. H. Mackenzie, 23 April 1796.
83. Thorne, *The House of Commons 1790–1820*, vol. 2, pp. 572, 619.
84. NRS, GD46/17/15, G. Gillanders to F. H. Mackenzie, 22 May and 17 June 1796.
85. NRS, GD46/17/15, C. Mackenzie to F. H. Mackenzie, 8 and 10 May 1796.
86. NRS, GD46/4/119/6, Sir H. Mackenzie to F. H. Mackenzie, 26 May 1796.
87. NRS, GD46/4/119/5, C. Mackenzie of Kilcoy to F. H. Mackenzie, 12 May 1796.
88. NRS, GD46/17/15, G. Gillanders to F. H. Mackenzie, 22 May and 12 June 1796.
89. Thorne, *The House of Commons 1790–1820*, vol. 2, p. 620.
90. Fry, *The Dundas Despotism*, pp. 203–4.
91. NRS, GD46/17/10, *London Gazette*, 7 October 1797; *London Chronicle*, 27 February 1798; *Star*, 10 March 1798 (BCN), accessed 6 December 2010.
92. NRS, GD46/17/18, A. Mackenzie to Lord Seaforth, 28 October 1797.
93. NRS, GD46/4/119/4, F. H. Mackenzie to K .Mackenzie of Cromarty, 3 May 1796.
94. NRS, GD46/18/1/51, Mary H. Mackenzie to F. H. Mackenzie, 23 April 1796.
95. Thorne, *The House of Commons 1790–1820*, vol. 2, p. 619.

96. NRS, GD46/4/119/7, W. Dundas to Lord Seaforth, 28 October 1797.
97. Thorne, *The House of Commons 1790–1820*, vol. 2, pp. 572, 619.
98. NRS, GD46/17/14, C. Mackenzie to Lord Seaforth, 24 April 1799.
99. NLS, MS 6396, fo. 31, Lord Seaforth to Lady Seaforth, 3 June 1799.
100. Newbury, C., 'Patronage and Professionalism: Manning a Transitional Empire, 1760–1870, *Journal of Imperial and Commonwealth History*, vol. 42, 2014, pp. 2, 195.
101. Namier and Brooke, *House of Commons 1754–1790*, vol. 2, pp. 550–1.
102. NRS, GD46/17/14, C. Mackenzie to Lord Seaforth, 17 May 1800.
103. NRS, GD46/17/14, C. Mackenzie to Lord Seaforth, 21 June 1800.
104. NRS, GD46/17/16/27, Duke of Portland to C. Greville, 11 August 1800.
105. *London Gazette*, 29 November 1800 (BCN), accessed 6 December 2010.
106. Devine, T. M., *Scotland's Empire 1600–1815* (London, 2003), p. 237.
107. Mackillop, 'Political Culture of Scottish Highlands', p. 513.
108. Fry, *The Dundas Despotism*, p. 55.
109. NRS, GD46/17/4/289, Mrs Mary H. Mackenzie to F. H. Mackenzie, 19 January 1792.
110. Harris, 'Scots in the Westminster parliament', pp. 126–7; Gambles, 'Free Trade and State Formation', pp. 293–7, 302, 304.
111. C. F. Papers, 1/1152, G. S. Mackenzie to A. Mackenzie Fraser, 5 March 1805.
112. Hague, *William Pitt the Younger*, pp. 464–72.
113. NRS, GD46/7/3, Lord Seaforth to H. Dundas, 7 February 1801.

6 The Soldier Chief

Raising the 78th

Most portraits of Francis Humberston Mackenzie show him as a portly figure in an elaborate military uniform wearing a hat with the flamboyant eagle's feather of a chief. His pretensions to active leadership of his clan may seem anomalous in a time when a chief's influence was much reduced. His pretensions to an army officer's career may seem surprising when he was profoundly deaf. Even some of his intimates did not take him seriously as a soldier. When in 1793 Seaforth was commissioned to raise a line regiment as its lieutenant colonel commandant, his friend Alexander Brodie wrote to Seaforth's brother-in-law Alexander Mackenzie, who was to be second-in-command, that 'when [Seaforth] becomes tired of playing the soldier, you might slip into the rank'.[1] It would also be easy to ascribe strictly pragmatic motives for Seaforth's recruiting. It is usually thought that landed proprietors could expect a secure income by recruiting a regiment. In addition to his own military salary Seaforth would receive bounties and equipment allowances for raising the troops and a regular income of off reckonings to maintain them. As has been shown in Chapter Four, Seaforth badly needed to find new sources of income.

Another motivation for Highland chiefs to recruit was as a political act to win favour with government and secure the various benefits that favour could bring. For example, the military commissions and other government posts which they could secure would increase their influence among the lesser gentry.[2]

Figure 6.1 Seaforth in uniform of colonel of the 78th Regiment, the Seaforth Highlanders, *c.*1800, after Thomas Lawrence. (Reproduced by generous permission of the National Trust for Scotland.)

It would be foolish to argue that Seaforth did not have pragmatic motives. However, there was more to his recruiting than that. He had a genuine ambition to lead his clan in a traditional way, which contemporaries regarded as outmoded and foolish. He wished to be thought of as 'a loyal honest chieftain calling out his friends to support their King and Country' and not as 'a jobber of the attachment my neighbours bear to me'.[3] Recruiting enabled him to play out the role of military leader of his clan in a modern context. As shown in Chapter One, he had an ambition to emulate the military exploits of his brother and his father. However, when he lobbied for an active command, a message was relayed to him from the Duke of York, the commander-in-chief, tactfully advising, 'H.R.H. has the highest opinion of your ability and integrity, but has an idea that your misfortune in a great measure incapacitates you for military command in time of actual service.'[4]

When in March 1793 he received the Crown commission to raise a regiment of foot,[5] it was part of the arrangement (discussed in Chapter Five) by which he switched his electoral influence to support Pitt and the king. Seaforth's commission was the first for a line regiment in the war with the French Republic.[6] This was considered to be a great coup financially. As the senior partner of Seaforth's Edinburgh lawyers, Alexander Mackenzie, wrote to him, a line regiment was more profitable and therefore far superior to a fencible one.[7] Nevertheless, he at first expressed a preference for a fencible regiment, which could only be used within Britain.[8] Alexander Brodie thought this was because 'his absence, in case of the regiment being ordered from Scotland, might be attended with material inconvenience to his private interests'.[9] He accepted a line regiment after receiving assurances on this matter and wrote to his wife that it was 'no more alarming than a fencible regiment as commanders of regiments are of course allowed to go abroad or not as they like'.[10] In congratulating Seaforth, Mira's sister Cathleen reported:

> My dear sister has written in better spirits lately, the certainty she feels your not going abroad is a great comfort to her and makes us all entirely enjoy the honor and happiness you receive from your new appointment. I fear you must have thought me lukewarm before, but I could not enter with glee into the pleasures of any plan I thought likely to deprive my beloved sister of her greatest comfort and delight, viz. your society.[11]

It appears that Seaforth had been under pressure from his wife not to go overseas with his regiment. It may seem surprising that a man who aspired to military glory deferred to a wife's natural fear of her husband going abroad on active service. Mira and the wider family no doubt believed that Seaforth's deafness disqualified him from commanding troops in action. They may have persuaded him on the less humiliating (and true) grounds that his estates needed his close management.

Henry Dundas, as Secretary of State for War, believed that the Highlander offered superior soldier material and that clan feeling would encourage recruitment if the chief was seen to be at the head of his troops.[12] This seems to have been an outdated view. The military aspects of clanship had been in long-term decay and the authority and influence of chiefs over their clan had been greatly diminished.[13] Nevertheless, Brodie wrote to Major Alexander Mackenzie, 'my motives for proposing Seaforth as the Commandant were first that his being in that situation would be popular with the clan.'[14] Dundas also believed that Highlanders were less likely to become infected with radicalism.[15] Government, in the interests of economy, had tied Seaforth's hands in significant respects. Most of the officers were to be selected from the half-pay list, which would mean that they would not have the usual incentive in a new unit for officers to raise men to pay for their commissions. In addition, the bounty paid by government was to be only 5 guineas. Brodie advised Dundas that 'notwithstanding Mr Mackenzie's great influence among his own clan, and over extensive districts of country his own property, he . . . will have to give a larger bounty than is allowed by Government'.[16] Initially he paid only an additional £1 per recruit.[17] There were, thus, signs from the start that raising the regiment might not be as easy or profitable as anticipated.

In 1793–4 Highland regiments of the line were raised also by the earl of Breadalbane, the duke of Gordon, the duke of Argyll and Sir James Grant. Why should Highlanders be seen as promising army recruits? It has been claimed that groups of young men from one Highland family would still exact vengeance on youths of another family alleged to have impugned their honour.[18] What success did Seaforth have in harnessing such aggressive impulses (if true) and mobilising tenants and subtenants from his estates? No time was lost. On 18 March, only eleven days after the commission was signed, Peter Fairbairn sent a beating order to Alexander Gillanders, the Lewis factor, in Stornoway and advised him that 'Seaforth has no doubt of you using your best endeavours to find a few good recruits'.[19] Alexander's father George, perhaps emboldened by having been superseded as chief factor by Fairbairn, advised Seaforth that 'without your own presence I expect little success' around Brahan. This was notwithstanding hints that providing recruits would ease the renewal of leases.[20] Subsequently Gillanders reported that tenants were removing to other estates rather than supply recruits.[21] Seaforth had immediately headed west in March, partly because he foresaw better prospects there and partly because his wife was at Seaforth Lodge expecting a birth. On 25 March he wrote to her, 'I shall be in Kintail above three days so keep up keep up my dear soul. I am harried to death morning noon and night and make more haste to Lewis.' He signed it proudly, 'Lt Col. Com, 78 Regt'.[22]

Peter Fairbairn had reservations about the prospects even in Kintail. He wrote to Seaforth that 'from what I can learn from a tenant . . . the people are not quite at ease, but your presence he apprehends will do away with all scruples'.[23] George Gillanders, having recruited for both Earl Kenneth and Frederick Mackenzie Humberston, was in a position to give practical advice:

> Seaforth should this night write his man of business in Lewis [Alexander] to make out lists immediately of all the men he knows can be spared and ought to enlist as sodjers with Seaforth . . . Seaforth should carry with him from Kintail six or eight young handsome men which will be a great encouragement and induce-ment for the Lewis men to enlist in case they should be refractory . . . Seaforth will instruct the factor and sergeant what levy money they are to give or what encouragement he may hold out to the parents of those young men in the lists made out.[24]

In this letter is another hint that parents might be given secu-rity of tenure if their sons joined the colours. There has been much criticism of Highland proprietors (for example, by James Hunter) for inducing tenants to 'give men for land' by offers of security of tenure, undertakings which the tenants believed were broken when these holdings were subsequently cleared.[25] New leases were certainly given in return for recruits throughout the Highlands, for example in Sutherland in 1799 and 1800[26] and on Lord Macdonald's lands in Skye and North Uist, on the Cromartie estate and on the duke of Gordon's lands in Badenoch.[27] However, it has also been suggested that, in con-trast to the clan levies of former times, landowners were now inclined to leave tenants and use less profitable individuals, namely cottars and day labourers.[28] Such a policy is indicated by Gillanders' advice that lists should be made of those who could be spared.

Recruiting in Kintail was considered to be highly satisfactory. The chief's presence there, although brief, had apparently done the trick. However, there was a major problem in Lewis, and it was to do with conditions of service. Seaforth did not start recruiting there until the end of April[29], after the birth of his daughter Augusta Ann on 24 April.[30] By this time resistance had developed, especially in the parish of Uig, where Seaforth reported more than 300 of the men of military age had taken to the hills (an estimate subsequently reduced to 200). This was the only occasion on which there was major, open and active opposition to him by the people of his estate. He believed it to be the work of radical agitators. Inflammatory posters and Thomas Paine's *The Rights of Man* were circulating in Stornoway.[31] The only other evidence was the word of one who had escaped from the hill that 'some evil minded persons' had told the people that Seaforth had no legal authority to recruit. Not for the only time, he responded to an emergency with energy and courage, despite his disability. He reported to Lord Adam Gordon, the military commander in Scotland, 'I am determined to be among them and set out early tomorrow morning. Though this step may be attended with some danger I . . . think it my duty to use any means to check in its beginning such a dangerous (and in this country unprecedented) association.'[32]

Donald Macleod of Geanies, the sheriff substitute, reported that Seaforth had courageously gone to the camp unarmed and unattended except by an interpreter. The protestors stated they had no complaint against him as their landlord, and their principal grievance related to the recruiting of the original 78th Regiment by Earl Kenneth in 1778. A promise had been made that the regiment would be disembodied in Ross-shire (the same promise Seaforth was making now for the new 78th[33]). This had been broken, the regiment had been sent to the East Indies and, it was alleged, the officers had made it difficult for those reaching the end of their term to take passage home. Some had returned to Lewis and Macleod reported that these were the leaders of the Uig protestors. They argued, brandishing their cudgels, that 'as the public had broken faith with the late 78th Regiment there was no reason but that they might do the same by this' and so they would not enlist. Seaforth apologised for the treatment of the original regiment and promised that the protestors would not be punished if they dispersed quickly to their homes and that 'no violence or sinister art whatever' would be used to make them enlist.[34] Although a later explanation was that they were afraid they would have no land to return to,[35] this contemporary evidence suggests that the grievance was a very specific one on the terms of service. Despite Seaforth's efforts the protestors remained on the hill, even after three other magistrates tried to persuade them. He and Geanies now asked for military help, which was refused. The Lord Advocate, Robert Dundas, pointed out that no strong act of violence had been committed and clearly believed that Seaforth and Geanies had panicked in making their request.[36] What Geanies referred to as 'your rebellious subjects in Uig' dispersed some time in early June.[37] Donald Macdonald, the historian of Lewis, claims that a deal was done that, if a family had only one son, that son would not be taken, but in a large family two might be taken.[38] If true, this may imply that co-operating tenants would be given some degree of security of tenure. Seaforth must have had his pride as clan chief battered by this experience. He reassured himself and Lord Adam Gordon that the protestors 'even at the height of their folly swore to a man that, if the country was invaded, they would all follow me to defend it'.[39]

By the time Seaforth's recruiting visit to Lewis ended on 8 June he had raised 220 men there.[40] This may not seem a large number set against a population of 6,300, especially as it seems probable there were at least hints that recruits would be rewarded by security of tenure. Furthermore, George Gillanders wrote to Seaforth that 'the wives of those who went with you have thrown their land away', being unable to work it.[41] This suggests that in desperation Seaforth ignored Gillanders' recommendation by taking tenants or at least sub-tenants.

In mid June an inspection of the regiment, numbered the 78th, was held at Fort George. Seaforth claimed to Mira that General Leslie had inspected the regiment and 'rejected only six men . . . we are 620 to 630 strong and my bacon is saved'.[42] However, a newspaper report stated that 400 men had been inspected and 'upwards of 300 of these men were raised from Seaforth's own estates'.[43] It is possible that some recruits had not yet reached Fort George. Certainly recruiting continued through the summer and early autumn. Peter Fairbairn wrote in early September to Sandy Mackenzie, 'I hope you get a good proportion of recruits in Edinburgh and neighbourhood for your augmentation.'[44] This suggests that the 78th was not filled up to its complement of 600 with Highlanders, still less by men from the Seaforth estates. In fact it had to be completed with Lowlanders. It is also clear that, under pressure, recruits had been taken who were subsequently rejected as unfit.[45] This indicates that Dundas had overestimated Seaforth's ability to raise men, and that he and his ally Brodie had mistaken the extent of clan sentiment. That recruitment had been better in Kintail than in Lewis or at Brahan might suggest that clan loyalty survived longer in that country from which the Mackenzies originally sprang. On the other hand (as shown in Chapter Two) this was the same year in which, Seaforth later alleged, the Glenshiel tenants banded together so as not to compete against one another for the new leases.

Seaforth was in his element at Fort George, realising at least some of his dreams of military service by drilling the troops. He wrote to Mira:

> I am upon parade every morning at about a quarter before or precisely at six, drill till half past eight, at ten drill the non-commissioned officers till twelve – from twelve to two drill the officers, at four dine, from six till nine drill the men again, so you see with . . . arranging the thousand details that concern a regiment . . . I have not many waste hours'.[46]

Presumably his orders were relayed by NCOs. By January, the 78th was at its first posting: Guernsey.[47] George Gillanders hoped that Seaforth was well there 'and free from your barbarous and ferocious enemies on the opposite coast'.[48] However, on the second day of 1794 he was at St. James's Palace being presented to the king by Dundas,[49] who had more important work for him than looking out for a French attack on the Channel Islands.

The second battalion – men for land?

On 10 February 1794, Seaforth received a Crown commission to raise a second battalion of the 78th Regiment.[50] There were rumours of a French invasion of Britain and, at home, increasing evidence of radical opposition. The army was being rapidly expanded,[51] with the consequence was that recruits became harder to find and more expensive to enlist. Notwithstanding Seaforth's problems in recruiting the first battalion, he had finally filled it. However, Peter Fairbairn warned him that 'people become more unwilling than ever in this country to enlist . . . at Carnoch [Ross-shire] Fairburn's tenants assembled in a tumultuous manner and deforced him of his recruits, saying they had nothing to do with kings nor would they serve any of them'.[52] The cost of recruiting was a major concern. Seaforth subsequently complained that he had been cheated by government, being given only 5 guineas bounty per man and only four months to raise the regiment, when other new regiments were 'set afloat' at 15 guineas bounty.[53] Other recruiters in the north-west were offering bounties of between £21 and £30[54] and Seaforth himself offered 15 guineas for quality recruits and even 20 guineas if the regiment's major could raise 100 men.[55] His bounties, therefore, seem to have been pitched at about the going rate. In the same year the duke of Gordon paid an average of £15, but reaching £21, in raising a line regiment.[56]

Bounties at this level were potentially ruinous. However, landlords did not always have to pay cash when drawing men from their own estates. For example, Maclean of Lochbuie in 1794 offered to reduce the rent by 30 shillings for five years on the holding of any family which produced a recruit. This deal attracted fifty men, a variation on the 'men for land' arrangement.[57] Seaforth seems to have done something similar in Lochalsh in 1794. Colin Mackenzie wrote later to the agent of a potential purchaser that 'in making the last set [in 1794] his Lordship was obliged to submit to some loss in consideration of the alacrity with which his people had enlisted in his regt. then newly raised'.[58]

The disadvantages of military service have often been emphasised. However, it not only provided secure income for many families, but also empowered tenants by enabling them to bargain with their landlords (as discussed in Chapter Two).[59] It has been suggested that Highlanders were more likely to be drawn to the colours by obtaining land in return for military service than by martial characteristics or patriotic motivation.[60] In other words, 'men for land' deals may actually have been attractive to recruits provided they were honoured. Seaforth does appear to have taken the terms of these arrangements seriously. In 1801 Colin Mackenzie suggested that at the new Glenshiel sett small tenants should be moved to 'small improvable spots' and their lands in the glen leased to sheep farmers. However, he asked for 'a copy of our letter promising the present tenants a continuance on equal terms'.[61] It seems clear that in 1794 Glenshiel tenants had been promised that they could keep their lands at the next sett in return for recruits. What happened in 1801 was that most of them were accommodated in six rearranged farms. Colin commented, 'we found ourselves tied up by an express promise given at the former sett to give the tenants of these farms a preference to strangers, reserving only a right to new model all the farms.' Eleven of the poorest tenants were squeezed into the farm of Morvich, but they may not have been entitled to the 1794 guarantee.[62] Seaforth seems to have largely (if not completely) honoured the promise made to the providers of recruits in 1794.

Highland proprietors have also been criticised for evicting as a punishment for not volunteering, as Alastair Ranaldson Macdonald of Glengarry did in 1794.[63] There is evidence that Seaforth, or his factors, threatened or at least hinted at this. Shortly after the commission for the second battalion Fairbairn advised Seaforth that the tenants of Dunglast (a farm near Brahan) would be warned to remove, and added, 'shall all the tenants on this estate [presumably the Easter Ross lands] be warned also? ... Of recruiting this is the most effectual check.'[64] That nothing further is heard of this in the estate correspondence suggests that tenants in Easter Ross were not actually evicted in 1794 for non-enlistment of their sons. In negotiations between the estate and tenants over recruiting, the threat of eviction must always have been in the minds of tenants even if not stated openly. The town of Stornoway was reported to be hostile to recruiting, perhaps because the estate did not have the same hold there as when dealing with rural tenants.[65] In the same month (March), Fairbairn reported on the 'tenants in Lewis who are warned to remove as refractory'.[66] The nature of the offence is not clear, and it was probably too early to have been a consequence of the 1794 recruitment. It might have been a delayed consequence of the 1793 campaign and the Uig protests. However, it is often difficult to establish motives for removals or indeed whether the warnings were carried out (frequently they were a tactic in rent negotiations). Probably when recruiting Seaforth was willing to use the threat of eviction, but less willing to carry it out. By 1804 the threat of removal was certainly being used in Lewis. The factor, F. A. Chapman reported that 'none almost are to be had without a threat that, if they do not come forward and enlist, they may depend upon it that their father will not get lands afterwards'.[67]

At first recruiting for the second battalion seemed to be going well. A report on 12 July stated that there were now 1,600 men in the two battalions.[68] However, on the death in September of Seaforth's eldest son George at the age of six and subsequent illness of his wife, he retreated to Brahan. The subsequent hiatus demonstrates the importance in recruiting of the personal involvement of the regimental commander. Still at Brahan on 1 December, Seaforth wrote to Mackenzie of Suddie, second-in-command of the new battalion, complaining that the officers had not fulfilled their engagements to recruit and that 'I have certainly paid for a vast proportion of men already'. Officers' commissions could raise large sums on the open market, but like other Highland landowners (for example the duke of Gordon)[69], Seaforth had to forego these in order to attract officers who promised to bring recruits with them. He would 'begin a brisk recruiting here' and was now prepared to pay a bounty of 20 guineas per man, but not for men the officers should have raised.[70] By March 1795 he had 100 waiting at Fort George for transport south, but the battalion was still not complete. He complained to Suddie:

> God knows if I had chosen to follow the course some of my neighbours have taken in filling up their regiment with the old, the lame, the halt and the blind I might have been complete two months ago, but I don't love to cheat the King and must therefore suffer for my folly . . . the only plan I can devise is to see what bounty we can get from Government and then to calculate what we can add.[71]

Profits from recruiting?

Seaforth's problems in completing his second battalion support the argument that recruiting was usually profitless for the chiefs who raised regiments in 1793–4 as the rush for men pushed the level of bounties well above the sum paid by government. Two other Highland regiments, the 90th and the 79th, raised in 1793–4, were said to have cost their proprietors £5,000–£6,000 and over £15,000 respectively.[72] As Andrew Mackillop has pointed out, it is difficult to quantify the revenue derived by commanders from the 'off reckonings' paid by government for the outfitting and maintenance of troops.[73] In July 1794 Seaforth bought clothing for his men amounting to the considerable value of £2,622.[74] He claimed that he made £1,000 in off reckonings. This may have been one of the few aspects of the regiment's finances from which he derived significant benefit. However, this claim was made (during a financial dispute with Colonel Sandy) when he had an incentive to maximise the figure.[75]

By January 1796, the 78th regiment was in danger of becoming bankrupt, and all the skills of Seaforth's military agent, Humphrey Donaldson, were required.[76] Military agents, stationed in London, were playing an increasingly important part in such matters at a price.[77] In July 1795 Seaforth asked Donaldson to urgently seek payment of balances due him from the officers on recruiting accounts. These were payments due by officers in lieu of the recruits they had committed to raise (in effect the bounties Seaforth complained he had paid himself): £1,592 was due from officers of the second battalion and, still outstanding, £330 from the first battalion. By far the largest sum due was £2,250 due from government, presumably unpaid because the battalion was not yet complete.[78] He commented to Suddie that 'all officers are like common whores, tho' venal to the last degree, they all love to be courted'.[79] However, this generalisation was unfair. In 1796 he was able to pass to Donaldson a total of £1,400 received, admittedly belatedly, from junior officers in the second battalion in payment for their commissions (six lieutenants and two ensigns).[80]

Landed proprietors who raised regiments also expected to benefit financially by receipt of their regimental salaries. The salary of a lieutenant colonel not in the field was a relatively modest £821.[81] In Seaforth's case this did not last long. The new commander-in-chief of the army, the Duke of York, began in the autumn of 1795 a programme of merging and disbanding many of the Scottish and Irish regiments recently raised by landed proprietors. The duke believed that private military patronage interfered with the claims of career officers and that such regiments found it difficult to maintain their recruiting after their initial formation. The disbanding of the 97th or Strathspey Highlanders is an illustration of what happened to some 'clan regiments'.[82] The 78th survived, at least in part (as suggested in Chapter Five) as a result of Seaforth's assiduous lobbying and use of his political contacts,[83] but at the cost of merging the two battalions.[84] The combined regiment was soon to embark for India and Colonel Sandy became lieutenant colonel commandant.[85] This transaction was accompanied by considerable rancour. Seaforth appears initially to have given his consent, but to have withdrawn it when his half-pay salary was not as high as he had anticipated and when he feared that the arrangement would not allow him to receive further promotion. He wrote rather curtly to Sandy that he expected him to 'look sharp to see that no change takes place till my fair interest is fully established'.[86] In his letters to Sandy, Seaforth displayed the self-pity in which he sometimes indulged in times of stress. He claimed that acquiring the rank of lieutenant colonel had been his sole object for himself and secured with great sacrifices (presumably financial). He wrote, 'can you ask me to give up almost the only thing I have to be proud of?' His sister Frances was less than sympathetic or tactful. She had told him, 'Pooh what was my rank to me who could not Serve [in action].' He complained to Sandy, 'it is rather hard to me to tell me the rank is . . . only nominal etc., etc. God knows I feel my own situation sufficiently without these hints.'[87] He blamed Sandy's 'exalted firmness' for his loss, despite his long exertions on Sandy's behalf. Sandy coolly replied that he assumed he had changed his mind 'and wished to retain the regiment notwithstanding our agreement'. In a draft letter he protested at being accused of total want of feeling by one he regarded as his best friend and advised Seaforth not to suppose that the whole world was in league against him.[88] Seaforth was mollified by a promise that his rank was permanent and unconditional and that he would receive promotion like any other army officer.[89] While he was soon on good terms again with Sandy,[90] his resentment at his treatment by the War Office remained unresolved. Two years later he was still complaining that 'a great deal of money was actually taken out of my pocket'.[91] He also lost the patronage belonging to a regimental commandant.

Seaforth's military ambitions were not satisfied by the status of a half-pay lieutenant colonel. He was involved in two of the forces raised for home defence at a time when a French invasion seemed a real possibility and domestic support for the French by no means impossible. One of these, the Volunteers, he was responsible for in his role as a proprietor. The Volunteers were civilian part-time soldiers, to whom the government provided arms and pay for regular drills.[92] Volunteering is claimed to have been particularly attractive in the north of Scotland because protection there from the regular forces (army and navy) was practically non-existent.[93] Nevertheless, a quota was imposed for each county and district to achieve and Seaforth did not find this easy to meet. Volunteering appears to have been more popular in smaller towns on the east coast.[94] Peter Fairbairn wrote from Stornoway in 1796 that men there 'will with much difficulty be made Volunteers at almost any bounty without pretty strong measures being used'.[95] Volunteers also proved a problem to Seaforth by their indiscipline. In Dingwall in 1795 several members of the Volunteer company met 'in an illegal manner and paraded to the storehouse of Fowlis wherein some grain the property of Mr Bertram of Mountrich was then lodged'. As no mention was made of grain being stolen, the purpose was presumably to protest at it being hoarded in a time of scarcity. The consequent reduction of the company was only reversed by Seaforth craving permission for it to be reformed to the home secretary, the duke of Portland. Portland had been his party leader in his Whig days and in his present position in government was now an important source of patronage. It must, therefore, have been a galling letter to write.[96]

The militia appears to have been a more enjoyable experience for Seaforth. It was established in Scotland in 1797 in the search for a home defence force more flexible and reliable than the Volunteers and was a compulsory levy by ballot. Its advantages over the Volunteers were that it could be used throughout the country and, although administered by the county, was more directly under the control of government than the Volunteers. Its compulsory element made it unpopular in Scotland. There were many areas where the introduction of the militia was not accompanied by violence, and Ross-shire was one of these.[97] However, there were riots in other areas in the late summer and autumn of 1797 (for example, in Atholl).[98] Even in peaceful areas, it was not always easy to implement. In Lewis in 1798, three who had undertaken to pay £10 for a substitute had paid up and others had not, and four men supplied as substitutes were rejected as unfit.[99] However, the militia enabled great proprietors like Seaforth to develop their public roles within their county, and through the nomination of officers bolstered their patronage in the local area.[100]

When the appointments were made in 1798 Seaforth became colonel of the Ross-shire or Second Scottish militia regiment.[101] He served with the regiment for over a year (although not continuously) while it was stationed at Banff and later at Aberdeen, and seems to have enjoyed his command. In Banff in December 1798 he wrote that 'I have a snug little regiment at present without risk' (by which he meant financial risk).[102] By the end of 1799 it was stationed at Aberdeen, where its colours were presented by Lady Augusta Leith. Major General Hay inspected the men and 'expressed his entire approbation' of their drill. As has been seen, Seaforth enjoyed drilling soldiers. That evening he gave a dinner and ball to the regiment and their friends.[103] One of the problems of army life was expensive hospitality and conviviality.[104] The following month he was able to demonstrate in Aberdeen his ability to take charge of a situation and instigate decisive action. In a storm of wind and snow two ships went ashore near the entrance to the harbour. According to the newspaper report, Seaforth 'exerted himself in an uncommon manner' to ensure that the crews were brought to safety. Furthermore, 'with a generosity which marks his character' he gave £10, which he could ill afford, to the rescuers.[105]

Conclusions

In December 1798, Seaforth offered to raise a regiment from Lewis, 'feeling anxious to promote a vigorous prosecution of the war' and boasted that 'I have a power of raising men'.[106] His offer was not taken up. Dundas almost certainly remembered how long it had taken to complete the second battalion of the 78th Regiment. Seaforth had indeed been able to raise men by his power over his tenants and by using what remained of clan sentiment, but not to the extent which he and the government had anticipated. It is possible to accept his assurance in 1798 that all he was looking for was to avoid a loss and that he saw a very feeble prospect of any profit. It is clear that he did not receive the direct financial benefit from his recruiting which had been anticipated and (as has been shown in Chapter Four) was badly needed. This confirms Cookson's view that Highland recruiting was often profitless.[107] However, as Mackillop has pointed out, the regular salary and off reckonings enabled him to secure the renewal of credit, essential to his financial survival.[108] Importantly, he was able to satisfy his ambition to lead troops, although not in action, and there were very significant indirect benefits. His raising of regiments added to his political influence (as has been explained in Chapter Five) and contributed to his receiving the lord lieutenancy of Ross in 1794 and peerage in 1797. This gave him the social position which (as shown in Chapter Four) he craved. These sort of rewards were clearly a motivation for raising regiments. The duke of Gordon, who raised the 92nd, became a Knight of the Thistle, lord lieutenant of Aberdeenshire and Keeper of the Great Seal of Scotland (reckoned to be worth £3,000 per annum).[109] Most importantly for Seaforth, his recruiting record, together with his political links, led to his appointment to the well-paid post of governor of Barbados in 1800. That marked a major turning point in his life, and that of his family, and its challenges and rewards will be the subject of Chapters Seven, Nine and Ten. As will be shown in Chapter Seven, one challenge was that his military experience had the effect of increasing the tensions which were liable to arise between the civil and military authorities in the Caribbean.

Notes

1. Edinburgh, National Records of Scotland (NRS), GD46/6/25/6, A. Brodie to A. Mackenzie of Balmudithy, 15 February 1793.
2. Cookson, J. E., *The British Armed Nation, 1793–1815* (Oxford, 1997), p. 130.
3. F. H. Mackenzie to H. Dundas, 8 February 1794, quoted in Mackenzie, A., *History of the Mackenzies* (Inverness, 1894 edn), p. 337.
4. NRS, GD46/17/20, A. Mackenzie to Lord Seaforth, 25 July 1801.
5. NRS, GD427/300/1, Printed Crown commission for raising 78th Regiment, 7 March 1793.
6. Cookson, *British Armed Nation*, pp. 133, 135; NRS, GD46/6/25/6, A. Brodie to A. Mackenzie of Balmudithy, 15 February 1793.
7. NRS, GD46/17/3, A. Mackenzie, Edinburgh, to F. H. Mackenzie, 21 February and 4 March 1793.
8. NRS, GD46/6/25/5, A. Brodie to F. H. Mackenzie, 11 February 1793.
9. NRS, GD46/6/25/8, A. Brodie to A. Mackenzie of Balmudithy, 18 February 1793.
10. Edinburgh, National Library of Scotland (NLS), MS 6396, fo. 13, F. H. Mackenzie to Mrs Mary Mackenzie, 24 February 1793.
11. NRS, GD46/15/1/5/1, Cathleen Proby to F. H. Mackenzie, 5 April 1793.
12. Cookson, *British Armed Nation*, p. 137; Mackillop, A., '*More Fruitful than the Soil': Army, Empire and the Scottish Highlands, 1715–1815* (East Linton, 2000), p. 64.
13. Mackillop, '*More Fruitful than the Soil*', p. 7.
14. NRS, GD46/6/25/6, A. Brodie to A. Mackenzie of Balmudithy, 15 February 1793.

15. Wold, A. L., *Scotland and the French Revolutionary War, 1792–1802* (Edinburgh, 2015), p. 73.

16. NRS, GD46/6/25/9, A. Brodie to H. Dundas, 19 February 1793.

17. NRS, GD427/307/3, F. H. Mackenzie to A. Gillanders, 1 April 1793.

18. Abrams, L., 'The Taming of Highland Masculinity: Inter-personal Violence and Shifting Codes of Manhood, *c*.1760–1840', *The Scottish Historical Review* (*SHR*), vol. 92, 1, 2013, pp. 101, 108, 121.

19. NRS, GD427/307/1, P. Fairbairn to A. Gillanders, 18 March 1793.

20. NRS, GD46/17/3, G. Gillanders to F. H. Mackenzie, 21 March 1793.

21. NRS, GD46/17/3, G. Gillanders to F. H. Mackenzie, 19 June 1793.

22. NLS, MS 6396, fo. 15, F. H. Mackenzie to Mrs Mary Mackenzie, 25 March 1793.

23. NRS, GD46/17/3, P. Fairbairn to F. H. Mackenzie, 27 March 1793.

24. NRS, GD427/307/2, Draft memo in George Gillanders's hand re. recruiting for the 78th Regiment in Lewis, 31 March 1793.

25. Hunter, J., *Set Adrift Upon the World: The Sutherland Clearances* (Edinburgh, 2015), pp. 143–4.

26. Mackillop, '*More Fruitful than the Soil*', pp. 146–7.

27. Richards, E., *A History of the Highland Clearances: Agrarian Transformation and the Evictions, 1750–1886* (London, 1982), p. 153; Richards, E. and Clough, M., *Cromartie: Highland Life 1650–1914* (Aberdeen, 1989), pp. 11–12; Taylor, D., *The Wild Black Region: Badenoch 1750–1800* (Edinburgh, 2016), pp. 230–1.

28. Mackillop, '*More Fruitful than the Soil?*', pp. 142–4.

29. NRS, GD427/307/4, MS annotation to printed 'instructions for officers recruiting for Seaforth's Highlanders'.

30. NRS, GD46/14/4, Notes of dates of birth and christening of the children of Lord and Lady Seaforth.

31. Logue, K. J., *Popular Disturbances in Scotland, 1780–1815* (Edinburgh, 1979), pp. 17–20.

32. NRS, RH2/4/207/465–7, F. H. Mackenzie to Lord A. Gordon, 27 April 1793.

33. NRS, GD427/307/4, 'Head Quarters instructions for the officers recruiting for Seaforth's Highlanders', n.d., but annotated 1793.

34. NRS, RH2/4/71/238–40, D. Macleod to R. Blair, 23 May 1793.

35. Macdonald, D., *Lewis: A History of the Island* (Edinburgh, 1978), p. 117.

36. NRS, GD46/4/232/2, R. Dundas to D. Macleod, 31 May 1793.
37. NRS, GD46/4/232/1, D. Macleod to F. H. Mackenzie, 12 June 1793.
38. Macdonald, *Lewis*, p. 117.
39. NRS, RH2/4/71/300–1, F. H. Mackenzie to Lord A. Gordon, 30 June 1793.
40. NRS, GD427/307/4, MS annotation to printed 'instructions for officers recruiting for Seaforth's Highlanders'.
41. Mackillop, A., 'The Outer Hebrides during the Wars of Empire and Revolution, 1790–1815' in *Island Heroes: The Military History of the Hebrides* (South Lochs, 2010), pp. 26–7.
42. NLS, MS 6396, fo. 19, F. H. Mackenzie to Mrs Mary Mackenzie, 17 June 1793.
43. *Diary or Woodfall's Register*, 21 June 1793, British Library Burney Collection of 17th and 18th Century Newspapers online (BCN), accessed 9 December 2010.
44. NRS, GD46/17/3, P. Fairbairn to Col. A. Mackenzie, 2 September 1793.
45. NRS, GD46/17/3, A. Gillanders to F. H. Mackenzie, 20 May 1794.
46. NLS, MS 6396, fo. 19, F. H. Mackenzie to Mrs Mary Mackenzie, 17 June 1793.
47. *Lloyd's Evening Post*, 27 January 1794 (BCN), accessed 9 December 2010.
48. NRS, GD46/17/3, G. Gillanders to F. H. Mackenzie, 28 December 1793.
49. *Lloyd's Evening Post*, 3 January 1794 (BCN), accessed 9 December 2010.
50. NRS, GD427/301/2, Printed Crown commission for raising 2nd Battalion, 78th Regiment.
51. Hague, W., *William Pitt the Younger* (London, 2004), pp. 345–9.
52. NRS, GD46/17/13, P. Fairbairn to F. H. Mackenzie, 1 March 1794.
53. NRS, GD46/17/4/373, Lord Seaforth to Sir H. Munro, 28 June 1799.
54. Mackillop, '*More Fruitful than the Soil*', p. 144.
55. NRS, GD427/307/7, 'Instructions for inlisting men for 2nd Bttn, 78th Regt.', 20 May 1794; London, British Library (BL) Add. MS 39200, fo. 107, F. H. Mackenzie to J. R. Mackenzie, 12 February 1794.
56. Taylor, *The Wild Black Region*, p. 230.
57. Mackillop, '*More Fruitful than the Soil*', pp. 145–6.
58. NRS, GD46/17/11, C. Mackenzie to J. Gibson, 17 December 1798.
59. Mackillop, '*More Fruitful than the Soil*', pp. 158–9.

60. Carr, R., 'The Gentleman and the Soldier: Patriotic Masculinities in Eighteenth-Century Scotland', *Journal of Scottish Historical Studies*, vol. 28 (2008), pp. 120–1.
61. NRS, GD46/17/20, C. Mackenzie to F. H. Mackenzie, 10 January 1801.
62. NRS, GD46/17/19/79, /82–3, C. Mackenzie to F. H. Mackenzie, 27 April 1801; see also Mackillop, *More Fruitful than the Soil'*, pp. 160–1.
63. Maclean, M., *The People of Glengarry: Highlanders in Transition, 1745–1820* (Montreal and Kingston, 1991), pp. 130–1.
64. NRS, GD46/17/3, P. Fairbairn to F. H. Mackenzie, 1 March 1794.
65. NRS, GD46/17/3, G. Gillanders, reporting advice from A. Gillanders, to F. H. Mackenzie, 21 July 1794.
66. NRS, GD46/17/3, P. Fairbairn to Mrs Mary Mackenzie, 27 March 1794.
67. Castle Fraser, Mackenzie Fraser Papers (C. F. Papers), F. A. Chapman to Maj. Gen. A. Mackenzie Fraser, 31 July 1804.
68. *Sun*, 22 July 1794 (BCN), accessed 9 December 2010.
69. Taylor, *Wild Black Region*, p. 230.
70. BL, Add. MS 39195, fos 67–8, F. H. Mackenzie to J. R. Mackenzie of Suddie, 1 December 1794.
71. BL, Add. MS 39195, fos 70–1, Col. F. H. Mackenzie to Major J. R. Mackenzie, 15 March 1795.
72. Cookson, *British Armed Nation*, pp. 130, 136.
73. Mackillop, '*More Fruitful than the Soil*', p. 137.
74. NRS, GD46/17/4/323–5, '1794 Francis Humberston Mackenzie Esq of the 78th Regt. to Alex Ross' (account).
75. C. F. Papers, F. H. Mackenzie to Lt Col. A. Mackenzie, 16 February 1796.
76. NRS, GD46/17/15, C. Mackenzie to Col. F. H. Mackenzie, 22 January 1796.
77. Nenadic, S., (ed.), *Scots in London in the Eighteenth Century* (Lewisburg, 2010), p. 239.
78. NRS, GD46/17/11, F. H. Mackenzie to H. Donaldson, 14 July 1795.
79. BL, Add. MS 39195, fo. 71, Col. F. H. Mackenzie to Major J. R. Mackenzie, 15 March 1795.
80. NRS, GD46/17/4/326, 'Seaforth, State of account with H. Donaldson, to 30 April 1796.
81. C. F. Papers, Lt Col. A. Mackenzie to F. H. Mackenzie, 18 February 1796.
82. Cookson, *British Armed Nation*, pp. 147–8.
83. NRS, GD51/1/658/2, A. Mackenzie to F. H. Mackenzie, 27 September 1795; GD51/1/658/1, A. Brodie to H. Dundas, 7 October 1795.

84. NRS, GD46/17/15, A. Mackenzie to F. H. Mackenzie, 9 December 1795.
85. C. F. Papers, 1/22, H. Dundas to F. H. Mackenzie, 4 March 1796.
86. C. F. Papers, F. H. Mackenzie to Lt Col. A. Mackenzie, 30 December 1795.
87. C. F. Papers, F. H. Mackenzie to Lt Col. A. Mackenzie, 15 January 1796.
88. C. F. Papers, Lt Col. A. Mackenzie to F. H. Mackenzie, 18 February 1796 and draft n.d.
89. C. F. Papers, 1/20, W. Adam to F. H. Mackenzie, 10 February 1796.
90. C. F. Papers, 1/21, H. Donaldson to Lt Col. Commandant A. Mackenzie, 4 March 1796.
91. NRS, GD46/17/11, 'Idea for a new Regt.', memo in Seaforth's hand, dated Banff 26 December 1798, no addressee, but clearly to military authorities.
92. Logue, *Popular Disturbances*, p. 76.
93. Cookson, *British Armed Nation*, pp. 142–4.
94. Wold, *Scotland and the French Revolutionary War*, p. 82.
95. NRS, GD46/17/13/131, P. Fairbairn to F. H. Mackenzie, 27 December 1796.
96. Macrae, N., *The Romance of a Royal Burgh: Dingwall's Story of a Thousand Years* (1923, reprint Wakefield: EP Publishing, 1974), pp. 241–2, Dingwall Town Council Minutes, 25 March 1795, 11 August and 10 September 1796.
97. Logue, *Popular Disturbances,* p. 76; Wold, *Scotland and the French Revolutionary War*, pp. 88–91.
98. Taylor, *Wild Black Region*, p. 231.
99. NRS, GD46/17/11, P. Fairbairn to Lord Seaforth, 13 December 1798.
100. Cookson, *British Armed Nation*, pp. 138–9.
101. *Star,* 25 April 1798 (BCN), accessed 6 December 2010.
102. NRS, GD46/17/11, 'Idea for a new Regt.', 26 December 1798.
103. *Star* 24 December 1799; *Morning Herald*, 25 December 1799 (BCN), accessed 6 December 2011.
104. Nenadic, S., *Lairds and Luxury: The Highland Gentry in Eighteenth-Century Scotland* (Edinburgh, 2007), pp. 101, 104–5.
105. *Aberdeen Journal*, 27 January 1800, 19th Century British Library Newspapers online, accessed 3 February 2011.
106. NRS, GD46/17/11, 'Idea for a new Regt.', 26 December 1798.
107. Cookson, *British Armed Nation*, p. 130.
108. Mackillop, *'More Fruitful than the Soil,* p. 137.
109. Taylor, *Wild Black Region*, p. 250.

7 Governor and Captain General

Passage to Barbados

When Lord Seaforth took the oaths as governor of Barbados at St James's Palace on 20 November 1800 he had mixed feelings. As has been shown in Chapter Four, he depended very much on his wife Mira and had a loving relationship with his children. It is doubtful if he could have coped on his own. He proposed to take wife and family with him, except for his elder son and heir, William (at school at Harrow), and his two youngest children. However, yellow fever, dysentry, smallpox and cholera were serious threats in Barbados.[1] Friends and family members were very conscious of the reputation of the West Indies as the white man's grave. In January 1801 his Ross-shire neighbour and friend Edward Satchwell Fraser of Reelig wrote that he hoped 'some happy occurance may occur to prevent Lady Seaforth and your family going abroad. I even hope you may not go' and reminded Seaforth of the dangers of the sea passage and the climate.[2] On 7 February 1801 he was ordered to Portsmouth to join the frigate *Topaz*, the warship which, according to custom, would take him as an imperial governor to his station. On the same day, William Pitt resigned as prime minister, with his government, over the king's refusal to accept Catholic emancipation. Seaforth wrote to Henry Dundas to assure him of his continuing support and offered to resign the governorship if Dundas said he could be useful.[3] Clearly he was clutching at the prospect of some political role at home, but the call from Dundas did not come. On 13 February he boarded the *Topaz* for Barbados.[4]

The passage to Barbados gave Seaforth time to think and write about some of the issues which faced him. In a letter to Charles Greville from the ship he expressed complaints about his personal position, which he was to follow up after he reached the island. As his new titles included captain general, commander-in-chief and vice admiral of Barbados and (as shown in Chapter Six) he had shown an enthusiasm for military leadership, it is not surprising that he hoped for a genuine military role as governor. A straw in the wind was that his request for promotion in the army from lieutenant colonel to brigadier general had been turned down. He complained to Greville that 'when I was ruining myself and my estates to serve the cause [by raising regiments] I was much encouraged, but when I ask that this service may tend a little to my own advantage' he was turned down.[5] There were policy reasons for this, but his disability was undoubtedly a factor. Another aspect of his personal position which concerned him was his salary. A table written in his hand of the salary of the governor of Barbados, part paid in London and part in Barbados, shows a total package of £4,800 in 1694 and only £3,500 in 1801. A note on it expresses his claim that the value of money was now less than half what it had been in 1694 and the cost of living thus doubled. On boarding the *Topaz* he complained to Colonel Sandy of the 'horrid inattention' which he claimed had brought on his 'distresses'.[6] He was also aggrieved by the refusal of the government to pay him outfitting money, which he claimed had been granted to his predecessor at the substantial rate of £1,500. The duke of Portland replied that it had been made clear Governor Ricketts would be the last to receive this.[7] Despite these financial disappointments, he was determined not to accept corrupt payments and wrote to Greville, 'how governors contrive it I do not know, but I much fear I have an enemy in my breast that will not follow the general line, I wish to get what I can fairly.'[8]

He had with him on the ship a lengthy set of 'Extracts from the King's orders and Instructions to Lord Seaforth', apparently written by a secretary in the Colonial Office to highlight particular items. For example, he was to inform himself of the Navigation Acts as they applied to plantation trade and ensure that they were punctually observed.[9] He wrote in his own hand, presumably on the voyage, a 'Rough abstract of instructions as Governor of Barbados'.[10] He found the prospect intimidating and complained to Greville that 'the project before me has quite broken me down and I shall not last long – I will however do my best'.[11] He soon discovered that written instructions issued to West Indian governors were, and had been for some time, highly formulaic and quite at variance with actual constitutional practice.[12] Why this was so and the consequences of the arrival of Lord Seaforth, who (despite his apprehensions) turned out to be an active and energetic governor, will be discussed in this chapter and in Chapters Nine and Ten.

Settling down in Barbados

The Barbados Assembly welcomed the new governor with fine words. At his first formal meeting with them on 14 April the Speaker described him as 'a nobleman whose fair fame comes . . . as combining the manners and dignity of the gentleman with the ability, diligence and conciliatory temper of the statesman, soldier and patriot'. However, they were not inclined to meet his request for an increase in the element of his salary paid in the island. A motion was passed fixing his salary at £3,000, the same as had been paid to Ricketts and to Assembly President Bishop, who had acted during the vacancy. The Speaker regretted that was unavoidable because of 'the visitation of the Almighty by two successive years of drought'. He hoped that this would be received as cordially as it had been offered. Seaforth replied that while 'cheerfully accepting what you are pleased to give . . . I am sorry for your sakes as well as my own for the causes'.[13] It was not a good start.

This less-than-cheerful response was occasioned by the desperation Seaforth felt for his finances (not being yet aware of the sale of the Kintail farms). He wrote in despair to his regimental agent:

> My fate oppresses me and I feel I cannot much longer be answerable for myself or my actions . . . I shall . . . send orders to sell everything I have, land and all and an order for dividing it between my wife and bairns and let them shift . . . it is all over and the straws are snatched from drowning me.[14]

He ordered Peter Fairbairn (now in Barbados and acting as his secretary) to write to Colin Mackenzie that the salary offered by the Barbados Assembly was insufficient to maintain him and his family there and requesting that at least £1,000 of the home salary should be sent across the Atlantic.[15] Colin replied sternly that he must live on the Barbados salary and stay there until it could be replaced by the profits from the plantations he was in the process of buying in Berbice, Guyana. He reminded him that it was not practicable to live on the rents of the Scottish estate and that, despite the revenue from land sales, the debt level was still high.[16] He advised that in the year to Whit 1802 net rents and kelp revenue were expected to total £6,000 and home salary and off reckonings about £2,600. Interest payable on debts was around £5,000, annuities £1,076 and £300 for board of sons William and Francis. Taking into account repayments due, a shortfall of £5,777 was anticipated.[17] Although Reelig wrote that he should 'stay long enough to do justice to your own character and show respect to the King',[18] he was, before long, looking for another job.[19] Greville put his position into context in lobbying on his behalf. He had been unhappy with not being appointed governor of Jamaica and now needed a higher salary than he was receiving. In addition, 'the inactive situation of governor of Barbados made him catch at any opportunity of active employment'. Greville asked that he be given the governorship of Trinidad, captured from Spain and about to become formally a British colony. This would enable 'his abilities and active mind to be employed to avert the serious dangers' anticipated there.[20]

Seaforth was offered no new position. Meantime, he had discovered that his role in Barbados was to be by no means inactive. An officer on a nearby island wrote to him that he seriously wished 'Your Lordship well clear of them [the Barbadians] – the levelling principle they show is too bad'.[21] John Poyer, a spokesperson for white Barbadians, recalled that they were at first inclined to underestimate their new governor:

> It appeared to them to be a kind of insult to be placed under a Commander in Chief whose ears no sound could penetrate and with whom no communication could be maintained but by writing or the fingers; the one too laborious, the other too imperfectly understood to facilitate the business of office.[22]

They may initially have been reassured. He promised Assembly members that 'I shall . . . preserve to you and your constituents all your just and constitutional rights and privileges . . . [and]

unite with you in every measure which tends to preserve the constitutional freedom of and necessary subordination in the Island . . .'[23] However, it soon emerged that the governor's and the Assembly's understanding of these rights and privileges was very different. He did not only seek to secure the subordination of enslaved labourers and free people of colour (which was how his hearers understood that remark), but also of the white islanders to royal authority (meaning the authority of the king's representative, the governor, and the government in Whitehall).[24]

It has been argued that real authority in the British West Indian islands (except for those captured after 1793) was in the early nineteenth century still in the hands of the colonists, as it had been in the previous century, and that the British government was still, in general, content that this should be so.[25] One of the early students of West Indian government argued that Barbados had in the eighteenth century the most complete system of self-government of any of the islands.[26] There was a high percentage of whites among the island's population, 19.3 per cent according to a calculation made in 1801.[27] It has been estimated that by 1807 at least 92 per cent of white Barbadians were creole (born on the island) and that in 1816 the population ratio of black to white was 4.8 to 1 in Barbados compared to 11.5 to 1 in Jamaica.[28] David Lambert has calculated that Barbados's upper-class of substantial planters and professionals represented less than one quarter of the white population and the middle class (lesser planters and merchants and plantation managers) a further quarter. The remainder were 'poor whites', many descended from indentured labourers and prisoners from British civil conflicts.[29] The ancestors of many white Barbadians had been on the island for several generations. For example, the Haynes family, from which came one of Seaforth's allies and one of his most prominent opponents, had been on Barbados and had owned the Newcastle plantation since at least 1643 (sixteen years after the first English settlement). Such longevity in one family was exceptional, but the tenure by the Hinds family of the Collins plantation since 1743 was a common situation.[30] Creole whites had a commitment to the island and to their role in it which was stronger than on other islands, where many whites were short-term sojourners. Their very varying interests were to complicate considerably Seaforth's role as governor.

An elected assembly first met in Barbados in 1639 and the colonists continued to be locked in a seventeenth-century style struggle between executive and legislature.[31] Their argument was that the original settlers (and their descendants) had not lost any of their rights as free-born Englishmen by crossing the Atlantic to colonies which they had established. In 1767 the Speaker of Assembly, Sir John Gay Alleyne, requested the privileges of the Assembly in conformity with those of the imperial House of Commons.[32] Alleyne admitted that Barbados was 'a small island containing only a handful of [free] men . . . [which] could not so much as exist without the constant Protection and Support of some superior state' (namely by Britain to prevent external attack or internal revolt by slaves).[33] Unlike the North American colonists, Barbadians were never going to declare independence. However, there were running battles in the 1770s between the Assembly and Governor Hay over his dismissal of officers of state, trade with the North American colonies after their revolt in 1776, and the island militia. The Assembly proclaimed, using seventeenth-century rhetoric, that they would not 'allow obedience to be enforced by a power congenial only with the habits of despotic sway'. There was total deadlock in relations between the Assembly and Governor James Cunningham for two years over the application of the duty applied to island exports. In 1783 he was recalled and the Assembly was triumphant.[34] The governors of the French islands also faced serious problems if they ignored the wishes of the wealthy planters as expressed in Council. The constitutional theory was different (France, until 1789, being in theory a royal absolutism), but the reality was similar. The governors of Dutch colonies were generally willing to act in co-operation with planters, who chose the members of the colony's Council. The Dutch political system being a decentralised one, the States General had little inclination to exercise a close control of their colonies.[35]

There has been discussion over the relationship between the British government and its West Indian colonies in the late eighteenth century. Arguably the peak of the power of the white settlers was in the 1760s and 1770s. The Jamaica Privilege controversy of 1764–6 was a particularly striking demonstration of the ability of an island assembly to successfully defy the wishes of Whitehall. This was over the right claimed by Assembly members to be immune from arrest (for example for debt) while in session. In 1778 the Declaratory Act, passed during the American War of Independence, gave the West Indian islands authority to levy taxation internally. This can be seen as demonstrating the wish of Parliament to avoid making again the mistakes which had provoked the North American colonists to rebel. However, it has recently been claimed that from the 1780s there was a renewed determination in London to treat colonists as subjects and to ensure that they obeyed.[36] It is certainly true that, thanks to the abolitionist campaign, British opinion was increasingly hostile to colonists who loudly proclaimed their own liberties, while often brutally denying liberty to their slaves. This was made clear in three great parliamentary debates on abolition of the slave trade in 1789, 1791 and 1792, in which the prime minister, William Pitt, professed a personal belief in abolition. However, in 1792, the House of Commons approved only gradual abolition and thus shelved the issue. The outbreak of war with revolutionary France in 1793 reduced support for apparently revolutionary proposals and reinvigorated the bargaining position of West Indian planters, whose product, sugar, played an important part in financing the war effort.[37]

It does not appear that the Westminster government deliberately attempted to increase its control in the years before Seaforth's arrival in Barbados. It did introduce 'West India Regiments' consisting of black troops (slaves compulsorily purchased from their owners) against the strenuous opposition of island assemblies. One of the earliest was raised in Barbados in 1795. John Poyer represented white opinion in protesting that 'should an enemy invade our shores, the arms of the black troops would be employed in murdering their former owners'.[38] Planters also resented losing valuable members of their labour force. However, the government's motivation was to provide sufficient troop numbers in an important but unhealthy theatre of war. It attempted to conciliate the white population by distributing soldiers on a ratio of two white men to one black man in each garrison.[39] Seaforth's predecessor, George Ricketts, did not attempt to increase Westminster control. He was described by John Poyer as 'a chief who governed by their affections . . . and the most perfect concord presided over the public councils'. He was for the most part accommodating to the interests of the white inhabitants and the wishes of the Assembly[40] and was described in private by Seaforth as 'a mean cowardly fellow'.[41]

The Barbados Assembly consisted of twenty-two members (two from each parish) elected annually by male owners of ten acres of land or property with a taxable value of £10 per annum.[42] Its power rested on its increasing control over taxation and public expenditure. All money bills originated with it, and it claimed a veto on amendments. It appointed the treasurer, the comptroller and all the collectors of the island revenue. It created boards and commissions under its control to supervise expenditure, thus severely limiting the governor's spending powers. It resisted any attempt by governors to initiate legislation.[43] It denied that the colony's constitution was founded solely on the king's commission to the governor, and became what has been called 'one of the most powerful representative bodies in the American colonies'.[44] It has been argued that in Barbados a governor's executive power was 'little more than sufficient negative voice in government to maintain British interests' and much more limited than was implied by his commission and official instructions as the king's representative.[45]

Seaforth was not the man to accept such limitations, despite his unhappiness about his appointment. He was unfortunate to arrive in Barbados at a time when the islanders were not used to the governor being an active executive. Relations between the island legislature and Seaforth, who turned out to be assertive and sometimes domineering, were thus likely to be fractious. He had little difficulty working with the island Council, composed of twelve members chosen from prominent planters and merchants and appointed by the Crown on governors' recommendations.[46] However, he soon formed the opinion that the Assembly had excessive powers and that it was trying to extend them. As early as May 1801 Seaforth alleged to the secretary of state that there was a 'most persevering struggle in the Assembly here to assume the whole Executive as well as Legislative powers' and this complaint became a regular feature of his despatches to Whitehall.[47]

Seaforth within his first few months in office worked out what he wanted to secure from the Assembly and made his views clear to them in two addresses. On 12 May he argued for measures to make better provision for aged and destitute free people of colour (mostly freed slaves and their descendants). He had been much affected by beholding the miserable state of such people, and felt action was required for the good of the country and called for by common humanity.[48] Seaforth was to devote much effort to attempting to improve the legal position of free people of colour. However, many Assembly members feared them as potential leaders of a slave revolt and as business rivals.[49] On 28 July he requested the establishment of a properly regulated police for Bridgetown and other towns and for country areas, but especially to curb the 'licentious, riotous and vicious' elements in the capital, Bridgetown.[50] This continued to be a concern. He later complained to the secretary of state that, while the lack of an effective police permitted among urban slaves 'a spirit of insolence and insubordination', this was provoked by 'the most barbarous and insulting oppression of the blacks and coloured people by the refuse of the whites'.[51]

Also on 28 July, Seaforth made his most contentious proposal of all, that the murder of any persons (free or slave) should become a felony without benefit of clergy, in other words that a white person should be hanged for the murder of a slave. He argued that this had already been enacted by neighbouring islands and that 'the Mother Country' was astonished it had not been done long ago.[52] This was not in his written instructions, but it is clear that he came to Barbados with orders to secure such an Act. In 1802 he emphasised to the secretary of state, Lord Hobart, that on this matter he was 'backed by the Instructions of the Sovereign at the instance of the Legislature of Great Britain'.[53] The government was under pressure from abolitionists over Barbados's intransigence on this issue. Seaforth also had a strong personal commitment to passing this legislation for humanitarian reasons.

To interfere with the relationship between the planters, who controlled the Assembly, and their slaves appeared to them to threaten the system on which their prosperity was based. That a mighty metropolitan campaign against that institution was now well established made the feeling of threat much greater. It may be taken as evidence of Seaforth's reforming zeal and humanitarian credentials that he laid before the Assembly so soon such a wide-ranging set of measures. An alternative view might be that he demonstrated arrogance, a lack of skill in political tactics and a failure to understand the island's constitutional history in asking so much of the Assembly so soon. What is certainly the case is that these proposals set the scene for a struggle with many members of the Assembly which dominated the whole period of his governorship.

Figure 7.1 *Slaves in Barbadoes*, c.1807–8, by R. Stennett. Their huts are in foreground, a sugar mill and planter's house in background. Representing an idealised view of plantation life, they are shown at work and play. (Copyright National Maritime Museum, Greenwich, London, Michael Graham-Stewart Slavery Collection. Acquired with the assistance of the Heritage Lottery Fund, E9895.)

Seaforth got off to a bad start also with the military commanders on Barbados. As has been seen above, his multiple titles of captain general, commander-in-chief and vice admiral gave him a real hope that he would secure an element of military leadership. He demanded information on the number of troops on the island and of troop movements in what the senior army officer, Brigadier General Romer, complained was an imperious manner. Romer refused the information and indicated that he regarded himself as entirely independent of the governor. Little more than a month after his arrival, Seaforth complained to the under secretary of state, that 'it would indeed be a strange thing to have a Governor in Chief here over whom every . . . Brigadier that came to the island was to be viceroy'.[54] Romer's superior officer, Lieutenant General Thomas Trygge, commander-in-chief in the eastern Caribbean, advised him uncompromisingly, 'Your Lordship derives no authority over the troops from your military rank – your situation is exactly similar to that of other civil governors who hold no commission in the army.'[55] Seaforth found himself in the middle of an ongoing dispute in the area over military jurisdiction between the civil administration and the military command. The military believed that in wartime it was essential to have a unified control of all forces. It was supported by the government, whose main concern was military success in what was a major theatre of the French Revolutionary and Napoleonic Wars.[56] There had been rivalry between Governor Parry of Barbados and the military commander in the late 1780s and early 1790s, but in recent years President Bishop and Governor Ricketts had not been inclined to press this issue.[57] Lord Hobart made clear to Seaforth that the civil governor could give orders for the marching of troops only in a situation in which no orders had been given by senior officers (for example, because they were absent or incapacitated).[58] Seaforth was unhappy with Hobart's decision that all he was entitled to was to receive the troop numbers. He wrote to Trygge, 'had I been honoured with the military command in my own Government it would have made me both proud and happy . . . but I know my duty too well to repine.' However, he complained that Romer still was not giving him the figures, and continued to argue his case. He asked what was to be done if an enemy should appear. Seaforth's argument was that, as his instructions specified how and why he should declare martial law, should he not command the troops thus mobilised? In the same letter he complained there was 'a wish in the Military to throw civil governors into the background'.[59] He instigated his friend William Adam to take the matter up with the Duke of York, the commander-in-chief. The answer was that 'Government had come to a determination to keep the two powers [civil and military] separate'.[60] Nevertheless, he came back again and again to the issue of command in the event of an invasion (by no means an impossible event).[61] He wrote to Romer, 'you have mistaken my character widely if you think any difficulty or mortification can make me give up a point when I hold it my duty to maintain it.'[62] He claimed in 1804 that co-operation with the military was one of his most important and pleasant duties. However, he added frankly that he must 'keep perfect and entire the powers of the Commission His Majesty entrusted to me . . . I am resolved never to voluntarily allow diminution of these'.[63] This determination to insist on every power contained in the governor's commission was contrary to current constitutional practice throughout the British Caribbean and explains many of the controversies which surrounded his governorship. It also seems clear that his military experience and ambitions, explained in Chapters One and Six, exacerbated the tension liable to arise between civil and military authorities in the British Caribbean.

The new governor very quickly got into dispute also with the naval authorities. The issue in this case was the 600 or 700 prisoners of war on the island. He feared that the prisoners were in a very mutinous state[64] and proposed a prisoner exchange with the French in Guadeloupe. This horrified the naval commander, Rear Admiral Duckworth, who protested that the French would be given back valuable seamen.[65] Sometimes in the colonies warrant and petty officers were excluded from exchanges, being experienced seamen they were the most difficult to replace.[66] Some sort of compromise seems to have been made and Duckworth agreed to an exchange. Perhaps because of his naval background, Seaforth was keen to avoid offence and assured Duckworth that all deference would be paid to his wishes for the good of the service.[67] Characteristically, he was unwilling to drop the issue of who had responsibility for POWs and asked the secretary of state that he should either be given clear responsibility for them or that they should be removed from the terms of his commission.[68] The net result was that within two months of his arrival he had alarmed both the local military and naval commanders.

Battling the militia

It has been shown above that soon after his arrival in Barbados in 1805 Seaforth began to alarm substantial elements in the island Assembly and in the wider white community. The most important reason was his strong personal mission to implement the government's policy that the murder of a slave by a white person should be a capital offence. This came to a head in the passing of the Slaves Protection Act in 1805 and the subsequent crisis over his allegedly illegal declaration of Martial Law when invasion threatened. These will be addressed in Chapters Nine and Ten. However, there were two other issues on which he struggled with white Barbadians before 1805, which will be considered in this chapter. The first was his attempts to reform the island militia, which threatened the privileges of many Assembly members.

Soon after his arrival, Seaforth received a very clear and damning account of the Barbados militia in a public letter from 'A Barbadian'. The author of the letter argued that in most parishes the militia had degenerated into an undisciplined rabble and become convivial clubs: 'The Gentlemen who compose these clubs are much less attentive to the manual and platoon exercises than to those of the glass. They manage their knives and forks with infinitely more dexterity than they do their swords'.[69] The author of this letter was John Poyer, an outspoken newspaper controversialist. This period saw the emergence of a two-party system among white Barbadians. The 'Salmagundis', of whom Poyer was to become a leading member, represented owners of the many small plantations, but owning ten acres or more and thus qualifying for the franchise, and less substantial merchants. They resisted the dominance of the large planters in the Assembly.[70] The 'Pumpkins' defended the great planters' interests, had a feeling of class superiority and accused the Salmagundis of 'levelling principles'.[71] It is no surprise that Poyer blamed the inadequacies of the militia on the behaviour of its regimental colonels, many of whom were large-scale planters and Assembly members. He accused them of creating as a means of patronage 'an indefinite number of nominee and superfluous officers', many of whom were given a military title but were exempted from front-line duty.

Seaforth could see with his own eyes the deficiencies of the militia. His commission authorised him to 'levy arms, muster command and employ all persons residing on the Island . . . for resisting and withstanding of all Enemies, Pirates and Rebels'.[72] His Instructions required him to 'take care that the Planters and Christian servants be well and fitly armed and that they be [en] listed under good officers and properly mustered and trained'.[73] In theory, he was commander of the island militia, but the Assembly laid down regulations on the sort of men who could be appointed. The Assembly also voted the funds to pay for weapons, equipment and fortifications, limited the time militia-men could be called on for training and specified the circum-stances in which martial law could be declared and the militia called out.[74] Regular complaints by Seaforth about the state of the island's fortifications[75] suggest that the Barbados Assembly was not prepared to make as large a financial investment in internal and external defence as in Jamaica.[76]

Seaforth wasted no time in trying to initiate reform. In August 1801 he insisted to the militia colonels that returns to him should be 'exactly according to order and that he shall look on all presented to him in other shapes as breaches of military discipline'.[77] Within days he realised that any attempt by him to control the militia caused offence to its colonels and, therefore, to a significant number of the Assembly. Of the twenty-two Assembly members six (representing six of the eleven parishes) were also militia colonels in 1802.[78] They were unwilling to send him the reports he requested. The colonels also resented any appearance of interference from the commanders of the royal forces, who would be in overall command in the event of an invasion. In Seaforth's view, lack of a unified effort had caused the disastrous failure to crush the revolt in Grenada in 1795 of slaves and French settlers. For a year Grenada was effectively, as he put it, 'a black republic under arms'.[79] The commanding officer had been unsuccessful in persuading the British planters to mobilise their loyal slaves into fighting units, and the Scottish governor, Ninian Home, had been murdered.[80]

In the autumn of 1802, Seaforth returned to the militia issue. As an experienced raiser of regiments, he was offended by the disproportionate number of officers in many of the parish militias. He pointed out to the secretary of state that, whereas the 1,500 royal troops had seven field officers, the militia of 3,000 men had 50 field officers.[81] He asked the Assembly to revise the current Militia Act, dating from 1799, to ensure that the number of officers be related to the size of each parish regiment, that uniforms be on a standard pattern and that appointment of officers and discipline should be in the hands of the king (in effect the governor). He argued that what was in practice the power of colonels to appoint officers gave them 'an opportunity of protecting a great number of people from the fair operation of the Militia Laws by giving them nominal commissions'. He sent a list of the 208 officers of the militia regiment, which included a colonel, a lieutenant colonel, a major, eight captains, ten lieutenants, six ensigns, two adjutants, two quartermasters and three surgeons.[82] This made it impossible for the militia to 'act with cordiality' with the royal forces. For example, a colonel in the royal forces would not defer to a militia general.[83]

Seaforth assured the secretary of state that the new bill would be built on the principles he had laid out. However, he seriously underestimated the powers of procrastination of the supporters in the Assembly of the existing militia order. He agreed to the Assembly's request that, because the existing law expired so soon (December 1802), the 1799 Act should be extended for a further year.[84] The current Peace of Amiens with France hardly helped his argument for urgency. The ambivalence of Whitehall on the issue soon emerged. Lord Hobart agreed that something should be done and praised Seaforth for the way he had proceeded. However, he advised that the governor should consult the colonels, the holders of patronage under the unreformed system, before submitting the question formally to the Assembly. He was unwilling to quarrel with the Assembly to reform what he believed to be a useless force.[85] The later view of the local commander of the royal forces was that, if the enemy appeared, the militia should be confined to a remote part of the island.[86] Seaforth found the failure to carry a new militia bill frustrating, not only because of the terms of his Commission and Instructions, but also because (as shown in Chapter Six) he had more control of the two battalions of the 78th Regiment which he raised in Scotland.

He had his allies. John Beckles, recently appointed by him chief justice, claimed in a speech in 1803 that Seaforth, 'by his rank and dignified deportment ... [and] the zeal and anxiety which he on every occasions displays' commanded respect. He hoped that, in view of the resumption of war with France at the end of the Peace of Amiens, all would contribute to making the militia 'as respectable and formidable for its discipline and good order as it is for its numbers'.[87] Seaforth pointed out that the establishment of the royal forces on the island of the eastern Caribbean headquarters made attack more likely and asked the Assembly to 'make our means of defence as respectable as possible'.[88] This was another request for the passing of a new Militia Act and by June he was making detailed suggestions.[89] Discussions again proceeded slowly. In early November 1803 Seaforth returned to the UK on sick leave,[90] and while he was away the 1799 Militia Act was twice extended.[91]

The *Barbados Mercury and Bridgetown Gazette* in early 1805 illustrated the state of the militia almost five years after Seaforth began campaigning for its reform. At a review by the governor a young militiaman by accident shot off a finger of one of his comrades. None of the numerous medical staff attached to the regiment had attended. The editor also appealed to young men of the militia to stop firing off their muskets in town as it was 'discreditable to themselves as soldiers and dangerous to the community'.[92] In early March, by which time a French fleet had appeared in the West Indies and was attacking British islands, the editor complained, 'we fritter out our Militia into numerous regiments and create supernumerary officers with useless rank. We want discipline.'[93] This could almost have been dictated by Seaforth, who argued to the Assembly that what was needed was system and discipline.[94] The Militia Act expired on 6 March. What was passed was again mainly a renewal of the 1799 Act. In one respect, through fear of the French fleet, it appeared to increase his authority. Whereas the 1799 Act permitted the governor to declare martial law only when enemy ships were in sight, this one allowed him to do so 'upon receiving information that an enemy's fleet is at sea, and that from the course it was steering, there would be no doubt in his mind that this island was likely to be attacked'. However, the effect of this was seriously limited by the provision that it would remain in force only for thirty days.[95] When it expired in early April, the French threat seemed to have passed. As a result it was the more restrictive 1799 Act which was now repeated, to be in force for six months.[96] It was not until over a month later that news came that a new and larger enemy fleet had arrived in the West Indies.[97] That it was the more restrictive Militia Act which was now in force was one of the factors which led to the greatest crisis in Seaforth's governorship, as will be explained in Chapter Ten.

Battling the island's officials and US trade

One of the early obstacles which surprised and annoyed Seaforth in Barbados was that he was unable to get copies of important documents such as previous Assembly and Council minutes. He complained to the secretary of state, 'There appears on this island . . . a most irregular and desultory method of conducting every branch of the public duty.' He was determined to ensure that 'public duties must not be assumed without being performed' and expected that he would have to make examples of two or three lax officials.[98] One was John Thomson, the auditor general. Seaforth saw from the accounts that 'very great irregularities existed in that department'. He threatened that cases of unpaid fines should come before him, which resulted in a prompt payment of arrears.[99]

The auditor general was one of the island officials appointed by the governor. With many other officials it was much more difficult for him to call them to task. A large number of government officers in Barbados were appointed by the Assembly or were deputies of UK based 'officials'. The latter had received their posts by patent as government patronage and had no intention of serving personally. Their deputies were mostly white Barbadians, often connected to Assembly members, over whom the governor had the ultimate power of suspension, but no control over day-to-day administration.[100] Spain attempted to address a similar problem around 1790 by replacing creole officials with men from Spain.[101] However, the British government was not inclined to interfere as long as the effective prosecution of the war was unimpeded. It has been suggested that Seaforth, without previous Caribbean experience, did not understand this, and asked successive secretaries of state to interfere in the internal administration of Barbados in ways they were unwilling to do.[102] It will be argued here that Seaforth understood very well how government had been conducted in Barbados and was determined to change it to increase the authority of the governor.

Seaforth's understanding of the distinction between the theoretical and the actual method of governing Barbados was shown in 1803. The Committee of the Privy Council for Trade queried his approval of an Act of Assembly appointing a temporary island treasurer (the post holder being on sick leave). He remarked that appointment by the Assembly 'has been so long submitted to that it is grown into a common usage ... my instructions from the King explicitly forbid me to encroach on the patronage of the Assembly'.[103] However, he was determined to gain some measure of control over officials appointed by patentees, whose revenue came mainly from payment of fees. This issue had come to a head in 1802, when Lord Dulcie, a patent holder as Provost Marshall (executive officer of the courts), gave to Sir Philip Gibbes, a member of the white plantocracy, a power of attorney to appoint and dismiss his deputy. This would give him supervisory powers over the deputy. It was alleged that patentees effectively auctioned the office to those who would pay most with no regard to qualifications. Seaforth argued that he should judge the qualifications of the nominee, assuring the secretary of state that he would 'object to no appointment ... where the character and abilities of the parties were equal to the appointments'.[104] Once the deputy was appointed, he claimed that only he should be able to remove him. If the patentee had the 'unlimited and despotic power of removing at pleasure the various and important officers of government ... [they] would be to all intents the real ruling power of the colony'.[105] There was a clause in Seaforth's instructions empowering him to inspect and enquire into the behaviour of all deputies and to suspend in case of misdemeanour. However, it is highly questionable at this period whether his instructions were intended to be fully and literally applied. Whitehall's judgement was that the patentee was entitled to appoint and remove his deputy as he saw fit, but the governor was judge of whether a suitably qualified person had been nominated and had the power to reject or suspend an insufficient deputy.[106] The patentees had received their posts as political patronage and had to be kept on side in the UK. However, that it was confirmed that the governor had some rights over the deputies may be a sign that Whitehall was beginning to be less comfortable with devolved government in slave-owning colonies such as Barbados. Seaforth, who had skilfully manipulated the patronage system to help control Ross-shire elections, was frustrated that the patronage available to him in Barbados was limited. He complained that the government was actually giving Barbados posts to his opponents.[107]

Seaforth continued to be frustrated in his dealings with government officers. In August 1805 he complained to Whitehall that 'from indolent and in my opinion ill judged (not to say criminal) indulgence, almost every department under Government in these parts seems to have imbibed an idea that they are uncontrollable except from home'.[108] One of his bitterest contests was with the customs-house officers. Here there was a fundamental difference over trade laws and economic policy, and not merely protocol. As shown in Chapter Two, the limited commercialism applied to his Highland estate showed that he did not share Adam Smith's belief in the free play of the market. His conservative world view included support for mercantilism, which, it has been claimed, 'legitimized commercial war, economic nationalism and rampant protectionism'.[109] His belief was that, where possible, goods should be supplied 'by British merchants in British bottoms [ships], and I think that ... in a British colony they are entitled to the preference'.[110] However, he had to attempt to balance the instructions of the metropolitan government and the legislation of the Westminster parliament with the often competing interests of the Barbados planters and the Bridgetown merchants.[111] The exclusion of the USA in 1783 from the protection of the Navigation Acts presented potentially critical problems for the British West Indian islands. They required North American timber for the barrels in which their sugar and rum were exported and provisions to feed their slaves, and the US was the cheapest source of supply.[112] Despite new Navigation Acts requiring the use of British produce delivered in British ships, the practical effects were variable. While imports of salt beef, pork and pickled fish from the US to the British West Indies had almost disappeared by 1793, in that year imports of American corn continued at a little over half the 1773 level and imports of flour and meal were hardly reduced at all. Critically for the planters, imports of American shingles and staves to make barrels reduced by only a quarter in aggregate between 1773 and 1793.[113] From the outbreak of war with France in 1793 American imports shot up and by 1800 were higher in all these categories than in 1773, except for pickled fish. It has long been known that the French Revolutionary War resulted in a breakdown of the system of restricted American trade with the British West Indies.[114] Between 1793 and 1800 imports of American corn, flour and meal almost doubled. The imperial requirement was now to maximise the output of Caribbean sugar to bolster the credit on which the war was being fought. The danger to British shipping through enemy action made it expedient to ensure security of supply of slave provisions and barrel timber in neutral (mainly American) vessels.[115]

This was the situation when Seaforth arrived in Barbados. He began to take an interest in trade with the USA in April 1802, when he enquired of the customs officers about its statutory basis. Samuel Reddish, the comptroller at Bridgetown, replied frankly that 'the whole system of the American trade to this country is in evident contradiction to every act of Parliament'. Only the governor's permission enabled the statutes to be bypassed. Seaforth's predecessors had done this by public proc-lamation, and Reddish clearly expected that the new gover-nor would do likewise.[116] The Shipping Returns show that the greater part of the grain and lumber imported to Barbados came from the US. In early 1802 (1 January to 19 February) sixteen American-registered ships arrived in Barbados. All of these carried some combination of the products planters needed – wooden staves and hoops, corn, flour and bread, salt beef, pork and fish and horses. This is true also of two American ships re-registered in Portsmouth within the previous six weeks. One Barbados-registered ship brought timber and corn from the US. While thirteen British ships brought some combination of these products from home or colonial ports, these did not constitute the greater part of their cargoes. More common cargoes for the thirty-seven British ships which arrived in this period were foodstuffs such as butter and cheese, various dry and luxury goods, and large quantities of bricks (probably for the new bar-racks being built to enable Barbados to become the army head-quarters for the eastern Caribbean).[117] This indicates that, while the Navigation Acts were not a dead letter, there was a degree of collusion by officials in Barbados and the UK in breaking them and at this point also acquiescence by Seaforth.

The issue came to a head on 5 September 1804 after Pitt's gov-ernment by Order in Council prohibited West Indian governors from opening their ports to goods from the USA which were not permitted by law 'except in cases of real and very great necessity'.[118] The influence of the West India planters with the imperial government appears to have been weakening, while that of British merchants and shipowners appears to have been rising. In part this may have been because the campaigns of British abolitionists damaged the image of the planters in the imperial parliament. The abolitionists attacked British protectionism on the basis of Adam Smith's argument that the slave system was economically inefficient. However, as the 1804 Order in Council showed, Pitt was no free trader.[119] Seaforth, as governor, was the point where free trade and mercantilism collided and served as arbiter between rival interests in Barbados. The planters asserted their right to obtain from America essential goods which could not be adequately supplied from British sources.[120] The Bridgetown merchants claimed American goods had been landed because they were cheaper, although there was not a shortage and the stores were full of (more expensive) British sourced articles.[121] This rivalry between merchants and planters was traditional in the British Caribbean.[122]

Shortly before the government's Order in Council was received in 1804, Seaforth made clear his personal preference for protectionism. Believing that there was now a good supply of provisions supplied by British merchants in British ships, he issued a proclamation on 16 October 1804 shutting the port against the admission of all articles of American provision and fish (corn and flour excepted). This, he believed, would give ships carrying sugar to Britain an outward cargo and thus reduce their freight rates. He was astonished by 'the torrent of obloquy and abuse that burst out against me'. Remonstrances came from almost every parish on the island, and at one of the parochial meetings a protester exclaimed, '"Mother Country"!! America is the natural mother of these colonies.' The island Council, usually supportive, presented a unanimous petition against his 16 October proclamation. Seaforth was aware that he could expect no aid from the Assembly and reminded the secretary of state that 'all these description are planters . . . and on the subject of the American intercourse [feelings] ran so high that those who were at other times the most impartial lost their tempers'. Showing either strength of character or obstinacy, he hoped to tough it out. At this juncture (on 17 October) the Order in Council providentially arrived and offered a compromise.[123] On 23 October he issued a new proclamation, which made clear that all forms of lumber, grain, bread and flour and livestock 'as being of the first necessity and such as the colony cannot exist without' (thus permissible within the Order in Council) could be imported from the United States on neutral vessels. But he stuck to his guns on salt meat and fish, which had to come from British sources.[124] He claimed to the secretary of state, 'I am happy to see good humour pretty generally restored.' This was an optimistic judgement.[125] When in the following year tension between governor and Assembly reached crisis point, it was evident that wounds over American trade had not healed and remained a major cause of grievance.

How far was American trade actually reduced by the Order in Council and Seaforth's subsequent proclamation? The official Shipping Returns, used above for the year 1802, are not extant for 1804–5. However, for 1805 they can, to some extent, be replaced by the 'marine and commercial intelligence' reports in the *Barbados Mercury and Bridgetown Gazette*, although these are unlikely to be as accurate. These show, between 4 January and 19 February 1805, thirty-five American and thirty-two British ships arriving at Bridgetown. Where the cargo of the American ships is given, the products are similar to those listed in the 1802 Shipping Returns: lumber, New England shingles, flour and bread, cattle and horses. The number of American and British arrivals was now roughly similar, whereas in the corresponding period in 1802 Americans were only half the British total.[126] This suggests that between 1802 and 1805 the balance of trade had, if anything, swung away from goods and ships from British territories.

After he attempted to curtail American imports, Seaforth became involved in frequent and acrimonious disagreements with customs-house officers Hew Dalrymple, the collector, and Samuel Reddish, the comptroller. Although they were appointed directly by the Crown, they were active supporters of the planters in trying to maximise trade with the United States (along, it has been alleged, with many other West Indian customs officers).[127] Dalrymple, who himself owned a plantation[128], argued to Seaforth that, if it was not possible for corn and grain to be brought from America in American ships, it would hardly be worth having an estate on Barbados and that government revenue would suffer. Planters would have to use a significant part of their land to grow provisions for their slaves and correspondingly would have less sugar to export and on which to pay duty.[129] Seaforth explained to the under secretary of state that 'they have become displeased with my conduct on American and other neutrals'. He also argued with the customs-house officers over who should authorise the landing of passengers from neutral ships. In May 1805 he complained to the secretary of state about them, enclosing the extensive correspondence and pointing out his difficulties in attempting to implement Camden's circular.[130] By June, Seaforth was claiming that all officers were liable to enforce his legal orders and the customs officers were arguing that in revenue matters they were responsible only to the commissioners of customs in London.[131] By September they were stating that they would not work with this governor.[132] Unusually, Whitehall took some action to support him in dealing with these officials. Because his agenda coincided with its own, the Board of Customs in London reprimanded Dalrymple and Reddish for preference given to American imports.[133] However, the government did not take any general action to increase the governor's authority over the officials he did not appoint. Seaforth wrote to the secretary of state, 'I knew before I came out that the Governor had no patronage,' (not entirely true) and complained that recently offices in the gift of the government had been given to members of the Barbados Assembly and their friends who were his most active opponents.[134] Being used to the Westminster system of patronage, he found it difficult to operate a system in which the executive had limited means of lubricating the political process.

The issue of US trade demonstrates that the metropole was wary of imposing on a long-established settlement colony an economic policy unpopular with its leading members. With the issue of slave rights in Barbados coming to a climax and in view of more general debates on the slave trade, it appears that ministers preferred not be battling with the Barbados planters on another front. The energy with which Seaforth tried to pursue the trade issue, contrary to the most powerful local interests and in advance of government instructions, demonstrates that he really believed in the restriction of trade to British producers, British ships and British merchants. It is not surprising that when he finally left Barbados it was the merchants of Bridgetown who sent him a complimentary address.[135] He had grievously offended the planters, the most powerful interest on the island, on three fronts – attempting to reform the militia, trying to impede trade between the island and the USA and, as will be explained in Chapter Nine, by insisting on a slaves protection act.

The governor at home

The more prominent islanders must have become very familiar with the interior of Pilgrim, the governor's residence, and with his heroic entertaining. In Barbados, Seaforth justified his long-standing urge to impress by arguing that the king's representative needed to be respected.[136] He also wished to woo influential opponents to his policies on US trade and the legal rights of slaves. In 1801, wine costing £669 (about one sixth of his net annual salary) was shipped from London to Barbados. This must have been regularly replenished, as in June 1802 the wine cellar at Pilgrim contained 2,810 bottles, mostly claret, Madeira, port and spirits.[137] Wine continued to be ordered from London. One order in 1805, for example, was for twenty-four dozen 'of the very first quality'.[138] Food was served on an extensive gold dinner service, which he had bought before leaving London.[139] The extent of his official entertaining is shown by his limitation of his birthday celebration in 1806 by inviting only sixty, being forty or fifty less than the usual number.[140] Such functions impressed at least the middle-class townsmen whose views were represented by the *Barbados Mercury and Bridgetown Gazette*. A ball was held in January 1805 following the wedding of Lord and Lady Seaforth's eldest daughter, Mary, to Sir Samuel Hood, the local naval commander. The editor reported that the party 'after enjoying with high spirits the enlivening dance . . . were conducted at one o'clock to a most prolific supper spread under a saloon formed by several tents . . . where the repast was considerably enlivened by the polite attention and cheerful demeanour of the elegant daughter of Lord Seaforth to every guest'.[141] When in April 1805 Sir Samuel Hood and Mary sailed for Britain at the end of his commission, a dinner was held. After toasts to the king and Sir Samuel, a third toast 'Lord Seaforth, with nearly the same marks of enthusiasm was drunk'. The editor referred to Hood's 'amiable consort, the elder daughter of our well approved governor'.[142] Seaforth would be delighted to read such comments, but whether the planters and leaders of the Assembly and militia felt this esteem as much as the town merchants may be doubted. His psychological need to excel, discussed in Chapter Four, was very much in evidence in Barbados. Colin Mackenzie was clearly misinformed when in 1803 he heard good reports of Seaforth's economic expenditure in Barbados.[143]

Despite the very real threat of disease posed by the Caribbean climate in the early nineteenth century, Seaforth, his wife and their daughters survived their five years in Barbados but suffered a constant undercurrent of worry about health issues. In 1802, about a year after his arrival, he wrote to Colonel Sandy, 'I wish to get home for, tho' we all keep tolerably well, yet I observe with grief the climate wears many of us very fast.'[144] On his return to Barbados in August 1804 after dental operations in London,[145] he was soon beset by further health concerns. In January 1805 he complained to Sandy that Mira was ill, their daughter Caroline not well and 'self tormented with bowel complaints and my eyes sadly affected by the tropical glare'. However, he added, 'Gen. Myers family still worse, out of sixteen, twelve have been buried.'[146] General Sir William Myers, Bart, was commander-in-chief of the land forces in the Windward and Leeward Islands. He himself died in July 1805 and his wife was immediately taken in by the Seaforth family at Pilgrim House.[147] This demonstrates that the Barbados climate did not spare even elite families living in what was regarded as high-class accommodation. The fate of the Myers family finally persuaded Seaforth that it was too dangerous to risk the health of his family longer in Barbados. He sought permission to take them home 'as it is really necessary for their healths and even lives to quit this colony'. This was particularly the case with Lady Seaforth, 'who has been quite broken down by the melancholy events of the last two seasons'.[148] Mira and the family sailed for home in April 1806, Seaforth himself staying on for a short while on the island.[149]

An interesting explanation for the family's survival was given in 1842 by Captain Ford, Seaforth's assistant private secretary from 1802. He pointed out that Pilgrim was situated on rising ground about 2,250 yards from the boat pier of Bridgetown. The military commander's residence, King's House, was 135 yards down the hill and close to a swamp, which in the wet season was fed by a stream. He explained the consequences as follows:

During his Lordship's residence in Barbados the yellow fever frequently prevailed, and in November 1803 at the King's House carried off Genl. Grinfield and his wife, most of his staff and servants ... Genl. Grinfield was succeeded by Sir William Myers from England. Sir William, several of his staff and servants, died of

Figure 7.2 *Carlisle Bay and Bridge Town Barbadoes*, c.1807, by John Augustine Waller. Seaforth's residence, Pilgrim, is the large house above Bridgetown. (Reproduced by permission of the National Library of Scotland.)

the fever. Lady Myers and a young lady her companion escaped. It was equally fatal also to the European residents and the garrison at both these periods ... His Lordship did not lose an individual or had one person alarmingly ill![150]

Ford concluded (using medical theories which were becoming popular in the 1840s) that the immunity of the Seaforth family was due to the elevated situation of Pilgrim well away from stagnant water. It was not until the 1890s that European medicine understood that the carriers of yellow fever were infected mosquitoes.[151] It is clear now that the mosquitoes on the King's House swamp sealed the fate of the Grinfield and Myers families.

Conclusions

Barbados was undoubtedly a disappointment to Seaforth. The salary was not as high as he expected. As he put it to his brother-in-law in 1805, 'how cruelly I have been disappointed here in a Government that does not afford me and my family bread.' He was trying to create a new job for himself as governor general of Guyana, and argued for 'such a share of patronage to the Governor as is necessary for carrying on such a Government'[152] He felt he had been handicapped by lack of patronage at his command. The military leadership to which he had long aspired (as shown in Chapters One and Six) did not materialise. The royal forces were determined to keep command in an important theatre of war in strictly professional hands and were supported in this by the imperial government. After the introductory pleasantries were over, it became clear that the Assembly members, the militia colonels and the island officials (often the same people or members of the same families) were unwilling to recognise in important matters the authority which Seaforth believed his royal Commission and Instructions gave him. There were also the continuous, and entirely realistic, health concerns.

It has been argued here that Seaforth, being a man of high intelligence, quickly understood the degree of devolved government which had been allowed to develop on the sugar islands. Possibly his disability made some of his personal relationships more brittle. Like some earlier governors of Barbados (but unlike the immediately preceding one) he was not willing to accept this. His motivation may have been influenced by his deafness in another way. He was a man of ability and energy, possibly greater than that of most Caribbean governors, who but for his disability might have reached high office in Britain. The frustrations created by this may have aggravated a natural urge to command and impatience when obstructed, and led to what appeared to his opponents a domineering style of governing. This may have been accentuated by his experience as a Highland proprietor used to having his instructions obeyed (as shown in Chapter Two). His psychological need to excel (suggested in Chapter Four) was certainly demonstrated by his style of entertaining in Barbados.

For Seaforth many of the issues which he faced in Barbados were matters of principle. The weaknesses of the island militia were evident to one who (as seen in Chapter Six) had experience and expertise in raising and training troops. At a period when invasion of the island by French forces was a very real possibility, he saw it as his duty to put the militia on a more effective and warlike footing. As an unreconstructed mercantilist, he thought it wrong that the descendants of American rebels should profit at the expense of British merchants and shipowners by selling provisions and wooden staves to the sugar planters. His service in the Royal Navy during the American War of Independence (discussed in Chapter One) may also have prejudiced him against Americans. He thought that the governor, as the king's representative, should be able to supervise and, if necessary, discipline government officials on the island. If he could not do this and if he could not bring pressure to bear on the Assembly members by more control over patronage (of the sort from which it has been shown in Chapter Five he had been used to benefitting), the governor's role would be strictly limited. He was frustrated by the comparison with his ability to control his regiment and manipulate patronage in Britain. More fundamentally, the governor's powers had been gradually eroded under his predecessors and he was trying to re-establish them. He was therefore bound to meet opposition.

How far were Seaforth's policies a personal crusade, possibly out of tune with the realities of Caribbean life? The issue of whether the metropolitan executive and parliament was trying to reassert control over the West Indian islands has been introduced in this chapter. Whitehall was most unwilling to upset vested interests whose sugar supported the credit on which the war was being fought. It thus failed to support Seaforth's attempts to reform the militia or to increase the governor's role in appointing island officials. On the other hand it did confirm his right to remove officials with good cause and took some steps (albeit with limited effect) to limit trade with the USA. A more definitive answer to this question will be offered in Chapter Ten. What is clear is that Seaforth's attempts to curb US imports and reform the militia grievously offended the Barbados planters. This seriously weakened his position when his policies reached a crisis point in 1805. As will be shown in Chapters Nine and Ten, this arose because his bill to protect slaves was finally forced through at the same time as a major French and Spanish fleet was approaching the Caribbean.

Notes

1. Devine, T. M., *Scotland's Empire 1600–1815* (London, 2003), p. 223.
2. Edinburgh, National Records of Scotland (NRS), GD46/17/20, E. S. Fraser to Lord Seaforth, 20 January 1801.
3. NRS, GD46/7/3, Lord Seaforth to H. Dundas, 7 February 1801.
4. NRS, GD46/17/16, '1801 – list of dates of journey to Barbados' (in Seaforth's hand).
5. London, British Library (BL), MS Add. 42071, vol. 2, fos 288–9, Lord Seaforth to C. F. Greville, 21 March 1801.
6. London, The National Archives (TNA), CO28/67, p. 19, 'Sketch of salaries of Governor of Barbados'; Castle Fraser, Mackenzie Fraser Papers (C. F. Papers) 1/289, Lord Seaforth to Col. A. Mackenzie, 13 February 1801.
7. TNA, CO29/27, Duke of Portland to Lord Seaforth, 1 December 1800.
8. BL, Add. MS 42071, vol. 2, fo. 289, Lord Seaforth to C. F. Greville, 21 March 1801.
9. NRS, GD46/17/24/307–8, 'Extracts from King's Orders and Instructions to Lord Seaforth', 24 December 1800.
10. NRS, GD46/17/80/224–30, 'Rough abstract of instructions as Governor of Barbados'.
11. BL, Add. MS 42071, vol. 2, fo. 289, Lord Seaforth to C. F. Greville, 21 March 1801.
12. Spurdle, F. G., *Early West Indian Government Showing the Progress of Government in Barbados, Jamaica and the Leeward Islands, 1660–1783* (New Zealand, 1962), pp. 210–13.

13. TNA, CO28/67, pp. 76–7, Minute of Barbados Assembly, 14 April 1801.
14. Aberdeen University Special Collections (AU), MS 3470/6/1/308, Lord Seaforth to H. Donaldson, 29 April 1801.
15. NRS, GD46/17/19/274–5, P. Fairbairn, 'Subjects for Lord Seaforth's attention', 31 July 1801.
16. NRS, GD46/17/19/351, /358, C. Mackenzie to Lord Seaforth, 20 October 1801.
17. NRS, GD46/17/19/363–7, 'Statement of Lord Seaforth's affairs made up to 15 October 1801'.
18. NRS, GD46/17/20, E. S. Fraser to Lord Seaforth, 7 June 1801.
19. TNA, CO28/67, p. 168, Lord Seaforth to Duke of Portland, 29 December 1801.
20. TNA, CO28/69, pp. 148–9, C. J. Greville to J. Sullivan, 11 March 1802.
21. NRS, GD46/17/16, Capt. Church, Port Royale, to Lord Seaforth, 31 July 1801.
22. Poyer, J., 'History of the Administration of the Rt Hon. Francis Lord Seaforth, late Governor', *Barbados Chronicle*, 1808, reproduced in *Journal of the Barbados Museum and Historical Society*, vol. 21, August 1954, p. 160.
23. TNA, CO28/67, p. 76, Minute of Barbados Assembly, 14 April 1801.
24. Lambert, D., *White Creole Culture, Politics and Identity during the Age of Abolition* (Cambridge, 2005), p. 91.
25. Murray, D. J., *The West Indies and the Development of Colonial Government 1801–1834* (Oxford, 1955), pp. xii, 32–3; Ward, J. R., 'The British West Indies 1748–1815' in P. J. Marshall (ed.), *The Oxford History of British Empire,* vol. 2, (Oxford, 1998), pp. 434–5.
26. Manning, H. T., *British Colonial Government after the American Revolution* (New Haven, 1933), p. 52.
27. Handler, J. S., *The Unappropriated People: Freedmen in the Slave Society of Barbados* (Baltimore, 1974), pp. 18–19 (quoting population figures from *Parliamentary Papers* 1814–15, vol. 7, rept. 478).
28. Beckles, H., *Black Rebellion in Barbados: The Struggle Against Slavery 1637–1838* (Bridgetown, 1987), pp. 54, 59.
29. Lambert, *White Creole Culture*, p. 37.
30. Black Rock, St James, Barbados Department of Archives, Planters Name Index.
31. Watson, M., 'The British West Indian Legislatures in the Seventeenth and Eighteenth Centuries' in P. Lawson (ed.), *Parliament and the Atlantic Empire* (Edinburgh, 1995), pp. 90–1.

32. O'Shaughnessy, A. J., *An Empire Divided: The American Revolution and the British Caribbean* (Philadelphia, 2000), p. 121.

33. Greene, J. P., 'The Transfer of British Liberty to the West Indies, 1627–1865' in J. P. Greene (ed.), *The Exclusionary Empire: English Liberty Overseas, 1600–1900* (Cambridge, 2010), pp. 55, 68.

34. Poyer, J., *The History of Barbados* (London, 1808), pp. 367–80, 490–525, 526–8; Spurdle, *Early West Indian Government*, pp. 92–3.

35. Boucher, P., 'The French and Dutch Caribbean, 1600–1800' in S. Palmie and F. A. Scarano, *The Caribbean: A History of the Region and Its Peoples* (Chicago, 2011), pp. 229–230.

36. Burnard, T., 'Harvest Years? Reconfigurations of Empire in Jamaica, 1756–1807', *Journal of Imperial and Commonwealth History (JICH)*, vol. 40, 4, 2012, pp. 534, 538–9, 541, 545, 547.

37. Hague, W., *William Pitt the Younger* (London, 2004), pp. 298–302.

38. Poyer, *The History of Barbados*, pp. 646–7.

39. Buckley, R. N., *Slaves in Red Coats: The British West India Regiments, 1795–1815* (New Haven, 1979), pp. 36–9, 69.

40. Poyer, *The History of Barbados*, pp. 632–40.

41. Edinburgh, National Library of Scotland (NLS), MS 6396, p. 42, Lord Seaforth to Lady Seaforth, 3 May 1804.

42. Lambert, *White Creole Culture*, p. 18, n. 44.

43. Manning, *British Colonial Government*, p. 136.

44. Greene, *Exclusionary Empire*, pp. 71–2.

45. Murray, *West Indies and Colonial Government*, p. 13.

46. Murray, *West Indies and Colonial Government*, p. 24.

47. TNA, CO28/67, p. 36, Lord Seaforth to Duke of Portland, 25 May 1801.

48. TNA, CO28/67, pp. 67, 111, Barbados Assembly Minute, 12 May 1801; CO28/68, p. 25, Barbados Council Minute, 12 May 1801.

49. Lambert, *White Creole Culture*, pp. 75, 78–9.

50. TNA, CO28/68, pp. 28–9, Barbados Council Minute, 28 July 1801.

51. TNA, CO28/71, p. 92, Lord Seaforth to Earl of Camden, 1 September 1804.

52. TNA, CO28/68, p. 29, Barbados Council Minute, 28 July 1801.

53. TNA, CO28/68, p. 78, Lord Seaforth to Lord Hobart, 28 June 1802.

54. TNA, CO28/67, p. 26, Lord Seaforth to J. King, 1 May 1801.

55. TNA, CO28/67, p. 41, Lt Gen. T. Trygge to Lord Seaforth, 5 May 1801.

56. Buckley, R. N., *The British Army in the West Indies: Society and the Military in the Revolutionary Age* (Gainsville, FL, 1998), pp. 197, 261–63.

57. Hall, N. A., 'Governors and Generals: The Relationship of Civil and Military Commands in Barbados, 1783–1815', *Caribbean Studies*, vol. 10, 4 (1971), pp. 95–102.

58. TNA, CO29/29, pp. 1–5, Lord Hobart to Lord Seaforth, 20 August 1801.

59. NRS, GD46/17/19/288–92, Lord Seaforth to Lt Gen. Trygge, 29 September 1801.

60. NRS, GD46/17/16, W. Adam to Col. A. Mackenzie, 31 December 1801.

61. For example, TNA, CO28/68, p. 66, Lord Seaforth to Lord Hobart, 27 June 1802.

62. NRS, GD46/7/4/33, Lord Seaforth to Br. Gen. Romer, 25 November 1801.

63. NRS, GD46/17/25/105, Lord Seaforth to General Sir William Myers, 8 October 1804.

64. NRS, GD46/17/4/6, Lord Seaforth to Rear Admiral J. T. Duckworth, 29 May 1801.

65. NRS, GD46/17/20/69, J. T. Duckworth to Lord Seaforth, 9 May 1801.

66. Rodger, N. A. M., *The Command of the Ocean: A Naval History of Britain, 1649–1815* (London, 2004), p. 319.

67. NRS, GD46/7/4/6, /12–14, Lord Seaforth to J. T. Duckworth, 29 May and 4 August 1801.

68. TNA, CO28/67, p. 39, Lord Seaforth to Duke of Portland, 27 May 1801.

69. NRS, GD46/7/5/15–19, 'A Letter addressed to H. E. the Rt Hon. Francis Lord Seaforth by a Barbadian', (Bridgetown, 1801).

70. Lambert, *White Creole Culture*, pp. 76–8, 170–1.

71. Watson, K., 'Salmagundis vs Pumpkins: White Politics and Creole Consciousness in Barbadian Slave Society, 1800 to 1834' in H. Johnson and K. Watson (eds), *The White Minority in the Caribbean* (Kingston, 1998), pp. 22–5.

72. NRS, GD46/7/2/17, 'Appointment of Lord Seaforth as Governor of Barbados – Powers, etc., 1800'.

73. NRS, GD46/17/80/229, Rough abstract of instructions as Governor of Barbados, clause 60.

74. Spurdle, *Early West Indian Government*, pp. 99–100; Murray, *West Indies and Colonial Government*, p. 25.

75. For example, NRS, GD46/7/11/137, Lord Seaforth to Lt Gen. Myers, 9 March 1805; /142, Lord Seaforth to Earl of Camden, 13 March 1805.

76. Graham, A., 'The Colonial Sinews of Imperial Power: The Political Economy of Jamaican Taxation, 1768–1838', *JICH*, vol. 45, 1, 2017, pp. 188–95.

77. NRS, GD46/7/4/17, Circular to colonels of militia, 30 August 1801.

78. NRS, GD46/17/21, 'Militia, Island of Barbados, Field Officers', 'General Assembly of Barbados', n.d., but from position, autumn 1802.

79. NRS, GD46/17/19/323–5, Lord Seaforth to Lord Hobart, 5 October 1801.

80. Hamilton, D. J., *Scotland, the Caribbean and the Atlantic World, 1750–1820* (Manchester, 2005), p. 38.

81. NRS, GD46/7/7/49–51, Lord Seaforth to Lord Hobart, 27 October 1802.

82. TNA, CO28/69, p. 42, Lord Seaforth to J. Sullivan, 27 October 1802.

83. NRS, GD46/7/7/49–51, Lord Seaforth to Lord Hobart, 27 October 1802.

84. TNA, CO28/69, p. 57, Barbados Assembly Minute, 2 December 1802.

85. TNA, CO29/29, pp. 27–8, Lord Hobart to Lord Seaforth, 6 January 1803.

86. NRS, GD46/7/11/61–2, W. Myers to Lord Seaforth, 27 December 1804.

87. NRS, GD46/17/23/30, Chief Justice Beckles charge to Grand Jury, n.d., but after resumption of war, May 1803.

88. TNA, CO28/70, p. 54, Address by Governor to Council and newly elected Assembly, 5 April 1803.

89. TNA, CO28/70, p. 68, Message from Governor on defective state of defence of the Island, Barbados Assembly Minute, 7 June 1803.

90. NRS, GD46/17/23/231, Lord Seaforth to Assembly, 1 November 1803.

91. TNA, CO28/70, p. 154, Barbados Council Minutes, 29 November 1803; CO30/17, pp. 123–4, Acts, Ordinances and Proclamations, Barbados, 31 July 1804.

92. *Barbados Mercury and Bridgetown Gazette*, 2 February 1805 (BL, MC1888).

93. *Barbados Mercury*, 2 March 1805 (BL, MC1888).

94. TNA, CO28/72, pp. 199–200, Speech by Lord Seaforth to Barbados Council and Assembly, 6 March 1805.

95. TNA, CO30/17, pp. 144–56, Barbados Militia Act, 7 March 1805; Schomburgk, R. H., *The History of Barbados* (London, 1848), pp. 360–1.

96. TNA, CO30/17, p. 169, Militia Act, 9 April 1804.

97. NRS, GD46/7/12/26, Lord Seaforth circular to members of Council, 15 May 1805.

98. NRS, GD46/7/4/14, Lord Seaforth to Duke of Portland, 25 August 1801.

99. NRS, GD46/7/7/67, Lord Seaforth to Lord Hobart, 23 December 1802.

100. NRS, GD46/17/21, Crown officers etc., Island of Barbados, n.d., but from position, autumn 1802.

101. Gibson, C., *Empire's Crossroads: The Caribbean from Columbus to the Present Day* (London, 2014), p. 149.

102. Murray, *West Indies and Colonial Government*, pp. 17–22, 33–4.

103. TNA, CO28/71, p. 242, Lord Seaforth to Sir Stephen Cottrell, 2 March 1804.

104. NRS, GD46/7/7/51, Lord Seaforth to Lord Hobart, 27 October 1802.

105. TNA, CO28/69, p. 124, Lord Seaforth to Sir P. Gibbes, 18 December 1802.

106. TNA, CO28/70, p. 165, S. Percival to Lord Hobart, 6 May 1803.

107. TNA, CO28/71, p. 147, Lord Seaforth to Lord Camden, 13 November 1804.

108. NRS, GD46/7/12/127–8, Lord Seaforth to E. Cooke, 29 August 1805.

109. Devine, *Scotland's Empire 1600–1815*, p. 30.

110. NRS, GD46/7/7/170, Lord Seaforth to S. Reddish, 1 October 1804.

111. Ryden, D. B., *West Indian Slavery and British Abolition, 1783–1807* (Cambridge, 2009), p. 35.

112. Crouzet, F., 'America and the crisis of the British imperial economy, 1803–1807' in J. J. McCusker and K. Morgan (eds), *The Early Modern Atlantic Economy* (Cambridge, 2000), pp. 290–2; Carrington, S. H. H., 'The United States and the British West Indian Trade, 1783–1807' in R. A. McDonald (ed.), *West Indies Accounts* (Kingston, 1996), pp. 151–60.

113. Ryden, *West Indian Slavery*, pp. 108–12.

114. Ragatz, L. J., *The Fall of the Planter Class in the British Caribbean, 1763–1833* (New York, 1929), p. 229, quoted Ryden, *West Indian Slavery*, p. 111.

115. Ryden, *West Indian Slavery*, pp. 112, 130.

116. NRS, GD46/17/21, S. Reddish to Lord Seaforth, 29 April 1802.

117. TNA, CO33/22, pp. 25–7, Shipping Returns, Barbados, 1801–2.

118. TNA, CO28/72, p. 150, Earl of Camden to Lord Seaforth, 5 September 1804.

119. Cain, P. J. and A. G. Hopkins, *British Imperialism: 1688–2000* (Harlow, 2002), p. 97.

120. TNA, CO28/71, pp. 258–60, G. W. Jordan to Secretary of State, 16 June 1804.
121. TNA, CO28/73, pp. 208–9, Mr Alderman Rowcroft to Board of Trade, 28 September 1804.
122. O'Shaughnessy, *An Empire Divided*, pp. 114, 122.
123. TNA, CO28/71, p. 197, Lord Seaforth to Earl of Camden, 12 December 1804.
124. *Barbados Mercury and Bridgetown Gazette*, 9 April 1805 (BL, MC1888).
125. TNA, CO28/71, p. 197, Lord Seaforth to Earl of Camden, 12 December 1804.
126. *Barbados Mercury and Bridgetown Gazette*, 8 January to 19 February 1805 (BL, MC1888).
127. Wrong, H., *Government of the West Indies* (Oxford, 1923), p. 50; Murray, *West Indies and Colonial Government*, p. 15.
128. NRS, GD46/17/25/175, H. Dalrymple to Lord Seaforth, 18 January 1805.
129. NRS, GD46/17/25/92, H. Dalrymple to Lord Seaforth, 20 October 1804.
130. NRS, GD46/7/12/24, Lord Seaforth to E. Cooke, 12 May 1805.
131. TNA, CO28/73, pp. 153–68, Lord Seaforth to customs officers and replies, 21 to 24 June 1805.
132. NRS, GD46/7/12/135, Lord Seaforth to P. Fairbairn, 11 September 1805.
133. TNA, CO28/73, p. 193, Lord Seaforth to E. Cooke, 22 December 1805.
134. TNA, CO28/71, p. 147, Lord Seaforth to Earl of Camden, 13 November 1804.
135. TNA, CO28/75, pp. 74–5, Address from merchants and inhabitants of Bridgetown, 21 July 1806.
136. NRS, GD46/7/11/170–1, Lord Seaforth to H. Dalrymple, Collector and S. Reddish, Comptroller, 9 April 1805.
137. NRS, GD46/7/6/63, /70, Accounts relating to Lord Seaforth's Barbados establishment.
138. NRS, GD46/17/28/1, P. Fairbairn to Urquhart and Robertson, 24 April 1805.
139. NRS, GD46/17/20/28, 'Memo re. plate', 5 February 1801.
140. NLS, MS 3696, fos 46–7, Lord Seaforth to Lady Seaforth, 4 June 1806.
141. *Barbados Mercury*, 8 January 1805 (BL, MC1888).
142. *Barbados Mercury*, 13 and 20 April 1805 (BL, MC1888).
143. NRS, GD46/17/23, C. Mackenzie to Lord Seaforth, 2 July 1803.
144. AU, MS 3470/6/2/53, Lord Seaforth to Col. A. Mackenzie, 31 July 1802.

145. AU, MS 3470/6/1/894, Lord Seaforth to Maj. Gen. A. Mackenzie Fraser, 20 August 1804.

146. AU, MS 3470/6/1/1084, Lord Seaforth to A. Mackenzie Fraser, 1 January 1805.

147. *Barbados Mercury*, 30 July 1805 (Barbados National Library, microfilm 20).

148. TNA, CO28/73, p. 111, Lord Seaforth to E. Cooke, 25 October 1805.

149. BL, Add. MS 40715, fos 211–2, Lord Seaforth to C. Greville, 19 April 1806.

150. NRS, GD46/7/17, 'Statement by Captain Ford on exemption from yellow fever of Lord Seaforth and his family during their residence in the West Indies', 1842.

151. Hamilton, *Scotland, the Caribbean and the Atlantic World*, pp. 129–130.

152. C. F. Papers 1/1186, Lord Seaforth to A. Mackenzie Fraser, 22 April 1805.

8 Slave Owner in Berbice

Plantations as a business venture

On his voyage to Barbados to take up his post as governor, Seaforth wrote a thirteen-page paper for the duke of Portland on the prospects for British planters in the former Dutch colonies in Guyana on the north-east coast of South America, which were now occupied by British forces.[1] The duke wanted to know how such 'rapid and large fortunes in Guyana could be made'. Seaforth had obtained information from knowledgeable owners of Guyana plantations, including his very successful neighbour, James Fraser of Belladrum, near Beauly[2] and Dr William Munro, who had property in and personal experience of Guyana and was an associate of Edward Fraser of Reelig (a friend of Seaforth's and subsequently his business partner). Reelig sent Seaforth a highly optimistic list, almost certainly from Munro, of the advantages of Guyana, some of which were repeated in the paper for Portland. It was claimed that far fewer slaves would be required than on comparable plantations in the West Indian islands, that the enslaved labourers would be healthier and that there would be abundant provision land to feed them. A cotton crop could be harvested six months after planting. Thus land and slaves could be bought on credit and paid from the profits on the first crop. In addition large profits could be made by buying and selling land.[3] Accordingly, he argued to Portland, the fortunes made in Berbice had not been built by dishonourable means. Portland wanted advice on whether Britain should aim to formally annexe Guyana when a peace treaty ended the war between the colonial powers. However, Seaforth had a personal interest in the issue. Before he left London he had made an agreement with partners (including the Highlanders Reelig and Belladrum) to invest in uncultivated land in Berbice to grow cotton.[4] The partners were encouraged by the growth of cotton manufacture in Scotland. As Reelig put it, 'cotton manufactures are getting on wonderfully, £150,000 of capital just now required for the newly erecting cotton mills by steam in Glasgow'. There seemed certain to be a good market for their Berbice cotton.[5]

Work is increasingly being published on Scotland and slavery.[6] Understandably, owners of slaves and merchants profiting from them have not received a good press. Although not many slave ships sailed to North America and the Caribbean from Scottish ports, Scots were intimately involved in trading voyages from English ports and as managers and owners of sugar and cotton plantations which depended on enslaved labour.[7] How can it be that Seaforth, who considered himself to be a humanitarian, and was so regarded by others, could have purchased plantations in Berbice to be cultivated by slave labour? As with his attitude to clanship and his clansmen (as shown in Chapter Two), his views on slavery were conservative and paternalistic. He was not an opponent of slavery or indeed of the slave trade. In 1802 he wrote. 'I am afraid there is no other mode under which any European nation can derive benefit from her West Indian colonies without the severe but necessary stimulus of compulsive labour.'[8] In 1805 he argued to the secretary of state that 'the abolition [of the slave trade] and the destruction of British interests . . . in the West Indies are synonymous'.[9] Seaforth has been accused of hypocrisy for owning slaves and professing humanitarian principles, despite the strong arguments being then made against slavery.[10] He had been an MP in 1789 when William Wilberforce delivered what has been regarded as his most celebrated speech against slavery, drawing on the researches since 1787 of the Society for Effecting the Abolition of the Slave Trade. There developed what has been seen as one of the first extra-parliamentary campaigns for reform.[11] It is particularly surprising that in this matter Seaforth opposed the views on slavery of his wife Mira, with whom he usually consulted. Their disagreement is shown by a letter to her in 1807 from Colin Mackenzie:

Were the Seaforth estate sufficient to afford . . . the means of merely comfortable support to Lord S. and his family it might be a matter of consideration whether he should retain a W.I. estate under any doubts or scruples – But as things are it would surely be unwise . . . to relinquish the benefits of a property . . . the doubts about which Lord Seaforth's own mind is unshaken.[12]

However, unlike many planters, Seaforth did believe in the conversion of slaves to Christianity, had by 1802 granted a licence in Barbados for a chapel for slaves on one estate and encouraged the sending of established church missionaries.[13] He was thereby recognising slaves as people rather than property. As will be shown in Chapter Nine, he put an enormous personal commitment into trying to make the killing of a slave by a white person in Barbados a capital offence. Furthermore, he seems to have envisaged a gradual transition to freedom. He suggested to Henry Dundas in 1804 that 'they would gradually add privilege to privilege and at last melt as it were into freemen, as the European serfs did of old'.[14] He certainly had no sympathy for sudden emancipation, as had been carried out on the French islands in the early years of the Revolution (but was revoked by Bonaparte in 1802–3).[15]

Hypocrisy was not usually one of Seaforth's vices. He was genuinely persuaded of the rightness of his views, or he had persuaded himself. If the latter, the reason was undoubtedly extreme financial pressure. As has been shown in Chapter Four, Lochalsh was sold only days before he left London for Barbados on 10 February 1801, and the critical cash-flow problems he faced on setting sail were not eased until the sale in April of three Kintail farms adjoining Lochalsh. However, the partnership agreement to buy Berbice lands was signed on 2 January 1801 (about a month before the sale of Lochalsh) and the purchase of these lands was made in March (well before the sale of the Kintail farms).[16] The Barbados governor's salary was not expected to do more than cover his and his family's living expenses. To significantly reduce his debt burden it would be necessary to find another and substantial income stream. This was the immediate purpose of the Berbice speculation. If this was successful, the effect on the Seaforth estate in Ross-shire would be that the forced labour of slaves would permit a policy of avoiding mass clearance of small tenants. Karly Kehoe has commented on the growing evidence of 'a rather unflattering picture of a nation that relied upon the exploitation of slaves in distant colonies and countries to secure its own financial survival'.[17]

Seaforth was encouraged by the success of Highland proprietors of Caribbean plantations, perhaps most notably the Malcolms of Poltalloch, but also – and probably better known to him – the Baillies of Bristol and Dochfour (near Inverness) and the Frasers of Belladrum.[18] Belladrum 'was said to have made £40,000 on his last trip'.[19] Another successful Guyana planter was Thomas Porter, who was one of the wealthiest dozen Britons to die in 1815 (the year of Seaforth's death).[20] David Alston suggests that once the stereotype of a successful Demerara planter had been established, then the appearance of men such as Belladrum confirmed the view that such success was common. Seaforth was also influenced by Reelig's list of the advantages of Guyana, which exaggerated the advantages and downplayed the disadvantages. A plantation was a hazardous business. It required a large capital investment in the purchase of land and slaves and incurred a wide range of risks, such as unfavourable weather and market conditions, the effects of military action and disease and unrest among the enslaved labourers. Alston has used behavioural economics to explain why Highland investors apparently ignored the potential dangers, citing, for example, the power of encouraging letters through kin networks.[21] Seaforth and his partners were undoubtedly over-optimistic. However, they were not unaware that they were taking a major risk. He explained to his friend Charles Greville that 'in the course of these enquiries [for Portland] such a scene of probable wealth was opened to me that I was tempted to ... try my fate'.[22] Reelig understood why he was taking the risk and wrote, 'I shall sincerely rejoice if this speculation should ... contribute to your reassembling the Fireside at Brahan in ample affluence.'[23] One element of risk became evident immediately. The partnership agreement included a provision that, if a partner did not pay his share of the purchase price within three months of the due date, the other partners could sell his land. Seaforth's share was £10,000 to be paid in instalments. The first of £3,800 was when the purchase was made in March 1801.[24] His finances were such that to put up his first payment he had to borrow from his mother[25] and a total of £2,000 from his father-in-law, Baptiste Proby, dean of Lichfield.[26]

Berbice was a narrow territory stretching inland along each side of the Berbice River. Most Dutch planters had settled well up the river for security and because cultivation was easier. The coastal lands were much harder and more expensive to work. The land was very low and had to be reclaimed from the sea by dykes and polder canals (known as poldering) and also by back dams to prevent flooding from inland water sources. However, the coast was potentially more fertile. The British military commander reported in 1802 that before it was brought into cultivation it was 'exposed to and lowered by the tides which by degree deposited that sediment which characterises the soil.'[27] He argued that it was British capital which brought sugar, coffee and especially cotton plantations to the coastal lands of Berbice and the adjoining colonies of Demerara and Essequibo, and this is confirmed by the contemporary and less immediately involved Jamaican historian Bryan Edwards.[28] David Alston has shown that Scottish (especially Highland) gentry families played a large part in the first Guyana boom, focussed on cotton, in the early years of the nineteenth century.[29]

It has been shown in Chapters Two, Three and Four that, although Seaforth was more interested in business development on his estates than in making economies in his lifestyle, his record in promoting development was patchy. How far was Berbice a wise speculation? A major problem was the difficulty of securing a watertight conveyance of land in a territory whose sovereignty was highly ambiguous. The Netherlands had been conquered by revolutionary France in 1795 and renamed the Batavian Republic, which thus became a French ally and consequently enemy of Britain. The Guyana territories, Demerara, Essequibo and Berbice, Dutch possessions, were captured by British forces in 1796, but not formally annexed by Britain until 1814. Under the terms of 1796 capitulation Dutch law continued to apply and Dutch governors remained in place.[30] Thus the purchase had to be registered in Berbice under Dutch law and also under the supervision of a Dutch official. Furthermore, Seaforth's partners were negotiating in early 1801 to buy the lands from a Dutch proprietor, resident in Holland.[31] A British statute required government permission to acquire landed property from parties resident in enemy countries. Seaforth claimed that, before he sailed, he had consulted the duke of Portland as the secretary of state responsible for the colonies and that he had 'hinted his good intention to me in the business'.[32] The partners decided that, since many sales in Guyana to British subjects had been made without any sanction, and given Portland's hints to Seaforth, there was no need for formal approval from the British government.[33]

By the summer of 1801 it became clear that, in Seaforth's words, 'a real bar is at present opposed to the business' by the British government.[34] The situation of the war was so fluid that ministers may have preferred not to be committed to one position or another on land sales in Guyana. Seaforth had almost certainly exaggerated his influence with government, and Portland ceased to be responsible for the colonies in July 1801. The opinion of Vicary Gibbs, Seaforth's brother-in-law and London legal agent, was that government consent should have been obtained before the purchase. So what was to be done? A majority of the partners proposed that the governor of Berbice, van Battenburg, should be asked to act for them and 'in a delicate manner some Douceur to obtain his sanction'. In other words, he should be bribed.[35] They thought that van Battenburg was about to accept the money. An agreement was made between them (signed for Seaforth by Colonel Sandy as his Berbice attorney in Britain) that 'whatever compliment or reward the parties shall think fit to give him for his trouble, care, pain or expenses' should be paid by them in proportion to their agreed share in the purchase.[36] However, these were murky waters. Van Battenburg refused to register the Seaforth partnership's purchase and demanded a share in the partnership.[37]

The conveyancing problem became more serious when, in October 1801, the British government signed preliminary articles of peace with the French Republic, the Peace of Amiens. It soon became clear that almost all colonies conquered by Britain during the war, including Guyana, would be returned to their former owners. At the time of the original purchase the Dutch Directory had given 'the handsomest and most decisive assurances if the Colonies revert to Holland in a peace'.[38] Van Battenburg tried to reassure the partners that their conveyance was safe[39] but it was not at all clear that he had yet completed the registration. He was presumably delaying in the hope of making as much from the transaction as possible. Munro had hopes that he would 'change his language and pocket his commission quietly'.[40] However, the net result for Seaforth at the end of 1801 was that he had paid £5,542 towards plantations whose ownership was still very uncertain – the initial payment of £3,800 and £1,742 paid for twenty 'Gold Coast Prime Negroes'.[41] Peter Fairbairn (now plantation attorney for the Berbice estates[42]) had bought them early so that they could be seasoned to the Berbice climate before use. However, at this point there was no certainty of having a plantation for them to work and there seemed no prospect of imminent access. This had serious consequences in view of Seaforth's lack of capital. He had bought more land than he intended to use with a view to selling some of the lots. In other words, he aimed to make money from land speculation as well as cotton planting. Fairbairn, now in Guyana, lamented that 'had the peace not taken place they would have sold readily and well', but the land market was now seriously depressed.[43] Henry Gibbs Dalton, the historian of British Guyana, reflected the views of the British planters when he argued that the British government had betrayed its countrymen, who were the very ones who were building up the economy of Guyana.[44] Fraser of Reelig had boasted to Seaforth in April 1801 that the partners had a bargain in their Berbice purchase.[45] By the end of the year the reasons for this had become clear, and the unwisdom of buying land in a territory of such uncertain sovereignty. Seaforth's lack of commercial acumen has been highlighted in Chapter Two. His Berbice purchase was not only the largest and most expensive, but also the most foolhardy purchase he ever made. In addition to the land price of £10,000, substantial capital expenditure (of which no adequate estimate was made at the outset) would be required to buy slaves and for reclamation work. It was estimated about the same time that a plantation in Guyana with 200 slaves would require a total capital of £20,000.[46]

At the end of December 1801 lots were drawn in London by the partners' agents to divide the purchase between them.[47] Two of Seaforth's plantations (lots 35 and 36 and A and B, in due course named respectively Brahan and Kintail after his Ross-shire seat and the original homeland of his kindred) were on the West Sea Coast, that is west of the Berbice River. The third (lots 1–4, subsequently named Seawell) on the East Sea Coast was the one earmarked for sale. Registration in Berbice seems to have been completed by April 1802.[48] However, surveys were required before the lands could be cultivated. This was delayed by a long spell of wet weather, which was a bad omen for future seasons.[49] In May it was recognised that the effects of the rain would prevent a crop being grown on Kintail during

Figure 8.1 Plan and division of A and B West Sea Coast, Berbice, 1803. This shows the coastal situation of Seaforth's Kintail plantation. (Reproduced by generous permission of Mr Andrew Matheson and the National Records of Scotland, ref. GD46/17/19.)

the ensuing season, but it was hoped operations on Brahan would begin before mid June and give a respectable crop in September 1803.[50] On 31 July 1802, Seaforth at last reported to Colonel Sandy that possession had been taken of Brahan and 'our operations go on well'. He hoped that the Berbice profits would enable him and his family soon to return to Britain.[51] Colin Mackenzie brought him down to earth, pointing out that the anticipated profits might not be to hand until 1805. It is not surprising that he described the state of Berbice as being 'all things considered a little precarious'.[52]

The position of British planters in Berbice was for a time extremely precarious after a Dutch squadron arrived at Berbice on 3 December 1802 to restore it to the sovereignty of the Batavian Republic.[53] The Republic threatened to dispossess Seaforth of his Berbice lands if he did not pay an instalment of £1,867 due in May 1803.[54] This issue was removed after war between Britain and France (and therefore also Holland) was resumed that month and Dutch forces in Berbice capitulated on 17 October 1803.[55] However, another potentially serious threat remained. A challenge was made to grants of land by the Dutch authorities since the preliminaries of peace had been signed on 1 October 1801.[56] Seaforth was doubly vulnerable. His grant had certainly not been approved by His Majesty's government, and there might be doubt as to whether it had been made by the Dutch authorities before or after October 1801.[57] After this he decided to pay van Battenburg £888, being his share of the commission promised in 1801, presumably on the grounds that the restored governor's goodwill was worth the money.[58]

It was not a straightforward matter to retain possession and establish clear ownership of the plantations on which Seaforth had staked his financial future and that of his family. To make a profit from them was another challenging issue. The business plan for the Berbice plantations drawn up by Seaforth and Colin Mackenzie was for all purchase instalments after the first to be paid by land and cotton sales. Seawell was intended to be sold at a sufficient profit to pay the second instalment of £2,262 due May 1802, but failed to find a market because of the return of the territory to the Dutch. The May 1803 instalment of £1,867 had been expected to be paid from the first crop.[59] However, this was prevented by the conveyancing problems and by delays in surveying caused by wet weather. The first cotton crop on the West Sea Coast lands was not harvested until late 1803 and early 1804. This was on Brahan and was of good quality but low yield, 24,000 lbs, caused by drought conditions. The average production of a good cotton plantation in Guyana was reckoned to be 50,000 lbs to 60,000 lbs per annum.[60] Fairbairn reported that 'appearances are very flattering for a second pick, but we must have rain. The pods and flowers are abundant, but do not come to perfection'. An additional 250 acres at Brahan had been impoldered for planting, but Fairbairn complained that because of the drought 'a spade could not be put into the ground in its then state'. At Kintail some draining had been done, but in January 1804 no crop had yet been planted.[61] In April 1804 Fairbairn explained to Lady Seaforth that this year the crop would not pay expenses 'because there is only one crop to two years expense'.[62]

Kintail was not got into cultivation until late in 1804. This meant that until then it was difficult to fully employ the existing force of slaves. Not only was this a waste of an expensive resource, but it also made it impossible meantime to purchase any more, which further delayed the business plan. Berbice planters were locked into a commitment to expansion.[63] Increases in output could be bought by the purchase of slaves on credit, with payment depending on the success of the next crop. One poor season thus caused cash flow problems. Colin Mackenzie envisaged that the funds needed to expand Seaforth's slave force (about £1,500) could not be accessed until after sale of the 1806 crop. Berbice had by April 1805 contributed nothing to the reduction of Seaforth's British debts, as had been planned. On the contrary, borrowing to pay instalments had been on the security of the Scottish estate and had thus increased the British debt. The Berbice concern was itself almost £4,000 in debt, besides more than £2,700 owing to Alexander Mackenzie Fraser (now General) on account of Berbice, who had paid this in 1803 'for the support of your interest in the concern', that is towards meeting instalments.[64]

This situation had been brought about partly by bad weather, alternating between excessive rain and drought which, with the losses, was to continue throughout the next decade. In 1809 Fairbairn reported that the weather had 'been not only wet but uncommonly cold. For several months the sun was only seen through a haze . . . another such season as the last, and former years, would render this country scarcely tenable'.[65] (The consequences of this will be shown in Chapter Eleven). This could not reasonably have been foreseen. The investment decisions had been taken on the basis of benign weather in 1799 and 1800.[66] However, Seaforth can certainly be accused of lack of judgement in staking so much in a territory of uncertain sovereignty and in misjudging the attitude of the British government. He was also criticised by one of his partners for the appointment of Peter Fairbairn as his Berbice attorney. Seaforth regarded highly his service as Ross-shire factor. His view then was that 'his habits were perfect clockwork, his diligence indefatigable and neither I nor anyone in my confidence had the slightest suspicion of his honesty'.[67] However, Reelig argued in 1801 that 'Fairbairn will prove a faithful servant . . . but you know experience in planting is not attained soon . . . He cannot instinctively be a West Indian or a cotton farmer'.[68] How far was this fair? B. W. Higman has suggested that a successful plantation attorney needed to have prior experience in supervisory roles on plantations and practical experience of plantation cultivation.[69] Clearly Fairbairn was not from this background. In 1812 James B. Fraser, Reelig's son and manager of his father's Berbice plantation, wrote a report on Fairbairn's management.[70] His view was that Fairbairn's 'zeal and integrity as a man of business far exceeded his skill and activity as a planter' and that his lack of local experience subjected him (especially at first) to excessive expense in carrying out his plans. He gave a number of examples. He had carried out an impolder on Brahan covering almost the whole estate, spending money (Fraser believed) on indifferent land which did not justify the expense. He had bought slaves at least six months before the partners gained access to the land on which they were to be used. He had, Fraser argued, resorted to 'the almost ruinous expense of hiring negroes' to speed cultivation. However, Fairbairn had very much in mind that the business plan was to expand cultivation as soon as possible. In his report Fraser admitted that in the years immediately after 1800 there was 'a general trend for expensive cultivation, a want of economy in justifying improvement'. Had it not been for the onset of unfavourable weather conditions, this might have been successful. Another adverse factor was increasing competition from cotton plantations in the American South.[71] For example, in 1809 Fairbairn complained to Seaforth of low prices, while assuring him 'I did my best to get the cotton to a good market'.[72] When in 1810 Seaforth considered dismissing Fairbairn, Inglis, Ellis and Co., his cotton agents, suggested that

Fairbairn's problems may have been caused entirely by adverse circumstances and bad crops and pointed out that many Berbice concerns were suffering from the poor seasons.[73] The responsibility for the financial problems of Seaforth's plantations may be shared mainly between his own ill judgement in making the purchase, the run of unfavourable seasons and possibly Fairbairn's inexperience. To attempt to make a profit while aiming to treat the enslaved labour force well was another challenge, which will be addressed in the next section.

Treatment of enslaved labourers

It has been argued in Chapter Two that Seaforth differed from the stereotypical Highland proprietor in the First Phase of Clearance by having a strong sense of responsibility for his small tenants. In Chapter One it was suggested that this sense may have resulted from his training in the Royal Navy in the 1770s, and specifically from the example of Admiral Mann. Is there evidence that, reflecting his policies in Scotland, his treatment of his enslaved labourers in Berbice differed from that of the stereotypical planter? David Alston has given an insight into that stereotype. Edward Fraser, younger son of Reelig, who worked on and managed Berbice plantations between 1803 and 1811 despised the harsh planters, but admitted that they were the successful ones. For example, the manager of the Baillies' Dochfour plantation, Mr Simpson, was 'a harsh disagreeable vulgar little creature', but was regarded as a good planter.[74] Seaforth had expressed the view in his report to Portland that slaves could perform strongly if well fed and treated.[75] How successful was he in implementing this policy? He thought he was succeeding, at least initially. In 1802 he welcomed the news that his slaves had survived without loss the 'seasoning' period after arriving from Africa as 'proof that my orders with regard to food and good treatment are adhered to'.[76] An examination will be made of the nature of the work done by his slaves, the extent to which their health was cared for, the provision made for feeding them and the extent to which slaves rebelled by running away.

The most detailed evidence is from the frequent reports of Seaforth's plantation attorney Fairbairn, from which his master's intentions mainly have to be deduced. Fairbairn regularly wrote, as in 1805, that 'all the negroes do well'.[77] But how far are we to believe this? In at least one respect Seaforth's instructions were quickly broken. In his 1801 paper on Berbice he had argued that renting slaves from other owners was bad practice. It was expensive, and the hirer had less incentive than the owner to treat the slaves well. However, in 1802, shortly after Fairbairn's arrival in Berbice, he decided to use a task gang to impolder. Digging the polder canals in the sea clay was regarded as the most arduous work for slaves, and he could have claimed he was saving Seaforth's own slaves from this.[78] The actual motivation appears to have been that he regularly suffered from insufficient funds or credit to buy enough slaves for the operations he planned.[79]

There seems to have been, as often on slave plantations, discrimination against female slaves in the allocation of tasks. A larger proportion of women was often used full-time for the arduous labour of field work. More men (especially as they got older) tended to be given easier jobs as craftsmen or specialists of one sort or another, possibly to buy their acquiescence.[80] The evidence for this on Seaforth's plantations can be seen in 'inventory and appraisements' carried out from time to time.[81] For example, on the Kintail plantation in 1810, of twenty-eight women only two were given non-field jobs full-time (as washerwomen). In contrast, nine of the forty-two male slaves did not labour in the fields. Two were the drivers, who kept the field slaves at work. Four were carpenters, one a gardener, one a stock-keeper and one a boatswain (to navigate the canals). In 1803 Fairbairn admitted to Seaforth that he was 'keeping the women and boys at the hoe, the labour of which for young cottons is great'. He claimed that this was to free adult males for drainage work.[82] Historians have taken as evidence of amelioration of conditions the easier work regime afforded to female slaves during pregnancy and after birth, thereby encouraging the health of the next generation of slaves. The inventories show a significant increase in the number of children on the Seaforth plantations (Brahan, five in 1805 to thirty in 1810, Seawell, three in 1807 to fifteen in 1810). By definition young children were non-productive, but they made business sense as the abolition of the British slave trade in 1807 prevented the purchase of fresh slaves from Africa.[83]

Plantation slavery was by its nature a brutal system. George Pinckard, who visited Berbice and Demerara in 1796, was

Figure 8.2 Plantation buildings and enslaved labourers, Mibiri Creek, Berbice, 1806, in this case for timber production. (From T. S. St Clair, *A Residence in the West Indies and America*. Reproduced by permission of the National Library of Scotland.)

shocked that 'in Guiana corporal punishment of slaves is so common that scarcely does it produce even the slightest glow of compassion'. He singled out a British planter in Demerara, Duggan of the Arcadia plantation, as one who treated his enslaved labourers well.[84] On the other hand, Alston quotes evidence that, despite what has been claimed to be an improvement of conditions after the abolition of the British slave trade in 1807, a quarter of the working slave population in Berbice were physically punished in the first half of 1828.[85] There is no direct evidence of the use of punishment on the Seaforth plantations. However, it is worth noting that, during five years (1801–6) as governor of relatively nearby Barbados, he never visited Berbice to check that his slaves really were being well treated. It is possible that he genuinely never had time. This is credible, as there were regular scares of French invasion and he was engaged in an arduous struggle to try to extend the legal rights of slaves and free people of colour in Barbados (as will be seen in Chapter Nine). On the other hand it could be that (as seems to have been the case with his partner Reelig), Seaforth was unwilling to test assurances of good treatment by seeing his plantations for himself.[86] However, a positive view of slave conditions in Berbice in 1806 was given by a Scottish army officer Thomas Staunton St Clair. He was horror-struck to watch the arrival of a slave ship and sick at heart that 'an Englishman [sic] could degrade himself so much as to traffic in human flesh'. On the other hand, after the Order in Council which in 1805 strictly limited the import of slaves to conquered territories like Berbice[87] and with slave trade abolition imminent, enslaved labourers were becoming a scarce and, therefore, valuable commodity. He thought that in general planters did not work them beyond their strength or punish them except for 'negligence, drunken-ness or some other fault'.[88]

An important issue in the treatment of slaves was the provision of food. The staple food of the slaves was plantains (sometimes supplemented with small quantities of salt fish and meat) which, as St Clair put it, 'either boiled or roasted, serves the negroes as a substitute for bread'.[89] In 1804 the Berbice Court of Policy (the local assembly) criticised planters, 'more particularly the new settled parts, who instead of having provision fields themselves or in sufficient quantity, purchase food for the slaves ... subject to many vicissitudes and disappointments', and made regulations intended to prevent this.[90] That these were not obeyed is suggested by the court's complaint in 1806 that the coastal planters had been relying on plantain purchases rather than allocate fertile and potentially profitable land for provision grounds.[91] It is true that Fairbairn regularly purchased flour, often American, for example in the particularly dry seasons of 1803 and 1804. The cost (presumably during the previous year) had been £1,000, which he rightly described as a heavy sum.[92] However, as early as 1804 (when the first cotton crop was being harvested) he reported extended searches for suitable ground for plantains, pointing out that this 'requires the first attention'[93] and he continued to devote much time and effort to developing plantain grounds. That this did not always succeed seems to have been due to the unfavourable weather. While the welfare of the slaves was set as a priority by Seaforth and energetic efforts made to maintain their food supply, there was at least an element of self-interest in safeguarding an asset which was rising in value. In 1811, Fairbairn pointed out that the value of slaves was rising after the abolition of the British slave trade, while the value of land was dropping fast because of the run of bad seasons.[94] For example, on Seawell the value of the slaves was estimated to be 82,820 guilders and the land 90,000 guilders (25 per cent below the previous valuation).[95] He reckoned that slaves could be sold at 20 per cent above that valuation, whereas it was very difficult to make a land sale.

Slaves were a valuable and (unlike land) marketable asset, and thus worth preserving.

Fairbairn gave Lord Seaforth regular and generally positive reports of the health of the enslaved labourers. For example, in 1806 'the negroes [on Seawell] are all well and cheerful'.[96] When he had to report in 1809 that three male slaves had died of pleurisy, he was very apologetic and insisted that every attention had been paid to them. As with the feeding of slaves, so with their healthcare there were mixed motives. For example, some slaves 'with all the care bestowed on them', were developing chigoes, a painful foot complaint. Fairbairn believed he was curing this with application of crab oil and immersing feet in salt mud.[97] Of course, slaves were a valuable business asset, but it is also reasonable to credit a man of Seaforth's humanitarian credentials with a genuine concern for their welfare. How effective was the healthcare on Seaforth's plantations? On the Brahan plantation in 1803 a doctor was being paid to provide medicine and attendance for 'each negro of all ages'.[98] This implies that care was being given to older slaves, contrary to suggestions elsewhere in Guyana that healthcare was given only to active and productive ones.[99] The annual doctor's fee, however, was £5 10s 0d per slave compared to £50 for each white patient.

There seems to have been a slow start to providing hospitals on the Seaforth plantations. In 1805 Fairbairn instructed his under-managers on Brahan and Kintail that permanent sick-houses 'must stand over for the present', but temporary ones should be erected in situations which would later be suitable for permanent structures.[100] However, at least Brahan already had some sort of 'sick house' in 1805, and in 1806 he reported 'the sick houses are almost deserted'.[101] Seawell had a logie (a type of sick house) in 1807 and in 1810 also a 'store and hospital'. In 1810, Brahan and Kintail both had a logie (Brahan's being of one-and-a-half storeys).[102] It has been pointed out that, although there are many accounts of inferior medical provision, there was also a stream of publications on slave medicine, which may suggest improvement was being seriously attempted.[103] Mortality figures would be one of the most telling measures of the effectiveness of healthcare. However, the data for the Seaforth estates is too fragmentary to be of statistical significance and there are no reliable figures for Berbice for comparison purposes until compulsory registration of slaves began there in 1819.[104] The most detailed evidence for the Seaforth plantations is for Brahan for a relatively short period (December 1801 to December 1803 inclusive):[105] 104 slaves were purchased, of whom four died (one of sores on the feet 'in spite of every effort of the doctor', one child 'supposed to have been improperly used' by its mother, and two of consumption).

What conclusions can be drawn about conditions on Seaforth's plantations? It can be pointed out that they were not so good as to prevent some slaves from running away. On Brahan in the period December 1801 to December 1803, of 104 slaves purchased six 'absented' (three of them on the same day, 20 September 1803). This may not have been as common as on other neighbouring estates. On the Union plantation five slaves ran away on the same day in January 1804.[106] One Brahan slave, Inverness, escaped and was recaptured at least twice. Alston has depicted Inverness as one of a group of well organised and determined slaves on the Seaforth plantations with the consistent aim of freeing themselves and others.[107] However, in the 1810 inventories no slaves on Brahan were shown as runaways, one on Seawell (absent three years) and two on Kintail. One of the Kintail absentees was Seaforth's former cook in Barbados, Quaco, who had a particular grievance over his transfer to plantation work after his master's return to Britain in 1806.[108] These figures, if they give a true picture, suggest that, as the plantations settled down and as there were no longer recent arrivals from Africa, there were fewer new absentees.

There is no doubt that Seaforth had commercial as well as humanitarian reasons for seeking to treat slaves well. It is also the case that financial pressures resulted in treatment and acts which he would have preferred to avoid, like the hiring of task gangs. His own perilous financial situation was, in the last resort, decisive. In 1805 he was horrified by the Order in Council strictly limiting the importation of slaves to conquered territories. The home government was under pressure from the opponents of the slave trade, but was not yet ready to abolish it completely and for all British territories. In a long letter of complaint Seaforth only briefly mentioned the interests of the enslaved, focusing instead on the larger number of slaves who he claimed would be imported to Trinidad and Jamaica.[109] Despite this, it can be argued that his concern for his slaves influenced at least to some extent decision-making on his plantations.

Conclusions

Kit Candlin has described Berbice as 'the last Caribbean frontier' and as 'the edge of the British world'.[110] David Alston called it a 'frontier land', and argued that the success of some Scottish planters there was contributed to by their greater appetite for risk.[111] It has been seen earlier in this volume (especially in Chapters Two and Six) that Seaforth demonstrated in Scotland a lack of business acumen. This was disastrously replicated in Berbice. His investment there, the largest he ever made, combined exceptionally high risk and poor business skill. It will be shown in Chapters Eleven and Twelve that the failure of the Berbice plantations had serious consequences, not only for his personal finances, but also for the future of the Ross-shire estate, with land sales becoming necessary in 1807 and again in 1813–14. It is clear that the initial decision to purchase the Berbice lots was rushed and fundamentally flawed. The London partners, Somarsall and Alves, had been in touch with the vendor, Ruysack, in May 1800. However, they do not appear to have come together with the Highland partners, including Seaforth, until mid November, the month in which he was appointed Barbados governor and about six weeks before the binding agreement was made between them.[112] The hurry was because he was about to sail for Barbados and because, as has been explained, his finances were in a particularly perilous state. He had to make some major change and he had to do it quickly. The consequence was that the potential dangers were given insufficient consideration.[113] The business projections, such as they were, were based on the very favourable results of season 1799–1800 and the advice (in some cases, self-interested) of Berbice planters resident in London. The dangers of buying land in what was still technically enemy territory from vendors who were certainly citizens of an enemy republic were not given sufficient weight. The subsequent problems, such as the effects of the Peace of Amiens (which should have been anticipated) and the decade of unfavourable weather (which could not have been foreseen) simply compounded what had been a highly imprudent initial decision. As Alexander Mackenzie, the late-nineteenth-century historian of the Mackenzies, put it, 'his faculties, penetrating as they were, had not the facility of detection which qualified him for cautious circumspection; he heedlessly ventured and lost'.[114]

It has been argued (especially in Chapter Two) that Seaforth differed from the stereotype of a Highland proprietor in the First Phase of Clearance in having a genuine concern for his small tenants. He had a similar concern for his enslaved labourers in Berbice, and thus cannot be regarded as a stereotypical Guyana planter. His continued admonitions to his attorney Fairbairn to treat them well, while never actually visiting to see for himself, has been seen as hypocrisy. We may criticise his belief in slavery. We may argue that some of his concerns for his slaves, such as for their food supply and health, were no more than enlightened self-interest. However, as will be shown in Chapter Nine, his commitment to the welfare of slaves and free people of colour was a real personal crusade, went well beyond the call of duty and caused him enormous stress and difficulty with white Barbadians. This entitles his wish to treat his slaves well to be taken at face value. It has been suggested that Seaforth's benevolent intentions towards his Highland small tenants were sometimes, under the pressures he faced, made less effective by inconsistent execution and unintended consequences.[115] A similar pattern can be seen in Berbice. For example, his disapproval of hiring task gangs of slaves was regularly ignored by Fairbairn, who had been unable to buy enough slaves because of Seaforth's lack of capital and poor credit-worthiness. The commercial pressures inherent in his personal situation were accentuated in Berbice by the decade of unfavourable weather and by declining cotton prices. Financial, commercial and climatic adversity could at times be more powerful than good intentions.

Notes

1. London, British Library (BL), MS Add. 42071, vol. 2, fos 295–308, 'Guiana – from Lord Seaforth', superscribed 'compiled for the Duke of Portland at sea – Feb. 1801'.
2. Alston, D. '"Very rapid and splendid fortunes"? Highland Scots in Berbice (Guyana) in the early nineteenth century', *Transactions of the Gaelic Society of Inverness*, vol. 63 (2006), pp. 212–3.
3. Edinburgh, National Records of Scotland (NRS), GD46/17/14/377, E. S. Fraser to Lord Seaforth, 14 and 15 November 1800; /387–8, 'Reelig on the state of the Berbice Co., end of 1800'.

4. NRS, GD46/17/19/552, Copy agreement between Lord Seaforth and others respecting the purchase of lands belonging to the Berbice Company, 2 January 1801. The partners were Lord Seaforth, E. S. Fraser of Reelig, J. Fraser of Belladrum, and A. W. Somarsall and A. Alves of London.

5. NRS, GD46/17/21, E. S. Fraser to Lord Seaforth, 30 December 1802.

6. Devine, T. M. (ed.), *Recovering Scotland's Slavery Past: The Caribbean Connection* (Edinburgh, 2015); Whyte, I., *Scotland and the Abolition of Black Slavery, 1756–1838* (Edinburgh, 2006); Cooke, A., 'An Elite Revisited: Glasgow West India Merchants, 1783–1877', *Journal of Scottish Historical Studies* (*JSHS*), vol. 32, 2, 2012; Mullen, S., 'A Glasgow–West India Merchant House and the Imperial Dividend, 1779–1867', *JSHS*, vol. 33, 2, 2013.

7. Devine, T. M. and P. T. Rossner, 'Scots in the Atlantic Economy, 1600–1800' in J. M. Mackenzie and T. M. Devine (eds), *Scotland and the British Empire* (Oxford, 2011), pp. 48–53; Devine, *Recovering Scotland's Slavery Past,* pp. 28–30, 227–32.

8. NRS, GD46/7/7/34, Lord Seaforth to M. Bertin, Prefect of Martinique, 12 September 1802.

9. London, The National Archives (TNA), CO28/73, pp. 15–16, Lord Seaforth to Earl of Camden, 22 July 1805.

10. Alston, '"Very rapid and splendid fortunes"?', pp. 228, 231.

11. Hague, W., *William Pitt the Younger* (London, 2004), p. 298; Lambert, D., *White Creole Culture, Politics and Identity during the Age of Abolition* (Cambridge, 2005), pp. 33–4.

12. NRS, GD46/17/31, C. Mackenzie to Lady Seaforth, 16 January 1807.

13. NRS, GD46/7/4/50–1, Lord Seaforth to Bishop Porteus of London, 8 March 1802.

14. NRS, GD46/7/10, Lord Seaforth to Lord Melville, 8 June 1804.

15. Gibson, C., *Empire's Crossroads: The Caribbean from Columbus to the Present Day* (London, 2014), pp. 162, 170–1.

16. NRS, GD46/17/20/46, E. S. Fraser to Lord Seaforth, 12 March 1801.

17. Kehoe, S. K., review of I. Whyte's *Send Back the Money! The Free Church of Scotland and American Slavery*, *The Scottish Historical Review* (*SHR*), vol. 93, no. 236, 1, 2014, p. 157.

18. Macinnes, A. I., 'Scottish Gaeldom from clanship to commercial landlordism, *c*.1600–*c*.1850' in S. Foster, A. Macinnes and R. Macinnes, *Scottish Power Centres from the Early Middle Ages to the Twentieth Century* (Glasgow, 1998), pp. 173–5; Hamilton, D. J., *Scotland, the Caribbean and the Atlantic*

World, 1750–1820 (Manchester, 2005), pp. 89–92, 199; Alston, '"Very rapid and splendid fortunes"?', pp. 212–3.

19. E. S. Fraser of Reelig to Lord Seaforth, 18 June 1801, quoted in Alston, '"Very rapid and splendid fortunes"', p. 212.

20. Draper, N., 'The Rise of a New Planter Class? Some Countercurrents from British Guiana and Trinidad, 1807–33', *Atlantic Studies*, vol. 9, 1, March 2012, pp. 71–2.

21. Alston, D., 'Behavioural Economics and the Paradox of Scottish Emigration', in A. McCarthy and J. M. Mackenzie (eds), *Global Migrations: The Scottish Diaspora since 1800* (Edinburgh, 2016), pp. 47, 51–5.

22. BL, Add. MS 42071, vol. 2, fos 285–7, Lord Seaforth, *Topaz* at sea, to C. F. Greville, 21 March 1801

23. NRS, GD46/17/20/60, E. S. Fraser to Lord Seaforth, 10 April 1801.

24. NRS, GD46/17/21, Lord Seaforth to C. Mackenzie, 21 May 1802; 'General State of the Berbice Concern' (P. Fairbairn), July 1802.

25. NRS, GD46/17/19/95, C. Mackenzie to Lord Seaforth, 27 April 1801.

26. NRS, GD46/17/19/41, B. Proby to C. Mackenzie, 1 June 1801.

27. TNA, CO111/4, fo. 94, Col. T. Hislop, 'Remarks and Observations relating to the Colonies of Berbice, Demerary and Esseqibo', 30 June 1802.

28. Edwards, B., *The History, Civil and Commercial, of the British Colonies in the West Indies* (London, 1819), vol. 4, pp. 245–6.

29. Alston, D., 'Enslaved Africans, Scots and the Plantations of Guyana' in Devine (ed.), *Recovering Scotland's Slavery Past: The Caribbean Connection*, pp. 103–6.

30. Dalton, H. G., *The History of British Guiana* (London, 1854), vol. 1, p. 249.

31. NRS, GD46/17/20/46, E. S. Fraser to Lord Seaforth, 12 March 1801.

32. NRS, GD46/17/19/371–3, Lord Seaforth to E. S. Fraser, 16 October 1801.

33. NRS, GD46/17/20/92, A. Alves to E. S. Fraser, 13 June 1801.

34. NRS, GD46/17/19/373, Lord Seaforth to E. S. Fraser, 16 October 1801.

35. NRS, GD46/17/20/92, A. Alves to E. S. Fraser, 13 June 1801.

36. NRS, GD46/17/19/566, Copy articles of agreement for altering intended division of Berbice lands between Lord Seaforth and others, 28 December 1801.

37. NRS, GD46/17/21, W. Munro to Lord Seaforth, 6 January 1802.

38. NRS, GD46/17/20/73, E. S. Fraser to Lord Seaforth, 13 May 1801.
39. NRS, GD46/17/20/206–7, P. Fairbairn to Lord Seaforth, 28 November 1801.
40. NRS, GD46/17/21, W. Munro to Lord Seaforth, 6 January 1802.
41. NRS, GD46/12/21, 'Negroes purchased for the Berbice concern', purchase made 1 December 1801.
42. NRS, GD46/17/11, Letter of attorney, Lord Seaforth to P. Fairbairn, 31 July 1801.
43. NRS, GD46/17/19/581–2, P. Fairbairn to Lord Seaforth, 24 December 1801.
44. Dalton, *History of Guiana*, vol. 1, pp. 257–8.
45. NRS, GD46/17/20/60–1, E. S. Fraser to Lord Seaforth, 10 April 1801.
46. Alston, '"Very rapid and splendid fortunes"?', p. 215.
47. NRS, GD46/17/19/585–8, Division of lands in Berbice, 28 and 31 December 1801; /568, Valuation between Lord Seaforth and E.S. Fraser, 28 December 1801.
48. NRS, GD46/17/21, Lord Seaforth to Governor van Battenburg, 5 April 1802.
49. NRS, GD46/17/21, H. Mackenzie to Lord Seaforth 30 March 1802, Lord Seaforth to Governor van Battenburg, 5 April 1802.
50. NRS, GD46/17/21, P. Fairbairn to Lord Seaforth, 1 May 1802, Lord Seaforth to C. Mackenzie, 21 May 1802.
51. Aberdeen University Special Collections (AU), MS 3470/6/2/53, Lord Seaforth to Col. A. Mackenzie, 31 July 1802.
52. NRS, GD46/17/21, C. Mackenzie to Lord Seaforth, 28 Oct. 1802.
53. TNA, CO112/1, fo. 2, Governor van Battenburg to Lord Hobart, 10 December 1802.
54. AU, MS 3470/6/1/691, J. Boaden to Maj. Gen. A. Mackenzie, 2 June 1803.
55. NRS, GD46/17/23/201, General Grinfield and Commodore Hood circular, 17 October 1803.
56. TNA, CO112/1, fos 7–13, Governor van Battenburg to Lord Hobart, 26 June, 14 July, 10 August and 30 October 1804.
57. NRS, GD46/17/26, P. Fairbairn to Lord Seaforth, 18 January 1804.
58. NRS, GD46/17/26, Governor van Battenburg to Lord Seaforth, 21 March and 2 April 1804.
59. NRS, GD46/17/21, C. Mackenzie to Lord Seaforth, 29 March and 28 October 1802, P. Fairbairn, 'General State of Berbice Concern, 1 July 1802'.
60. Dalton, *History of British Guiana*, vol. 1, p. 254.

61. NRS, GD46/17/26, P. Fairbairn to Lord Seaforth, 18 January 1804.

62. NRS, GD46/17/26, P. Fairbairn to Lady Seaforth, 12 July 1804.

63. Alston, '"Very rapid and splendid fortunes"?', p. 216.

64. NRS, GD46/17/26, C. Mackenzie to Lord Seaforth, 26 April 1805; Castle Fraser, Mackenzie Fraser Papers 1/1440, C. Mackenzie to A. Mackenzie, 28 October 1802.

65. NRS, GD46/17/35/86, P. Fairbairn to Lord Seaforth, 29 July 1809.

66. Alston, '"Very rapid and splendid fortunes"?', pp. 216–7; Dalton, *History of British Guiana*, vol. 1, p. 329.

67. NRS, GD46/17/37/32, Lord Seaforth to Inglis, Ellis and Co., 9 February 1811.

68. NRS, GD46/17/20/73, /98, E. S. Fraser to Lord Seaforth, 13 May and 7 June 1801.

69. Higman, B. W., *Plantation Jamaica 1750–1850: Capital and Control in a Plantation Economy* (Kingston, 2005), pp. 92–3.

70. NRS, GD46/17/36, J. B. Fraser to Lord Seaforth, 14 December 1812.

71. Alston, 'Enslaved Africans, Scots and the Plantations of Guyana', p. 113.

72. NRS, GD46/17/35/86, P. Fairbairn to Lord Seaforth, 29 July 1809.

73. NRS, GD46/17/37/27, J. Inglis to Lord Seaforth, 11 February 1811.

74. Alston, '"Very rapid and splendid fortunes"?', pp. 223–4, 228, 232.

75. BL, Add. MS 42071, vol. 2, fos 295–308, 'Guiana – from Lord Seaforth, 1801'.

76. NRS, GD46/17/21, Lord Seaforth to C. Mackenzie, 21 May 1802.

77. NRS, GD46/17/27/20, P. Fairbairn to Lord Seaforth, 2 February 1805.

78. NRS, GD46/17/21, P. Fairbairn to Lord Seaforth, 'Memorandums, Berbice' (n.d., but from context, summer 1802); Sheridan, R. B., 'The condition of the slaves on the sugar plantations of Sir John Gladstone in the colony of Demerara, 1812–49', *New West Indian Guide*, vol. 76, 3–4, 2002, pp. 245, 266.

79. NRS, GD46/17/25/5, P. Fairbairn to Lord Seaforth, 17 January 1805.

80. Ryden, D. B., *West Indian Slavery and British Abolition, 1783–1807* (Cambridge, 2009), pp. 143–6.

81. NRS, GD46/17/25/169–70 (Brahan, 22 January 1805); GD46/17/32/63–4 (Seawell, 27 January 1807), /206–7 (Kintail,

20 December 1810), /210–11 (Seawell, 13 December 1810), /215 (Brahan, 20 December 1810).

82. NRS, GD46/17/24/126, P. Fairbairn to Lord Seaforth, 25 April 1803.

83. Paton, D., 'Enslaved women and slavery before and after 1807', *History in Focus*, 12, 2007 (electronic resource); Ward, J. R. *British West Indian Slavery 1754–1834: The Process of Amelioration* (Oxford, 1988), pp. 166, 187–8, 208.

84. Pinckard, G., *Notes on the West Indies including observations relative to the Creoles and slaves of the western colonies* (London, 1816), vol. 2, pp. 343, 349–53.

85. Alston, 'Enslaved Africans, Scots and the Plantations of Guyana', p. 110.

86. McKichan, F., 'Lord Seaforth: Highland Proprietor, Caribbean Governor and Slave Owner', *SHR*, vol. 90, 2, October 2011, pp. 218–9.

87. NRS, GD46/17/25/284–6, Order in Council 15 August 1805 prohibiting import of slaves to conquered colonies.

88. St Clair, T. S., *A Residence in the West Indies and America* (London, 1834), pp. 189–90, 196–7.

89. St Clair, *A Residence in the West Indies,* p. 125.

90. NRS, GD46/17/25/15–16, Regulations Berbice for Proper Sustenance of the Slaves, enacted 30 April 1804.

91. Thompson, A. O., *A Documentary History of Slavery in Berbice 1796–1834* (Georgetown, 2002), p. 75.

92. NRS, GD46/17/24/125–6, P. Fairbairn, 'Particulars re the Berbice concerns', 25 April 1803.

93. NRS GD46/17/26, P. Fairbairn to Lord Seaforth, 18 January 1804.

94. NRS, GD46/17/37/257–8, P. Fairbairn to Lord Seaforth, 17 April 1811.

95. NRS, GD46/17/25/210–11, Inventory and Appraisement, Seawell, 13 December 1810.

96. NRS, GD46/17/24/443, P. Fairbairn to Lord Seaforth, 1 September 1806.

97. NRS, GD46/17/26, P. Fairbairn to Lord Seaforth, 18 January 1804.

98. McKichan, 'Highland Proprietor, Caribbean Governor and Slave Owner', 216–7.

99. Sheridan, 'Condition of slaves on sugar plantations of Sir John Gladstone', p. 257.

100. NRS, GD46/17/25, P. Fairbairn, instructions for managers, plantations Brahan and Kintail, 1 April 1805.

101. NRS, GD46/17/24/326, P. Fairbairn to Lord Seaforth, 10 January 1806.

102. NRS, Inventory and Appraisements, GD46/17/25/169 (Brahan, 22 January 1805); GD46/17/32/63 (Seawell, 27 January 1807), /206, (Kintail, 20 December 1810), /210 (Seawell, 13 December 1810), /215 (Brahan, 20 December 1810).

103. Ward, *British West Indian Slavery*, pp. 146–7, 163.

104. Higman, B. W., *Slave Populations of the British Caribbean, 1807–1834* (Baltimore, 1984), pp. 413–4.

105. NRS, GD46/17/25/11–12, 'List of negroes purchased for Plantation Brahan and their state 1 Jan. 1804'.

106. NRS, GD46/17/26, P. Fairbairn to Lord Seaforth, 18 January 1804.

107. Alston, 'Enslaved Africans, Scots and the Plantations of Guyana', pp. 111–12.

108. NRS, Inventory and Appraisements, GD46/17/32/207 (Kintail, 20 December 1810), /210–11 (Seawell, 13 December 1810), /215 (Brahan, 20 December 1810); NRS, GD46/17/35/247, P. Fairbairn to Lord Seaforth, 15 February 1810. The author is grateful to Dr Alston for drawing the case of Quaco to his attention.

109. NRS, GD46/17/25/308–10, Lord Seaforth to Sir S. Hood, 27 November 1805.

110. Candlin, K., *The Last Caribbean Frontier, 1795–1815* (Basingstoke, 2012), pp. 26–9, 45.

111. Alston, 'Enslaved Africans, Scots and the Plantations of Guyana', p. 102.

112. NRS, GD46/17/14/407, 'History of Berbice and of the lots of land reserved to its Company – from Ruysack, 26 May 1800'; /377, E. S. Fraser to Lord Seaforth, 14 and 15 November 1800.

113. NRS, GD46/17/14/377, /381, E. S. Fraser to Lord Seaforth, 14 and 15 November and 2 December 1800.

114. Mackenzie, A., *History of the Mackenzies* (Inverness, 1894 edn), p. 343.

115. McKichan, F., 'Lord Seaforth and Highland Estate Management in the First Phase of Clearance (1783–1815)', *SHR*, vol. 86, 1, 2007, pp. 67–8.

9   Seaforth's Great Matter: the Rights of Enslaved Labourers and Free People of Colour

Forces for change

Lord Seaforth's reputation as a prominent colonial governor and indeed as a humanitarian arises from his efforts to increase the legal rights of enslaved labourers and free people of colour in Barbados. As has been shown in Chapter Seven, he set about this within months of landing by arguing for better provision for aged and destitute free people of colour and, most controversially, that the murder of any persons (free or slave) should become a felony without benefit of clergy, that is, a capital offence. The latter became a personal mission. His view, expressed in a despatch, was that 'it is proper that he who sheds a man's blood should have his blood shed by man'.[1] The Assembly was dominated by planters, whose major concern was resistance from and possible rebellion by their slaves. To interfere with the relationship between planters and slaves appeared to threaten the system on which their prosperity and even their lives depended. The free people of colour were feared by many planters as potential leaders of a slave revolt.

Experience on other West Indian islands gave good grounds for such fears. The slave revolt in French Saint-Domingue in 1791–2, supported by free people of colour, had led to the deaths of thousands of whites and the flight of many more. This sent through the British West Indies what has been described as 'a shudder of terror'.[2] In the 1790s slaves and free people of colour had taken part in rebellions in the British islands of Grenada (1795–7), St Vincent (1795) and St Lucia (1796–7).

There had been a Maroon war (against escaped slaves) in Jamaica in 1795–6 and a black military mutiny in Dominica in 1802.[3] Seaforth would have in mind that another Scottish governor (Ninian Home of Grenada) had been murdered in the slave rising in 1795.[4] In 1802 he assured Lord Hobart, Secretary of State for War and the Colonies, that in general the Barbados slaves appeared very quiet and well disposed. However, that a man might kill his slave for a small fine (£11 4s sterling) was an 'irritating circumstance' and it was necessary to prevent the unrest which this might cause. Furthermore, the routine 'riot, turbulence and insolence' of the Bridgetown black communities might mean that conspiracies there would go undiscovered.[5] Urban slaves might earn money and tended to less under the control of their owners than rural slaves.[6] It has been argued that all slaves were becoming more anxious and restless at this period as their knowledge of the metropolitan campaign against the slave trade opened the prospect of freedom,[7] and that rumours of black revolts circulated around the colonies, making Barbados part of a wider 'Revolutionary Atlantic'.[8] In 1804 Saint-Domingue became the independent black republic of Haiti, a serious challenge to planter domination of the Caribbean.[9] By that year Seaforth regarded the danger presented by the slaves as increasingly serious and potentially imminent. He complained to the secretary of state, Lord Camden, that 'the laxity of the Police promotes among the slaves a spirit of insolence and insubordination that spreads fast, particularly in the towns, while wanton crueltys [sic] irritate them to extremity' and asked for Camden's help in pressing the Assembly to pass a slaves protection bill.[10]

Seaforth's motivation and that of the British government has to be examined in the light of the long-running controversy over the reasons for the abolition of the British slave trade in 1807. The current balance of opinion is that it was due to pressure from abolitionists in Britain, fear of slave revolt and political pressures from free people of colour.[11] The leading Barbadian historian argues that measures of amelioration were because of fears that a rebellious minority of slaves might otherwise become a majority.[12] The British government had a strong incentive to improve the legal position of the slaves. The credit on which Britain was fighting Napoleon depended to a significant extent on the sugar cargoes from the West Indies. Times of particular danger were when major French fleets were active in the Caribbean. Then the invasion of British islands was a real possibility and the likely response of the slaves to this would be a critical factor.[13]

One of the most influential metropolitan campaigners against the slave trade, James Stephen, argued that only amelioration of slave conditions could retain the loyalty of slaves and enable the sugar islands to be defended against France.[14] Barbados stood out because other British West Indian colonies had already legislated to improve the legal position of slaves.[15] Parliament in 1797 had called on West Indian governors to secure for slaves the active protection of the law, and it was only in Barbados that this had not been done.[16] The campaign for abolition of the slave trade made it important for a government which was trying to balance competing interests that there should not be outbreaks of slave revolt.[17] Seaforth was accordingly backed on the Slaves Protection Bill by two successive secretaries of state (Hobart and Camden) under two prime ministers (Addington and Pitt). The government's support was most evident in 1802, when a public message of support from Hobart induced the Assembly to hold joint talks on the issue with the Council (unproductive) and in 1805, when the Slaves Protection Act was finally passed.[18]

Free people of colour

Free people of colour were mainly freed slaves and their descendants. Their numbers were small – estimated in 1801 at 2,209, representing 2.7 per cent of the population of Barbados, compared to whites 19.3 per cent and slaves 78 per cent.[19] However, about half the population of Bridgetown, the island capital, were free people of colour, and they were also a significant presence in the smaller urban centres of Speightstown and Holetown.[20] Most were in manual occupations or scraped a living by huckstering. A small but increasing number had become prosperous, especially in the hospitality trades, and were owners of land and slaves. A sense of the tensions between whites and free people of colour is given in an open letter addressed to Seaforth on his arrival by 'a Barbadian', in reality John Poyer speaking for urban and poorer whites. He asserted that free people of colour 'should not be suffered to exceed the bounds of that subordinate state in which divine Providence has placed them' and that it was dangerous for the future security of the colony that they should be allowed to accumulate land and slaves.[21]

Seaforth lost no time in forming his own view, and explained with characteristic clarity and force to Lord Hobart:

> There is . . . a third description of people from whom I am more suspicious of evil than either from the whites or slaves, and yet whom I cannot bring myself to call free. I think unappropriated people would be a more proper denomination for them . . . their evidence cannot be taken either in civil or criminal cases . . . and they experience the most shocking outrages and unprovoked ill treatment both in their families and persons . . . yet these people . . . are allowed to acquire and possess land and other real property. This is a combination of circumstances that I cannot look upon without terror, thinking I see in it the seeds of inevitable future destruction to the colony.[22]

Both Poyer and Seaforth were concerned that free people of colour might lead a slave revolt. But whereas Poyer wished to reduce their rights, Seaforth aimed to extend them. He recommended in May 1801 'some measure which . . . might insure to those people the means of existence when age, sickness or misfortunes render them incapable of procuring it by their own exertions'. Poyer was not amused. He asked, 'why should the emancipated African be exempt from the common lot of humanity, to eat bread in the sweat of his brow?'[23] The Assembly passed a bill which substantially increased the sums payable to the parish on the manumission (freeing) of slaves to £300 for a female and £200 for a male, intended to cover the cost of relief to pauper free people of colour.[24] Poyer believed the governor had been tricked into accepting this, thinking it would help poor free people of colour, when in reality it was designed to reduce their number by making it less attractive to free old and broken-down slaves.[25] However, Seaforth was not naive. He wrote to the secretary of state that 'the bill for the better provision of freed negroes was loudly called for both by humanity and good policy as the smallness of the sum attending manumission of slaves was accumulating the number of freed people of colour to an alarming extent'.[26] On the French Caribbean islands also 'liberty taxes' were imposed on manumissions, but with very limited success.[27] On Saint-Domingue by 1789 *gens de couleur* had reached a much higher proportion of the free population than in Barbados (one of the lower estimates for that date being 40 per cent).[28]

Seaforth made clear to the Assembly in July 1801 that he wished to encourage the 'worthy, peaceable and industrious' free people of colour, of whom he 'finds with pleasure there is considerable numbers'. They would be the potential leaders of a revolt if their position was not ameliorated, and their ownership of land and slaves increased their potential to do harm. He asked 'how far it may be advisable to permit them, to acquire real property'.[29] There might seem to be as much pragmatism as idealism here. However, there is considerable evidence of Seaforth intervening on behalf of people of colour whose free status was challenged by whites. In 1802 he told one of the justices that such cases should be investigated with moderation and humanity and insisted that 'I will most assuredly do my utmost to protect every description of the public'.[30] There is evidence of him doing this. For example, he was petitioned by a free man of colour who had been imprisoned for assaulting a white man and liberated him on the grounds of self-defence.[31]

Seaforth's main ambition for free people of colour was that they should be permitted to give evidence in court against white men so as to be able to enforce debts owed them. He argued to the secretary of state in 1802 that this should be corrected for 'the purposes of Justice and Humanity' and because the free people of colour might facilitate a black revolt as they had done on other islands.[32] In an impassioned letter to Prime Minister William Pitt in 1804 he wrote that 'all that is wanted to create confusion is heads and hands to lay the train and give effect to the explosion, and these are only to be found among the free coloured people'.[33] Signs of growing political mobilisation by free people of colour were petitions in 1799, 1801 and 1803 in favour of the right to testify against whites and against attempts to restrict their property rights.[34] The Samaritan Charitable Society of the Free People of Colour, formed in 1798, was also a reflection of the political aspirations of wealthy non-white men.[35] In May 1805 Seaforth argued again to Camden that by failing to improve the legal position of the free people of colour 'we compel a considerable part of our population to be necessarily our Enemies who are highly desirous of being our friends'.[36]

The view of a majority of the Assembly was that free people of colour were more of a threat than an ally. It was only with difficulty that in 1803 Seaforth managed to resist a bill sent up twice by the Assembly which would have limited the number of slaves they could own to five and their acres of land to ten.[37] This was John Poyer's scheme to protect the interests of urban and poorer whites as small traders, innkeepers and tradesmen. It reflected actions taken earlier in the French Caribbean, where free people of colour lost rights in the 1780s. After the Revolution (in 1790) they were declared to have equal rights with whites. Taking a different approach, in 1795 a Spanish royal order enabled free people of colour to buy certain white privileges, thus ensuring that only rich members of that community could benefit.[38] In Barbados, Seaforth was able to have the 1803 bill rejected by the Council. Its plantocratic members shared his concern to keep free people of colour on side and were also nervous of any legal limitation on the right to own slaves.[39] Attorney General Beckles declared that the bill was cruel and unconstitutional in depriving free persons of rights and privileges incident to freedom.[40] However, Seaforth had no direct support from Whitehall in protecting the existing rights of free people of colour, in which he succeeded. Nor did he have government support in increasing

Figure 9.1 Sunbury plantation house, Barbados – home in Seaforth's time to John Henry Barrow, owner of a substantial sugar plantation, member of the island Council and supporter of the governor. (© Finlay McKichan)

their rights, in which he failed.[41] In contrast the government showed great concern for the rights of free people of colour in Trinidad. The needs of this recently conquered island were seen as more pressing. The free people of colour there were a much higher proportion of the population than in Barbados, where, it is likely, they were not considered in London a sufficient danger to justify a struggle with the Assembly.[42]

The Slaves Protection Bill

Seaforth's speech to the island Assembly on 28 July 1801 was the defining moment of his governorship. By proposing that the murder of any persons (free or slave) should be a capital offence, he launched what was to be his most vigorously pursued and divisive policy. Although he had orders from the Westminster government to promote this measure, it created the enemies who were to plague him as long as he remained on the island. He raised the issue by pointing out, incontrovertibly, that most neighbouring islands had already passed such a law. Warming to the theme, he argued:

> An act to this purpose is not only loudly called for to protect the character of the island and to remove the astonishment of the Mother Country that it has not long ago been done, but is self evidently consistent with honour, honesty and Christianity, for none but villains can be benefited by the want of such an act . . . A code may be formed . . . than which nothing would more contribute to the Governor's own ambition of happiness.[43]

This message was highly offensive to those he sought to win over. The shocked reaction is shown by their failure to make any immediate response. The message was neither acknowledged nor even mentioned in the Assembly Minutes.[44] Seaforth was soon told that it had offended and that it sounded like the clauses of a bill, which by convention the governor did not initiate. He justified it to the secretary of state by arguing that:

> He wished fairly and candidly to impress on the Assembly the sense the rest of mankind entertains of their perseverance in a point not only so utterly contrary to every implied principle of Christianity, but to the positive and explicit commands of God.[45]

It is fortunate that he did not make these comments to the Assembly. As shown in Chapter Eight, Seaforth has been accused of hypocrisy in owning slaves but professing principles of humanity. However, his conservative world view gave him a sense of obligation towards people for whom he believed he was responsible, whether slaves in Barbados or (as shown in Chapter Two) small tenants in Ross-shire. A link can be seen between his attitude to his Highland tenants and to enslaved labourers in Berbice (discussed in Chapter Eight) and in Barbados. He demonstrated regular concern for the welfare of black people in Barbados. When a black regiment, the 8th West Indian, mutinied in Dominica in 1802 over arrears of pay and poor food, Seaforth wrote, 'the treatment these poor devils met with is really shocking … it is highly disgraceful both to the Nation and the service'. He was horrified when six of the black mutineers were brought to Barbados for execution and described this as a 'massacre'.[46] When in 1802 a slave was found starving by the roadside, he instructed the justices to take action 'to enforce justice and common humanity'.[47] Seaforth was not unique in being a landowning governor with the same concern for black people as for his small tenants at home. Sir Richard Bourke, a paternalistic Irish landlord and acting governor of the Cape Colony in the late 1820s, sought to protect the Khoi people, who were under pressure from advancing European colonists.[48]

At the next Assembly meeting after 28 July 1801, on 13 October, Seaforth's allies knew they were on the defensive. The island's treasurer proposed that a committee of Assembly be appointed to meet a committee of Council to consult on a consolidation of the slave laws. The Council was composed mainly of owners of large plantations, chosen by the governor, and aware of the political need to demonstrate at least a measure of amelioration to the imperial government. This attempt to pour oil on troubled waters was probably not helped by the assertion of John Beckles, attorney general, and a Seaforth ally, that:

No man can sincerely think the present punishment sufficient. A law which empowers a proprietor to make a slaughter house in his plantation, and to butcher in cold blood as many of his slaves as he may think proper without suffering any other punishment than the paying a sum not equal to what he must pay for killing his neighbour's bull or his ox, must be a disgrace to any community.

Robert James Haynes was determined that the Assembly should meet the governor's July message head-on with 'an answer moderate and respectful, but calculated to repel insult and evince that the House understands its interests and asserts its rights'. He complained of 'the European Governor's interference between the white inhabitants of the island and their slaves'. This was to be the nub of Seaforth's problems in Barbados. The treasurer's proposal was defeated by a small majority, but Haynes did not secure enough support for as robust a reply as he had hoped. The message finally approved informed Seaforth that the Assembly would take his message into consideration, but observed that it had been 'expressed in language unusual in communications between the Governor and the Assembly'.[49] Colonists used to a great measure of self-government were not likely to respond well to such language. The defeat of the treasurer's motion was crucial as it showed that a majority in the Assembly had no intention of considering reforms to the slave laws. At the November 1801 Assembly meeting, Seaforth (characteristically thin-skinned) described the Assembly's relatively mild rebuke as 'a solemn and deliberate vote of censure on that part of the Legislature which represents the sovereign' (ie the governor). More constructively, he stated his belief that most Barbados planters treated their slaves well, and enquired what, therefore, was the basis of their opposition? If he had tactfully led with this argument in July, the opposition might have been more limited.[50]

Who were the leading opponents of the Slaves Protection Bill? Robert James Haynes was a substantial planter and militia officer born in Barbados. He also voted against the bill in 1805. Four other Assembly members voted against both the treasurer's motion in 1801 and the bill in 1805 – Thomas Williams, William Culpepper, James Scott Payne and Thomas Piggott.[51] These were the core of the opposition to the bill and to the governor. Haynes, Culpepper, Payne and Williams represented between them the three adjoining parishes of St Joseph, St Andrew and St Thomas.[52] St Joseph and St Andrew were remote eastern parishes comprising the district known as 'Scotland'. The land there was poor and much of it unsuitable for sugar cultivation. Many of the whites in these parishes had small farms, just sufficient to qualify for the ten acres required to have a vote for the Assembly.[53] The core of the opposition to Seaforth came from the representatives of poorer whites (a larger proportion

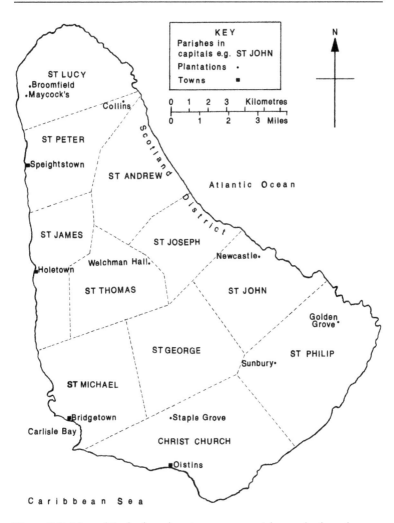

KEY
Parishes in capitals e.g. ST JOHN
Plantations ·
Towns ■

0 1 2 3 Kilometres
0 1 2 3 Miles

N

ST LUCY
·Broomfield
·Maycock's

Collins

ST PETER

■Speightstown

ST ANDREW

Scotland District

Atlantic Ocean

ST JAMES

ST JOSEPH

Newcastle·

Welchman Hall·

▲Holetown

ST THOMAS

ST JOHN

Golden Grove·

ST GEORGE

Sunbury·

ST PHILIP

ST MICHAEL

■Bridgetown

Carlisle Bay

·Staple Grove

·Oistins

CHRIST CHURCH

■Oistins

Caribbean Sea

Figure 9.2 Map of Barbados, showing towns, parishes and selected plantations *c.*1800. (© Joan C. McKichan)

of the white population than on other islands),[54] with one or two richer leaders, notably Robert James Haynes and Thomas Williams. Most of the less affluent whites did not have a sufficiently sophisticated knowledge of British politics to understand how to come to terms with a governor and an imperial government which demanded amelioration of the condition of the slaves. John Poyer was a spokesman of such people. He hoped that Seaforth had 'come among us with a mind superior to those prejudices on the subject of slavery which have unhappily found so general and favourable a reception among our mistaken and misinformed fellow subjects on the other side of the Atlantic'.[55] But Poyer was to be disappointed. Seaforth did not approve of laws which permitted slaves to be seriously ill-treated.

Before Seaforth approached the Assembly again he was determined to have more open support from Whitehall, such as a strong order to the Assembly. He reminded the secretary of state that, although the practice of the Barbadian planters in treating their slaves was at least as lenient as their neighbours, their laws 'are by far the most illiberal and harsh of any of the colonies'.[56] He believed he would have the support at least of nine of the twenty-two Assemblymen, but admitted that the prejudices of others reflected the views of a large part of the white community: 'They have written ridiculous . . . pamphlets against me as "a barbarous wretch . . . for wishing to hang an amiable white man and a respectable member of the community for killing a rascally negro".'[57] This was offensive to Seaforth as one whose attitudes were humanitarian if conservative. He was now rewarded with the first of two major interventions in this controversy by the secretary of state. Hobart wrote to commend 'the humane disposition which has elsewhere been manifested to make a serious and effective reform for the advantage and comfort of the negroes' and expressed astonishment that the Barbados Assembly had deliberately refused to address this.[58] The government was balancing the opposing pressures of British ante-slavery campaigners and the metropolitan representatives of the planters, and advocating by way of compromise a policy of amelioration. Thus armed, Seaforth was able to press the issue again on the Assembly in December 1802, this time tactfully assuring them that he had 'the greatest deference to their superior opportunities of information'. However, he emphasised 'the strong instructions he had received from His Majesty's Principal Secretary of State for the Colonial Department' and illustrated this with extracts. The Assembly's response was to appoint a committee to join a Council committee to take the slave laws into consideration, and thus effectively kick the issue into the long grass. It was not a good omen that the Assembly's immediately following item of business was to pass the bill 'to prevent the accumulation of real property by free negroes' (subsequently rejected by the Council, as shown above).[59]

In November 1803 Seaforth sailed for England on sick leave, and no further legislative steps were taken until after his return in August 1804. He had prolonged dental treatment in London, which involved extractions and then the implant of false teeth ('pulling out and putting in' as he described it).[60] Shortly before he left to return, the Barbados situation was highlighted in a House of Commons debate on slave-trade abolition. The Barbados Assembly's unwillingness to address the issue of slave murders was used in the House 'to show how little assistance was to be derived from the colonial assemblies in any endeavour to ameliorate the condition of the slaves'.[61] When Seaforth landed at Bridgetown he learned that during his absence there had been a series of particularly brutal and callous killings of slaves by whites. He wrote to the secretary of state, the earl of Camden:

> I would humbly beg that some strong instructions should be sent from home. Nothing can be expected to be effectually done on this side of the water. I have often vainly tried but I find it impossible either to rouse them from the torpor they are in or shake their barbarous and almost incomprehensible prejudices.[62]

He set about collecting evidence, asking the parish clergy and various legal officials to give him reports on cases which he named.[63] However, when the next packet ship was due to sail, he was still struggling to receive detailed reports, and argued to Camden that the murders were 'not only really disgraceful to the British character but I think . . . highly dangerous to the safety of the colony'. He had returned to find 'a spirit of insolence and insubordination' spreading fast among the slaves, particularly in the towns.[64] The evidence of increasing restlessness among slaves as they learned of metropolitan campaigning has been discussed earlier in this chapter. These murders might be the spark which ignited a slave revolt.

Seaforth went well beyond the call of duty in investigating these slave murders against resistance and in expressing his disgust at the findings. In one case, a pregnant black woman had been bayoneted and killed on the road by a drunk estate overseer because she did not get out of his way quickly enough.[65] Seaforth was especially shocked that the employer of the overseer, a female planter, declined to take action on the grounds that she would gain nothing by it, 'thereby putting the interest of humanity and the dignity and honour of the community you

belong to completely out of the question'.[66] In another case, a
runaway boy had been shot in a pond and then buried alive
by Crone, a plantation manager. Seaforth expressed his revul-
sion by writing to the owner that this was a disgrace to the
colony and that such horrors were un-Christian.[67] In a third
case, Thomas Howell, a butcher in St Andrews parish and notorious for his cruelty to his slaves, had cut out the tongue of and
thereby killed a female house slave who had released his wife
after he had locked her up.[68] Seaforth's strong personal commitment prevented him using the soft words and the techniques
of political persuasion which might have won a better hearing
from men whose status and prosperity appeared to them to
depend on maintaining the subordination of the slaves. The difficulty he had in getting this information undermines the claim
by a mid-nineteenth-century British historian that he had been
fed exaggerated stories by reformers.[69]

Seaforth still feared the Slaves Protection Bill would be thrown
out by the Assembly.[70] However, his detailed reports had their
intended effect in Whitehall and in early 1805 he received a
second public statement of support from the imperial government, and a much clearer and more explicit one than in 1802.
The secretary of state wrote:

> I am commanded by His Majesty to convey to you his royal appro-
> bation of the zeal and vigour with which you have proceeded, and
> that it is his royal pleasure that you do send a message in his name
> to the Council and House of Assembly . . . to pass laws which, fol-
> lowing up the system adopted in Jamaica and other islands, shall
> produce regulations favourable to the wellbeing and protection of
> the negroes tending to rescue them from the danger of improper
> usage by their masters and constituting the maiming and murder of
> a negro by any person whatever to be a capital felony.[71]

Seaforth was quick to use this backing to seek the Assembly's
approval of the Slaves Protection Bill on 9 April 1805. He did
so with the remarkably brief statement, 'I am particularly and
expressly ordered by His Majesty in his name to recommend to
you the passing of some act to protect the lives of his slave subjects in this colony.'[72] He now had the political guile to leave the
talking to his island supporters and thus avoid the earlier accu-
sation that he was a European governor interfering between
long-established islanders and their slaves. On this occasion

the circumstances were much more propitious to securing the Assembly's co-operation. The declaration of independence of the black republic of Haiti in 1804 had been a blow to the confidence of Europeans throughout the Caribbean. More recently, in February 1805, a French fleet of five ships of the line and 4,000 troops had arrived in the Caribbean and attacked a series of British islands, the first being Dominica.[73] The *Barbados Mercury* frightened its readers with detailed accounts of how the French had extracted large sums from Dominica, St Kitts, Nevis and Montserrat.[74] Seaforth persuaded the Assembly to approve a series of measures for the defence of Barbados by highlighting that at Dominica the French had added 'the cruelty of individual pillage and extortion to the unavoidable horrors of war'.[75] In the event, Barbados escaped attack, but the defence measures had been notable for the strong support of slaves conscripted to support the militia. Seaforth was impressed by the 'armed blacks of whom we have 2000, I assure you fine trusty fellows'.[76]

John Beckles, now the Assembly Speaker, made the principal speech on behalf of the bill and declared:

> Our slaves showed the strongest attachments, they came forward with the greatest cheerfulness and alacrity to fight by our sides in defence of our lives and properties. Does not this call for some return from us? Justice and Gratitude call upon us to do something for the protection of the lives of those who are so ready and willing to protect our's.[77]

It was not only a matter of gratitude for services rendered. Seaforth pointed out the same day, in an attempt to secure an extension and a strengthening of the Militia Act, that other French squadrons were believed to be trying to escape the Royal Navy blockade and might soon be in the Caribbean. The attitude of the slaves would be crucial in the event, which seemed not unlikely, of a French attack on Barbados. The bill, Beckles declared, would 'endear us more strongly to them and will add to our security'.[78] He also pointed out that if the Assembly again refused to pass a bill for the protection of slaves, the imperial parliament was likely to do it with such a preamble 'as will be a perpetual monument to our disgrace and dishonour'. The implications of this were emphasised by John Pollard Mayers, another supporter of the bill. If the right of the Westminster parliament to legislate for the colonies was exercised, 'there is no saying to what extent it might be carried'.[79] His listeners would not be slow to see in this a threat to the existence of slavery itself, emphasised by events in Haiti.

At last, a combination of powerful circumstances persuaded the Barbados Assembly to vote for the Slaves Protection Bill by thirteen votes to eight after four years of pressure by the governor. This moment could be seen as the high point of Seaforth's governorship and indeed of his entire public career. He wrote to Lord Camden, 'it is with great pleasure that I inform you that, contrary to universal expectation, the bill to make murdering of slaves felony passed the Assembly.'[80]

How had it been achieved? Seaforth sent Camden a detailed analysis showing that he had anticipated that ten members would be against the bill and eight for it. Four others he described in advance of the vote as 'intimidated . . . could not be depended on and might be hostile'. All four of these voted for the bill, as did two on the 'hostile' list of Assembly members. These were the men whose minds were changed by the circumstances discussed above.[81] Seaforth's supporters on the Slaves Bill were mainly the wealthier planters, who had a sufficiently wide view to understand both the strategic and the British political context. Such men were hoping to preserve the slave system by amelioration (even if limited)[82], and that Seaforth himself was a supporter of slavery may have helped him to build a winning coalition. The representatives of the five prosperous southern parishes (St Michael, Christchurch, St Philip, St George and St John) voted solidly for the bill. The seconder of the bill, John Pollard Mayers, owned the Staple Grove plantation in Christchurch.[83] Five of the eight members who voted against were from the group of mostly poor parishes (St Andrew, St Joseph and St Thomas), which, it has been argued, had been at the core of the opposition to amelioration since 1801.[84] Seaforth described Robert James Haynes (a representative of St Joseph parish) as 'the most violent senseless man on the Island – he has been and I think always will be in opposition'. Thomas Piggott (St James parish) he called 'a low illiterate man'. Thomas Williams was described by Seaforth as 'of low origin but opulent and in a part of the country where there were no real gentlemen'. Williams' plantation, Welchman Hall, was in St Thomas, which he represented in the Assembly, but near the boundary with St Joseph and thus close to the Scotland district. He, like Robert James

Haynes, was a substantial planter who chose to represent the views of the poorer whites who dominated his area. He had consulted on parade the St Thomas militia regiment, of which he was colonel, asking those opposed to the bill to shoulder arms. All did so, declaring that their arms would remain there if the bill passed until it was repealed.[85] Such men were the foundation of opposition to Seaforth and to the nuanced policies of the imperial government.[86]

Why did the secretary of state issue a much stronger message of support for the Slaves Bill than in 1802 and why did it appear that, if the Barbados Assembly again refused to act, the Westminster parliament would this time do so? As has been seen, the British government had been unwilling to offend the planters by supporting Seaforth either on the status of the free people of colour or on the reform of the militia. However, it was suggested in Chapter Seven that the September 1804 Order in Council limiting imports from the US showed that the influence of the West Indian planters was weakening. The campaigns of British abolitionists damaged the image of planters at Westminster. They had seen themselves as respectable and respected members of the British nation, and were horrified to find that many British people, including MPs, now regarded the slaves and not the planters as their brothers.[87] To his chagrin, extracts from Seaforth's letter to Lord Camden on slave murders were printed in a London newspaper and turned into an abolitionist pamphlet.[88] While William Pitt was by no means reconciled to passing an abolitionist measure, it was politically necessary for him to make concessions on this issue, which had given so much scope for abolitionist propaganda.[89] It was also important for the war effort to reduce the danger of slave revolt. Was this a purely tactical initiative or is it possible to see it as evidence of longer term determination by Westminster to reduce the freedom of action by West Indian assemblies? It has been generally believed that this trend did not develop until after 1815.[90] The Secretaryship of State for War and the Colonies had been established in 1801 and a Colonial Office to support him. However, this has usually been seen simply as a political tactic in the creation of a new government, and until after 1815 the office was manned only by junior clerks.[91] An alternative view is that the initiative in colonial government was shifting away from the West Indian assemblies to Whitehall before 1815.[92] Whether Seaforth's relationship with Whitehall gives evidence of this will be assessed in Chapter Ten, when a judgement can be made from the whole period of his governorship.

Seaforth had declared at the start of the campaign in 1801 that nothing would more contribute to his own ambition of happiness than an Act to protect slaves, which he had now achieved.[93] Or had he? His surprised delight at the result of the Assembly vote in April 1805 was understandable, but how great a victory was it? The Slaves Protection Act 1805 stated in clear humanitarian terms in its preamble that 'the wilful and malicious murder of any fellow creature whether it be a free person or a slave ought to be punished with the death of the murderer', but conviction was to be dependent on the evidence of a white person.[94] Not only the members who voted for it, but also Seaforth, were fully aware of this. His ally John Beckles, in moving the bill, made clear that it 'does not alter the rules of evidence, and no man can be convicted under it, but by a verdict of twelve freeholders, his peers' (that is, whites).[95] If the only witnesses to the murder of a slave were black, as might well be the case, their evidence was inadmissible. It can only be concluded that Seaforth agreed to this concession because he was by now desperate to have a slaves bill passed and believed this could only be achieved by winning over some of the opposition. It was not to be until 1830 that all restrictions on the admission of slave evidence were removed.[96]

Conclusions

It has been argued in Chapter Two that Seaforth dealt with his small tenants in Ross-shire in a conservative but humanitarian manner. Chapter Eight and this chapter suggest that his approach to enslaved labourers in Berbice and Barbados was similar. He supported slavery, at least for the foreseeable future, but attempted to ensure (with very mixed success) that slaves were well looked after. In Berbice his intentions were hampered by unfavourable weather and shortage of capital. In Barbados the benefits of the Slaves Protection Act were diluted by planter resistance. He was not the first to promote the amelioration of slave conditions in Barbados. In the 1780s Joshua Steele had forbidden the use of the whip and paid his slaves. This was anathema even to other planters who considered themselves enlightened. Their idea of amelioration was to treat female slaves well enough to enable them to breed the next generation of slaves, so that by the early 1800s Barbados, uniquely, had barely any need to import slaves from Africa.[97] Most today would consider that Seaforth and those who had similar ideas were trying to humanise a system which was fundamentally inhumane.[98] It has been argued in Chapter Eight that he was sincere. His opposition to the ending of the slave trade or speedy emancipation was not driven only by his commercial interests. The anti-slavery campaign was based on new forms of political action (mass agitation and large public meetings) which he disliked and for which he was not equipped. This was very different from politicking behind the scenes and the use of influence, at which, in Britain, it has been shown in Chapter Five, he was skilful, and from which he had achieved so much.

As with his Highland tenants, the benefits to enslaved labourers of the Slaves Protection Act were limited. Despite the concessions he had to make, Seaforth expected that the passing of the Slaves Act would facilitate progress on other issues which it has been shown in Chapter Seven he considered necessary. He wrote to the secretary of state:

> Now this stumbling block is out of the way I have little doubt of being able to convince the Assembly how necessary it is to pass a Police Bill that shall be strong and humane and that shall ensure the safety of the whites and the happiness of the blacks by introducing and regularly enforcing a spirit of good order, regular habits, discipline and subordination, upheld by humanity and protection.

It may have been a sense of realism which led him to add 'luckily some bill must now pass'.[99] However, this did not happen. Only a particular, and in many respects temporary, combination of circumstances, coupled with direct pressure from Whitehall, secured the passing of the Slaves Bill, and that by a majority of only five votes. A police bill would have limited the freedoms of whites as well as addressing what they saw as increasing insolence and disorder among the black population. In Chapter Ten, Seaforth's continued attempts to reform the militia will be referred to. A judgement will be made there on whether Whitehall at this time had any consistent purpose to reassert imperial control over the internal governance of the West Indies. As has been shown in Chapter Seven, the resilience of Seaforth himself and more particularly his family to the Barbados climate was coming under increasing strain and, consequently, his governorship was nearing its end. What he had desperately feared and laboured to avert – a slave rebellion – occurred in 1816 and was to be the largest enslaved uprising in two centuries on Barbados.[100]

Notes

1. Edinburgh, National Records of Scotland (NRS), GD46/17/80/235–6, 'Argument for Lord Seaforth in defence of his message to the Assembly', n.d.
2. Craton, M., *Testing the Chains: Resistance to Slavery in the British West Indies* (Ithaca, 1982), pp. 11–13, 164–5.
3. Ibid., pp. 183–90, 190–204, 211–26, 228–9.
4. Hamilton, D. J., *Scotland, the Caribbean and the Atlantic World 1750–1820* (Manchester, 2005), p. 38.
5. London, The National Archives (TNA), CO28/68, pp. 48–50, 52–3, Lord Seaforth to Lord Hobart, 6 June 1802.
6. Welch, P. L. V., *Slave Society in the City: Bridgetown, Barbados, 1680–1834* (Kingston, 2003), pp. 157, 162.
7. Beckles, H., *Black Rebellion in Barbados: The Struggle Against Slavery 1637–1838* (Bridgetown, 1987), pp. 68, 83; Beckles, H., *Afro-Caribbean Women and Resistance to Slavery in Barbados* (London, 1988), pp. 75–9.
8. Lambert, D., *White Creole Culture, Politics and Identity during the Age of Abolition* (Cambridge, 2005), p. 32.
9. Nicholls, D., *From Dessalenes to Duvalier: Race, Colour and National Independence in Haiti* (Cambridge, 1979), p. 3.
10. TNA, CO28/71, pp. 92, 94, 147, Lord Seaforth to Earl of Camden, 1 and 30 September, 13 November 1804.
11. Petley, C., 'Rethinking the fall of the planter class', *Atlantic Studies*, vol. 9, 1, 2012, pp. 1–9; Ryden, D. B., *West Indian Slavery and British Abolition, 1783–1807* (Cambridge, 2009), pp. 7–18; Hilton, B., 'And all that: why Britain outlawed her slave trade' in D. R. Peterson (ed.), *Abolitionism and Imperialism in Britain, Africa and the Atlantic* (Athens, OH, 2010), pp. 69–75
12. Beckles, *Black Rebellion in Barbados*, p. 8.
13. Duffy, M., 'World-Wide War and British Expansionism, 1793–1815' in P. J. Marshall (ed.), *Oxford History of British Empire*, vol. 2 (Oxford, 1998), pp. 190–2.
14. In J. Stephen, *The Crisis of the Sugar Colonies* (1802), quoted Whyte, I., *Scotland and the Abolition of Black Slavery, 1756–1838* (Edinburgh, 2006), p. 118.

15. Watson, K., *The Civilised Island: Barbados, a Social History 1750–1816* (St George, Barbados, 1979), p. 67; Ward, J. M., *Colonial Self-Government: The British Experience 1759–1856* (London, 1976), p. 91; Goveia, E. V., *Slave Society in the British Leeward Islands at the End of the Eighteenth Century* (New Haven, 1965), p. 191.
16. Schomburgk, R. H., *The History of Barbados* (London, 1848), p. 358.
17. Bayly, C. A., *Imperial Meridian: The British Empire and the World, 1780–1830* (Harlow, 1989), p. 221.
18. TNA, CO28/68, pp. 10–11, Lord Seaforth to Lord Hobart, 18 March 1802; CO29/29, p. 17, Lord Hobart to Lord Seaforth, 5 September 1802; CO28/69, pp. 51–3, Barbados Assembly Minute, 9 November 1802; CO28/72, p. 123, *Barbados Mercury and Bridgetown Gazette*, 16 April 1805.
19. Handler, J. S., *The Unappropriated People: Freedmen in the Slave Society of Barbados* (Baltimore, 1974), pp. 18–19.
20. Welch, *Slave Society in the City*, pp. 95, 169.
21. NRS, GD46/7/5, 'A Letter addressed to H. E. the Rt Hon. Francis Lord Seaforth by a Barbadian' (Bridgetown, 1801), p. 24.
22. TNA, CO28/68, p. 49, Lord Seaforth to Lord Hobart, 6 June 1802.
23. Poyer, J., 'History of the Administration of the Rt Hon. Francis Lord Seaforth, late Governor, etc. etc.', *Barbados Chronicle*, 20 April–3 August 1808, *Journal of the Barbados Museum and Historical Society*, vol. 21, August 1954, p. 164.
24. TNA, CO28/67, pp. 67–8, Minute of Barbados Assembly, 12 May 1801.
25. Poyer, 'History of Administration of Lord Seaforth', p. 165.
26. TNA, CO28/67, p. 60, Lord Seaforth to Duke of Portland, 27 July 1801.
27. Dubois, L., *A Colony of Citizens: Revolution and Slave Emancipation in the French Caribbean, 1787–1804* (Chapel Hill, NC, 2004), pp. 32–3.
28. Boucher, P., 'The French and Dutch Caribbean, 1600–1800' in S. Palmie and F. A. Scarano (eds), *The Caribbean: A History of the Region and Its Peoples* (Chicago, 2011), p. 230.
29. NRS, GD46/17/19/241, Address by Lord Seaforth to Barbados Assembly, 28 July 1801.
30. NRS, GD46/7/7/24, Lord Seaforth to H. Olton, 14 July 1802.
31. NRS, GD46/17/25/73, J. Belgrave to Lord Seaforth, 3 September 1804.
32. TNA, CO28/68, p. 49, Lord Seaforth to Lord Hobart, 6 June 1802.
33. NRS, GD46/17/25/22, Lord Seaforth to W. Pitt, 17 June 1804.

34. Handler, *The Unappropriated People*, pp. 76–9; Beckles, H., 'Freedom without Liberty: Free Blacks in the Barbados Slave System' in V. E. Shepherd (ed.), *Slavery without Sugar: Diversity in Caribbean Economy and Society since the 17th Century* (Gainesville, Fla., 2002), pp. 204–8.

35. Newton, M., 'Philanthropy, Gender and the Production of Public Life in Barbados, ca.1790–ca.1850' in P. Scully and D. Paton (eds), *Gender and Slave Emancipation in the Atlantic World* (Durham, NC, 2005), p. 229.

36. TNA, CO28/72, p. 122, Lord Seaforth to Earl of Camden, 4 May 1805.

37. Handler, *The Unappropriated People*, pp. 71–2; Welch, P. L. V. with R. A. Goodridge, *'Red' and Black over White: Free Coloured Women in Pre-Emancipation Barbados* (Bridgetown, 2000), p. 102.

38. Gibson, C., *Empire's Crossroads: The Caribbean from Columbus to the Present Day* (London, 2014), pp. 149, 155, 164.

39. Handler, *The Unappropriated People*, pp. 80–1; Welch and Goodridge, *'Red' and Black over White*, p. 105.

40. TNA, CO28/70, p. 145, Barbados Council Minutes, 1 November 1803.

41. TNA, CO28/71, pp. 92, 94, Lord Seaforth to Earl of Camden, 1 September 1804; CO28/72, pp. 121–2, Lord Seaforth to Earl of Camden, 4 May 1805.

42. Manning, H. T., *British Colonial Government after the American Revolution* (New Haven, 1933), pp. 522–3.

43. NRS, GD46/17/19/241, Address to Barbados Assembly, 28 July 1801.

44. TNA, CO28/68, pp. 18–19, Minute of Barbados Assembly, 28 July 1801; CO28/68, p. 29, Minute of Barbados Council, 28 July 1801.

45. NRS, GD46/17/19/254–8, 'Argument for Lord Seaforth in defence of his Message to the Assembly submitted to H. M. with greatest humility by Lord Seaforth', n.d.

46. Buckley, R. N., *Slaves in Red Coats: The British West Indian Regiments, 1795–1815* (New Haven, 1979), pp. 76–8; Aberdeen University Special Collections, MS 3470/6/2/53, Lord Seaforth to Col. A. Mackenzie, 31 July 1802.

47. NRS, GD46/7/7/60, Lord Seaforth to justices of the peace, 6 December 1802.

48. Laidlaw, Z., 'Richard Bourke: Irish liberalism tempered by empire', in D. Lambert and A. Lester (eds), *Colonial Lives across the British Empire: Imperial Careering in the Long Nineteenth Century* (Cambridge, 2006), pp. 121–125.

49. TNA, CO28/68, pp. 21–2, Barbados Assembly Minute, 13 October 1801.

50. TNA, CO28/68, pp. 81–2, Barbados Assembly Minute, 10 November 1801.

51. TNA, CO28/68, pp. 21–2, Barbados Assembly Minute, 13 October 1801; CO28/72, p. 123, *Barbados Mercury and Bridgetown Gazette*, 16 April 1805, report on passing of bill for better protection of slaves on 9 April 1805.

52. TNA, CO28/72, pp. 131–2, 'List of members of Barbados Assembly who supported or opposed bill re murdering of slaves', 1805.

53. Lambert, *White Creole Culture*, pp. 19, 78.

54. Beckles, *Black Rebellion in Barbados*, pp. 68–9.

55. NRS, GD46/7/5, 'Letter addressed to Lord Seaforth by a Barbadian', pp. 21–2.

56. TNA, CO28/68, pp. 52–3, Lord Seaforth to Lord Hobart, 6 June 1802.

57. NRS, GD46/7/7/21, Lord Seaforth to Lord Hobart, 28 June 1802.

58. TNA, CO29/29, pp. 18–19, Lord Hobart to Lord Seaforth, 6 September 1802.

59. TNA, CO28/69, pp. 51–2, Barbados Assembly Minute, 9 November 1802; Lambert, *White Creole Culture*, pp. 96–7.

60. Edinburgh, National Library of Scotland, MS 6396, fo. 42, Lord Seaforth to Lady Seaforth, 3 May 1804.

61. *Caledonian Mercury*, 2 July 1804, 19th Century British Library Newspapers online, re House of Commons debate 27 June 1804 on third reading of Slave Trade Abolition Bill, accessed 3 February 2011.

62. TNA, CO28/71, p. 92, Lord Seaforth to Earl of Camden, 1 September 1804.

63. NRS, GD46/7/7/161, Lord Seaforth circular to clergy, judges, Attorney General, Advocate General, etc., 19 September 1804.

64. NRS, GD46/17/10, Lord Seaforth to Earl of Camden, 30 September 1804.

65. NRS, GD46/17/25/76, 'Statement in the case of Henry Halls'; /115–16, Advocate General M. Coalthurst to Lord Seaforth, 25 October 1804.

66. NRS, GD46/17/25/61, Lord Seaforth to Attorney for Mrs Clarke, 27 September 1804.

67. NRS, GD46/7/7/164, Lord Seaforth to H. Crowe, 27 September 1804.

68. NRS, GD46/17/25/115–16, M. Coalthurst to Lord Seaforth, 25 October 1804.

69. Schomburgk, *History of Barbados*, p. 359.

70. TNA, CO28/71, p. 147, Lord Seaforth to Earl of Camden, 13 November 1804.
71. TNA CO29/29, pp. 46–7, Earl of Camden to Lord Seaforth, 21 January 1805.
72. NRS, GD46/7/11/169, Addresses by Lord Seaforth to Barbados Council and Assembly, 9 April 1805.
73. Schomburgk, *History of Barbados*, pp. 360–1.
74. *Barbados Mercury and Bridgetown Gazette*, 30 March and 2 April 1805, British Library (BL) microfilm MC1888.
75. TNA, CO28/72, p. 199, Lord Seaforth, address to Barbados Council and Assembly, 6 March 1805.
76. Castle Fraser, Mackenzie Fraser Papers, 1/1168, Lord Seaforth to A. Mackenzie Fraser, 13 March 1805.
77. TNA, CO28/72, p. 123, *Barbados Mercury and Bridgetown Gazette*, 18 April 1805, report of Barbados Assembly meeting, 9 April 1805.
78. Duffy, 'World-Wide War and British Expansionism', pp. 190–2.
79. TNA, CO28/72, p. 123, *Barbados Mercury*, report of Barbados Assembly meeting, 9 April 1805.
80. TNA, CO28/72, p. 121, Lord Seaforth to Earl of Camden, 4 May 1805.
81. TNA, CO28/72, pp. 131–2, List of members of Barbados Assembly who supported and opposed Slaves Protection Bill.
82. Lambert, *White Creole Culture*, pp. 43–7, 69–72.
83. Black Rock, St James, Barbados Department of Archives (BDA), Planters Name Index.
84. TNA, CO28/72, p. 131, List of members of Barbados Assembly who supported and opposed Slaves Protection Bill.
85. TNA, CO28/72, pp. 126–7, Lord Seaforth to Lord Camden, 4 May 1805; BDA, Planters Name Index.
86. Lambert, *White Creole Culture*, p. 170.
87. Petley, C., '"Devoted Islands" and "That Madman Wilberforce": British Proslavery Patriotism During the Age of Abolition', *Journal of Imperial and Commonwealth History (JICH)*, vol. 39, 3, 2011, p. 406; Hilton, B., 'And all that: why Britain outlawed her slave trade', D. R. Peterson (ed.), *Abolitionism and Imperialism in Britain, Africa and the Atlantic* (Athens, OH, 2010), pp. 73–5.
88. NRS, GD46/7/12/120–1, Lord Seaforth to G. W. Jordan, Barbados agent in London, 27 July 1805.
89. Ehrmann, J., *The Younger Pitt*, vol. 8 (London, 1996), p. 667.
90. Murray, D. J., *The West Indies and the Development of Colonial Government 1801–1834* (Oxford, 1955), pp. xii, 13, 32–3, 46; Laidlaw, Z., *Colonial Connections, 1815–45: Patronage, the*

Information Revolution and Colonial Government (Manchester, 2005), p. 41.

91. Newbury, C., 'Patronage and Professionalism: Manning a Transitional Empire, 1760–1870', *JICH*, vol. 42, 2, 2014, pp. 195–6.

92. Buckley, R. N., *The British Army in the West Indies: Society and the Military in the Revolutionary Age* (Gainsville, FL, 1998), p. 201.

93. TNA, CO28/68, p. 29, Barbados Council Minute, 28 July 1801.

94. TNA, CO30/17, pp. 161–3, Act for Better Protection of Slaves of this Island, 9 April 1805.

95. TNA, 28/72, p. 123, *Barbados Mercury,* report of Assembly meeting 9 April 1805.

96. TNA, CO323/44, pp. 26–7, J. Stephen to Earl Bathurst, 29 January 1827; CO323/48, pp. 127–8, J. Stephen to Viscount Godrich, 15 November 1831.

97. Lambert, *White Creole Culture*, pp. 41–4.

98. For example Devine, T. M., 'Scotland and Transatlantic Slavery', in T. M. Devine (ed.), *Recovering Scotland's Slavery Past: The Caribbean Connection* (Edinburgh, 2015), pp. 7–11.

99. TNA, CO28/72, p. 121, Lord Seaforth to Earl of Camden, 4 May 1805.

100. Lambert, *White Creole Culture*, pp. 105–7.

10 Martial Law, a Governor's Crisis

The combined French and Spanish fleet commanded by Villeneuve arrived at Martinique on 16 May 1805 with orders to capture British West Indian islands. The Militia Act in force in Barbados after 9 April 1805 authorised the governor to introduce martial law only if the enemy was in sight of the island. The first news of a sighting came from Sir Francis Laforey, commander of the naval force based at Barbados, on 13 May. One of his two ships had encountered off Martinique three frigates, two of them very large ones, which had not been seen before in these waters. He concluded that these were the advanced guard of the combined fleet, whose approach was anticipated.[1] On 17 May he received news from the Diamond Rock, a British outpost off the coast of Martinique, that sixteen ships of the line and six large frigates were at anchor at Port Royale. He warned the Council that the combined fleet 'may be expected here every hour' as Barbados was now the British military depot for the area.[2]

The crucial decisions were taken on 18 May by Seaforth and the Council, there being no Assembly in place pending the annual election. Seaforth, asking Council members to 'consider the very perilous present situation of the colony', reported information from Laforey 'that six sail of the line, one of these a three decker, had been seen near the island'.[3] However, they had not come any closer and had not been seen from Barbados. It appears that Seaforth, already apparently in something of a panic, was pressured by General Myers, commander of the island garrison, into declaring martial law. Martial law was military government, by which military courts martial could try any who refused to serve in the militia or supply slaves to support the militia or who disobeyed the governor's orders as militia commander. The governor advised the Council that 'the Country cannot be defended by voluntary contributions . . . and I submit to you the necessity of putting the Country under martial law, without which neither Sir Wm Myers or myself will be responsible for the safety of the colony'. While agreeing unanimously, members of Council were very well aware of the terms of the Barbados Militia Act and of the potential for controversy. They made a public statement that they had agreed because of assurances 'that the Enemy were actually in sight yesterday evening and that he [the governor] has not a doubt that they are at this moment not far from us'.[4] In fact they had not been seen from Barbados and were now apparently heading back to Martinique. Martial law, which was supposed to last for only forty-eight hours after the enemy had disappeared, came into force on 19 May and was continued until the evening of 25 May.[5] This was a hardship to poor whites, who were unable meantime to earn a living following their trades and crafts, and to planters whose male slaves were called up.

Seaforth's declaration of martial law raised important issues of imperial governance. As has been seen in Chapter Seven, he was painfully aware of the provisions of the Militia Act and must have been conscious of the vague nature of the intelligence. The *Barbados Mercury,* supporting him, felt it necessary to assert 'the anxious desire of the Governor and Council . . . to maintain the liberties and promote the happiness of the People'.[6] Throughout the British Caribbean colonists resented martial law because they were suspicious that governors used it to increase their own authority. Acts had been passed in Jamaica, St Vincent and Grenada increasing their assemblies' authority over martial law.[7] Why did Seaforth not wait a week or so for the election of the new Assembly? In addition to the pressure from the military, he may have seen it as an opportunity to bolster the governor's authority at the expense of the Assembly. He later argued that the danger to the colony was real and potentially imminent, that this overrode local law and, using delegated royal prerogative, entitled him to act with the consent only of the Council.[8] Had he possessed the sensitivity to danger of a more adept politician, he might have concluded that the Barbados Assembly was a greater and more imminent threat to him than Admiral Villeneuve and the combined fleet.

Some islanders were prepared to give Seaforth the benefit of the doubt. The *Barbados Mercury*, which usually reflected the views of the Bridgetown merchants, argued on 21 May that such a large enemy fleet must have as its aim the conquest of British islands.[9] The first sign of trouble was on 22 May, when the St Thomas militia regiment was reported to be in a state 'little short of mutiny'. The officers passed a series of resolutions, one of which was that they would not hold any commission during Lord Seaforth's administration. The commander was Thomas Williams (as has been seen in Chapter Nine, a leading opponent of Seaforth), who told his men that 'the Country was oppressed, tyrannised and insulted by the Governor'. Seaforth promptly dismissed him as colonel[10] and was now feeling the pressure. On 25 May he wrote to his brother-in-law General Sandy, 'I sometimes ride 16 or 18 miles before breakfast, seldom less than double that in the day – then with the fag of writing, thinking etc. works me to an oil – and I have little but vexation in return'.[11] By this date the flimsiness of the original intelligence had become general knowledge. Colonel Beckles, son of Speaker Beckles and like him a loyalist, told his regiment that 'it is certain the enemy never were in sight', but insisted, 'we are in the most imminent danger'.[12] The Council now demanded, 'wishing to exonerate the Governor and themselves from any blame whatsoever' that Sir Francis Laforey give details of the 17 May sighting because 'grave jealousy and anxiety has been excited in consequence of the public conceiving themselves deceived on the information of a French fleet'.[13] General Myers observed that martial law was in force in all the surrounding British colonies, and only in Barbados was thought to be unnecessary.[14]

This was merely a curtain raiser for the storm which broke when the newly elected Assembly met on 29 May. Seaforth asserted that despite 'the censures of the unreflecting' there had been no alternative, but gave no other justification.[15] In reality, he was in no position to justify his actions in terms of the April 1805 Militia Act. The Assembly now passed resolutions asserting that any other declaration was unconstitutional and contrary to law. It requested him to give an explanation of his conduct, 'which has justly created great ferment and uneasiness in the public mind'.[16] Dissent was put on hold by the arrival of Admiral Nelson on 4 June and his embarkation of General Myers and his entire force of 2,000 royal troops. Seaforth was left in command on the island, with only the militia at his disposal and facing the very real possibility of a French invasion.[17] This gave him the opportunity, which as shown in Chapter Six he had long desired, of leading troops on active service.

Seaforth admitted to General Myers, 'with the little resource I have here much cannot be done if they [the enemy] come before your return – however, it shall not be my fault if they get us without a little brush for it.'[18] He was determined to make a fight of it because 'while I have life I will not see the colony entrusted to me lost without doing all I can to defend it'.[19] Given his chance, he now demonstrated his capacity for energetic command and sheer hard work. He envisaged a defence which was far from passive. He instructed the colonels, 'we must first meet the Enemy with every force we can muster at the shore . . . I shall charge them if possible before they form.' If forced back, they must render the enemy's advance as hard as they could make it, using every gully as an obstacle. Artillery would be brought to bear if practicable and conscripted slaves used occasionally 'to harass and distress the Enemy'.[20] Colonel Straker was ordered, 'if at your station at Hole Town you have certain intelligence that the Enemy will land to leeward, you will march that way with the St James's and St George's Regiments'.[21] He demonstrated a detailed knowledge of the topography of the island by ordering Colonel Cadogan to:

> Take post at Maycocks [plantation] and, if the Enemy show the least indication of landing to leeward of Mrs Colleton's store, you will immediately employ your negroes . . . with axes and bills in felling trees . . . that they may fall across the road . . . If they continue their march round by Broomfield . . . you will take every opportunity of annoying and insulting them by harassing their rear in defiles.[22]

Fortunately the militia's ability to fulfil these spirited and detailed orders was never tested. Villeneuve soon learned that Nelson was in the West Indies and thereupon quit the Caribbean to return to Europe.[23] Nelson became a hero of white Barbadians and one of the first statues of him outside Britain was erected in Bridgetown in 1813.[24] Myers and the royal forces arrived back at Barbados on 22 June, bringing Seaforth's military command to an end after eighteen days.[25] He now asked General Sandy to lobby for him to be given the military command in Barbados on the grounds that 'I was sole in command during all the real danger'.[26]

Figure 10.1 Statue of Lord Nelson, Bridgetown. Nelson was seen by white Barbadians as their saviour, having driven the combined French and Spanish fleet from the Caribbean in 1805. (© Finlay McKichan.)

Some Barbadians shared Seaforth's satisfaction. The *Barbados Mercury* carried a letter describing Seaforth as 'a gallant chief' and argued that 'even if a 'vigour beyond the law' was exercised, 'the dreadful calamity that hung over us was sufficient to excite our united co-operation in every means of defence'.[27]

He was painfully aware that this did not reflect the universal view. Articles of war had to be approved by the Council that 'any officer, NCO or soldier who shall behave himself with contempt or disrespect towards the Governor' should be subject to court martial.[28] He found it necessary to assure the Assembly on 18 June that he had 'not any intention of extension of personal power', but claimed that he was only answerable to the king.[29] By mid July it was evident that the combined fleet had left the Caribbean, and on the 16th the Assembly renewed its demand for an explanation of the declaration of martial law. As one member, William Grassett, put it, 'the chief question . . . is whether Lord Seaforth is not blameable in withholding from us . . . the necessary information . . . to judge the expediency of the measure.' Grassett was not a regular opponent of the governor, nor from one of the parishes at the heart of the opposition (that is, those dominated by poor whites). His Golden Grove plantation[30] was in the rich south-east parish of St Philip, which he represented in the Assembly, and he had seconded the Slaves Protection Bill in April. Speaker John Beckles gave an extended defence of Seaforth's position. Nevertheless, the Assembly carried a motion, with only four voting against, that the governor's claim that he was answerable only to the king was unsatisfactory and highly disrespectful to the House.[31] Relations between governor and Assembly were effectively deadlocked.

At one level this was a straightforward constitutional struggle between the powers of the island Assembly and of the governor (and, by extension, the imperial government). The Assembly asserted its right to legislate on the circumstances in which a governor could declare martial law and, when it appeared that its law had been broken, to call a governor to account. Seaforth's view, expressed to the secretary of state, was that 'if no opposition is made to such violent encroachments on the forms and rights of the different branches of the Legislature, the Government of the Colonies would be soon purely Democratic'.[32] He could reasonably claim that in May 1805 the danger to the colony was real and that if he had not taken the action he did and the French had captured Barbados, the secretary of state's duty would have been to pursue 'me till I lost my head for betraying the colony entrusted to me, and sheltering my cowardice under the pretence of forms'.[33] The speed and extent of the reaction to martial law, despite the seriousness of the threat, was undoubtedly because he, by now, had thoroughly offended certain Assembly members and interests in the community. Seaforth wrote to the secretary of state that 'there were some men in the Assembly who had long been anxious for an opportunity to show their resentment to me . . . with respect to the American intercourse and . . . on the subject of murdering negroes'.[34] The eight Assembly members who voted against the Slaves Protection Bill (especially Robert James Haynes, Thomas Williams and his son George) were the core of the opposition to martial law.[35] He claimed his Assembly opponents and the customs officers had coalesced and that Samuel Reddish, the comptroller, had been 'the publisher of many rascally libels' on the martial law controversy.[36] The imperial government clearly had an interest in defending its West Indian colonies when they were genuinely in danger. An official despatch and a public message supporting Seaforth's declaration of martial law was sent by the new secretary of state, Lord Castlereagh. It authorised him to dissolve the Assembly if necessary.[37] In public it supported him. However, the despatch was accompanied by a private letter from the under secretary. This told him that he should have offered a full explanation and advised that 'persons who are in violent opposition to Government require much caution in management'.[38] He could not claim he had not been warned. Lord Hobart advised him in 1803 that 'an open contest with (the Assembly) cannot be too cautiously avoided'.[39] Seaforth's unquestioned decision-making powers on his Highland estate and his irascible personality (almost certainly accentuated by his disability) had not given him practice in diplomacy.

In October 1805, Seaforth thanked the secretary of state for his support 'in the late disputes between the Assembly and me . . . I am happy to add that every shadow of them seems now to be dissipated'.[40] How far was this true, and to what extent did the imperial government support the other reforms which (showing remarkable resilience) he pursued in the closing stages of his governorship? He was not supported by government in his attempt to reform the island's legal system by setting up a Court of King's Bench. The secretary of state's view on this continued to be what his predecessor's had been in 1802: 'any change or innovation should be attempted with extreme caution'.[41] Judges of most courts were prominent islanders without legal expertise. Seaforth knew that the Assembly was opposed to a King's

Bench because it would reduce the influence of its members, and admitted he was in favour because 'it would strengthen the King's [that is, the governor's] hand here'.[42]

It is a tribute to Seaforth's dedication to duty, or else to his obstinacy, that he returned to the thorny issue of militia law.[43] By March 1806 it looked as if the issues of whether each of the eleven parishes should retain its own regiment and how many officers each should be allowed were being seriously addressed. All the clauses had been agreed, but on 18 March wrecking amendments were inserted. These were that the articles of war should only be in force when the enemy was in sight of the island (the major item of dissension throughout 1805) and that members of Assembly and Council should be exempt from military duty in their own persons.[44] It had been alleged that, while invasion threatened, 'the gentlemen of the Militia, the proud lords of the soil . . . were indolently lolling at their ease . . . idle spectators of the busy scene'.[45] Characteristically, the wrecking amendments were made after news was received that a renewed French naval threat had been defeated by Admiral Duckworth, who had destroyed a squadron of five ships of the line off St Domingo.[46] The Assembly was still willing to consider meaningful reform to the militia only when and only for as long as there was imminent danger of invasion. In September 1805 the secretary of state had given general approval to reform of the militia subject to the exercise by Seaforth of 'discretion'.[47] However, a governor needed more than this. He wrote to the under secretary that he could only throw out hints 'till I know for certain how the business will be received at home . . . where private interests seem so strongly counter to public duties the labour . . . to amend is not small'.[48] But clear instructions from Whitehall never arrived.

To the end of his time in Barbados, Seaforth never gave up the struggle to rectify what he saw as the imbalance between the powers of the imperial government and the Barbados Assembly. In March 1806 he complained once again of the increasing assertion of authority by colonial assemblies and recommended a parliamentary commission to enquire into the constitution of colonies.[49] However, his time in Barbados was now running out and this was merely a parting shot.

Figure 10.2 *Duckworth's action off San Domingo, 6 February 1806*, by Nicholas Pocock. Naval warfare was a constant background to life in the Caribbean at this period. With the French threat thus removed, the proposed reform of the Barbados Militia Act was dropped. (Copyright National Maritime Museum, Greenwich, London, BHC0571.)

Conclusions

The most generally held view of the relationship between the imperial government and the West Indian colonies was expressed by Murray in 1965. As has been shown in Chapter Seven, he argued that by the late eighteenth century the initiative in the government of the Caribbean colonies had been allowed to pass to the colonies themselves. His view was that, until the end of the Napoleonic Wars, after which the demands of metropolitan emancipationists became its main concern, Britain's strategic and economic needs required that the colonists be kept happy.[50] In 1998, Roger Norman Buckley argued that the initiative was shifting towards London as early as 1795, when black West Indian regiments began to be raised against the wishes of the colonists. He saw this process continuing with the appointment in 1801 of a Secretary of State for War and the Colonies (which Murray saw simply as an exercise in ministry building) and in 1807 with the abolition of the British slave trade.[51] More recently, in 2012, Trevor Burnard has argued that from as early as the 1780s there was an increased determination in London to treat colonists as subjects and ensure that they obeyed, reinforced by a decline in sympathy for planters caused by the emancipation campaign.[52]

It has been suggested in Chapter Seven that the Whitehall government did not deliberately attempt to increase its control in the years before Seaforth's arrival in Barbados. For example, Governor Cunningham had been recalled in 1783 when his relationship with the Assembly had broken down.[53] Douglas Hamilton has shown that even in the islands ceded by France in 1763, in which governors were initially given greater powers than in settled colonies, the colonists gradually acquired more and more authority.[54] As also shown in Chapter Seven, the government's motivation in raising black regiments was to solve a serious manpower problem, and it did its best to conciliate white opinion in the manner of implementation.[55]

How far does Seaforth's experience suggest that Whitehall was trying to reassert control? It might be argued that the secretary of state's public backing for him over the Slaves Protection Bill and the martial law crisis was evidence of this. Earlier governors (in Barbados and Jamaica) had been recalled in such situations. Alternatively, the evidence may indicate that support in summer 1805 was what has been called 'an unplanned liberal response to settler pressures'?[56] Whitehall's backing for Seaforth on these issues may have been only because his views happened to coincide with its agenda. By contrast, as has been seen in Chapter Nine, he lobbied long and hard to increase the rights of free people of colour, including when he was home on sick leave in 1804, and had finally to admit to 'not being honoured with the least notice. I fear my ideas were disapproved of'.[57] As shown above, to keep the Assembly members onside by preserving their privileges and powers of patronage was more important for the secretary of state than to reform a militia which he believed to be of limited support to the professional military.[58] Whitehall continued to ignore Seaforth's general schemes for an increase in the powers of the governor. It may be evidence of a changing attitude in Whitehall that William Windham, the new Secretary of State for War and the Colonies, in his first despatch in March 1806, complimented Seaforth on 'the zeal and perseverance with which you have applied yourself to the correction of all irregularities in the Departments within your Government'.[59] It is also true that the abolition of the British slave trade in 1807 significantly altered the balance of power between the Westminster parliament and the Caribbean settler colonies, and demonstrated the will and ability of Westminster to impose reforms on the colonies.[60] Britain was not the first colonial power to abolish the slave trade. Denmark had done so in 1803. Two others followed soon after Britain – Sweden in 1813 and the Netherlands in 1814.[61] However, British abolition was still in the future when Seaforth left Barbados for the last time on 25 July 1806.[62] Until that point the imperial government's failure to support him on important issues shows that there was still no systematic policy to recover power from the island assemblies.

Ten days before he left Barbados, the Council praised the purity of Seaforth's motives and asserted that he had never exercised power 'to the danger of injury of the constitutional liberties of the subject'.[63] He would have taken that as vindication of his struggles, although the Assembly would have been unlikely to pass such an address. Seaforth's view two years later was that in Barbados 'I experienced great friendship and likewise great ingratitude and injustice'.[64] His governorship was undoubtedly the high point of his career. How can it be judged? At one level, his successes were negative. He prevented the rights of free people of colour being reduced and there was no slave revolt. Accordingly, Barbados continued to contribute its sugar profits and revenues to the war effort. On the other hand, the enormous effort to pass the Slaves Protection Act (described in Chapter Nine) did not in the short term materially increase the safety of slaves. He failed in his frequent efforts to secure a more effective Militia Act, although he saw this as essential to the island's security, to increase the rights of free people of colour or the constitutional powers of the governor. On a personal level, his ambition to achieve military leadership was only realised for eighteen days in the summer of 1805. Due to his extravagant entertaining on Barbados and (as shown in Chapter Eight) the failure of the Berbice plantations, he returned to Britain with even higher debts than in 1801. This was to have serious effects on the future of his Highland estates, as will be seen in Chapters Eleven and Twelve.

And yet, there was cause for satisfaction. He and his close family survived the dangerous climate for five years (a remarkable achievement, as shown in Chapter Seven). He maintained the momentum of his efforts until his last days in Barbados. One of the paradoxes of his governorship is that, while his frustrations led him regularly to seek new posts, they did not lessen his energy in seeking to implement his policies and in confronting his opponents. He would have thought this justified his position in society at a time when aristocracies were under threat across Europe.[65] Cain and Hopkins refer to a 'justificatory model of an elite dedicated to public service'. Bayly comments on the 'prevailing ethos of loyalism, royalism and aristocratic military virtue' among the colonial governors of this period.[66] Seaforth certainly subscribed to this. He was unique in one respect in showing that such a demanding public position could be actively filled by a man with his disability (although his deafness may have contributed to his lack of flexibility). And this was in a major theatre of war, not a backwater, and at a highly delicate stage in race relations as the abolition of the British slave trade approached. In brief, he consistently did what he saw as his duty and thus demonstrated the main justification for aristocracy in the revolutionary age.

Notes

1. Edinburgh, National Records of Scotland (NRS), GD46/17/25/216, Capt. Sir F. Laforey to Lord Seaforth, 13 May 1805.
2. NRS, GD46/7/12/31, Lord Seaforth circular to Council, 17 May 1805.
3. *Barbados Mercury and Bridgetown Gazette,* 28 May 1805 – British Library (BL), microfilm MC1888.
4. *Barbados Mercury,* 28 May 1805, Report of Council meeting 18 May, BL, MC1888.
5. *Barbados Mercury,* 28 May 1805, Reports of Council meetings 21 and 22 May, BL, MC1888; Schomburgk, R. H., *The History of Barbados* (London, 1848), p. 362.
6. *Barbados Mercury,* 21 May 1805, BL, MC1888.
7. O'Shaughnessy, A. J., *An Empire Divided: The American Revolution and the British Caribbean* (Philadelphia, 2000), p. 193.
8. London, The National Archives (TNA), CO28/72, p. 179, Lord Seaforth to Earl of Camden, 27 June 1805; NRS, GD46/7/2/17–19, 'Appointment of Francis Humberstone Lord Seaforth as Governor of Barbados – Powers, etc., 1800'.
9. *Barbados Mercury,* 21 May 1805, BL, MC1888.
10. NRS, GD46/7/12/38, Lord Seaforth to Col. Harvey, 22 May 1805; /39–40, Lord Seaforth to T. Williams, 25 May 1805.
11. Aberdeen University Special Collections (AU), MS 3470/6/1/1206, Lord Seaforth to Major General A. M. Fraser, 25 May 1805.
12. *Barbados Mercury,* 25 May 1805, BL, MC1888.
13. TNA, CO28/72, p. 215, Barbados Council resolution 25 May 1805.
14. NRS, GD46/17/25/209, Sir W. Myers to Lord Seaforth, 28 May 1805.
15. TNA, CO28/72, p. 233, Speech of Lord Seaforth to both houses of legislature on opening of sessions, 29 May 1805.
16. TNA, CO28/72, pp. 211–2, Assembly resolutions of 29 May recorded in Council Minutes of 7 June 1805; Schomburgk, *History of Barbados,* p. 363.
17. Edwards, B., *The History, Civil and Commercial, of the British Colonies in the West Indies,* vol. 4 (London, 1819), p. 146.
18. NRS, GD46/7/12/54, Lord Seaforth to Sir W. Myers, 6 June 1805.
19. TNA, CO28/72, p. 198, Lord Seaforth to Earl of Camden, 27 June 1805.
20. NRS, GD46/7/12/61–3, Lord Seaforth circular to colonels of militia, 6 June 1805.
21. NRS, GD46/7/12/57–8, Lord Seaforth to Col. Straker, 6 June 1805.

22. NRS, GD46/7/12/58–9, Lord Seaforth to Col. Cadogan, 6 June 1805.
23. Rodger, N. A. M., *The Command of the Ocean: A Naval History of Britain, 1649–1815*, (London, 2004), p. 535.
24. Alleyne, W., *Historic Bridgetown*, (Bridgetown, 2003), pp. 97–8.
25. *Barbados Mercury*, 25 June 1805, Barbados National Library (BNL) microfilm 20.
26. AU, MS 3470/6/1/1275, Lord Seaforth to A. M. Fraser, 24 July 1805.
27. *Barbados Mercury*, 18 June and 9 July 1805, BNL microfilm 20.
28. *Barbados Mercury*, 22 June 1805, BNL microfilm 20.
29. NRS, GD46/17/25/231, Messages between Lord Seaforth and Assembly on subject of defence, 18 June 1805; *Barbados Mercury*, 3 August 1805, BNL microfilm 20.
30. Black Rock, St. James, Barbados Department of Archives (BDA), Planters Name Index.
31. BDA, microfilm BS7, Barbados Assembly Minutes, 16 July 1805.
32. TNA, CO28/72, p. 195, Lord Seaforth to Earl of Camden, 27 June 1805.
33. TNA, CO28/73, p. 10, Lord Seaforth to Earl of Camden, 22 July 1805.
34. TNA, CO28/72, p. 179, Lord Seaforth to Earl of Camden, 27 June 1805.
35. TNA, CO28/73, pp. 7–8, Lord Seaforth to Earl of Camden, 30 June 1805.
36. TNA, CO28/73, p. 193, Lord Seaforth to E. Cooke, 22 December.1805.
37. TNA, CO29/29, pp. 59–63, Lord Castlereagh to Lord Seaforth, 6 September 1805.
38. TNA, CO28/73, p. 72, E. Cooke to Lord Seaforth, 7 September 1805.
39. TNA, CO29/29, p. 26, Lord Hobart to Lord Seaforth, 6 January 1803.
40. TNA, CO28/73, pp. 99–100, Lord Seaforth to Lord Castlereagh, 21 October 1805.
41. TNA, CO29/29, p. 20, Lord Hobart to Lord Seaforth, 6 September 1802.
42. TNA, CO28/73, p. 116, Lord Seaforth to Lord Castlereagh, 7 November 1805.
43. TNA, CO28/73, p. 12, Lord Seaforth to Earl of Camden, 22 July 1805.
44. BDA, microfilm BS7, Barbados Assembly Minutes, 11 and 18 March 1806; BNL microfilm 20, *Barbados Mercury*, 11 March 1806.
45. *Impartial Expositor*, 13 July 1805, reprinted *Barbados Mercury*, 16 July 1805, BNL microfilm 20.

46. NRS, GD46/7/13/184, Lord Seaforth to E. Cooke, 23 March 1806; Rodger, *Command of the Ocean*, p. 546).

47. TNA, CO29/29, pp. 70–1, Lord Castlereagh to Lord Seaforth, 21 September 1805.

48. TNA, CO28/73, pp. 93–4, Lord Seaforth to E. Cooke, 4 October 1805.

49. TNA, CO28/73, pp. 23–5, Lord Seaforth to E, Cooke, 3 March 1806.

50. Murray, D. J., *The West Indies and the Development of Colonial Government, 1801–1834* (Oxford, 1955), pp. xii, 10, 13.

51. Buckley, R. N., *The British Army in the West Indies: Society and the Military in the Revolutionary Age* (Gainsville, FL, 1998), p. 201.

52. Burnard, T., 'Harvest Years? Reconfigurations of Empire in Jamaica, 1756–1807', *Journal of Imperial and Commonwealth History (JICH)*, vol. 40, 4, 2012, pp. 541–5.

53. Poyer, *The History of Barbados* (London, 1808), p. 528.

54. Hamilton, D. J., *Scotland, the Caribbean and the Atlantic World, 1750–1820* (Manchester, 2005), pp. 146–9.

55. Buckley, R. N., *Slaves in Red Coats: The British West India Regiments, 1795–1815* (New Haven, 1979), pp. 36–9, 69.

56. Newbury, C., 'Patronage and Professionalism: Manning a Transitional Empire, 1760–1870', *JICH*, vol. 42, 2, 2014, p. 195.

57. NRS, GD46/7/12/15, Lord Seaforth to Earl of Camden, 4 May 1805.

58. Young, D. M., *The Colonial Office in the Early Nineteenth Century* (London, 1961), p. 16.

59. NRS, GD46/17/24/366, W. Windham to Lord Seaforth, 5 March 1806.

60. Petley, C., '"Devoted Islands" and "That Madman Wilberforce": British Proslavery Patriotism During the Age of Abolition', *JICH*, vol. 39, 3, 2011, pp. 406, 408.

61. Gibson, C., *Empire's Crossroads :The Caribbean from Columbus to the Present Day* (London, 2014), p. 173.

62. TNA, CO28/7, p. 20, Lord Seaforth to W. Windham, 27 July 1806; CO28/75, p. 22, President J. Spooner to W. Windham, Barbados, 1 August 1806.

63. *Barbados Mercury*, 19 July 1806, BNL microfilm 20.

64. NRS, GD46/17/28/57, Lord Seaforth to J. Maxwell, Barbados, 8 November 1808.

65. Colley, L., *Britons: Forging the Nation 1707–1737* (London, 1994 edn), p. 188.

66. Bayly, A., *Imperial Meridian: The British Empire and the World, 1780–1830* (Harlow, 1989), p. 194; Cain, P. J. and A. G. Hopkins, *British Imperialism: 1688–2000* (Harlow, 2002), p. 646.

Coming home

As early as 1802, Seaforth was looking forward to leaving Barbados with his family to return to their life in Britain.[1] Colin Mackenzie found it necessary to explain to him the financial unwisdom of this. In the next year (1803) the revenue of the Highland estate was likely to amount to £7,175 and the demands in interest payments, annuities, taxes and management £7,965, leaving a likely deficit of about £800. He advised that if Seaforth came home soon 'all the prospects of ease and comfort which could alone render tolerable the separation from your country and the voyage to a burning climate must be blasted'. Land sales, he argued, were essential unless profits from Berbice could at least meet the family's living expenses.[2]

With his characteristically optimistic view of business ventures, Seaforth wrote to General Sandy in 1805 that he had just seen someone from Demerara and Berbice with excellent accounts of their state, and asserted, 'I truly pride myself on my financial abilities with regard to that place, and we shall all make rich by it.'[3] At this point even Colin was more hopeful. The cotton agents had rated highly the quality of the last (albeit small) crop.[4] However, Fairbairn reported in March 1806 that 'rains exceed anything previously experienced. This estate has been and still is in a very critical situation'.[5] By this time the decision had been made to return to Britain in 1806, and Colin now calculated the net income of the estate to be £6,536, about £600 less than in 1802.[6] Lady Seaforth and the family left Barbados in late April 1806 and Seaforth himself left on 25 July.[7]

Colin reported in October 1806 that 'the Berbice accounts will this year only just balance, if that'.[8] The dilemma facing Seaforth as he adjusted to life in Britain was that the revenues of the Highland estate could not be touched, but Berbice was still not delivering and he was, as yet, unwilling to sell land. An answer seemed to be offered by the death of Governor van Battenburg of Berbice in November 1806.[9] Seaforth proposed to William Windham, that he should resign his Barbados post (from which he was technically on leave of absence) and be given instead a combined governorship of the three Guyana colonies.[10] Despite the health risks, the prospect of supervising personally his Berbice plantations, hopefully bringing them into profit, and of earning a good salary meantime seemed too good to miss. Windham offered only a direct exchange of Berbice for Barbados. Lord Grenville, now prime minister, had expressed 'the sense which he entertains of the claims which your lordship had to the attention and support of His Majesty's Government'.[11] This was almost certainly an acknowledgement of Seaforth's support for the Ministry of All the Talents established after Pitt's death in January 1806.[12] It was dominated by Whig magnates (one of whom Seaforth had previously been) and it hoped to secure the support of docile Scottish MPs in the way Pitt and Dundas (now Viscount Melville) had hitherto done.[13] At the 1806 general election Melville's relative Sir Charles Lockhart Ross moved from Ross-shire to fight another constituency and was replaced by Seaforth's brother-in-law General Sandy.[14] Melville maintained his professions of friendship for Seaforth, but admitted that his 'unalterable veneration for the memory of Mr Pitt' might be 'not altogether consistent with connexions which you may have formed'.[15] In a House of Lords speech Grenville complimented Seaforth for promoting the Slaves Protection Bill 'in conformity to the instructions he had received, and with a proper regard for the British character'. As this was an argument for the bill to abolish the British slave trade, Seaforth would have mixed feelings about the endorsement.[16]

The Berbice appointment immediately came under attack from Lady Seaforth's cousin Lord Carysfort, although a long-term supporter of Grenville and an unwilling conduit for Seaforth's application.[17] He now wrote to him that 'if you take your children with you, you will deprive your fine girls of the best years of their lives, and if you leave them here you will lose the society which you know so well how to value'. This is an interesting reference to Seaforth's good relationships with his children. In Britain he would be in a better position to forward the career of his son William, 'who, by the by, is one of the best boys I ever saw'. The estate in Scotland would 'suffer from the want of a master's care'. As serious as any of these arguments, he wrote that Lady Seaforth 'seems to me to have so little idea of it'.[18] Mira would be horrified that he was proposing to return to and possibly take his family to the Caribbean climate they had been so keen to escape. Seaforth vacillated for several months, to the irritation of Windham, and characteristically argued about the salary.[19] The Ministry of All the Talents fell on 25 March 1807 and Grenville and Windham left office. There was no further discussion of employment for Seaforth.

Land sales and purchase

In a memo on his finances in March 1807 Seaforth promised that he would 'make the garter stretch the furthest possible', but this was not enough.[20] Moves were already under way to plan for a land sale. In February Archibald Macrae, as factor, supplied detailed advice on parts of Kintail which could be sold without damaging the integrity of the property. However, as tacksman of Ardintoul and as one of the Kintail Macraes, who had fought under Seaforth chiefs for centuries, he deeply regretted the need 'to sell off any more of these ancient domains of your family and see them translated to a stranger'.[21] Colin Mackenzie's view was very different. He wrote to his brother William (now the active partner in the legal firm) that 'the constant and endless recurrence of embarrassment must I think justify his disposing of Kintail if he can sell it to any advantage'. Rents and kelp sales would be insufficient to meet current demands, especially as it had been agreed to pay directly to Lady Seaforth (not a frugal spender) £1,000 per annum. He advised William only to pay out when he had funds in hand, but recognised that this could have fatal consequences for Seaforth's credit, and then 'the estate must be torn in pieces'.[22]

On 4 April 1807 Lachlan Mackinnon of Corryachatan offered £13,700 for Ardintoul and (on behalf of Kenneth Mackenzie) for Inverinate, two portions of Kintail on opposite sides of

Loch Duich. Both Mackinnon and Seaforth were in London, and the sale was completed by 11 April.[23] Despite Seaforth's sentimental attachment to Kintail, he was prepared to continue nibbling away at its periphery (a process started in 1801 with the sale to Hugh Innes of Kintail farms adjoining Lochalsh). With Berbice still not providing a significant income and the governorship gone, bankruptcy could only be avoided by selling land. At least on this occasion he seems to have made a good deal. Mackinnon complained that 'the lands you have sold are the dearest purchase ever made on the West Coast'.[24]

Seaforth believed that his lands in Easter Ross were more improvable than in Kintail. On his first return he had discussed a plan for a village at Ussie on the west bank of the river Conon near Dingwall, to be named Maryburgh after his wife. He had to be reminded twice about the scheme by his Brahan gardener William Gibbs. A village would increase rent rolls and provide craftspeople and labourers to support improved farms and a market for their food output. It was a relatively cheap form of capital investment, costing perhaps only a few hundred pounds. Another motivation may have been Sir Hector Mackenzie of Scatwell's plan for a village on the other side of the river (which became Conon Bridge).[25] In July 1808 the terms were published and applications for feus invited. An advertisement in the *Inverness Journal* claimed that 'the situation is healthy and pleasant in a fertile and highly improvable country'. A stream nearby could drive machinery. 'Industrious tradesmen' were encouraged to apply and the first settlers were promised 'great advantages'. One of these was the opportunity to lease small parcels of excellent arable land close by.[26] The success of many planned villages was dependent on the villagers being in a position to grow at least part of their own food and perhaps to keep a horse or cows. Many villages were intended to take advantage of transport improvements, and new roads were being built around Maryburgh as it was being planned.[27]

Maryburgh did modestly well. The parish minister believed it was a considerable factor in the growth of the population of Fodderty from 1,730 in 1794 to 2,292 in 1831. In 1838 it had a school with an average attendance of 120.[28] The village still thrives today and is arguably the greatest surviving legacy of Seaforth's schemes. It might have grown faster if at the outset all the farms in the area had been large, modern and profitable. On the contrary, the lands of the Ussies and Kildun were let 'in small farms of from 50 to 60 acres each that a fair trial may be given to the natives of improving their mode of farming . . . without being expelled by strangers'.[29] Despite all his troubles, Seaforth was still concerned to enable his small tenants to make a living on the estate at the expense of maximising profits.

As shown in Chapter Two, Seaforth gradually added to his Easter Ross estate lands surrounding Brahan Castle – Ussie, to the north of Brahan around Loch Ussie (1784) and Moy to the west of Brahan (1794). In the autumn of 1808 he was determined to complete the process by buying Arcan, opposite Brahan on the south side of the river Conon.[30] This was owned by an elderly widow, Mrs Mackenzie of Lentron, and he sought to ensure a quick deal by offering her extremely good terms. The purpose, he wrote to her, was to exclude 'any possibility of a stranger becoming the purchaser of it'. She would receive the good price of £12,000 and an annuity for life of the present net rental (£280) with the use of the house and garden.[31] William Mackenzie commented wryly that 'the transaction is such as will tend very materially to her advantage'.[32] Seaforth was himself aware that he had paid well above the going rate. Shortly after the purchase was concluded he asked his London bankers, Coutts and Co., to continue his overdraft because 'I have just purchased a <u>very dear</u> bit of land close to me'.[33]

It is curious that Seaforth was so keen to buy Arcan and was prepared to pay so highly. At this time William Mackenzie was demanding prompt repayment of £2,000 from him and he was 'sorry to see you [William] so very peremptory and short with me'. If necessary he would sell his London plate and also some of his precious books. At the same time he was humiliating himself by asking for a loan of a few thousand pounds from his son-in-law, Admiral Sir Samuel Hood.[34] That his kelp revenues reached a peak in season 1808 (as analysed in the next section), may have been the most important factor in making the Arcan purchase possible. These funds would begin to become available as the purchase was being finalised. In June 1809 he asked for £2,000 of Lewis rents to be sent to permit the agreed payments. It was 'a matter of life and death to me as my honour is pledged and I am determined to raise it . . . for Arcan must not go out of my power again'.[35] What was Seaforth's motivation? He had a tendency when in financial difficulty, not to reduce expenditure, but to enter new and hazardous business ventures to try to raise revenue, most notably (as seen in

Chapter Eight) the purchase of the Berbice plantations. Probably the major motivation was to prevent anyone else buying land adjoining Brahan and to increase his prestige among the proprietors of Easter Ross. As seen in Chapter Four, he also had a record of spending large sums if he believed his standing and prestige required it, irrespective of financial problems, as with the building of the kitchen wing at Brahan in 1796.

Now in his fifties, Seaforth still demonstrated an extravagant wish to excel, notably at Brahan. A neighbouring proprietor wrote in 1810 that 'the pleasure grounds are beautiful, and are every year becoming more extensive'.[36] When Robert Brown (now acting as a virtual chief factor) complained in 1811, 'there are twenty two persons ... employed in that branch [the garden], which is quite ruinous', he received the response, 'there must be labourers or nothing considerable can be done in the time it ought to be done'.[37] Although, after his return from Barbados, his political activities were mainly limited to Ross-shire, Seaforth retained a fashionable London house as a base for elite social activities. For example, in 1807 he played a prominent part in the annual dinner of the long-established London charitable foundation, the Scots Corporation.[38] The company was 'as usual, very select and respectable and subscriptions ... equally liberal'.[39] A considerable element in his London expenditure at this time was keeping his two surviving sons at Harrow School. William and Francis were both there is 1808.[40] Attendance at such an institution was by this time almost essential for access to the British aristocratic elite.[41]

Saved by kelp

Berbice was still not producing good profits. Not only had prices dropped[42], but output was well below expectations. After a poor season in 1808, Fairbairn had reported in April that both the first and second crops had failed due to the weather.[43] Indeed, there was no prospect of a payment by the agents. In April 1809 the balance against Seaforth on the Brahan and Kintail plantations was £3,112. The sum realised from the 1809 cotton sales to reduce this balance was only £1,100.[44] How did Seaforth avoid bankruptcy while his expenditure remained high? The answer is that kelp revenue from Lewis was now at such a level that he could draw on his kelp sales agents (S. And

J. Mackenzie of Leith) when there was a financial emergency. When in 1809 Coutts complained about the size of his bank overdraft, he directed Messrs Mackenzie to send him £1,000 'as they have plenty of mine in their hands'.[45]

Malcolm Gray was the first to point out that in the first decade of the nineteenth century, island proprietors could make far more from kelp sales than from their farm rents. Macdonald of Clanranald, proprietor of South Uist and Benbecula, in 1809 had a net income from kelp of £10,047 compared to a land rental of around £7,500.[46] Lord Macdonald's kelp from North Uist was estimated to be worth nearly double the island's land rent.[47] Seaforth was late to join this elite group. As recently as 1797–8 Lewis output had been less than 50 per cent that of the Clanranald estates (290 tons compared to 620 tons)[48], but was in 1808 (at 880 tons) about 90 per cent of the Clanranald estates. In cash terms, Seaforth's net kelp profit in 1808 was £8,484, more than the theoretical rental of the whole estate (£7,362 for year to April 1809).[49] This was made possible by what John MacAskill has described as a 'patriotic partnership', in which the fiscal military state maintained high duties on alternative forms of soda for soap and glass to enable proprietors to retain a reserve of population to supply soldiers and sailors for the war effort against Napoleon.[50] Table 11.1 shows how the Lewis kelp harvest produced such a remarkable profit. Manufacturing costs were paid mainly in cash and oatmeal to the kelpers.

Kelp income was so vital to Seaforth's financial survival that he paid close attention to the price his kelp was fetching. He now followed the conventional marketing system, instead of selling

Table 11.1 Kelp prices, costs and revenue, Lewis, season 1808

Output (tons)	880
Total receipts	£13,370
Total manufacturing cost	£2,246
Manufacturing cost per ton	£2.55
Freight, insurance and commission cost	£2,640
Freight, insurance and commission per ton	£3
Total net profit	£8,464
Net profit per ton	£9.64

Source: National Records of Scotland, GD46/17/35/82, W. Mackenzie to A. Mackay, 4 July 1809.

at the port of loading as in the 1780s and 1790s. His agents sought the best price for each cargo, and deducted the cost of freight, insurance, commission, etc. before paying him the balance. The variable factors and unpredictable forces involved made this a hard task.[51] In 1807 Seaforth complained that 150 tons of Lewis kelp had been sold for £12 per ton when Lord Macdonald subsequently sold 200 tons for £14 or 14 guineas. Sutherland Mackenzie, the agent, apologised and gave a highly technical explanation of market conditions. Briefly, the London soapmakers had banded together to push up the price of kelp to make it impossible for the Scottish soap manufacturers to buy. As soon as this had been achieved and they themselves had acquired 1,000 tons, they stopped offering high prices for kelp unseen. Mackenzie also described what was an agent's dilemma every year – how much to send and when to the two main markets, Liverpool and London. He had managed to sell a small cargo of 82 tons at Liverpool for the high price of £14 17s 6d. However, he had sent the rest of Seaforth's kelp to London as Irish kelp usually swamped the Liverpool market at the end of the season. This year, most unusually, the Liverpool prices ended the season higher than London. Mackenzie asserted that 'the circumstances in which I was placed must have puzzled the most judicious and experienced agent'.[52]

As a consequence of these problems, Seaforth insisted that consignments of the 1808 crop should not be sold without his agreement on the price. His direct involvement was unhelpful in two characteristic respects. His financial problems were sufficiently pressing for him to request a remittance of £2,000 from the first sales. Notwithstanding this, he was slow to let the agents know the minimum price at which he would sell. By June it was clear 1808 was going to be a bumper season. Sutherland Mackenzie believed he could command 20 guineas for Loch Roag kelp (recognised to be of high quality) and was frustrated that he could not act. He wrote, 'if we had been completely in possession of your Lordship's instructions . . . we should have made good use of the present moment.'[53] When Seaforth's views were obtained they obstructed the agents with their unrealistic expectations. He was apparently looking for 18 guineas per ton for Loch Roag and a pound or two less for other Lewis shores. The agents had to store in hope of prices rising. By September they had more than 400 tons (half the year's crop) in store at Leith.[54] Although some of Seaforth's 1808 sales were at £18

and even £20, the average price of the Lewis kelp crop of that
year was £15 19s per ton.[55] It is possible he could have realised
a figure near his expectations if he had been more nimble-footed
in the summer.

Seaforth may have expected more in 1808, but one of the
factors which was to weaken kelp prices was already evident. In
November 1806, Napoleon, by his Berlin Decree, had declared
Britain to be in a state of blockade. As Spain, the major source
of barilla, was an ally of France, supplies could only reach
Britain in small quantities by indirect routes and were therefore
expensive. Despite high import duties, the London soap boilers
favoured barilla because its alkali content was about twice
as high as good kelp. In May 1808 Napoleon deposed King
Ferdinand IV of Spain and replaced him by his own brother-in-
law Joseph Bonaparte. The result was a Spanish uprising, which
opened the prospect that Spanish ports might again welcome
British ships.[56] Sutherland Mackenzie anticipated that a great
quantity of barilla would be imported unless Napoleon was
able to establish firm control over Spain, which, it soon became
evident, he could not.[57] The ensuing Peninsular War was to be
a major source of volatility in the kelp market. Mackenzie complained of the effects of 'the fluctuating and uncertain state of
political events'.[58]

Even at the peak of kelp profits there were signs of another
damaging consequence of the war – economic recession.
Mackenzie reported to Seaforth in early 1810 that there was
little demand for soap and that 'many of the most respectable soap manufacturers, particularly in London, who had purchased at high prices, have been obliged to stop payment'.[59] The
French 'Continental Blockade' was seriously reducing imports
to Britain of such commodities as cotton and grain. The cotton
shortage caused short-time working in manufacturing areas
such as Lancashire. The shortage of grain was exacerbated by
bad harvests in 1809 and 1810. A peak in the economic war
came in 1811. Stricter enforcement of French controls, and
the inclusion in them of Sweden, significantly reduced British
exports. The consequences included high domestic prices, widespread hardship and a drop in soap sales.[60]

It was during the 1811 economic crisis that kelp prices began
to dramatically decline. From a plateau of around £15 per ton
since 1808, most of Seaforth's 1811 crop sold for 10 guineas
per ton, a drop of around a third, from a sale of 621 tons (over

250 tons less than in 1808).[61] This confirms Malcolm Gray's view that the turn in prices came about 1810 or 1811[62] and a report that in Tiree (a major kelp-producing island) in 1811 there would be 'much difficulty in selling kelp even at reduced prices' because glassworks were refusing to buy.[63] Mackenzie warned Seaforth at the beginning of the 1811 season that 'the situation of mercantile affairs is such that I am not justified in treating with your Lordship on the terms proposed'. At this point he was only offering 8 guineas per ton for Loch Roag kelp.[64] By the autumn of 1811 France was feeling the strain of the trade war as much as Britain and the restrictions were eased.[65] This was not good news for kelp producers. Together with the increasing success of British, Spanish and Portugese forces in the Peninsula, it became easier to import barilla. By 1812 Sutherland Mackenzie was lobbying Seaforth to press for an increase in the customs duties on barilla and ashes. He pointed out, 'while it is notorious that in soap manufacture much less kelp is now used, the quantity of Scotch kelp burnt has been at the same time annually increasing . . . some of poor quality.'[66] In other words, some kelp proprietors were increasing output to try to maintain income. This does not appear to have been the case on Lewis. In 1811 an annual output of 700 tons was forecast, below the 1808 peak of 880 tons, and an annual profit of £3,500.[67] In the event net proceeds in 1814 were £2,300, compared to £8,483 at the peak in 1808.[68] The boom was now well over.

Political operator

One of the uses to which Seaforth's kelp money was put was to maintain his political supremacy in Ross-shire. For this he needed also government patronage to satisfy his clients. The Ministry of All the Talents fell in March 1807, to be succeeded by an administration led by the duke of Portland.[69] Seaforth had no difficulty giving his loyalty to Portland, with whom he had been allied in the 1780s when they both were Whigs. In December 1808 Seaforth was ready to call in what he regarded as Portland's political debt to him. He wanted his supporter Macleod of Geanies to be replaced as sheriff of Ross by Colin Mackenzie, his former legal adviser and still his political agent, in order to have a more effective ally on the ground at election times. He wrote to Portland, 'we have at present far the predominant interest in this county and have had this twenty five years back.' He pointed out that he and his brother-in-law General Sandy were 'warm adherants of your grace'. He claimed that Macleod wished to give up for health reasons. He referred to 'the pretensions the General and I might think ourselves entitled to on a subject of this kind in Ross-shire'.[70] However, in a very revealing letter to Sandy, Geanies complained that he had not received the £3,150 promised him and was not going to resign until he had it (through an intermediary).[71] A transaction which depended on Seaforth paying a large sum was liable to fail. Nevertheless, the strength of his political influence in the county is shown by a letter from Sir George Mackenzie of Coull. He had first opposed Sandy in the county election of 1807, but had in the event voted for him. He wished to assure Seaforth that he could 'safely restore any share of friendship he may have withdrawn from me'.[72] In a letter to another brother-in-law, Sir Vicary Gibbs, Seaforth was revealing of the way the patronage system worked. He argued that 'under all circumstances of the politics of this county we had a fair right to expect attention to be paid to our pretensions . . . we should ourselves be furnished with the means of affording . . . support in the bounds of our own operations'.[73]

However, times were changing. Depending on a patron's ability to supply posts in the gift of government was becoming an embarrassing business. William Mackenzie complained to Seaforth in 1809 that 'the rage against jobs is so strong'.[74] During the Ministry of All the Talents, the Scottish Whigs had argued in the *Edinburgh Review* for a cleansing of politics. Practical change came with the appointment of Melville's son, Robert Dundas, as president of the Board of Control [for India] in 1807. In contrast to his father, he was loath to use his influence to find posts for clients and indeed dismissed East India Company officials who had purchased their appointments. The passing in 1810 of an Act to prevent abuse in Scottish pensions was further evidence of a trend to curb 'jobbery'.[75]

In September 1809 Seaforth suffered a severe personal blow which was also a political problem. Alexander Mackenzie Fraser ('General Sandy') was posted to the Low Countries on the disastrous Walcheren expedition and a few months after his return died of fever contracted on campaign.[76] Seaforth was devastated. Sandy was not only his brother-in-law, but also one

Figure 11.1 Lieutenant General Alexander Mackenzie Fraser, Seaforth's brother-in-law and close confidant until his death in 1809. (Reproduced by generous permission of the National Trust for Scotland.)

of his closest personal friends. He could tell Seaforth unpalatable truths which others would not have dared to utter, and was also one of the few permitted to address him as 'Frank'. Colin Mackenzie, the general's nephew, wrote to Seaforth, 'we never shall again meet a friend so kind, so warm, yet so dispassionate, in short so much everything that can fill up the idea of friendship.'[77] The resulting by-election is an interesting case study of a closely fought county contest at this period. The plan had been for Seaforth's son William Frederick to inherit the seat at the first election after he came of age at twenty-one in 1812. Who would be willing to fill the gap? Seaforth's long-term political rival Sir Charles Ross of Balnagown was quickly into the lists and impudently invited Seaforth's support.[78] He replied that, in addition to their 'already numerous disagreements ... imperious family duty compels me to keep open the door for another turn'.[79] In addition to his well-oiled Ross-shire machine, Seaforth could rely on at least the neutrality of the Dundas interest. Ross was not only a relative of Henry Dundas, Lord

Melville, but had also been a political protégé of his. However, he was believed to have deserted his patron in the parliamentary votes on his impeachment[80] and had veered towards the 'democratic principles' of Fox.[81]

Struggling to find a candidate who was willing to fill the seat for possibly only three years, Seaforth chose Hugh Innes, who had purchased the Lochalsh estate in 1801.[82] Many freeholders were of gentry families which had been in the county for generations, and Hugh Ross, brother of Alexander Ross of Cromarty, wrote that 'Innes being unconnected with the County was a great barrier'.[83] There may have been a degree of personal dislike, caused by the clearances Innes had made immediately after taking possession. John Matheson of Attadale, reluctantly agreeing to vote for Innes, wrote, 'it is with infinite regret I see the estate of Lochalsh and the representation of this county walk together'.[84] Another problem was that recent Court of Session decisions held that liferent qualifications were nominal and fictitious unless there was evidence to the contrary. After taking counsel's opinion Colin Mackenzie reported that 'our liferent votes are <u>bad bad</u>'. He would not advise liferent voters to take the oath as 'I do verily believe it would be perjury'.[85] Colin's skill, energy and judgement as campaign manager was a major asset. In an earlier letter to Seaforth, Lady Stafford referred to Colin's 'real sagacity and good way of conducting these sorts of business ... [which] render him really a most valuable person'. She also suggested that he 'may be more cautious than you might like'.[86]

Both sides tried to undermine the qualifications of genuine freeholders. The sale of a small piece of land might have inadvertently brought the value of the holding below the necessary £400 Scots. Colin arranged for his partner Alexander Monypenny to check whether 'any alteration of circumstances ... may have occurred among our own friends and also to discover flaws if such there be among the adversaries'.[87] William Mackenzie promised to be at Tain in good time to examine minutely the records there.[88] A Ross supporter, Sir John Leslie, appears to have been disqualified.[89] The opposition was taking similar action. Only three days before the election Sir Charles Ross 'with a strong force' came to Tain to check the qualification of an Innes supporter, Pitcalnie, but he still held a superiority of £413 Scots.[90] However, with fictitious superiorities meantime unusable, legal challenges could only succeed on the margin.

A part was played by offers of transport to the election at Tain. Dundonald was to be provided a carriage from the west coast 'as usual'[91] and the very sick George Mackenzie of Avoch a cutter to bring him by sea.[92] Avoch died on 2 December before he could be got home. Colin tried to reassure Seaforth, a grieving personal friend, that 'the opportunity of marking his decided and manly feelings towards yourself and your family evidently gilded his later hours and brightened his spirits'.[93] Major efforts were made to canvass the voters in person and by post. A notable feature of the Seaforth canvassing was the emphasis on clanship. For example, Colin Mackenzie's mother wrote to Mackenzie of Letterewe that 'Now becomes us all to rally ... that nothing can overcome the good old fashioned feeling of sticking to our Chief – for if we once let the enemy into our country we shall rue after, when I trust our young chief may be the candidate for Ross-shire'.[94] Letterewe was unwilling to leave London, but agreed to write to his nephew Strathgarve, also a freeholder, to advise him to vote 'in favour of Lord Seaforth'.[95] It is clear that Seaforth was in the constituency at Brahan directing operations and attempting to win votes by his presence.[96] As anticipated, the election (held on 28 November) was tight, Innes winning by twenty-three to Ross's nineteen.[97] Although it might appear anomalous by this period, Andrew Mackillop has argued that 'concepts of elite kindred clearly influenced [the] political sensibilities' of freeholders. Mackillop quotes Melville: 'it has always struck me that during the life of this Lord Seaforth, Sir Charles had not the chance of beating that powerful Clan in Ross-shire.'[98] He almost did beat it in 1809, but the exploitation of clanship may have been decisive in Innes's election.

Managing the militia

Seaforth's first involvement in military matters after his return from Barbados, and also his resumption of the active exercise of his lord lieutenancy, did not come until 1808. The motivation was the passing of the Act to establish the local militia, when it was clear that valuable patronage would become available in the commissioning of officers.[99] J. E. Cookson has noted that militia regiments were regarded by their raisers as patronage fiefs, 'immensely valuable to them as county magnates and

public men'.[100] When in 1808 the Volunteers were being trans-
formed into local militia regiments, Seaforth in his capacity
as lord lieutenant of Ross-shire insisted that all the applications for commissions should go through him.[101] He had just
become a lieutenant-general, having been promoted twice since
retiring in 1795 as lieutenant colonel commandant of the 78th
Regiment.[102] His command of the Ross-shire militia demonstrated both his weaknesses and his strengths.

He had serious trouble in consequence of the reduction from
three Ross-shire Volunteer units to two local militia ones. In the
Black Isle the Volunteers refused to enrol in the militia unless
they could have their own battalion. Seaforth complained that,
since the militia exercise would only be annual, it was not unrea-
sonable for a man to march 24 miles to Dingwall. He had seen
three companies of Volunteers at Munlochy and had left under
the impression (possibly a misunderstanding caused by his deafness) that they had promised to enrol.[103] He was outraged that
four officers sent to him for transmission to Lord Hawkesbury,
the home secretary, a memorial arguing for the retention of a
Black Isle battalion.[104] He replied that he would make his own
justifications to the king and ministers 'against the charges of
injustice and impropriety . . . and having exceeded my authority', which he claimed had been implied by the memorialists.[105]
He argued to the home secretary, with his characteristic use of
hyperbole, that this was 'the total loss of all weight of authority'
and 'a strong attempt to disturb the peace of the county'.[106] The
officers denied that they had any intention to criticise Seaforth
for the decision, which they did not believe had been taken
by him. Their only criticism of him was that a court of lieutenancy should have been held to discuss the issue[107] Seaforth
did not come out of this dispute well. It was an example of the
high-handed behaviour which he had demonstrated on many
occasions. It was also an illustration of his tendency to take
personal offence, which seems to have been accentuated as he
got older. The provision in the Act for a compulsory ballot had
to be implemented in the offending parishes.[108] In Lewis and
Lochalsh, from where men would have to travel much further
(to Dingwall), Volunteers had come forward for the local militia
'without a murmur'.[109] This may have been because he made it
known to all his Lewis tenants that he would 'befriend' all
Volunteers who agreed to transfer.[110] This was no doubt inter-
preted as a promise that they would retain their land.

If the disputes over the local militia in 1808 did not reflect well on Seaforth, it was a different story in 1809. On 1 August, he received at Brahan a report from its colonel, Donald Macleod of Geanies, that a mutiny was under way among the 2nd, or Easter Ross, Regiment, assembled at Tain for annual exercise. The primary cause of the mutiny appears to have been that some men had given up their claim to a bounty when transferring and others had received it. Characteristically, after time for reflection, Seaforth sympathised with 'the poor fellows [who] had lost the bounty they so generously gave up'.[111] However, at the time of the mutiny and at the age of fifty-five, he demonstrated that he could still take energetic action and show decisiveness, physical resilience and indeed courage. He immediately sat down to write a number of letters. One was to Geanies, assuring him that 'I will be with you directly' and advising him not to make any promises of general pardon 'for their conduct stands contrary to all necessary subordination to be overlooked'.[112] Of greater immediate importance was a letter to Lieutenant Colonel Macleod, commander of the 78th Regiment stationed at Fort George. He asked him to send 100 men quickly via the Invergordon ferry and assured him that 'in six hours after they get to Tain all will be as quiet as possible'.[113] He also wrote to Lord Cathcart, the army commander in Scotland, telling him he was setting out directly for Tain and seeking authorisation to hold courts martial.[114] He left Brahan at 9 p.m., presumably on horseback, and rode to Invergordon, where he spent the night at Cadboll House. However, it must have been a short night. At 4 a.m., the regular troops (100, as he had asked) arrived at Invergordon ferry. At 5 a.m., they and Seaforth set off for Tain, where they arrived between 9 a.m. and 10 a.m. He found that the 'judicious steps' taken by Geanies (probably negotiating a compromise) had nearly settled the mutineers. The presence of the regular troops 'quite did the business' and at 11.30 a.m. he left for Brahan with 'all quiet, orderly and penitent'.[115] It is possible that another factor in the mutiny was that the Black Isle members of the regiment had been balloted. The use of the ballot, which involved a form of conscription, was among the most important reasons for hostility to the Militia Act. In Aberdeenshire there had been a riot against the use of the ballot only six weeks before.[116]

Conclusions

Seaforth had come home from Barbados in 1806 despite warnings that he should first have sufficient income from the Berbice plantations to support his family. The run of bad seasons there which has been described in Chapter Eight persisted and it consistently underperformed. Since he turned down the governorship of Berbice, something had to give financially. Ardintoul and Inverinate in Kintail were sold in 1807, continuing the process of nibbling away pieces of the ancestral lands, which (as shown in Chapter Four) had begun in 1801. An economical and moderately successful development was the planned village at Maryburgh. However, it has been argued that its potential growth was limited by retaining small farms around it (continuing Seaforth's earlier attempts to protect small tenants analysed in Chapter Two). Despite the Kintail sales, he was again under financial pressure in 1808 when he paid a high price for the Arcan estate. As before when in financial trouble he entered a new and risky business venture in an attempt to raise revenue (as notably in Berbice, explained in Chapter Eight). The terms of sale meant that no profit could be anticipated from Arcan in the short term. The most immediate motivation was to increase his status among Ross-shire landowners. In the same way, extravagant expenditure continued in London and at Brahan to meet his psychological need to excel, as argued in Chapter Four. He was saved from bankruptcy when the price of Lewis kelp reached a peak in 1808 and continued until 1810 on a plateau of around £15 per ton. A comparison has been made with earlier prices and marketing methods, as analysed in Chapter Three. Kelp kept him afloat financially until 1811, the year when prices began to drop. An attempt has been made here to explain this decline which, as will be shown in Chapter Twelve, had catastrophic financial consequences for Seaforth, impacting the future of the estate.

In Ross-shire politics Seaforth was still a highly influential force and in many respects an effective one. A case study has been made of the 1809 Ross-shire by-election, comparing the techniques used to those employed earlier (as described in Chapter Five). It is argued that clanship was still an important force in electioneering. The creation of a local militia in 1808 enabled Seaforth to continue a military role which, it has been shown in Chapters One and Six, was important to his sense of self-worth. However, the disputes with the Black Isle officers and men showed that his tendency to take personal offence when opposed increased as he got older. By contrast, his performance in addressing the militia mutiny at Tain in 1809 was impressive. This illustrated that he still had the ability in emergencies to demonstrate energy and personal courage (as shown in Chapter Six in the Uig recruitment riot in 1793 and in Chapter Ten when Barbados was under threat of French attack in 1805).

Notes

1. Aberdeen University Special Collections (AU), MS 3470/6/2/53, Lord Seaforth to Col. A. Mackenzie, 31 July 1802.
2. Edinburgh, National Archives of Scotland (NRS), GD46/7/21, C. Mackenzie to Lord Seaforth, 28 October 1802.
3. AU, MS 3470/6/1/1275, Lord Seaforth to Gen. A. M. Fraser, 24 July 1805.
4. NRS, GD46/17/26, C. Mackenzie to Lord Seaforth, 26 April 1805.
5. NRS, GD46/17/24/368, P. Fairbairn to Lord Seaforth, 6 March 1806.
6. NRS, GD46/17/24/375–7, C. Mackenzie to Lord Seaforth, 26 March 1806.
7. London, British Library (BL), Add. MS 40715, fos 111–12, Lord Seaforth to C. H. Greville, 19 April 1806; London, The National Archives (TNA), CO28/75, p. 22, J. Spooner to W. Windham, 1 August 1806.
8. NRS, GD46/17/24, C. Mackenzie to Lord Seaforth, 3 October 1806.
9. TNA, CO112/1, fo. 29, Brigadier Montgomerie to Secretary of State, 21 November 1806.
10. TNA, CO28/75, fo. 87, Lord Seaforth to E. Cooke, 25 December 1806.
11. NRS, GD46/17/31/5, W. Windham to Lord Seaforth, 12 January 1807.
12. Thorne, R. G., *The House of Commons 1790–1820* (London, 1986), vol. 2, p. 621.
13. Fry, M., *The Dundas Despotism* (Edinburgh, 2004 edn), pp. 280, 284–5.
14. Thorne, *The House of Commons 1790–1820*, vol. 2, p. 572.
15. NRS, GD46/17/16, Lord Melville to Lord Seaforth, 6 January 1807.

16. *Morning Chronicle*, 6 February 1807, 19th Century British Library Newspapers online (19BLN), accessed 3 February 2011.
17. Barker, G. F. R., 'Proby, John Joshua, first earl of Carysfort (1751–1828)', rev. E. A. Smith, *Oxford Dictionary of National Biography (ODNB)*, Oxford 2004, online edition, <www.oxforddnb.com>, article no. 22832, accessed 3 February 2011.
18. NRS, GD46/17/16, Lord Carysfort to Lord Seaforth, 1 January 1807.
19. BL Add. MS 37886, fo. 185, W. Windham to Lord Seaforth, 22 March 1807; fo. 187, Lord Seaforth to W. Windham, 22 March 1807.
20. NRS, GD46/17/31, Memo by Lord Seaforth, March 1807.
21. NRS, GD46/17/31, A. Macrae to Lord Seaforth, 21 February 1807.
22. Quoted in NRS, GD46/17/31, W. Mackenzie to Lord Seaforth, 6 April 1807; GD46/17/16, T. Coutts to Lord Seaforth, 8 June 1807.
23. NRS, GD46/17/80/245, Contract Lord Seaforth/L. Mackinnon for sale of lands of Inverinate, etc.; Register of Sasines Ross-shire Abridgements, Inverinate, Easter Leckmelm and Mill of Croe to K. Mackenzie W.S., Ardintoul, Wester Leckmelm and Croe of Kintail to L. Mackinnon, 23 October 1807.
24. NRS, GD46/17/31, L .Mackinnon to Lord Seaforth, 4 and 11 April 1807.
25. Lockhart, D., *Scottish Planned Villages* (Edinburgh, 2012), pp. 1, 7, 23, 67.
26. *Inverness Journal*, 1 July 1808 (NLS – the author is indebted to Dr Lockhart for transcripts); *Caledonian Mercury*, 15 October 1808 (19BLN), accessed 7 February 2011.
27. Lockhart, *Scottish Planned Villages*, p. 15; NRS, GD46/17/28/93–6, Lord Seaforth to Sir G. Mackenzie, 15 December 1808.
28. *New Statistical Account of Scotland*, vol. XIV, <http://stat-acc-scot.edina.ac.uk/link/1834-45/Ross and Cromarty/Fodderty>, accessed 12 March 2015.
29. *Inverness Journal* (NLS), 15 January 1808.
30. McKichan, F., 'Lord Seaforth and Highland Estate Management in the First Phase of Clearance', *The Scottish Historical Review*, vol. 86, 1, 2007, p. 63.
31. NRS, GD46/17/28/46–7, Lord Seaforth to Mrs Mackenzie of Lentron, 5 October 1808.
32. NRS, GD46/17/32, W. Mackenzie to Lord Seaforth, 22 October 1808.
33. NRS, GD46/17/28/51, Lord Seaforth to Coutts and Co., 26 October 1808.

34. NRS, GD46/17/28/48–50, Lord Seaforth to W. Mackenzie, 18 October 1808.

35. NRS, GD46/6/72, Lord Seaforth to R. Brown, 26 June 1809.

36. Mackenzie, Sir G. S., *A General Survey of the Counties of Ross and Cromarty drawn up for the Consideration of the Board of Agriculture* (London, 1810), p. 110.

37. NRS, GD46/17/80/219, 'Statement made up by Mr Brown and given in to Lord Seaforth on the expense of keeping up Brahan', n.d., but from context, 1811.

38. Nenadic, S. (ed.), *Scots in London in the Eighteenth Century* (Lewisburg, 2010), p. 26.

39. *Caledonian Mercury*, 30 April 1807 (BLN), accessed 3 February 2011.

40. NLS, MS 6396, fo. 78, W. F. Mackenzie, Harrow, to Lady Seaforth, 4 March 1808; fo. 94, F. Mackenzie, Harrow, to Lady Seaforth, 4 March 1808.

41. Nenadic, *Scots in London*, p. 38; Nenadic, S., *Lairds and Luxury: The Highland Gentry in Eighteenth-Century Scotland* (Edinburgh, 2007), pp. 52–3, 98–9; Colley, L., *Britons: Forging the Nation, 1707–1837* (London, 1994 edn), p. 167.

42. Cooke, A., *The Rise and Fall of the Scottish Cotton Industry 1778–1914* (Manchester, 2010), p. 54.

43. NRS, GD46/17/35/51, P. Fairbairn to Lord Seaforth, 20 April 1809.

44. NRS, GD46/17/35/276–7, Lord Seaforth and others re plantations Brahan and Kintail with Inglis, Ellis and Co., 20 April 1810.

45. NRS, GD46/17/28/98, Lord Seaforth to Coutts and Co., 26 September 1809.

46. Gray, M., *The Highland Economy 1750–1850* (Edinburgh, 1957), p. 135.

47. Hunter, J., *The Making of the Crofting Community* (Edinburgh, 1976), p. 16.

48. NRS, GD46/13/126, State of Lewis kelp from 1794–1799; GD201/1/365/2, 'State of Clanranald's Affairs January 1798'.

49. NRS, GD46/17/35/82, W. Mackenzie to A. Mackay, 4 July 1809; GD46/17/35/119, Note of Lord Seaforth's Property Duties, year to 5 April 1809 (by property tax assessor, A. Mackenzie).

50. MacAskill, J., 'The Highland Kelp Proprietors and their Struggle over the Salt and Barilla Duties, 1817–1831', *Journal of Scottish Historical Studies*, vol. 26, 2006, p. 61.

51. Thomson, W. P. L. and J. R. Coull, 'Kelp', in J. R. Coull, A. Fenton and K. Veitch (eds), *Scottish Life and Society: A Compendium of Scottish Ethnology*, vol. 4 (Edinburgh, 2008), p. 157.

52. NRS, GD46/17/16, S. Mackenzie, Leith to Lord Seaforth, 8 Oct. 1807.
53. NRS, GD46/17/16, S. Mackenzie, Leith to Lord Seaforth, 9 June 1808.
54. NRS, GD46/17/16, S. Mackenzie, Leith to Lord Seaforth, 16 July and 22 September 1808.
55. NRS, GD46/17/32/143, Account sales of kelp crop 1808 shipped from Lewis for account of Lord Seaforth.
56. MacAskill, 'The Highland Kelp Proprietors', p. 63; Thomson and Coull, 'Kelp', p. 158.
57. Longford, E., Wellington: The Years of the Sword (London, 1971), pp. 182, 190; NRS, GD46/17/16, S. Mackenzie, Leith to Lord Seaforth, 16 July 1808.
58. NRS, GD46/17/16, S. and J. Mackenzie to Lord Seaforth, 22 September 1808.
59. NRS, GD46/17/16, S. and J. Mackenzie to Lord Seaforth, 27 March 1810.
60. Watson, J. S., The Reign of George III (Oxford, 1960), p. 469.
61. NRS, GD46/17/16, S. and J. Mackenzie, Leith, to Lord Seaforth, 12 September 1809, J. Stewart and Co., London, to Lord Seaforth, 18 April 1810; GD46/17/32/191–2, Account sales for cargoes, August–September 1810; GD46/17/37/478–80, Account sales J. Stewart and Co., London, September–October 1811; GD46/17/35/208, Account of kelp shipped from Lewis, 1810.
62. Gray, Highland Economy, pp. 155–6.
63. Macdonell, C., 'Kelp and the Argyll Estates, 1780–1847' in The Secret Island: Towards a History of Tiree (Lewis, 2014), p. 73.
64. NRS, GD46/17/16, S. and J. Mackenzie to Lord Seaforth, 6 April 1811.
65. Watson, Reign of George III, p. 470.
66. NRS, GD46/17/16, S. and J. Mackenzie to Lord Seaforth, 4 March 1812.
67. NRS, GD46/17/36, Minute of Seaforth Trustees, Edinburgh, July 1811.
68. NRS, GD46/17/35/82, Kelp Crop 1808; GD46/1/141, Minutes of Seaforth Trustees 1815.
69. Fry, The Dundas Despotism, p. 286.
70. NRS, GD46/17/28/75–7, Lord Seaforth to Duke of Portland, 4 December 1808.
71. Castle Fraser, Mackenzie Fraser Papers (C. F. Papers) 1/2062, D. Macleod to A. M. Fraser, 18 February 1809.
72. C. F. Papers 1/2016, Sir G. S. Mackenzie to A. M. Fraser, 16 January 1808.
73. NRS, GD46/17/28/68–70, Lord Seaforth to Sir V. Gibbs, 4 December 1808.

74. NRS, GD46/17/35/71, W. Mackenzie to Lord Seaforth, 26 June 1809.

75. Fry, *The Dundas Despotism*, pp. 289, 294–5.

76. Thorne, *The House of Commons 1790–1820*, vol. 4, p. 494.

77. NRS, GD46/17/35/113, C. Mackenzie to Lord Seaforth, 30 September 1809.

78. NRS, GD46/17/35/110, Sir C. Ross to Lord Seaforth, 10 September 1809.

79. NRS, GD46/17/35/108, Lord Seaforth to Sir C. Ross, 26 September 1809.

80. AU, MS 3470/6/1/1275, Lord Seaforth to Maj. Gen. A. M. Fraser, 24 July 1805.

81. NRS, GD46/17/28/81, Lord Seaforth to Lord Melville, 5 December 1808.

82. NRS, GD46/17/35/11, C. Mackenzie to Lord Seaforth, n.d., but from context, early October 1809.

83. NRS, GD46/17/35/157, H. Ross to Lord Seaforth, October 1809.

84. NRS, GD46/17/35/174, J. Mathieson to W. F. Mackenzie, 7 October 1809.

85. NRS, GD46/17/35/169, C. Mackenzie to Lord Seaforth, 12 October 1809.

86. NRS, GD46/17/16, Lady Stafford to Lord Seaforth, 2 April 1807.

87. NRS, GD46/17/35/12, C. Mackenzie to Lord Seaforth, n.d., but from context, late September or early October 1809.

88. NRS, GD46/17/35/167, W. Mackenzie to Lord Seaforth, 12 October 1809.

89. NRS, GD46/17/35/175–6, /179, W. Mackenzie to Lord Seaforth, 17 and 18 October 1809.

90. NRS, GD46/17/35/194, G. Munro to Lord Seaforth, 25 November 1809.

91. NRS, GD46/17/35/148, C. Mackenzie to Lord Seaforth, 5 October 1809.

92. NRS, GD46/17/35/171–2, C. Mackenzie to Lord Seaforth, 12 October 1809.

93. NRS, GD46/17/35/196, C. Mackenzie to Lord Seaforth, 8 December 1809.

94. NRS, GD46/17/35/182, Mrs A. Mackenzie, Edinburgh to A. Mackenzie of Letterewe, 13 October 1809.

95. NRS, GD46/17/35/180, A. Mackenzie of Letterewe to Mrs A. Mackenzie, n.d.; /183, C. Mackenzie to Lord Seaforth, 13 October 1809.

96. NRS, GD46/17/35/2, C. Mackenzie to Lord Seaforth, n.d., but clearly 1809.

97. Thorne, *The House of Commons 1790–1820*, vol. 2, p. 572.
98. Mackillop, A., 'The Political Culture of the Scottish Highlands from Culloden to Waterloo'. *The Historical Journal*, vol. 46, 3, 2003, p. 529.
99. NRS, GD46/6/71/4, Lord Seaforth to Lord Hawkesbury, 23 September 1808.
100. Cookson, J. E., *The British Armed Nation, 1793–1815* (Oxford, 1997), p. 7.
101. NRS, GD46/6/71/2, Lord Seaforth to D. Macleod, 23 September 1808.
102. Chichester, H. M., rev. J. Spain, *ODNB*, online edition, <www.oxforddnb.com>, article no. 14126, accessed 29 September 2004.
103. NRS, GD46/6/71/11–14, Lord Seaforth to Sir R. Mackenzie of Scatwell, 25 October 1808.
104. NRS, GD46/17/16, Sir R. Mackenzie of Scatwell, C. Mackenzie of Kilcoy, J. Mackenzie of Allangrange and J. Leslie of Findrassie, memorial to Lord Hawkesbury, 15 October 1808.
105. NRS, GD46/6/71/15, Lord Seaforth to J. Mackenzie of Allangrange, 31 October 1808.
106. NRS, GD46/6/71/24, Lord Seaforth to Lord Hawkesbury, 2 December 1808.
107. NRS, GD46/17/16, Scatwell, Allangrange and Kilcoy to Lord Seaforth, 1 November 1808.
108. NRS, GD46/6/71/29, Lord Seaforth to Lord Hawkesbury, 4 December 1808.
109. NRS, GD46/6/71/24–6, Lord Seaforth to Lord Hawkesbury, 2 December 1808.
110. NRS, GD46/6/71/16, Lord Seaforth to J. Robertson, 31 October 1808; GD46/17/16, J. Robertson to Lord Seaforth, 28 December 1808.
111. NRS, GD46/6/72/104–5, Lord Seaforth to D. Macleod, 16 September 1809.
112. NRS, GD46/6/72/73–4, Lord Seaforth to D. Macleod, 1 August 1809.
113. NRS, GD46/6/72/74, Lord Seaforth to Lt Col. Macleod, Fort George, 1 August 1809.
114. NRS, GD46/6/72/72–3, Lord Seaforth to Lord Cathcart, 1 August 1809.
115. NRS, GD46/6/72/80, Lord Seaforth to Lord Cathcart, 4 August 1809.
116. Logue, K. J., *Popular Disturbances in Scotland, 1780–1815* (Edinburgh, 1979), p. 107.

12   Shadows Lengthen

Financial shadows

In March 1811 Seaforth, reflecting on his finances, wrote, 'my state of mind is the most exquisite torture . . . I see some daylight, but I am palsied and cannot open the shutters.'[1] The most serious of all his financial crises was about to break. How had it come to this? In 1810 his solvency was already on a knife edge and highly dependent on kelp. Lewis and Kintail rents yielded £4,758, only a little over half the sum of £8,119 paid to him by his kelp agents that year. The rents did not even cover interest payments on debt (£5,350).[2] William Mackenzie calculated in June 1810 that payments due to be made on Seaforth's account for various purposes totalled £12,656. He could not make any further advances and, despite every possible exertion, had been unable to negotiate a loan from elsewhere. He advised that 'there is much difficulty at present . . . particularly where an estate is at all burdened . . . and we found a strong prejudice in the money market against Highland securities'.[3] The crisis came in 1811, by which time there were two major issues.

The first was Berbice, which had turned out to be liability rather than salvation. For the year 1809 cotton sales totalled £1,097, but the balance due the cotton agents, Inglis, Ellis and Co., in April 1810 was £3,112.[4] By March 1811 that balance had increased to £7,387.[5] Peter Fairbairn's letters contained the usual news of poor weather and harvest failures, while making optimistic forecasts. As Colin Mackenzie commented, his letters were 'only gay as to the future'.[6] Seaforth now doubted

Fairbairn's honesty because he never submitted accounts. He asked Inglis, Ellis to recommend a man to send to Berbice to investigate and, if necessary, remove Fairbairn.[7] Inglis, Ellis did not doubt his honesty, pointed out that many Berbice concerns were suffering from poor seasons and advised they could make no further advances.[8] What put the cat among the pigeons was news that Fairbairn had bought the Ross plantation at the same time as he was complaining that he had 'been yearly sunk deeper in trouble and difficulty'.[9] Colin Mackenzie's view was that, if Fairbairn was really buying Ross for himself, 'I could think anything ill of him.'[10]

This was a critical moment. The Berbice speculation, on which the finances of the family had been gambled, looked in danger of collapse. At the age of fifty-seven Seaforth now proposed to travel to Berbice for the first time to see for himself, and in March 1811 actually booked a passage.[11] His business skills could be doubted, but never his courage. William Mackenzie regretted that 'you should think it necessary to expose your health to the climate of Berbice'.[12] He did not go, and a year later (in 1812) a full report was obtained from James Baillie Fraser, son of Seaforth's friend and partner Edward Satchwell Fraser of Reelig. J. B. Fraser had a decade's experience as a planter in Berbice and had known Fairbairn well. He had no doubts about his honesty or probity, and he was known as 'a most exact accountant'. His explanation for his remissness in reporting was that it must be an unpleasant task to continually describe misfortunes. Fairbairn, he said, had bought the Ross plantation as a speculation with borrowed money, and 'has I believe been sorely disappointed'. On Seaforth's plantations he may have made 'a few grand errors, partly the result of inexperience and partly of the sanguine turn common to all Guinea adventurers at that period'. However, a major factor was 'a ten years series of the most dreadful and impracticable seasons ever known'.[13]

J. B. Fraser had himself come home in 1812 after his father had concluded that 'Berbice is a poison' and had given up. Another Scottish planter who failed in Berbice was William Macpherson. He had borrowed to buy a half share in the Rising Sun plantation. The first payment was due in 1812, which he was quite unable to meet because of the unfavourable seasons and low cotton prices caused by the economic recession and the war. He returned to Britain in early 1813, having persuaded his major creditor to accept the land and slaves as full payment.[14] By that time Seaforth also was keen to 'get rid as quickly as possible upon the best terms I can of my West Indies Estates'. He wrote to Sir Alexander Mackenzie of Avoch (son of his old friend) to ask him 'owing to my infirm state of health' to handle the business. The new agent, John Gladstone of Liverpool, was to be asked to send a man to Berbice to sell the lands and slaves and to advance (to Inglis, Ellis and Co.) enough to clear British debts on the plantations.[15] However, it seems clear that no sales in Berbice were concluded during Seaforth's lifetime.[16]

Berbice was not the only financial issue in 1811. The other was whether Seaforth would allow the estate to be managed for the maximum return and lands sold to repay debts. In 1810 Robert Brown, now chief factor, advised that some of the Glenshiel leases (dating from the 1801 sett) should be bought out to free the land for commercial sheep farming. He estimated that double or even treble the current rent could be expected – for example, Torlysich £190 to £565 and Cluanie £130 to £468.[17] As this proposal was not taken up, it is clear that Seaforth, as in the past, was still unwilling to bring in large-scale graziers at the cost of clearing small tenants. This had been his approach to sheep farming since the 1780s, as shown in Chapter Two. He was now also opposed to selling land in Kintail, which he had previously done in 1801 and 1807 (as shown in Chapters Four and Eleven). He wrote to Brown, 'I will fight and claw to the last to save Kintail or perish myself . . . books, trees [at Brahan], plate and all shall vanish before I will look that way'.[18] He may have been influenced by the admiration felt in Britain for the guerrilla fighters in the Peninsular War. Peter Womack has argued that this was translated into a romantic enthusiasm for traditional Highland warriors, as illustrated by the popularity of Scott's historical poems.[19] Seaforth would be particularly susceptible as a traditionally minded Highland proprietor and a friend of Scott in Edinburgh society.

The reality was that in 1811 Seaforth could not afford the luxury of romantic notions. The capital debt had increased to £118,714, the highest yet, and his personal debts to £18,837. As in 1810, demands for payment were 'very peremptory' and it was almost impossible to replace debts with new loans.[20] With these issues unresolved and with Seaforth apparently about to disappear to Berbice, from which he might not return, it was time for his creditors and advisers to act. Some of the advisers, such as the Mackenzie brothers and Thomas Coutts the banker, were also substantial creditors. William Mackenzie co-ordinated the assembling of the trustees and a trust deed was signed on 30 April 1811. Seaforth gave the trustees the right of property of all his Scottish estate, except immediately around Brahan.[21] Some of the trustees, such as Coutts and Sir Vicary Gibbs, would pay off immediate demands and in return the trustees would have control of rents, kelp receipts and other income.[22] Seaforth would be paid an allowance of £6,000 per annum for the use of himself, Lady Seaforth and their family.[23] This was only a stopgap. The trustees were agreed there needed to be land sales to repay debts. Given that the Berbice plantations could not be disposed of for an acceptable price, the best option was to sell part of Kintail and keep Lewis, the source of kelp wealth. The trouble was, as Colin put it, the trustees were authorised to sell land 'with Lord Seaforth's consent, which is plainly no authority at all'. A subsequent trust deed completed on 17 June gave a majority of the four trustees power to make sales for seven years.[24] This marked the end of Seaforth's career as an active proprietor in Ross-shire. He could make suggestions, but he no longer made the major decisions. Financial necessity obliged him to agree, but he was not happy. He made clear to Colin his attitude at that time to clanship and proprietorship:

> If it regarded only myself I should certainly think selling a part the wisest project, but I will tell you the reasons I have for wishing to make a strong struggle just now at almost any sacrifice . . . Plain sense and good management have almost kicked sentiment and attachment out of doors . . . but there is another feeling . . . I mean that incomprehensible feeling by which we are led to value antiquity of family and permanence of property.

Had this occurred to him sooner, he wrote, he would have sold lands in Easter Ross and Lewis in 1801 and 1807 rather than parts of Kintail, the country from which the Mackenzies sprang. With characteristically unfounded optimism, he claimed that 'should things go on as they do I look on a rise equivalent to a double rent as certain in the course of ten years'. However, he had an immediate reason for not wanting to sell – to retain votes needed to elect William to Parliament after he came of age in 1812. Here, Seaforth gave Colin an insight into his attitude to politics in the later part of his life:

For those who have not yet plunged into the vortex, the clearer they keep from it the happier they may be, but for me it would be worse than death, after having worked so hard and succeeded so long in procuring for my family that local consideration . . . to see myself slipping back with tenfold rapidity – I could not sustain it.[25]

He could not give up the drug of politics and the local dignity it brought to his family any more than he could agree to the sale of any more of the ancestral lands in Kintail. The situation was worsened in September 1811, when (as shown in Chapter Eleven) a substantial drop in kelp prices became clear. The price realised for most of the Lewis kelp fell from £15 per ton in 1810 to £10 10s in 1811, a drop of about 34 per cent in Seaforth's largest source of income.[26] The trustees believed that land sales were essential and must go ahead without Seaforth's approval[27], but they were not achieved quickly. An auction in January 1813 was apparently unsuccessful, but by March negotiations were underway (subsequently concluded) for a sale by private treaty of South Glenshiel to a Jamaica planter, David Dick.[28] At the same time lands in the west part of Kintail were advertised. These included the villages of Dornie (described in the advertisement as now having 400–500 inhabitants) and Bundalloch. These were purchased by Hugh Innes at some time before January 1815 to extend his 1801 Lochalsh purchase.[29]

Final days

Seaforth's fascination with politics, shown in Chapters Five and Eleven and in the previous section of this chapter, continued into the final years of his life. One political triumph was still to come. On 22 July 1812, William Frederick Mackenzie, Seaforth's eldest son, reached his twenty-first birthday. Very conveniently, there was a general election in the autumn of that year. Seaforth could hope for an early realisation of his long-held ambition to install William as MP for Ross-shire, and thus carry forward the Seaforth domination of Ross-shire politics into the next generation. The family had high hopes of his success against Sir Charles Ross, but was slightly nervous of the majority in view of Ross's strong performance in almost capturing the seat in 1809, as seen in Chapter Eleven.[30] The *Caledonian Mercury* envisaged a close contest.[31] However,

William was a strong candidate. Like his father, he was a man of ability and a keen student. On arriving in Cambridge in 1809 he reported to Seaforth that 'for a person who is at all fond of reading it is very pleasant'.[32] He was also very personable, as Lady Seaforth's cousin Lord Carysfort testified. After visiting him in Cambridge he reported that 'his modesty and good sense and his natural courtesy and good manners will introduce him with every advantage'.[33] William soon showed his ability to win over some of the more sceptical Ross-shire proprietors. He was already in the county in July for the exercises of the East Ross local militia, of which he had become lieutenant colonel.[34] He made a good impression, even though this event was held at Tain in Easter Ross, described by his sister Caroline as 'the heart of enemy country'. William, as the representative of 'the Western interest', covered many miles in central and Wester Ross to canvass support.[35] The election, held on 3 November was a triumph. William won by twenty-nine votes to Ross's twelve.[36] Colin Mackenzie, who had acted as his agent, was jubilant. He reported to Lady Seaforth that William's acceptance speech was 'well considered, well expressed, well delivered and well received . . . the clan had reason to be proud of their young chief'.[37] At Brahan joy was unconfined. Caroline wrote to her sister Mary that 'we have been very gay since this happy event' and was sure she 'shared in the delight of dear Mackenzie's [his family nickname] brilliant election'.[38]

William's election was Seaforth's last hurrah. His morale and physical health was becoming a constant matter of concern for the family, as shown by letters written by his daughter Caroline to her sister Mary in Madras. In early February 1812, when he was at Brahan, his spirits were 'sadly low' because of 'broken promises and his disappointed hopes'.[39] He still had the power to rally. In March 1812 he was in Edinburgh and 'enjoying himself enormously with all his old friends'.[40] In September 1812 he made an impressive speech at the Northern Meeting in Inverness. Nevertheless, at the very time of William's election in November, Caroline reported to Mary that their father's 'strength has failed him sadly of late'.[41] There is a sense of doors gradually closing on his activities. In January 1813 Colin and William Mackenzie advised William of the forthcoming land sales. William informed his mother rather than his father.[42] Seaforth was evidently aware of his failing powers. In May 1813

Figure 12.1 William Frederick Mackenzie, Seaforth's son, who was elected MP for Ross-shire in 1812. (Reproduced by generous permission of the National Trust for Scotland.)

he wrote to the home secretary, Lord Sidmouth, offering his resignation as lord lieutenant of Ross-shire 'finding my health so much impaired as to make it painful to me to discharge the duties'. However, he was still sufficiently aware of the status of the family to make this conditional on William being his successor,[43] a proposal which was turned down.[44]

Despite this, Caroline reported in April 1813 that her father's health was improving every day. He was now driven around Brahan in a low carriage specially built for him and held 'levees' of the family in his bedroom in the evenings, in which he enjoyed himself, cracking jokes.[45] These were to be his last months at Brahan, which he had loved so much and to which he had devoted so much time and money.

In November 1813 came the first of two hammer blows which almost certainly shortened Seaforth's life. His younger surviving son, Francis John (known as Frank) had appeared keen to become a midshipman, following in his father's footsteps, and to make the Royal Navy his profession.[46] However, in a letter from Bombay in February 1813 he announced that, being on bad terms with the captain of a ship which he had joined for the East Indies, he 'had taken a strong aversion to the Navy' and, even more worryingly, had been 'rather unwell for some time'.[47] His father arranged for him to come home. He arrived at Brahan in the autumn of 1813 and died there on 7 November at the age of seventeen.[48] Seaforth was at Brahan at the time of Frank's death. There is evidence that he had been his favourite. He admired William's conscientious and studious nature, but the high-spirited Frank setting out (as he had thought) on a career of action was the man he himself would have liked to be. Sir Walter Scott reported the following month that 'Poor Caberfae is in Edinburgh – very ill indeed and quite broken in mind and spirits.'[49]

Seaforth was to remain in Edinburgh for the rest of his life. If he was now not in a position to make decisions, his attitudes were still highly influential. When the family moved to Edinburgh in late 1813, it was to a rented property at 21 George Street.[50] However, in the spring of 1814 a house was bought in the newest and most fashionable part of the New Town, Charlotte Square. No. 23, on the west side of the square, had been built in 1810 for Colonel, subsequently Major General Dyce.[51] It was purchased at the upper end of the going rate (£4,000) and that sum was borrowed back from the vendor.[52] Presumably No. 23 was bought, despite continuing financial problems, in recognition that it would be Seaforth's permanent abode. Not only was this expense undertaken, but also Warriston House, a mile outside Edinburgh, was leased as a summer residence. Perhaps Seaforth was involved in these very characteristic decisions. Caroline claimed to Mary in April that he was 'wonderfully improved . . . now I trust he will be long spared to us'.[53]

It was at Warriston that the final blow struck. William had been a delicate child and his health a subject of continuing comment in the family. He was much affected by Frank's death. Possibly worn down by this, by a visit to Paris in April 1814

Figure 12.2 No. 23 Charlotte Square, Edinburgh, in the newest and most fashionable part of the New Town, purchased by Seaforth in 1814. (© Finlay McKichan.)

after Napoleon's abdication[54] and finally by a mail-coach journey from London, he died at Warriston on 25 August. He was carried to the family burial ground at Fortrose Cathedral accompanied by most of the gentlemen of Ross-shire and all the Brahan tenants, but not by his father.[55] For Seaforth it was a mortal blow. Not only was the death in quick succession of his two surviving sons a personal tragedy for a man with a particular affection for his family. In addition, William had shown promise of becoming a conscientious and judicious proprietor and a successful public man. By no means least, his death ensured the extinction of the peerage Seaforth had struggled so hard to acquire. Coming so soon after the death of his beloved Frank, it was not to be borne. Seaforth died at 23 Charlotte Square on 11 January 1815 at the age of sixty, and the press was quick to attribute it to the recent loss of William.[56] On 21 January, Scott reported to Morritt, friend of Seaforth's son William, that he had watched from his Castle Street house as Seaforth's uncharacteristically modest cortège made its way to Leith to be taken by sea for him to lie with his sons at Fortrose: 'There is something very melancholy in seeing the body pass, poorly attended and in the midst of a snow storm whitening the sable ornaments of the undertaker, and all corresponding with the decadence and misfortunes of the family.'[57]

Because of the continuing snowstorm, the intended procession from Inverness was cancelled and the advertised date of the funeral postponed. An excise yacht took the coffin direct to Cromarty, from which messages of when to come to Fortrose were sent to those nearby.[58]

Scott wrote to Lady Stafford, proprietor of the Sutherland estate and longstanding political ally and friend of the Seaforth family, 'It is a mercy that the curtain is dropped. All the Highlands ring with the prophesy that when there should be a deaf Caberfae the clan and chief shall all go to wreck.' He was judicious enough to add that 'these predictions are very apt to be framed after the event'[59], and this is indeed the judgement of modern scholarship on the prophecies of 'the Brahan Seer'.[60]

Postscript

How did the Seaforth estate fare after his death? Joseph Mitchell wrote in the 1880s that in the course of his professional travels in the Highlands since the 1820s he had seen nearly two-thirds of the estates change hands.[61] Despite his deep affection and concern for his wife and children, Seaforth left to his heir Mary in 1815 and to her second husband from 1817, James Alexander Stewart Mackenzie, what they regarded as an impossible task.

At around £145,000, his debts were almost identical on his death to the mid 1780s.[62] In 1817 an Act of Parliament had to be obtained to permit land sales to meet debts notwithstanding an entail created in 1810. Annuities under Seaforth's will amounted to £4,009 per annum, £2,000 of which was for Lady Seaforth. Kelp proceeds had dropped from a peak of £8,494 in 1808 to £2,221 in 1815. Annual interest payments on debt in 1817 were £11,882, almost as much as the rental of £13,196.[63] Robert Brown's advice in 1817 was that the Seaforths should sell Brahan and Kintail, draw income from Lewis and live at Glasserton, Stewart Mackenzie's family home in Wigtonshire. Mary wrote that they had not done so to avoid criticism and 'as it is, the best years of life are spent in fruitless struggle against an overwhelming tide of disappointments and vexation'.[64]

The struggle eventually overcame them. Glasserton was sold in 1820 despite Stewart Mackenzie's understandable reluctance.[65] Agricultural depression in the years after 1815 caused growing rental arrears. Stewart Mackenzie complained in 1823 on 'the difficulty of getting rents from a Highland estate in bad times'.[66] In 1825 the creditors brought the three parishes of the island of Lewis (excluding Stornoway parish) to a judicial sale, at an upset price of £136,000. At the auction Stewart Mackenzie, probably unwisely, bought them back for £160,000.[67] Thereafter Lewis was in trust, with trustee approval being required for capital expenditure.[68] By 1826 at the latest, Lachlan Mackinnon had purchased Letterfearn, on the south side of Loch Duich, to add to the adjoining lands at Ardintoul, which he had bought from Seaforth in 1807.[69] Lewis was finally disposed of in 1844 for £190,000 to an East India merchant James Matheson, whose fortune was based on the opium trade.[70] In 1847 the Seaforth family was discussing with their London agent Hugh Innes Cameron a plan to sell lands in Kintail and Glenshiel (Morvich, Inchcroe, Invershiel and other farms on the north side of Glenshiel) to Alexander Matheson, nephew of James and former partner with him in Jardine, Matheson and Co., for £43,000. This was intended to help pay for the purchase of Fairburn, Bridge Park and Scatwell near Brahan, and believed to be more improvable. Following the death of her husband in 1843, Mary Stewart Mackenzie was making decisions aided by her son Keith William, now aged twenty-nine. Both Mary and Keith at first vacillated. Mary finally gave her approval. Perhaps surprisingly, Keith still resisted[71] and no sale was made at this point.[72] Although Fairburn etc. was purchased, part of it was sold to Alexander Matheson only months later.[73]

In 1853 the Seaforths were still the largest landowners in the parish of Glenshiel[74] and continued to have holdings there on Mary's death in 1862. Invershiel, Morvich, Inchcroe, Achnagart and Cluanie were finally sold by Keith in November 1869. Ironically, they were purchased for £30,000 by James Thompson Mackenzie, a London merchant, who thereafter styled himself 'of Kintail'.[75] However, the farms in Easter Ross near Brahan were all that was left of the Seaforth wide acres. The lands from which they had sprung had now passed out of their hands for ever.

Final conclusions

As indicated in the Preface, this has been a thematic study of the life and career of Francis Humberston Mackenzie, placing him in the historiographical context of the issues he faced. Specific conclusions have been given at the end of previous chapters, and in these links have been made to similar topics and issues arising in other chapters. General conclusions will now be made on the overarching arguments developed in the book.

It has been argued that Seaforth differed significantly from the stereotype of a Highland proprietor and clan chief of what Allan Macinnes has called 'The First Phase of Clearance'.[76] Seaforth had a traditional view of clanship, believing that it was his duty to be concerned for the welfare of his clansmen and small tenants. Accordingly, he was most unwilling to introduce large-scale sheep farming and carry out the consequent clearances, as so many of his fellow chiefs were doing in the late eighteenth and early nineteenth centuries. He resisted offers from sheepmasters for Glenshiel in the 1780s, and continued this policy until as late as 1808, when small tenants were given preference around the village he was establishing at Maryburgh. He was still asserting this eloquently (but now unsuccessfully) in 1811 when the trust was being created which took the management of the estate out of his hands. The only large-scale sheep farm set up on lands owned by him was at Valamos, Lewis, in 1802, when he was in Barbados and the estate was in the hands of trustees. He was, similarly, slow to end the traditional multiple landholdings at a time when other Highland proprietors were hurrying to 'lot' township land into individual smallholdings and thus create the crofting system.

Seaforth was regarded by himself and others as a humanitarian, and there is no doubt that his intentions towards his small tenants were benevolent. In addition to other motivations for his humanitarianism, his deafness may have helped to give him a sympathetic view of people disadvantaged in other ways. However, the benefits to the intended recipients were sometimes limited. He had inherited large debts, which were never seriously reduced because of his less-than-commercial (and sometimes contradictory) estate policies. The consequence was land sales, which started a decade before the next two similarly embarrassed Highland proprietors and two decades before most others. It has been argued that this was caused by Seaforth's psychological need to counter his deafness by excelling in expenditure. The land sales were often followed quickly by clearance. For example, within six months of purchase in 1801, extensive sheep farms in Lochalsh and Kintail were advertised by the new owner, Hugh Innes.[77] Colin Mackenzie reported to Seaforth, 'I am sorry to say that the farms of Lochalsh etc. sold to Mr Innes which were out of lease have been let in such a way as to turn out many good people, whose honest attachment to you interested me warmly.'[78] An attempt was made to salve Seaforth's conscience by trying to make room for as many as possible in the new villages of Dornie and Bundalloch.[79] However, it is difficult to avoid the conclusion that part of the motivation, as with subsequent sales, was to avoid clearance on Seaforth's watch. Seaforth is one of the clearest examples of a proprietor whose ambition was to look after his small tenants and clansmen in the traditional way, but whose experience illustrates the pitfalls which faced those who did not maximise their income by turning over their lands to large-scale sheep farming.

The stereotype of a Highland chief is also of a man who made large profits by forcing the sons of his small tenants to join the regiment he raised to fight the French. There is evidence that Seaforth used the threat of eviction to win recruits (and mainly kept promises to the families of those who joined the 78th). However, he did not profit financially from his recruiting, while military service did bring additional income to small tenants. Probably the most commercial aspect of his management was the kelp trade. Nevertheless, he does not appear to have followed some of the practices of which kelp landlords have been accused, such as forcing families into tiny coastal plots to oblige them to gather kelp. One of the most successful aspects of Seaforth's activities in Ross-shire was his domination of the politics of the county. Here it might appear that in his active use of fictitious votes and patronage to secure votes he came nearest to the stereotype of a Highland proprietor of his time. Even here there is evidence of his wish to follow his principles, especially from 1784 to 1792, when his support for Charles James Fox and the Whigs was ill-calculated to win favours from the government he opposed.

D. J. Murray argued that Seaforth, because of his lack of experience in the Caribbean, did not understand that governors were expected to rub along as best they could with the planter elite.[80] It has been argued here that he well understood recent trends in the governance of Barbados, and was determined to reverse them, specifically in order to increase the legal rights of free people of colour and enslaved labourers. This seems anomalous to modern eyes in a man who continued to believe in slavery. We may believe that he was trying to ameliorate what was an inherently evil system. However, there is clear evidence of his sincere concern for the welfare of people of colour. For example, in 1804 he went to great trouble, against sustained resistance, to uncover the details of murders of enslaved labourers by whites. To make such murders a capital offence was the principal theme of his governorship. He had been instructed by his Whitehall masters to have such an Act passed by the island Assembly. However, that this became a personal mission is shown by the empassioned (and possibly counter-productive) language which he used to persuade the Assembly. It is also true that the Act passed in 1805 lost a good deal of its force by the requirement for there to be a white witness. His continued attempts to increase the legal rights of free people of colour (based on both humanitarianism and a concern that they might join a slave rising) received no government support and came to nothing. It is fair to say that Seaforth's principal achievements in Barbados were to prevent certain things happening. He successfully resisted pressure to reduce the rights of free people of colour and there was no slave rising in his time. His active promotion of the rights of people of colour was not what white Barbadians had expected of a governor of his background, and it horrified many of them. He did what he regarded as his duty in a job which he had not particularly wanted with great conscientiousness, and was unique in his time in holding such a post while being profoundly deaf. His years in Barbados illustrate the complex tensions which unsettled slave societies (owners and slaves) in the run up to the abolition of the British slave trade, which occurred a year after his departure. They also give an insight into the governance of British Caribbean territories during the Napoleonic Wars.

It has been argued that Seaforth was hypocritical in claiming to be a humanitarian while being a partner in cotton plantations in Berbice worked by enslaved labourers.[81] That he did so was undoubtedly due to financial desperation. This may have further clouded his already imperfect commercial judgement and led him to buy land in a colony whose sovereignty was highly questionable. He was determined not to appear as a stereotypical slave owner of the type then being criticised in abolitionist campaigning. It is clear that instructions were given to his plantation attorney Peter Fairbairn that slaves should be treated well. To some extent this was achieved. However, his intentions were sometimes nullified by adverse circumstances and, it has to be said, by his failure to give any supervision on the spot. The venture was underfinanced from the start because of delays, caused in part by difficulties in securing land titles for which he was to some extent responsible. What he could not have anticipated was the long series of unfavourable seasons. This made it more difficult to treat slaves as he had hoped and led to financial disaster. The investment which was intended to repay his debts and pay his living costs on his return to the UK in fact added to the debt burden.

It has been shown that there were strong links between Seaforth's policies and attitudes in the Highlands of Scotland and in the Caribbean. His concern for his small tenants in Ross-shire was matched by his attempts to increase the rights of people of colour in Barbados and to provide good treatment for his own enslaved labourers in Berbice. Another common feature, regrettably, was that in all these places the practical improvements for the intended beneficiaries were partial or short-term. Seaforth's conservative economic views were reflected both in limited commercialism in Ross-shire and strong support for the Navigation Laws in Barbados. On the other hand, local conditions in Barbados prevented him behaving in some of the ways he had been used to. A tradition of local self-government and an insufficient supply of patronage prevented him controlling the politics of the island as he had done in Ross-shire. His attempts to mould the Barbados militia into something like his 78th Regiment in Scotland were obstructed by powerful local interests.[82]

The Berbice purchase was probably the worst decision he made. Its failure led to the land sales of his later years and, because of the burdens passed to his heirs, played a part in the gradual disappearance of the estate in Lewis and mainland Ross-shire described above. Culminating in the tragic loss of his two surviving sons in 1813 and 1814, all his ambitions and efforts to re-establish the Seaforth peers as the predominant figures in Ross-shire and influential players in the British polity and military crumbled to ashes. And yet there is something heroic in his failure. Such luminaries as Sir Walter Scott admired his 'talents of a high order'.[83] His family, who arguably lost most from his failures, regarded him with admiration as well as love. His daughter Caroline wrote on his death, 'when one considers what a man he had been and how all who knew him had been accustomed to look up to him with admiration and reverence, one cannot see the change without feeling the greatest misery.'[84] They had felt his affection, but also admired the way in which he overcame his deafness to become a man of science and culture, a popular figure in society and to carve out a career as a public man in revolutionary and demanding times.

Notes

1. Edinburgh, National Records of Scotland (NRS), GD46/17/36, Lord Seaforth to R. Brown, 11 March 1811.
2. NRS, GD46/17/35/274–5, Stuart and Co., Sketch of kelp account to 12 January 1811; /300, W. Mackenzie to Lord Seaforth, 19 June 1810.
3. NRS, GD46/17/35/298–9, W. Mackenzie to Lord Seaforth, 28 June 1810.
4. NRS, GD46/17/35/276–7, Lord Seaforth et al. in account with Inglis, Ellis and Co. 20 April 1810.
5. NRS, GD46/17/37, T. Coutts to Lord Seaforth, 19 March 1811.
6. NRS, GD46/17/36, C. Mackenzie to Lord Seaforth, 12 June 1811.
7. NRS, GD46/17/37/32, Lord Seaforth to Inglis, Ellis and Co., 9 February 1811.
8. NRS, GD46/17/37/27, J. Inglis to Lord Seaforth, 11 February 1811.

9. NRS, GD46/17/37/52, P. Fairbairn to Lord Seaforth, 8 February 1811.
10. NRS, GD46/17/37, C. Mackenzie to Lord Seaforth, 18 March 1811.
11. NRS, GD46/17/36, Lord Seaforth to R. Brown, 11 March 1811.
12. NRS, GD46/17/37/126, W. Mackenzie to Lord Seaforth, 17 March 1811.
13. NRS, GD46/17/36, J. B. Fraser to Lord Seaforth, 14 December 1812.
14. Foster, S., *A Private Empire* (Millers Point, 2011), pp. 159–66.
15. NRS, GD46/17/41, Lord Seaforth to Sir A. Mackenzie of Avoch, 30 May 1813.
16. NRS, GD46/1/143, C. Mackenzie 22 July 1815 and W. Mackenzie 24 July 1815 to Lady Hood Mackenzie.
17. NRS, GD46/17/16, 'Tables showing farms . . . in Glenshiel and Kintail . . . with present and expected rent', n.d., but from internal evidence, after Whit 1810.
18. NRS, GD46/17/36, Lord Seaforth to R. Brown, 11 March 1811.
19. Womack, P., *Improvement and Romance – Constructing the Myth of the Highlands* (Basingstoke, 1989), pp. 2, 56.
20. NRS, GD46/17/36, Minute of meeting of Lord Seaforth's trustees, Edinburgh, July 1811.
21. NRS, GD46/1/28, Act authorising sale of parts of estate of Seaforth, 27 June 1817, 57 Geo. III cap. 23, 406.
22. NRS, GD46/17/36, W. Mackenzie and R. Brown to Lord Seaforth, 30 April 1811.
23. NRS, GD46/17/36, Minute of meeting of Lord Seaforth's trustees, July 1811.
24. NRS, GD46/1/28, Act authorising sale of parts of estate of Seaforth, 27 June 1817, 57 Geo III cap. 23, 406.
25. NRS, GD46/17/36, Lord Seaforth to C. Mackenzie, 1 July 1811.
26. NRS, GD46/17/32/191–2, Account sales kelp, 8–9/1810; GD46/17/37/478–80, Account sales J. Stuart and Co., September–October 1811.
27. NRS, GD46/17/36, Minute of meeting of Lord Seaforth's trustees, July 1811.
28. Advertised *Inverness Journal,* 20 November 1812, 19 and 26 March 1813; NRS, Register of Sasines Ross-shire Abridgements, 22 February 1814. David Dick purchased Torlysich, those parts of Invershiel and Cluanie south of the rivers Shiel and Cluanie, Shielhouse Inn, Ratagan at the head of Loch Duich and the Glenlunie grazings.
29. NRS, Register of Sasines Ross-shire Abridgements, 30 January 1815. Advertised *Inverness Journal*, 20 November 1812, 19 and 26 March 1813.

30. NRS, GD46/17/29, Caroline Mackenzie to Lady Hood, 2 September 1812.
31. *Caledonian Mercury*, 19 October 1812, 19th Century British Library Newspapers online (19BLN), accessed 7 February 2011.
32. Edinburgh, National Library of Scotland (NLS), MS 6396, fos 84–5, W. F. Mackenzie to Lord Seaforth, 26 November 1809.
33. NLS, MS 6396, fo. 144, Lord Carysfort to Lady Seaforth, 7 November 1811.
34. NRS, GD46/17/29, W. F. Mackenzie, Brahan, to Lady Hood, 13 July 1812.
35. NRS, GD46/17/29, Caroline Mackenzie, Brahan, 27 October 1812, to Lady Hood.
36. *Caledonian Mercury*, 7 November 1812 (19BLN), accessed 7 February 2011.
37. NLS, MS 6396, fos 137–8, C. Mackenzie to Lady Seaforth, 5 November 1812.
38. NRS, GD46/17/29, Caroline Mackenzie, Brahan, 21 November 1812, to Lady Hood.
39. NRS, GD46/17/29, Caroline Mackenzie to Lady Hood, n.d. and 6 February 1812.
40. NRS, GD46/17/29, Caroline Mackenzie to Lady Hood, 17 March 1812.
41. NRS, GD46/17/29, Caroline Mackenzie to Lady Hood, 2 September and 21 November 1812.
42. NLS, MS 6396, fo. 90–1, W. F. Mackenzie to Lady Seaforth, 24 January 1813.
43. NRS, GD46/17/41, Lord Seaforth to Lord Sidmouth, 12 May 1813.
44. NRS, GD46/17/41, Lord Sidmouth to Lord Seaforth, 20 May 1813.
45. NRS, GD46/17/29, Caroline Mackenzie to Lady Hood, 16 April 1813.
46. NLS, MS 3696, fos 94–6, F. J. Mackenzie to Lady Seaforth, 25 June 1808.
47. NRS, GD46/17/9/310–13, F. J. Mackenzie to Lord Seaforth, 1 February 1813.
48. *Caledonian Mercury*, 25 November 1813 (19BLN), accessed 9 February 2011.
49. Grierson, H. J. C. (ed.), *The Letters of Sir Walter Scott, 1811–1814* (London, 1932), vol. 3, p. 393, Scott to Miss Clephane, 11 December 1813.
50. NRS, GD46/17/29, Caroline Mackenzie, 21 George St., to Lady Hood, 20 January 1814.
51. RCAHMS Canmore website, ID 114491, <www.canmore.rcahms.gov.uk>; *Post Office Annual Directory – Edinburgh*, 1809–16, <www.nls.uk>, both accessed 8 April 2015.

52. NRS, Edinburgh Sheriff Court Inventories, 21 November 1815, Will of Francis Mackenzie alias Lord Seaforth; GD46/17/80/25, List of debts, n.d.; Youngson, A. J., *The Making of Classical Edinburgh, 1750–1840* (Edinburgh, 1988), p. 224.

53. NRS, GD46/17/29, Caroline Mackenzie to Lady Hood, 20 and 25 April 1814.

54. NRS, GD46/17/29, Caroline Mackenzie to Lady Hood, 20 April 1814.

55. *Caledonian Mercury*, 3 and 15 September 1814 (19BLN), accessed 9 February 2011; NRS, GD46/17/41, R. Brown to A. Mundell, 3 September 1814.

56. *Morning Chronicle*, 18 January 1815; *Caledonian Mercury*, 21 January 1815 (19BLN), accessed 9 February 2011.

57. Grierson, *Letters of Scott*, vol. 4, p. 19, W. Scott to J. B. S. Morritt, 21 January 1815.

58. *Caledonian Mercury*, 30 January 1815 (19BLN), accessed 9 February 2011.

59. Grierson, *Letters of Scott*, vol. 4, p. 22, W. Scott to Lady Stafford, 21 January 1815.

60. Sutherland, A., *The Brahan Seer: The Making of a Legend* (Bern, 2009), pp. 192–3.

61. Mitchell, J., *Reminiscences of my Life in the Highlands* (Chilworth: Gresham Press, 1884, reprint Newton Abbot: David and Charles, 1971), vol. 2, p. 114.

62. Seaforth's calculation of his debts 1786, NRS, GD46/17/4/74; debts on his death GD46/17/82, 'Memo for Lady Hood Mackenzie', n.d., but apparently 1815.

63. NRS, GD46/1/28, Act authorising sale of parts of estate of Seaforth, 27 June 1817, 57 Geo III cap. 23, 406; GD46/17/52, 'Present state of Seaforth debts, 29 January 1819'.

64. NRS, GD46/17/80/137, Mrs Mary F. E. S. Mackenzie to Lord Mackenzie, n.d.

65. NRS, GD46/17/52, P. Cockburn to J. Tod, 22 December 1819; C. Selkrig to J. Tod, 22 December 1819; J. Tod to C. Selkrig, 5 January 1820.

66. Quoted in Hunter, J., *The Making of the Crofting Community* (Edinburgh, 1976), p. 37.

67. *Inverness Courier*, 17 March 1825.

68. NRS, GD46/1/528, J. Adam to J. A. S. Mackenzie, 17 August 1825.

69. NRS, Ross-shire Sasine Abridgements, 6 November 1833.

70. *Inverness Courier*, 17 January 1844; NRS, Ross-shire Sasine Abridgements, 17 August 1846.

71. NRS, GD46/1/401, H. I. Cameron to K. W. S. Mackenzie, 8 July and 30 August 1847.

72. NRS, Ross-shire Sasine Abridgements, search made for Alexander Matheson sasines 1847–8.
73. NRS, Ross-shire Sasine Abridgements, 11 September 1847.
74. Mackenzie, K. S., 'Changes in the ownership of land in Ross-shire, 1756–1853', *Transactions of the Gaelic Society of Inverness* (*TGSI*), vol. 12, 1885–6, p. 313.
75. NRS, Ross-shire Sasine Abridgements, 23 December 1870 to 5 January 1871; Mackenzie, A., *History of the Mackenzies* (Inverness, 1894 edn), pp. 345–7.
76. Macinnes, A. I., 'Scottish Gaeldom: The First Phase of Clearance', in T. M. Devine and R. Mitchison (eds), *People and Society in Scotland, Volume 1, 1760–1830* (Edinburgh, 1988), pp. 70–90.
77. *Aberdeen Journal*, 9 September 1801 (19BLN), accessed 3 February 2011.
78. NRS, GD46/17/20/204–5, C. Mackenzie to Lord Seaforth, 24 November 1801.
79. NRS GD46/17/21, 'Plan of distribution of Dornie and Bundalloch', 23 March 1802.
80. Murray, D. J., *The West Indies and the Development of Colonial Government 1801–1834* (Oxford, 1955), pp. 21–2, 33.
81. Alston, D., '"Very rapid and splendid fortunes"? Highland Scots in Berbice (Guyana) in the early nineteenth century', *TGSI*, vol. 63, 2006, pp. 228, 231.
82. These arguments developed in McKichan, F., 'Lord Seaforth: Highland Proprietor, Caribbean Governor and Slave Owner', *The Scottish Historical Review*, vol. 90, 2, 2011, pp. 204–35.
83. Grierson, *Letters of Sir Walter Scott*, vol. 3, pp. 393–4, Scott to Miss Clephane, 11 December 1813.
84. NRS, GD46/17/29, Caroline Mackenzie to Lady Hood, 29 January 1815.

Bibliography

Manuscript Sources

Aberdeen, Aberdeen University Special Collections – Manuscripts and Archives (AU)   MS 3470, Castle Fraser Archive.

Black Rock, St James, Barbados Department of Archives (BDA) microfilm BS7, Barbados Assembly Minutes, 1782–1815. Planters Name Index.

Castle Fraser, Sauchen, Aberdeenshire (C. F. Papers) Mackenzie Fraser papers and transcripts.

Edinburgh, National Library of Scotland (NLS) MS 6396, Seaforth Papers.

Edinburgh, National Records of Scotland (NRS) NRS, E106/28, Ross-shire Valuation Rolls, 1756–1802.

NRS, E326/5–6, Male and Female Servants Tax, Ross and Cromarty, 1786–7, 1791–2, 1797–8.

NRS, E326/8, Carriage Tax Rolls, Ross-shire, 1792–3, 1797–8.

NRS, GD9/1, British Fisheries Society Records, 1787.

NRS, GD46, Seaforth Papers.

NRS, GD51, Papers of Dundas of Melville Family.

NRS GD201/1/365, Macdonald of Clanranald Papers, Correspondence re debts, 1797–1837.

NRS, GD427, Gillanders of Highfield Papers.

NRS, RH2/4/71, 207, Home Office Supplementary Papers, Scotland, 1793.

NRS, Register of Sasines Ross-shire Abridgements (digitised).

NRS, Will of Francis Mackenzie alias Lord Seaforth, Edinburgh Sheriff Court   Inventories, 21 November 1815 available at <www.scottishdocuments.com>.

Glasgow, Mitchell Library Special Collections ref. 591706, –711, –837, Mackenzie Miscellanea.

London, British Library (BL)

BL, Add. MS 33978, Banks Correspondence, vol. II, 1785–89.

BL, Add. MS 37886, Windham Papers, vol. XLV.

BL, Add. MS 39191, Mackenzie Papers, vol. V.

BL, Add. MS 39195, Mackenzie Papers, Correspondence of Maj. Gen. J. R. Mackenzie, vols VIII and IX.

BL, Add. MS 39200, Mackenzie Papers, vol. XIV.

BL, Add. MS 40715, Add. MS 42071, Hamilton and Greville Papers.

London, The National Archives (TNA)

ADM106/1225, /1240, letters re storing of squadron of Vice Admiral R. Mann in Mediterranean, 1774, 1777.

TNA, CO28/67–75, Colonial Office (CO) Correspondence Original, Barbados, 1801–6.

TNA, CO29/27, /29 Barbados Entry Books, 1801–6.

TNA, CO30/17–18, Acts, Ordinances and Proclamations, Barbados, 1797–1811.

TNA, CO33/22, Shipping Returns, Barbados, 1801–2.

TNA, CO111/2, /4, /73, /74, Original Correspondence, Berbice, Demerara and Essequibo, 1799–1803.

TNA, CO112/1, Berbice Governor's Correspondence, 1801–7.

TNA, CO112/8, Berbice Despatches (letters from Secretary of State to Governor), 1801–15.

TNA, CO323/43–4, Law Officers Reports on Colonial Acts, 1825–7.

TNA, T71/437, Office of Registry of Colonial Slaves and Slave Compensation Commission Records, Berbice (1818).

London, Royal Society Library

EC/1794/05, election certificate of Francis Humberstone Mackenzie, 26 June 1794.

Printed Primary Sources

Aberdeen Journal, 19th Century British Library Newspapers online (19BLN).

Adam, R. J. (ed.), *Papers on Sutherland Estate Management 1802–1816*, 2 vols, (Edinburgh: Scottish History Society, 1972).

Anderson, James, *An Account of the Present State of the Hebrides and Western Coasts of Scotland* (Edinburgh: G. Robinson and C. Elliott, 1785).

Aspinall, A. (ed.), *Correspondence of George, Prince of Wales, 1770–1812*, vol. 2 (London: Cassell, 1964).

Barbados Mercury and Bridgetown Gazette, 1805 Barbados National Library, microfilm 20; 1805–6 British Library microfilm MC1888.

Barker, G. F. R. and A. H. Stenning (eds), *The Westminster School Register from 1764 to 1883* (London: Macmillan, 1892).

Barron, James, *The Northern Highlands in the Nineteenth Century: Newspaper Index and Annals,* (Inverness: R. Carruthers, 1903) vol. 1.

Caledonian Mercury, Edinburgh, NLS microfilm Mf. N.776, paper copies 1812–4 and 19BLN.

Cregeen, E. R. (ed.), *Argyll Estate Instructions: Mull, Morvern and Tiree, 1771–1805* (Edinburgh: Scottish History Society, 1964).

Daily Advertiser, London, British Library Burney Collection of 17th and 18th Century Newspapers online (BCN).

Diary or Woodfall's Register (BCN).

Dingwall Town Council Minutes, 1786–1813, in Appendix, Norman Macrae, *The Romance of a Royal Burgh: Dingwall's Story of a Thousand Years* (1923, reprint Wakefield: EP Publishing, 1974).

Gazetteer and New Daily Advertiser, London (19BLN).

Ginter, Donald E. (ed.), *Voting Records of the House of Commons, 1761–1820* (London: Hambledon Press, 1995), vol. 5.

Grierson, H. J. C. (ed.), *The Letters of Sir Walter Scott, 1811–1814* (London: Constable, 1932), vols 3, 4.

General Evening Post, London (BCN).

Gun, W. T. J. (ed.), *The Harrow School Register, 1571–1800* (London: Longmans Green, 1934).

Headrick, James., *Report on the Island of Lewis* (Edinburgh: Adam Neill, 1800).

Inverness Courier, 1812–13 and 1825 (NLS).

Inverness Journal, 1808 (NLS microfilm Mf. N.157).

Knox, John, *A Tour through the Highlands of Scotland and the Hebride Isles in 1786* (1787, reprint Edinburgh: James Thin, 1975).

Kyd, James Gray, *Scottish Population Statistics including Webster's Analysis of Population 1755* (Edinburgh: Scottish History Society, 1952).

Lloyd's Evening Post, London (BCN).

London Chronicle (BCN).

London Evening Post (BCN).

London Gazette (BCN).

Mackenzie, Sir G. S., *A General Survey of the Counties of Ross and Cromarty drawn up for the Consideration of the Board of Agriculture* (London: Board of Agriculture, 1810).

Mitchell, Joseph, *Reminiscences of my Life in the Highlands,* (Chilworth: Gresham Press, 1884, reprint Newton Abbot: David and Charles, 1971), vol. 2.

Morning Chronicle, London (BCN).

Morning Herald, London (BCN).

Morning Post and Gazetteer, London (BCN).

New Statistical Account of Scotland (Edinburgh: Blackwood, 1845), vol. XIV, <http://stat-acc-scot-edina.ac.uk/link/1834-45/Ross and Cromarty> and <http://stat-acc-scot-edina.ac.uk/1834-45/Inverness>.

Oracle and Public Advertiser, London (BCN).

Pappalardo, B., *Royal Navy Lieutenants' Passing Certificates, 1691–1902* (Kew: List and Text Society, 2001).

Pinckard, G., *Notes on the West Indies including observations relative to the Creoles and slaves of the western colonies* (London: Baldwin, Craddock and Joy, 1816), vol. 2.

Post Office Annual Directory – Edinburgh, 1809–16 (Edinburgh: Postmaster General, <www.nls.uk>, accessed 8 April 2015).

Poyer, John, 'A Letter addressed to H. E. the Rt Hon. Francis Lord Seaforth by a Barbadian' (Bridgetown: William Williams, 1801).

Poyer, John, 'History of the Administration of the Rt Hon. Francis Lord Seaforth, late Governor', *Barbados Chronicle*, 20 April–3 August 1808, reproduced in *Journal of the Barbados Museum and Historical Society*, vol. 21, August 1954.

Public Advertiser, London (BCN).

St Clair, Thomas Staunton, *A Residence in the West Indies and America* (London: R. Bentley, 1834).

St James Chronicle, London (BCN).

Say's Weekly Journal, London (BCN).

Sinclair, Sir John, *General View of the Agriculture of the Northern Counties and Islands of Scotland* (Edinburgh: Colin Macrae, 1795).

Star, London (19BLN).

Statistical Account of Scotland (OSA), ed. Sir John Sinclair (Edinburgh, 1791–9) vols VI, VII, IX, XI, XIX, <http://stat-acc-scot.edina.ac.uk/link/1791-99/Ross>.

Sun, London (BCN).

Thompson, Alvin O., *A Documentary History of Slavery in Berbice 1796—1834* (Georgetown: Free Press, 2002).

True Briton, London (BCN).

Welsh, R.C. (ed.), *The Harrow School Register 1801–1883* (London: Longmans Green, 1894).

Whitehall Evening Post, London (BCN).

Secondary Sources

Abrams, Lynn, 'The Taming of Highland Masculinity: Inter-personal Violence and Shifting Codes of Manhood, *c*.1760–1840', *The Scottish Historical Review (SHR)*, vol. 92, April 2013.

Adamson, J. W., *English Education 1789–1902* (Cambridge: Cambridge University Press, 1930).

Alleyne, Warren, *Historic Bridgetown*, (Bridgetown: Barbados National Trust, 2003).

Alston, David, '"Very rapid and splendid fortunes"? Highland Scots in Berbice (Guyana) in the early nineteenth century', *Transactions of the Gaelic Society of Inverness*, vol. 63, 2006.

Alston, David, 'Enslaved Africans, Scots and the Plantations of Guyana', in T. M. Devine (ed.), *Recovering Scotland's Slavery Past: The Caribbean Connection* (Edinburgh: Edinburgh University Press, 2015).

Alston, David, 'Behavioural Economics and the Paradox of Scottish Emigration', in A. McCarthy and J. M. Mackenzie (eds), *Global Migrations: The Scottish Diaspora since 1800* (Edinburgh: Edinburgh University Press, 2016).

Barker, G. F. R., 'Proby, John Joshua, first earl of Carysfort (1751–1828), rev. E. A. Smith, *Oxford Dictionary of National Biography (ODNB)*, Oxford, 2004, online edition, <www.oxforddnb.com>, article 22832.

Barker, G. F. R., 'Hamilton, Lord Archibald (1770–1827)', rev. H. C. G. Matthew, *ODNB*, Oxford, 2004, online edition, <www.oxforddnb.com>, article 12051.

Bayly, A., *Imperial Meridian: The British Empire and the World, 1780–1830* (Harlow: Longman, 1989).

Beckles, Hilary, *Black Rebellion in Barbados: The Struggle Against Slavery 1637–1838* (Bridgetown: Antilles Publications, 1987).

Beckles, Hilary, *Afro-Caribbean Women and Resistance to Slavery in Barbados* (London: Karnack House, 1988).

Beckles, Hilary, 'Freedom without Liberty: Free Blacks in the Barbados Slave System' in Verene E. Shepherd (ed.), *Slavery without Sugar: Diversity in Caribbean Economy and Society since the 17th Century* (Gainesville, Fla.: University Press of Florida, 2002).

Bew, John, *Castlereagh Enlightenment, War and Tyranny* (London: Quercus, 2011).

Boucher, Philip, 'The French and Dutch Caribbean, 1600–1800' in Stephen Palmie and Francisco A. Scarano (eds), *The Caribbean: A History of the Region and Its Peoples* (Chicago: University of Chicago Press, 2011).

Branigan, Keith, *The Last of the Clan* (Stroud: Amberley, 2010).

Brown, Ian Gordon, 'James Hall's Paris Day', *Scottish Archives*, vol. 17 (2011).

Buckley, Roger Norman, *Slaves in Red Coats: The British West India Regiments, 1795–1815* (New Haven: Yale University Press, 1979).

Buckley, Roger Norman, *The British Army in the West Indies: Society and the Military in the Revolutionary Age* (Gainesville: University Press of Florida, 1998).

Burnard, Trevor, 'Harvest Years? Reconfigurations of Empire in Jamaica, 1756–1807', *Journal of Imperial and Commonwealth History (JICH)*, vol. 40, 4, 2012.

Cain, P.J., and A. G. Hopkins, *British Imperialism: 1688–2000* (Harlow: Longman, 2002).

Campbell, Stuart D., 'Post-medieval settlement in the Isle of Lewis: a study in adaptability or change?', *Proceedings of Society of Antiquaries of Scotland*, vol. 139, 2009.

Candlin, Kit, *The Last Caribbean Frontier, 1795–1815* (Basingstoke: Palgrave Macmillan, 2012).

Carr, Rosalind, 'The Gentleman and the Soldier: Patriotic Masculinities in Eighteenth-Century Scotland', *Journal of Scottish Historical Studies*, vol. 28, 2008.

Carrington, Selwyn H. H., 'The United States and the British West Indian Trade, 1783–1807' in Roderick A. McDonald (ed.), *West Indies Accounts: Essays on the History of the British Caribbean and the Atlantic Economy in Honour of Richard Sheridan* (Kingston: University of West Indies Press, 1996).

Carter, Harold B., *Sir Joseph Banks, 1743–1820* (London: British Museum, 1988).

Cavell, S. A., *Midshipmen and Quarterdeck Boys in the British Navy, 1771–1831* (Woodbridge: Boydell Press, 2012).

Chichester, H. M., 'Mackenzie, Francis Humberston, Baron Seaforth and Mackenzie of Kintail (1754–1815)', rev. Jonathan Spain, ODNB, Oxford, 2004, online edition, <www.oxforddnb.com>, article 14126.

Clifford, Timothy, Michael Gallagher and Helen Smailes, *Benjamin West and the Death of the Stag* (Edinburgh: National Galleries of Scotland, 2009).

Colley, Linda, *Britons: Forging the Nation 1707–1837* (London: Pimlico, 1994).

Cooke, Anthony, *The Rise and Fall of the Scottish Cotton Industry 1778–1914* (Manchester: Manchester University Press, 2010).

Cooke, Anthony, 'An Elite Revisited: Glasgow West India Merchants, 1783–1877', *JSHS*, vol. 32, 2, 2012.

Cookson, J. E., *The British Armed Nation, 1793–1815* (Oxford: Clarendon Press, 1997).

Cookson, J. E., 'The Napoleonic Wars, Military Scotland and Tory Highlandism in the Early Nineteenth Century', *SHR*, vol. 78, April 1999.

Coull, James R., 'Fishery Development in Scotland in the Eighteenth Century', *Scottish Economic and Social History (SESH)*, vol. 21, 2001.

Craton, Michael, *Testing the Chains: Resistance to Slavery in the British West Indies* (Ithaca, NY: Cornell University Press, 1982).

Cregeen, Eric R., Annie Tindley (ed.), 'The Creation of the Crofting Townships in Tiree', *JSHS*, vol. 35, 2, 2015.

Crouzet, François, 'America and the crisis of the British imperial economy, 1803–1807' in John J. McCusker and Kenneth Morgan (eds), *The Early Modern Atlantic Economy* (Cambridge: Cambridge University Press, 2000).

Dalton, Henry Gibbs, *The History of British Guiana,* 2 vols (London: Longman Brown Green, 1854–5).

Devine, T. M., *Clanship to Crofters' War: The Social Transformation of the Scottish Highlands* (Manchester: Manchester University Press, 1994).

Devine, T. M., *The Scottish Nation 1700–2000* (London: Allen Lane, 1999).

Devine, T. M., *Scotland's Empire 1600–1815* (London: Allen Lane, 2003).

Devine, T. M., *Clearance and Improvement: Land, Power and People in Scotland, 1700–1900* (Edinburgh: John Donald, 2006).

Devine, T. M., and Philipp T. Rossner, 'Scots in the Atlantic Economy, 1600–1800', John M. Mackenzie and T. M. Devine (eds), *Scotland and the British Empire* (Oxford: Oxford University Press, 2011).

Devine, T. M. (ed.), *Recovering Scotland's Slavery Past: The Caribbean Connection* (Edinburgh: Edinburgh University Press, 2015).

Dodgshon, Robert A., *From Chiefs to Landlords: Social and Economic Change in the Western Highlands and Islands, c.1493–1820* (Edinburgh: Edinburgh University Press, 1998).

Dodgshon, Robert A., *No Stone Unturned: A History of Farming, Landscape and Environment in the Scottish Highlands and Islands* (Edinburgh: Edinburgh University Press, 2015).

Dooley, Terence E. M., *The Decline of the Big House in Ireland: A Study of Irish Landed Families* (Dublin: Wolfhound Press, 2001).

Draper, Nicholas, 'The Rise of a New Planter Class? Some Countercurrents from British Guiana and Trinidad, 1807–33', *Atlantic Studies*, vol. 9, 1, March 2012.

Dressler, Camille, *Eigg: The Story of an Island* (Edinburgh: Birlinn, 1998).

Dubois, Laurent, *A Colony of Citizens: Revolution and Slave Emancipation in the French Caribbean, 1787–1804* (Chapel Hill, NC: University of North Carolina Press, 2004).

Duffy, Michael, 'World-Wide War and British Expansionism, 1793–1815' in P. J. Marshall (ed.), *The Oxford History of the British Empire*, vol. 2 (Oxford: Oxford University Press, 1998).

Dunlop, Jean, *The British Fisheries Society, 1786–1893* (Edinburgh: John Donald, 1978).

Edwards, Bryan, *The History, Civil and Commercial, of the British Colonies in the West Indies*, vol. 4 (London: Whittaker, 1819).

Ehrmann, John, *The Younger Pitt*, vol. 3 (London: Constable, 1996).

Farrell, S. M., 'Pratt, John Jeffreys, first Marquess Camden (1759–1840)', *ODNB*, Oxford 2004, online edition, <www.oxforddnb.com>, article 22705.

Ferguson, W., 'Dingwall Burgh Politics and the Parliamentary Franchise in the Eighteenth Century', *SHR*, vol. 126, 1959.

Flinn, Michael, (ed.), *Scottish Population History from the 17th Century to the 1930s* (Cambridge: Cambridge University Press, 1977).

Forte, Angelo and James R. Coull, 'Fishing and Legislation' in J. R. Coull, A. Fenton and K. Veitch, (eds), *A Compendium of Scottish Ethnology*, vol. 4, Boats, Fishing and the Sea (Edinburgh: John Donald, 2008).

Foster, Stephen, *A Private Empire* (Millers Point, NSW: Pier 9, 2011).

Fry, Michael, *The Dundas Despotism* (Edinburgh: John Donald, 2004 edn).

Gambles, Anna, 'Free Trade and State Formation: The Political Economy of Fisheries Policy in Britain and the United Kingdom, circa 1750–1850', *Journal of British Studies,* vol. 39, 3, 2000.

Gascoigne, John, *Joseph Banks and the English Enlightenment* (Cambridge: Cambridge University Press, 1994).

Gascoigne, John, 'Banks, Sir Joseph, baronet (1743–1820)', *ODNB,* Oxford, 2004, online edition, <www.oxforddnb.com>, article 1300.

Gibson, Carrie, *Empire's Crossroads: The Caribbean from Columbus to the Present Day* (London: Macmillan, 2014).

Goveia, Elsa V., *Slave Society in the British Leeward Islands at the End of the Eighteenth Century* (New Haven: Yale University Press, 1965).

Graham, Aaron, 'The Colonial Sinews of Imperial Power: The Political Economy of Jamaican Taxation, 1768–1838', *JICH,* vol. 45, 1, March 2017.

Graham, Bill and Mary-Margaret Sharp-Pucci, 'The special challenge of late-deafened adults: another deaf way' in C. J. Erting, R. C. Johnson, D. L. Smith, and B. D. Snider (eds), *The Deaf Way: Proceedings from the International Conference on Deaf Culture* (Washington, DC: Gallaudet University Press, 1994).

Gray, Malcolm, 'The Kelp Industry in the Highlands and Islands', *Economic History Review*, New Series, vol. 4, 2 (1951).

Gray, Malcolm, *The Highland Economy 1750–1850* (Edinburgh: Oliver and Boyd, 1957).

Gray, Malcolm, *The Fishing Industries of Scotland, 1790–1914* (Aberdeen: University of Aberdeen, 1978).

Greene, Jack P., 'The Transfer of British Liberty to the West Indies, 1627–1865' in J. P. Greene (ed.), *The Exclusionary Empire: English Liberty Overseas, 1600–1900* (Cambridge: Cambridge University Press, 2010).

Hague, William, *William Pitt the Younger* (London: HarperCollins, 2004).

Hall, Neville A., 'Governors and Generals: The Relationship of Civil and Military Commands in Barbados, 1783–1815', *Caribbean Studies,* vol. 10, 4 (1971).

Hamilton, Douglas J., *Scotland, the Caribbean and the Atlantic World, 1750–1820* (Manchester: Manchester University Press, 2005).

Hamilton, Henry, *Economic History of Scotland in the Eighteenth Century* (Oxford: Clarendon Press, 1963).

Handler, Jerome S., *The Unappropriated People: Freedmen in the Slave Society of Barbados* (Baltimore: Johns Hopkins University, 1974).

Harris, Bob, 'The Scots in the Westminster parliament and the British state in the eighteenth century' in Julian Hoppit (ed.), *Parliaments, Nations and Identities in Britain and Ireland, 1660–1850* (Manchester: Manchester University Press, 2003).

Harris, Bob, *The Scottish People and the French Revolution* (London, 2008).

Harris, Bob, 'Landowners and Urban Society in Eighteenth-Century Scotland', *SHR*, vol. 92, 2013.

Herman, Arthur, *The Scottish Enlightenment: The Scots' Invention of the Modern World* (London: Harper, 2006 edn).

Higman, B. W., *Slave Populations of the British Caribbean, 1807–1834* (Baltimore: Johns Hopkins University Press, 1984).

Higman, B. W., *Plantation Jamaica 1750–1850: Capital and Control in a Plantation Economy* (Kingston: University of West Indies Press, 2005).

Hilton, Boyd, 'And all that: why Britain outlawed her slave trade' in Derek R. Peterson (ed.), *Abolitionism and Imperialism in Britain, Africa and the Atlantic* (Athens, OH: Ohio University Press, 2010).

Hunt, John Dixon, *Gardens and the Picturesque: Studies in the History of Landscape Architecture* (Cambridge, MA: MIT Press, 1992).

Hunter, James, *The Making of the Crofting Community* (Edinburgh: John Donald, 1976).

Hunter, James, *Set Adrift Upon the World: The Sutherland Clearances* (Edinburgh: Birlinn, 2015).

Hutchison, Iain, *A History of Disability in Nineteenth-Century Scotland* (Lampeter: Edwin Mellen Press, 2007).

Kehoe, S. Karly, review of I. Whyte, *Send Back the Money! The Free Church of Scotland and American Slavery*, *SHR*, vol. 93, April 2014.

Laidlaw, Zoe, *Colonial Connections, 1815–45: Patronage, the Information Revolution and Colonial Government* (Manchester: Manchester University Press, 2005).

Laidlaw, Zoe, 'Richard Bourke: Irish liberalism tempered by empire' in David Lambert and Alan Lester (eds), *Colonial Lives across the British Empire: Imperial Careering in the Long Nineteenth Century* (Cambridge: Cambridge University Press, 2006).

Lambert, David, *White Creole Culture, Politics and Identities during the Age of Abolition* (Cambridge: Cambridge University Press, 2005).

Lang, Andrew M., 'Dempster, George, of Dunnichen (1732–1818)', *ODNB*, Oxford, 2004, online edition, <www.oxforddnb.com>, article 7472.

Little, J. I., 'Agricultural Improvement and Highland Clearance: The Isle of Arran 1766–1829', *SESH*, vol. 19, 1999.

Lockhart, Douglas, *Scottish Planned Villages* (Edinburgh: Scottish History Society, 2012).

Logue, Kenneth J., *Popular Disturbances in Scotland, 1780–1815* (Edinburgh: John Donald, 1979).

Longford, Elizabeth, *Wellington: The Years of the Sword* (London: Panther, 1971).

MacAskill, John, 'The Highland Kelp Proprietors and their Struggle over the Salt and Barilla Duties, 1817–1831', *JSHS*, vol. 26, 2006.

MacAskill, John, '"The most arbitrary, scandalous act of tyranny": The Crown, private proprietors and the ownership of the Scottish foreshore in the nineteenth century', *SHR*, vol. 85, 2006.

MacCoinnich, Aonghas, '"Kingis rabellis" to Cuidich' n' Righ; the emergence of Clan Choinnich, *c*.1475–1508' in S. Boardman and A. Ross (eds), *The Exercise of Power in Medieval Scotland, 1200–1500* (Dublin: Four Courts Press, 2003).

MacCoinnich, Aonghas, 'Siol Torcail and their lordship in the sixteenth century' in *Crossing the Minch: Exploring the Links Between Skye and the Outer Hebrides* (Lewis: Islands Book Trust, 2007).

MacCoinnich, Aonghas, *Plantation and Civility in the North Atlantic World: The Case of the Northern Hebrides, 1570–1639* (Leiden: Brill, 2015).

McCullough, Katie Louise, 'For the Good and Glory of the Whole': The Highland Society of London and the Formation of Scoto-British Identity' in Jodi A. Campbell, Elizabeth Ewan and Heather Parker, *The Shaping of Scottish Identities: Family, Nation and the Worlds Beyond* (Guelph: University of Guelph Centre for Scottish Studies, 2011).

Macdonald, Donald, *Lewis: A History of the Island* (Edinburgh: Gordon Wright, 1978).

Macdonell, Charles, 'Kelp and the Argyll Estates, 1780–1847' in Donald E. Meek, author of foreword, *The Secret Island: Towards a History of Tiree* (Lewis: Islands Book Trust, 2014).

McGilvary, George. K., *East India Patronage and the British State: The Scottish Elite and Politics in the Eighteenth Century* (London: Tauris Academic Studies, 2008).

Macinnes, Allan I., 'Scottish Gaeldom: The First Phase of Clearance' in T. M. Devine and Rosalind Mitchison (eds), *People and Society in Scotland, Volume 1, 1760–1830* (Edinburgh: John Donald, 1988).

Macinnes, Allan I., *Clanship, Commerce and the House of Stuart, 1603–1788* (East Linton: Tuckwell Press, 1996).

Macinnes, Allan I., 'Scottish Gaeldom from clanship to commercial landlordism, *c.*1600–*c.*1850' in S. Foster, A. Macinnes and R. Macinnes, *Scottish Power Centres from the Early Middle Ages to the Twentieth Century* (Glasgow: Cruithne Press, 1998).

Macinnes, Allan I., 'Jacobites and Empire: Highland Connections, 1707–1753', paper at ESHSS conference 'The Scottish Highlands: an Historical Reassessment', September 2012.

Mackenzie, Alexander, *History of the Mackenzies* (Inverness: A. and W. Mackenzie, 1894).

Mackenzie, K.S., 'Changes in the ownership of land in Ross-shire, 1756–1853', *Transactions of the Gaelic Society of Inverness*, vol. 12, 1885–6.

McKichan, Finlay, 'Lord Seaforth and Highland Estate Management in the First Phase of Clearance (1783–1815)', *SHR*, vol. 86, April 2007.

McKichan, Finlay, 'Lord Seaforth: Highland Proprietor, Caribbean Governor and Slave Owner', *SHR*, vol. 90, October 2011.

McKichan, Finlay, 'Lord Seaforth (1754–1815): The Lifestyle of a Highland Proprietor and Clan Chief', *Northern Scotland*, New Series, vol. 5, 2014.

Mackillop, Andrew, *'More Fruitful than the Soil': Army, Empire and the Scottish Highlands, 1715–1815* (East Linton: Tuckwell Press, 2000).

Mackillop, Andrew, 'The Political Culture of the Scottish Highlands from Culloden to Waterloo', *The Historical Journal*, vol. 46, 3, 2003.

Mackillop, Andrew, 'The Highlands and the Returning Nabobs: Sir Hector Munro of Novar, 1760–1807', in M. Harper (ed.), *Emigrant Homecomings: The Return Movement of Emigrants, 1600–2000* (Manchester: Manchester University Press, 2005).

Mackillop, Andrew, 'The Outer Hebrides during the Wars of Empire and Revolution, 1790–1815' in *Island Heroes: The Military History of the Hebrides* (Lewis: Islands Book Trust, 2010).

McLean, Marianne, *The People of Glengarry: Highlanders in Transition, 1745–1820* (Montreal: McGill-Queen's University Press, 1991).

Macrae, Norman, *Highland Second-Sight* (Dingwall: George Souter, 1909).

Manning, Helen Taft, *British Colonial Government after the American Revolution* (New Haven: Yale University Press, 1933).

Massie, Alastair W., 'Alexander Mackenzie Fraser (1758–1809)', *ODNB*, Oxford 2004, online edition, <www.oxforddnb.com>, article no. 10103.

Miers, Mary, *The Western Seaboard: An Illustrated Architectural Guide* (Edinburgh: Rutland Press, 2008).

Miller, Edgar, 'A community approaching crisis: Skye in the eighteenth century' in Christopher Dyer et al. (eds), *New Directions in Local*

History since Hoskins (Hatfield: University of Hertfordshire Press, 2011).

Mowat, Ian R. M., *Easter Ross 1750–1850: the Double Frontier* (Edinburgh: John Donald, 1981).

Mullen, Stephen, 'A Glasgow–West India Merchant House and the Imperial Dividend, 1779–1867', *JSHS*, vol. 33, 2, 2013.

Munro, Jean, 'The Mackenzies' in Richard D. Oram and Geoffrey P. Stell (eds), *Lordship and Architecture in Medieval and Renaissance Scotland* (Edinburgh: John Donald, 2005).

Murdoch, Alexander, *'The People Above': Politics and Administration in Mid-Eighteenth-Century Scotland* (Edinburgh: John Donald, 1980).

Murray, D. J., *The West Indies and the Development of Colonial Government 1801–1834* (Oxford: Clarendon Press, 1955).

Mutch, Alistair, 'A Contested Eighteenth-Century Election: Banffshire, 1795', *Northern Scotland*, New Series, vol. 2, 2011.

Namier, Sir Lewis and John Brooke, *The House of Commons 1754–1790* (London: History of Parliament Trust, 1964), vols 1 and 2.

Nenadic, Stana, *Lairds and Luxury: The Highland Gentry in Eighteenth-Century Scotland* (Edinburgh: John Donald, 2007).

Nenadic, Stana (ed.), *Scots in London in the Eighteenth Century* (Lewisburg: Bucknell University Press, 2010).

Newbury, Colin, 'Patronage and Professionalism: Manning a Transitional Empire, 1760–1870, *JICH*, vol. 42, 2, 2014.

Newton, Melanie, 'Philanthropy, Gender and the Production of Public Life in Barbados, ca. 1790–ca. 1850' in Pamela Scully and Diana Paton (eds), *Gender and Slave Emancipation in the Atlantic World* (Durham, NC: Duke University Press, 2005).

Newton, Melanie J., *The Children of Africa in the Colonies: Free People of Colour in Barbados in the Age of Emancipation* (Baton Rouge: LSU Press, 2008, e-book).

Nicholls, David, *From Dessalenes to Duvalier: Race, Colour and National Independence in Haiti* (Cambridge: Cambridge University Press, 1979).

O'Shaughnessy, Andrew Jackson, *An Empire Divided: The American Revolution and the British Caribbean* (Philadelphia: University of Pennsylvania Press, 2000).

Paton, Diana, 'Enslaved women and slavery before and after 1807', *History in Focus*, 12, 2007 (electronic resource).

Petley, Christer, '"Devoted Islands" and "That Madman Wilberforce": British Proslavery Patriotism During the Age of Abolition', *JICH*, vol. 39, 3, 2011.

Petley, Christer, 'Rethinking the fall of the planter class', *Atlantic Studies*, vol. 9, 1, 2012.

Poyer, John, *The History of Barbados* (London: J. Mawman, 1808).

Ragatz, Lowell Joseph, *The Fall of the Planter Class in the British Caribbean, 1763–1833* (New York: Century Co., 1929).

Randall, John, *The Historic Shielings of Pairc* (Lewis: Islands Book Trust, 2017).

Rendall, Jane, 'The Reputation of William Cullen (1710–1790): Family, Politics and the Biography of an "Ornate Physician"', *SHR*, vol. 93, October 2014.

Richards, Eric, *The Leviathan of Wealth* (London: Routledge, 1973).

Richards, Eric, *A History of the Highland Clearances: Agrarian Transformation and the Evictions, 1746–1886* (London: Croom Helm, 1982).

Richards, Eric and Monica Clough, *Cromartie: Highland Life 1650–1914* (Aberdeen: Aberdeen University Press, 1989).

Richards, Eric, *The Highland Clearances: People, Landlords and Rural Turmoil* (Edinburgh: Birlinn, 2016).

Richards, Eric, *The Highland Estate Factor in the Age of the Clearances* (Lewis: Islands Book Trust, 2016).

Robertson, J. I., *The First Highlander: Major-General David Stewart of Garth CB* (East Linton: Tuckwell Press, 1998).

Rodger, N. A. M., *The Command of the Ocean: A Naval History of Britain, 1649–1815* (London: Penguin, 2005).

Rothschild, Emma, *The Inner Life of Empires* (Princeton: Princeton University Press, 2011).

Royal Commission on the Ancient and Historical Monuments of Scotland Canmore website, ID 114491, <www.canmore.rcahms.gov.uk>.

Ryden, David Beck, *West Indian Slavery and British Abolition, 1783–1807* (Cambridge: Cambridge University Press, 2009).

Schomburgk, R. H., *The History of Barbados* (London: Longman Brown Green, 1848).

Sheridan, Richard B., 'The condition of the slaves on the sugar plantations of Sir John Gladstone in the colony of Demerara, 1812–49', *New West Indian Guide*, vol. 76, 3 and 4, 2002.

Spurdle, F. G., *Early West Indian Government Showing the Progress of Government in Barbados, Jamaica and the Leeward Islands, 1660–1783* (Palmerston North, New Zealand: published by author, 1962).

Stewart, David, *Sketches of the Character, Manners and Present State of the Highlanders of Scotland*, vol. 1 (Edinburgh: Constable, 1822).

Sutherland, Alex, *The Brahan Seer: The Making of a Legend* (Bern: Peter Lang, 2009).

Tague, Ingrid H., 'Aristocratic women and ideas of family in the early eighteenth century' in Helen Berry and Elizabeth A. Foyster (eds), *The Family in Early Modern England* (Cambridge: Cambridge University Press, 2007).

Taylor, David, *The Wild Black Region: Badenoch 1750–1800* (Edinburgh: John Donald, 2016).

Thomson, William P. L. and James R. Coull, 'Kelp' in James R. Coull, Alexander Fenton and Kenneth Veitch (eds), *Scottish Life and Society: A Compendium of Scottish Ethnology*, vol. 4 (Edinburgh: John Donald, 2008).

Thorne, R. G., *The House of Commons 1790–1820*, vols 2 and 4 (London: History of Parliament Trust, 1986).

Thorne, Roland, 'Robert Hobart 4th Earl of Buckinghamshire (1760–1816)', *ODNB,* Oxford, 2004, online edition, <www.oxforddnb.com>, article no. 13396.

Tindley, Annie and Heather Haynes, 'The River Helmsdale and Strath Ullie, *c.*1780–*c.*1850: a historical perspective of societal and environmental influences on land management', *Scottish Geographical Journal*, vol. 130, 1, 2014.

Ward, J. R., *Colonial Self-Government: The British Experience, 1759–1856* (London: Macmillan, 1976).

Ward, J. R., *British West Indian Slavery, 1754–1834: The Process of Amelioration* (Oxford: Clarendon Press, 1988).

Ward, J. R., 'The British West Indies 1748–1815' in P. J. Marshall (ed.), *The Oxford History of British Empire,* vol. 2, (Oxford: Oxford University Press, 1998).

Watson, J. Steven, *The Reign of George III* (Oxford: Oxford University Press, 1960).

Watson, Karl, *The Civilised Island: Barbados, a Social History 1750–1816* (St George, Barbados: Caribbean Graphic, 1979).

Watson, Karl, 'Salmagundis vs Pumpkins: White Politics and Creole Consciousness in Barbadian Slave Society, 1800–34' in Howard Johnson and Karl Watson (eds), *The White Minority in the Caribbean* (Kingston: Ian Randle, 1998).

Watson, Michael, 'The British West Indian Legislatures in the Seventeenth and Eighteenth Centuries' in Philip Lawson (ed.), *Parliament and the Atlantic Empire* (Edinburgh: Edinburgh University Press, 1995).

Welch, Pedro L. V. with Richard A. Goodridge, *'Red' and Black over White: Free Coloured Women in Pre-Emancipation Barbados* (Bridgetown: Carib Research and Publications, 2000).

Welch, Pedro L. V., *Slave Society in the City: Bridgetown, Barbados, 1680–1834* (Kingston: Ian Randle, 2003).

Whyte, Iain, *Scotland and the Abolition of Black Slavery, 1756–1838* (Edinburgh: Edinburgh University Press, 2006).

Wilkinson, D., 'Adam, William (1751–1839)', *ODNB*, Oxford, 2004, online edition <www.oxforddnb.com>, article no. 108.

Withers, C. W., *Placing the Enlightenment: Thinking Geographically about the Age of Reason* (Chicago: University of Chicago Press, 2008).

Wold, A. L., *Scotland and the French Revolutionary War, 1792–1802* (Edinburgh: Edinburgh University Press, 2015).

Womack, Peter, *Improvement and Romance – Constructing the Myth of the Highlands* (Basingstoke: Macmillan, 1989).

Wrong, Hume, *Government of the West Indies*, (Oxford: Clarendon Press, 1923).

Young, D. M., *The Colonial Office in the Early Nineteenth Century* (London: Royal Commonwealth Society, 1961).

Youngson, A. J., *The Making of Classical Edinburgh, 1750–1840* (Edinburgh: Edinburgh University Press, 1988).

Index